Mormonism and the Making of a British Zion

Matthew Lyman Rasmussen

MORMONISM *and the* MAKING *of a* BRITISH ZION

THE UNIVERSITY OF UTAH PRESS
Salt Lake City

The Defiance House Man colophon is a registered trademark of the University of Utah Press. It is based on a four-foot-tall Ancient Puebloan pictograph (late PIII) near Glen Canyon, Utah.

20 19 18 17 16   1 2 3 4 5

LIBRARY OF CONGRESS CATALOGING-IN-PUBLICATION DATA

Name: Rasmussen, Matthew Lyman, author.
Title: Mormonism and the making of a British Zion/Matthew Lyman Rasmussen.
Description: Salt Lake City : University of Utah Press, 2016. | Includes bibliographical references and index.
Identifiers: LCCN 2015047852| ISBN 9781607814870 (pbk. : alk. paper) | ISBN 9781607814887 (ebook)
Subjects: LCSH: Church of Jesus Christ of Latter-Day Saints—Great Britain—History. | Mormon Church—Great Britain—History. | Great Britain—Church history.
Classification: LCC BX8617.G7 R37 2016 | DDC 289.3/41—dc23
LC record available at http://lccn.loc.gov/2015047852

Printed and bound by Sheridan Books, Inc., Ann Arbor, Michigan.

For Roger John Halhead,

whose door is always open

By the rivers of Babylon, there we sat down, yea, we wept, when we remembered Zion. . . . For there they that carried us away captive required of us a song; . . . saying, Sing us one of the songs of Zion. How shall we sing the Lord's song in a strange land?

—Psalm 137

Contents

Illustrations

Figures

Maps

Acknowledgments

I EXPRESS HEARTFELT appreciation to the following individuals, without whom this book could not have been produced: Professor Emeritus Michael Mullett of the University of Lancaster for his expert supervision, thorough editorial remarks, and willingness to stave off full retirement to see me through my interminable doctoral studies; Professor Douglas Davies of the University of Durham for his essential criticism; Ronald Watt of the Church History Department for his enduring interest in my research and for helping me identify and access crucial primary sources; Professor Richard Bennett of Brigham Young University for his thoughtful review and morale-boosting endorsement of my work at a key stage in its development; Emily Bailey for her cheerful and timely assistance with data collection and graphing; Tom Child for his quality map design; Dan Skoubye for his advocacy and enthusiasm when this project was little more than a proposition; John Alley, Kelly Neumann, and the production staff at the University of Utah Press for their professional treatment of my manuscript and careful attention to the finishing touches; and the dear members of the Kendal Branch of the Preston England Stake for their boundless hospitality during each of my many research trips.

I owe special thanks to my parents, David and Susan Rasmussen, for sponsoring my first expedition to the British Isles in 1996 and for providing every form of needed support thereafter. Theirs is a legacy of steady devotion and unmatched generosity. Finally, I acknowledge the key contributions of my wife, Jessica, and my children, Jonah, Caroline, Cecily, and Ewan. Their patience and encouragement were invaluable. May this book long remind them of who we are and why.

Map 1. Great Britain. Map by Tom Child.

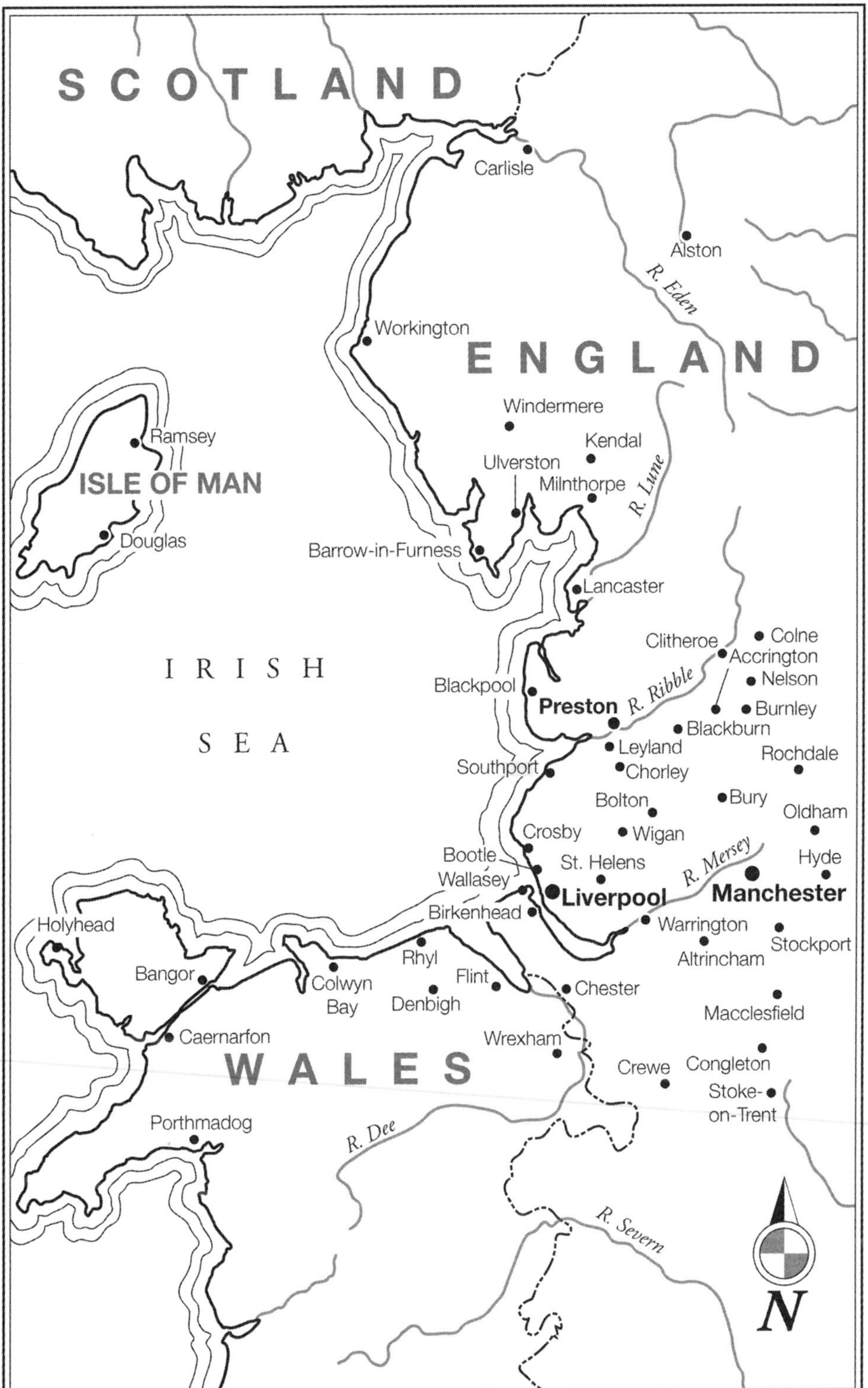

Map 2. Lancashire and the English North West. Map by Tom Child.

Chapter 1
"Among These Dark Satanic Mills"
Britain as Babylon

> The spread of the Gospel throughout England is certainly pleasing; the contemplation of which cannot but afford feelings of no ordinary kind.
>
> —Joseph Smith, 1841

Established in 1830 by the Prophet Joseph Smith, The Church of Jesus Christ of Latter-day Saints has relentlessly pursued global expansion and has found in its history a powerful and sustaining spiritual base from which to spring. Nowhere outside North America is this more evident than the British Isles—and nowhere within the British Isles is this more evident than Lancashire and North West England. Although the church is distinctly American in origin, the enduring Mormon experience in Britain has created its own parallel history, one that has never been fully explored. British Mormonism claims Lancashire as its birthplace, and throughout its storied history the English North West has become a place of profound significance for the international church.

Before taking root in Lancashire, Mormonism spread from its point of origin in upstate New York throughout New England and into the Ohio valley. Joseph Smith, as prophet and church president, commissioned elders to preach the Mormon message of restored Christianity throughout as much of North America as travel routes allowed. In 1832, the movement spread to Canada. The cluster of converts in the Toronto area held familial ties to Britain, which hastened the exportation of Mormonism to England during the first overseas mission of the church in July 1837.[1]

The original band of missionaries, led by Apostle Heber C. Kimball, quickly established their headquarters in Preston, Lancashire. Their nine-month campaign resulted in a wave of converts—around 1,500—the majority of whom were found within Preston and the Ribble Valley. This success was enhanced in 1840, when nine members of the church's Quorum of the Twelve Apostles arrived in Liverpool. They strengthened the Lancashire base and extended the movement throughout the rest of Britain. Before returning to America in 1841, the apostles authorized local converts to preside over the newly formed congregations and encourage the proselytizing effort. Over the next three decades, successive waves of local converts spearheaded an effective, expansive thrust that originated from its major administrative bases in Preston, Manchester, and Liverpool, and carried the Mormon message to every major population center in the country. Sustained and directed by periodic visits from upper church leadership from the Utah territory, Mormonism's mid-nineteenth-century expansion rode largely on the backs of its local membership.

Among the effects of this multigenerational, transatlantic missionary endeavor was the formation of a powerful connection between Mormonism and the English North West. Thousands of converts in Victorian Lancashire gave the church its footings in Britain, where it has remained in continual operation since the first congregation was established in Preston in 1837.

Joseph Smith's call to establish Zion in various locations throughout the American frontier carried with it an urgent sense of millenarianism that spurred the mass emigration of church members.[2] Although emigration removed the initial convert generation from the English North West, they and their posterity retained a powerful sense of attachment to the region, a connection bound up equally in the dynamism of their newfound faith and the customs of their ancestral homeland. Many of the children and grandchildren of early converts returned to the region as missionaries, seeking to further the work among relations and friends. Thus, a profound spiritual and familial connection between Mormonism and Great Britain has defined the island as a place of enduring significance to subsequent generations of Latter-day Saints on two continents—a place where ancestry blends seamlessly with spirituality, and family with faith.

The British Mormon emigration commenced in 1840 and the exodus sapped church membership so severely that by the late 1890s fewer than seven hundred scattered members remained. Onlookers speculated that the movement was on the brink of collapse. Notwithstanding the impact of two world wars, an economic depression, and a steady increase in secularism, a century later the highest concentration of Latter-day Saints in Britain was again in Lancashire.

To what can this gradual yet remarkable resurgence be attributed? More broadly, what is the survival story of this religious minority that has successfully carved out a distinct and enduring niche within Britain's variegated religious landscape? Why has British Mormonism flourished when so many nineteenth-century revivalist movements have long since diminished? As this book will demonstrate, the institutional endurance of Mormonism in North West England may be one of the least researched and least understood aspects of Britain's religious history. Mormonism's inception, perpetuation, and maturation in Britain make it a compelling case study of a so-called "new religious movement" with staying power.

This book is built upon the premise that Mormonism's continuity in Great Britain is a function of endogenous factors—specifically the implementation and adaptation of its own doctrine-driven perspectives, policies, and programs. This premise establishes the primacy of Mormon doctrine within and upon British Mormon history and asserts that the development of Mormon theology has, over time, assured two things: first, Mormonism's survival within a host culture whose regard for it has swung from indifference to hostility and back again; and second, the sacralization of the English North West within the minds of many Latter-day Saints. These factors that have sustained British Mormonism and the resulting sacralization of the North West region are among the major focal points of this book.

Justification and Scope

As Alan Rogers notes, "Whenever an identifiable community can be isolated, possessing a coherence and identity of its own, that community is a subject worthy of the attention of the historian."[3] Because Mormonism is well established and actively practiced throughout all parts of Britain, any regional study of the faith requires the consideration of a few key questions: First, why center a study of British Mormonism on Lancashire and the English North West? Second, why extend the scope to the end of the twentieth century?

The integrity of this book's thematic structure requires a certain geographic specificity. Again, why Lancashire? When the LDS Church is compared with the major Nonconformist denominations of the nineteenth and twentieth centuries, Mormonism's impact on the broader social and religious history of the British Isles seems relatively slight. Inasmuch as the LDS Church has never transcended the status of a minority religion anywhere in Britain, this is quite understandable. Its minority status notwithstanding, Mormonism's nineteenth-century emigration agenda captivated the imaginations (and fueled the suspicions) of Britons at all social levels. For believers, the impact of this tenet cannot be overstated. It influenced thousands of lives within individual families as well as smaller, rural communities, many of which were divided by conversion to the faith. As Hugh McLeod notes, many of the smaller Nonconformist denominations in Britain, "though apparently insignificant nationally, were important in particular regions or localities."[4] Such a case can easily be made for Mormonism in rural east Lancashire, particularly the villages of the upper Ribble Valley. And yet, the justification for basing a study of British Mormonism on the English North West does not extend from Mormonism's impact on Lancashire, but from Lancashire's outstanding impact on Mormonism. It is, in that sense, a case for Lancashire exceptionalism from the LDS point of view and traditions.

The significance of Lancashire to the Latter-day Saints originates in 1837 to 1838 in what was, from the Mormon perspective, a powerful realization of an ancient prophecy. This proclamation was elucidated by modern-day revelators and fulfilled by divinely authorized, apostolic endeavors. At the center of this unique relationship between the Mormons and the English North West is Heber C. Kimball, an unassuming potter-turned-apostle from upstate New York.

In April 1838, near the end of his first mission to England, Kimball toured the villages of Lancashire's upper Ribble Valley and bade farewell to his recent converts. He recounted his departure scene as follows:

> I went and visited the branches in the regions of Clithero [*sic*] and Chatburn, and on the morning when I left Chatburn many were in tears, thinking they should see my face no more. When I left them, my feelings were such I cannot describe. As I walked down the street I was followed by numbers; the doors were crowded by the inmates of the houses to bid me farewell, who could only give vent to their grief in sobs and broken accents. While contemplating this scene I was constrained to take off my hat, for I felt as if the place was holy ground. The Spirit of the Lord rested down upon me and I was constrained to bless that whole region of country. I was followed by a great number to Clithero, a considerable distance from the villages, who could then hardly separate from me. My heart was like unto theirs, and I thought my head was a fountain of tears, for I wept for several miles after I bid them adieu. I had to leave the road three times to go to streams of water to bathe my eyes.[5]

In addition to conveying the affection that existed between missionaries and converts in early Mormon proselytizing, Kimball's account also illustrates that this bucolic corner of east Lancashire was as "holy ground" to its Mormon members. As an original member of the church's Quorum of the Twelve Apostles, Kimball's perspective of the striking spirituality of the upper Ribble Valley would have resonated with local converts, if for no other reason than his high standing in the church. If Kimball's perspective was to endure, however, it would require both clarification and validation from Mormonism's founding prophet.

At some point following his return to Ohio, Kimball shared his experience in Chatburn and Clitheroe with the Prophet Joseph Smith and puzzled openly at the root cause of Mormonism's popularity in the upper Ribble Valley. The prophet's response not only buttressed Kimball's earlier sentiment, but also galvanized the relationship between Lancashire and the Mormon people. "Did you not understand it?" Joseph replied. "That is the place where some of the old Prophets traveled and dedicated that land, and their blessing fell upon you."[6] This proclamation by Mormonism's foremost revelator has permanently secured the significance of the English North West in British Mormon history.

The Latter-day Saint interpretation of Lancashire as holy ground is inextricably linked with the church's broader restorationist claims. Accordingly, there are distinct parallels between the apostolic ministry of the original church of Christ and the latter-day, restored counterpart now regarded as "Mormonism." Confirming LDS belief in this parallel, historian James Moss wrote:

> The revelation to the Prophet Joseph Smith to send the gospel to the British Isles was similar to the revelation to Peter in former days to take the gospel beyond the society in which it was first established. As the apostle Paul became the herald of the gospel message to foreign lands in that day, so Elder Heber C. Kimball was the chosen minister to Britain in our day. The branches of the early church in Corinth, Ephesus, and Thessalonica had their British counterparts in Preston, Chatburn and Eccleston.[7]

Joseph Smith's association of the English North West with the prophets of the previous Christian epoch had both immediate and long term significance for British Mormonism. For the faithful, Smith's capacity to discern this fact further validated his status as God's anointed prophet whose perspective was neither bounded by time nor restricted by geography (Smith never visited the British Isles). Lancashire's upper Ribble Valley became a spiritual symbol to the British saints, and one that further evidenced the veracity of Mormonism as the vehicle through which the primitive truth, simplicity, and authority of Christ's gospel were restored. In its earliest years in Britain, Mormon prophets laid a special claim upon Britain—a claim that emboldened successive generations of converts and missionaries as they sought to perpetuate the church within a sacred space, or, more accurately, a space made sacred.

Although from a doctrinal point of view there may be nothing inherently sacred about the English North West, the region will be regarded as sacred space as long as this perspective is embraced by local members and encouraged by church historians and apologists. However significant the Latter-day Saint interpretation of Lancashire has become, it should be noted that the Ribble Valley—the spiritual and historical center of British Mormonism—is similarly associated with other groups as a site of abiding importance, though these groups are varied and little understand one another.

In particular, the Pendle Hill region of the upper Ribble Valley is steeped in historical significance, both as a former hub of witchcraft in the early seventeenth century and, a few generations later, as the site of George Fox's pivotal vision that fueled the expanse of the Quaker movement throughout northern England. It is a region blanketed with layers of interpretation, memory, and nuance.

Subsequent generations of church leaders have endorsed Joseph Smith's interpretation of the "blessedness" of the English North West. At a church conference in Manchester in 1976, the Prophet Joseph's pronouncement concerning the upper Ribble Valley was refreshed and added upon by Spencer W. Kimball, then president of the LDS Church and grandson of Heber C. Kimball. Referring to the exchange between his grandfather and the Prophet Joseph, President Kimball declared, "I should like to think that the whole of this great land is blessed and still carrying a blessing from our Heavenly Father from great and holy men who have walked upon its shores."[8] This statement effectively extended the sacredness of the English North West to all of Great Britain, and reinforced the view that the Latter-day Saints of the twentieth century had as much reason as their nineteenth-century forebears to regard Lancashire as the historical center of British Christian spirituality.

This enduring importance was manifested further in the 1980s as the church prepared for and celebrated its sesquicentennial year in Britain. The church's formal campaign to commemorate Mormon history throughout the British Isles included the identification of those sites with the greatest meaning. Accordingly, at Avenham Park in Preston the church erected a plaque to commemorate its first convert baptisms in England, which took place in the River Ribble in July 1837. Another plaque in Beetham (near Milnthorpe, now in south Cumbria) marks the site of the boyhood home of John Taylor, a convert who later became the third president of the church. In Downham, near Clitheroe, the church installed a bench with a plaque that memorializes the early converts from the upper Ribble Valley. More recently, the church donated to the Museum of Liverpool a bronze statue of a Mormon convert family on the eve of their emigration. It stands near the Albert Dock and portrays Latter-day Saint emigration as an underrepresented aspect of the city's maritime history.[9] Perhaps of greater significance, the statue helps assure Merseyside's present-day church members, many of whom are first-generation Latter-day Saints, that their sense of religious heritage has its own local roots and should be as tied to Liverpool as to Salt Lake City.

The abiding significance of the English North West to the Latter-day Saints was augmented during the presidency of Gordon B. Hinckley. His personal relationship with the region began in 1933 when he labored as a missionary in Preston and Nelson for nine months.[10] The immediate fruits of these labors were quantifiably meager, and fully characteristic of the time. Mission records indicate that during his time in

Lancashire Hinckley distributed three copies of the Book of Mormon and performed one confirmation, but did not baptize any converts.[11]

Hinckley's ties to the English North West were of little relevance until he was ordained to the church presidency in 1995. As the most widely traveled church president in Mormon history, Hinckley visited Preston four times in his thirteen-year ministry (1995, 1996, 1998, 2004), more than any other single location outside the United States.[12] His missionary residence at 15 Wadham Road in Preston has become a revered place among the LDS historic sites in Lancashire, and is visited frequently by members and missionaries.[13] Hinckley's death in 2008 again drew the attention of the worldwide church to the English North West as his widely publicized funeral and graveside service revealed that a box of Lancashire soil, given to him early in his presidency, was placed atop his casket.[14]

As with John Walton's social history of Lancashire, I too have found that this book "cannot shelter behind the Lancashire boundary: its basic terms of reference must range a little more widely."[15] As it concerns the history of British Mormonism, these terms of reference are doctrinal, cultural, and geographical. Although this book refers to Lancashire and the English North West almost interchangeably, there are a few reasons why the two require differentiation. For instance, Lancashire County's 1974 boundary reform reflects the importance of incorporating Liverpool, Manchester, and their surrounding conurbations into the geography of this book. Indeed, the history of Lancashire Mormonism cannot be adequately explored independent of the LDS congregations formed in the metropolitan counties of Merseyside and Greater Manchester. Organizationally, there is a need to recognize and work within the ecclesiastical boundaries of Lancashire-based Mormonism which, at various times, extended into parts of Westmorland, Cumberland, Yorkshire, Cheshire, Flintshire, and the Isle of Man. Because the LDS interpretation of British culture is central to this book, I do not hesitate to examine Mormon activity outside of Lancashire itself.

The dates of this study, 1837 through 1998, are based upon endogenous factors that are significant to the development and maturation of the church in Great Britain. These dates represent the commencement and culmination of what could be described by Mormons and scholars as Britain's "Babylon-to-Zion" transformation. This transformation revolves around Mormonism's doctrine of gathering—the theological crux of the church's early history—and a tenet that shaped its sense of purpose, identity, and geography. The year 1837 marks the beginning—when the Mormon apostles brought their restored gospel to England. For much of the nineteenth-century, the objective of the church was to gather Israel's elect in one, with the intent of establishing Zion in the providentially preserved expanse of the American Intermountain West and prepare for Christ's second coming.[16] Zion's crown jewel was her temple, and only when sufficient faith, membership, and means were gathered could the "House of the Lord" be constructed. The presence of the temple signified the institutional and spiritual maturation of the kingdom of God in both Utah and Britain.

In the twentieth century, Mormon leaders shifted the gathering away from the Intermountain West and toward localized centers of strength worldwide, wherever sufficient numbers of Latter-day Saints had congregated. In June 1998, President Gordon B. Hinckley dedicated the Preston England Temple, constructed at Hartwood Green, Chorley. The second temple in England, the Preston Temple represents the full maturation of British Mormonism and the zenith of the church's regional history.

It may be more accurate to say that the temple represents Britain's very redemption. Lancashire's "blessedness," as identified by Heber C. Kimball and certified by Joseph Smith, did not endure in the minds of local converts and the missionaries who brought them into the fold. Throughout much of the nineteenth century, Britain was a literal Babylon to the Latter-day Saints, a place of corruption, pollution, and depravity that the Mormons were quick to condemn and, as convert emigrants, eager to forsake. And yet, the dedication of the Preston Temple in 1998 signifies that the same region had become a veritable extension of Zion—a place of peace, unity, and consecrated prosperity that former generations of church members had associated only with Utah.

With its temples built and its stakes organized, the Babylon-to-Zion transformation of the British Isles was complete. The LDS perspective of Britain has thus evolved from a land that was initially blessed, subsequently cursed, and ultimately redeemed. The intervening years between British Mormonism's inception in 1837 and its maturation in 1998 reveal themes of endurance, commitment, and adaptability, which have sustained British Mormonism's perpetuation and broader progress.

Extending this study into the late twentieth century may surprise scholars who associate British Mormon history primarily with the Victorian period. Victorian-era studies of Mormonism, although crucial, are the most common. These studies typically highlight Mormonism's mid-nineteenth century heyday—characterized by the astonishingly high numbers of converts from northern industrial districts—and acknowledge that the church's emigration program facilitated its own diminution.[17] This view, while accurate within a certain period, is nevertheless shortsighted. The "spectacular yet short-lived" perspective neglects to consider British Mormonism's impressive continuity and its determination to maintain a presence in a place typically associated with a brief season of remarkable growth.

Growth, it must be said, is only part of British Mormon history. Because it is among the more apparent and quantifiable aspects of Mormonism's past, it is understandably an attractive area of research. A broader and more inclusive historical perspective argues that British Mormonism is equally concerned with establishing institutional and cultural depth—and depth takes time. In this context, depth is a powerful and highly subjective quality that is central to the perpetuation of Mormonism in Britain. It is a potent cultural influence encouraged by the tradition's leadership, historians, and apologists.

Broadening the dates of this study to include the second half of the twentieth century allows the major themes pertaining to Mormonism's perpetuation to emerge. To study British Mormon history independent of its post-World War II revitalization would neglect its most critical and climactic phase. Of course, all of this requires that British Mormonism be studied on its own terms, as it were, and in keeping with its historical agenda.

It is important to note that the dates of this study are strictly associated with LDS endogenous factors. Examples include the impact and sequence of key events: Joseph Smith's martyrdom; the arrival of the church in the Salt Lake Valley; the years of administration of a particular church, mission, or conference president; the emergence of a new proselytizing method; the publication of a new series of tracts; and the construction of meeting houses.

Proper examination of British Mormonism's perpetuation requires that The Church of Jesus Christ of Latter-day Saints be considered simultaneously as a global and local religious organization, and one that possesses a uniquely transatlantic identity. Admittedly, this is a complicated point of view to maintain—it requires keeping a finger on the pulse of the main body of the church in America while also monitoring its local activity in Britain, its most important European satellite.[18]

Over time, British Mormonism's American orientation became less pronounced as its leadership and membership stopped looking westward and started looking homeward and inward. Of course, British Mormonism cannot be studied wholly independent of its affiliation with and—for much of its history—dependence upon the American church. Only by resisting the temptation to follow the nineteenth-century British converts westward to Utah, and by fixing the historical spotlight firmly upon the English North West, can British Mormonism's survival story be comprehensively uncovered and examined.

There is an underlying deficiency in the historiography of British Mormonism that has both marred the corpus and restricted much needed developments. Much of it is decidedly American-centric and accentuates "the [American] missionary's sacrifice, his abject poverty, his sacred manifestations, and his successful baptismal record" while failing to "communicate the magnitude of the contribution made by the individual English convert."[19] This is problematic in that it fundamentally Americanizes what could otherwise be considered the *British* history of an *international* church. As one historian notes:

> With the general lack of historic recognition of the British Saints, the personal history of church members in Britain is left to American-born descendants to tell. They repeat from generation to generation the unwritten stories of their ancestors. Through this process they have often enlarged upon facts and created moralistic fables and traditional legends of their ancestry. Through their efforts the legendary "British gospel hero" has often emerged as less than a credible figure.[20]

Notwithstanding the productive rush of articles published in conjunction with the British church's sesquicentennial celebration in 1987, historian David J. Whittaker lamented that there remained "no adequate one-volume history of Mormonism in Great Britain".[21] Whittaker leveled this criticism in the face of the only book-length piece produced in 1987, *Truth Will Prevail*, a collaborative work of eleven historians and bearing the imprimatur of the church. Whittaker proclaimed the work unsatisfactory and "marred by the uneven scholarship of [its] essays."[22] The book's debatable failings aside, *Truth Will Prevail* was a welcome contribution to British Mormon historiography, which had not seen any significant additions since Richard L. Evans's *A Century of "Mormonism" in Great Britain* and P.A.M. Taylor's *Expectations Westward* were published in 1937 and 1965, respectively.

Today, a comprehensive history of British Mormonism continues to elude the corpus. This reinforces the justification of this book as a narrower study, and partially defines its place and purpose. Its regional emphasis aims to improve the accessibility of British Mormon history to the lay reader and reveal many of its dominant themes. Lamentably, owing to its limitations, this book is not the long-sought-for comprehensive history. It is, however, a step in that direction and should provide a template of historical themes intended to inform and enable additional research.

Centrality of Endogenous Factors

Mormonism can be, and indeed has been, examined as a social movement, an emerging religious tradition, and even a distinct ethnicity.[23] In recent years, examination of this American-born faith has taken on an interdisciplinary tone. This is valuable when exploring the intricacies of the faith. And yet, the examination of Mormonism from myriad points of view and from within the frameworks and agendas of differing disciplines has also encouraged an academic myopia. In an effort to explain the history of British Mormonism, some historians have sought to contextualize its progress in relation to the broader and fundamentally irreligious social, cultural, and economic influences at play in British society. While this approach is essential, when taken to excess it detaches Mormonism from its doctrines and fails to account for the relationship between the doctrine of the church and the lives and actions of its members. Mormonism is, above all, a religion. Mormonism as a system of belief is what sustains and influences Mormonism as a movement. As Vladimir Nabokov says, "the pattern of the thing precedes the thing."[24] To examine Mormonism while excluding its doctrinal context is to separate the "thing" from its sustaining, defining, and preceding "pattern." Of greater significance, therefore, is this question—what are the patterns of British Mormonism and what events have influenced them?

There is a single argument that addresses this question, expressed in the varied attempts scholars have made to explain British Mormonism's success. There are two directly opposing theories. The first credits environmental influences that have, over time, predisposed individuals to convert. This position is validated by research comparing LDS Church growth to the growth patterns of other denominations in Britain. These studies reveal seasons of religious receptivity in Britain that are manifest broadly and not just within a distinct group or sect, Mormonism included.[25] Of note, these studies are endorsed by historians outside the faith.

Within the LDS tradition, historians typically accentuate the importance of internal factors by maintaining that Mormonism's success is a function of the truthfulness of its doctrines, the divine authority of its prophets and apostles, the committed labors of its missionaries, and the spiritual power that attends its covenant membership. Indeed, for many LDS historians, the spiritual verities of Mormonism are a dominant reality that cannot be fully subjugated by temporal considerations, however pervasive these considerations may be. The renowned Utah historian Dean May asserts that the scholar cannot presume to write upon the validity of personal religious experience, which by its nature is "quite beyond the world of scholarly inquiry."[26] More fruitful, May posits, is the consideration of the *consequences* of religious belief and the change it works upon human beings and societies.[27]

To consider this matter more fully and determine its relationship to British Mormon history, it is necessary to cite specific examples of the "exogenous versus endogenous" debate. Sociological and theological case studies occupy opposing ends of the theoretical spectrum. Considering patterns of general church growth in Britain, Robert Curie, Alan Gilbert, and Lee Horsley concede that individual church policy (itself among the more important endogenous factors) does influence a given denomination's growth. Nevertheless, "whatever efforts are expended by a church, increased recruitment cannot be obtained in unfavorable exogenous conditions."[28]

Curie, Gilbert, and Horsley present Mormonism in mid-twentieth-century Britain as a successful example of "the effects of a church's policy on its growth." They note that the rapid increase in LDS membership in the 1950s and 60s was a direct result of action taken by church administration in Salt Lake City. They attribute the inability of the church to maintain thereafter a growth rate of over fifty percent a year to "the same obstacles, insuperable by any policy, that so severely reduced the numbers of other churches" during the mid-1960s. Thus, from a sociological perspective, internal influences can initiate or encourage church growth, but it is only a phase, and at all times is subordinate to broader, more influential exogenous or environmental factors.

Theologically, the matter of Mormonism's growth is dictated by a different set of determinants. The only other period of British Mormonism to compare with the mid-twentieth-century growth analyzed by Curie, Gilbert and Horsley occurred a century earlier, between the late 1830s and the early 1850s. British church membership increased from around 1,500 in 1838[29] to over 32,000 at the time of the religious census in 1851.[30] To a Latter-day Saint audience, James Moss offered the following explanation of the rapid rise of Mormonism in early Victorian Britain:

> Social, economic, and political considerations in Britain also provided a setting conducive to the gospel message, although these were secondary in their impact on the success of the mission. . . . New members of the Church in the United States and Canada retained close ties with friends and family remaining in Britain. Correspondence between them brought the good news of the Restoration, and these family referrals provided the early missionaries with their first opportunities for sharing the gospel in places such as Preston, Liverpool, Manchester, and London. Equally important were the missionaries, prepared in most cases with extensive experience and bearing the keys of apostolic authority to open the doors of the nation for the gospel. These factors alone would have assured the success of the mission.
>
> But there is a deeper reason for the great response of the British people to the restored gospel. It is a spiritual reason largely hidden from the world but known among those who are aware of God's purposes and sensitive to the workings of the Spirit. These people had been spiritually prepared to receive the gospel because they were among those foreordained to be gathered first in the house of Israel. They were of Ephraim, to whom was given the birthright in order that he might lead out in sharing the gospel with his brethren of Israel in the last days.[31]

Moss's emphasis on doctrines pertaining to apostolic authority, spiritual preparation, foreordination, and Israelite lineage clearly overrides the significance of concomitant exogenous factors, which, although acknowledged, receive passing attention.

While sociological and theological hypotheses occupy the extreme ends of the argument, wide-ranging historical explanations occupy the space between them. Historical analyses synthesize internal and external considerations and account for the relevance of both the spiritual and the temporal. One might assume that hypotheses accentuating the role of Mormon doctrine and other matters of religious significance come exclusively from academics within the LDS tradition. However, this is not the case. Two important examples are found in the writings of Douglas Davies and P.A.M. Taylor. In seeking to account for Mormonism's popularity in industrialized Wales, Davies sounds an important caution to historians who overemphasize exogenous factors:

> Change rather than custom emerged as the keynote of the Restoration. This was precisely the right note for those local inhabitants who were unhappy with the status quo. But here we need to be careful not to slip too easily into that position of the deprivation theory which places excessive stress on the poverty and on the pitiable aspects of life from which converts sought release. Doubtless many poor people did see America as a secular land of economic promise. This is a well known feature of nineteenth century emigration. But to it must be added the further, and perhaps more significant element of religious longing for salvation. The critical scholar can find it too easy to reduce the wish to be in Zion to nothing more than economic desire. That kind of reductionism strips away too quickly the very human yearning for a quality of experience and fulfillment which is best described as spiritual.[32]

P.A.M. Taylor's contribution is particularly valuable because it emphasizes what some have seen as a temporal aspect of Mormonism—emigration—which was a clear consequence of conversion throughout much of the nineteenth century. After accounting for the various social, political, and economic factors that influenced British Mormon emigration, Taylor notes:

> In the face of all these considerations, we have to acknowledge the plain fact, that before emigrating these people went through a process of conversion which marked them as a strange minority within British religious life; that they lived in the Church for some time, under the scrutiny of leaders; that they had to gain those leaders' approval, in many cases, before receiving financial aid. . . . If any assumption has to be made, or if any subjective addition has to be made after statistical or other proofs have been exhausted, it should be that of religious purpose and not, as a pure historian's dogma, that of economic motive.[33]

Other historians of Mormon migration have reached similar conclusions. LDS writers Leonard Arrington and Davis Bitton also address the relationship between spiritual and temporal matters:

> One must remember that in many ways Mormonism was the least attractive of the several means of emigration to a new country. Demanding of the emigrant strict obedience and continuing economic sacrifice, it offered in return a home in one of the least inviting regions of the hemisphere. Clearly the Mormon religion itself, if not the sole factor behind the emigration, was the key to the process.[34]

Primary source material from the peak years of British Mormon emigration indicate that church leaders were aware of the varied motives converts had for emigrating, and that powerful discontent with the status quo in the British Isles could not be disregarded. A letter written in 1855 by Franklin D. Richards, then president of the British Mission, takes stock of the sad realities within British society that impacted church members' attitudes toward emigration: "I would say again in reference to the emigration of the Saints to the [United] States, that the horrors of [the Crimean] war, the prevalence of hunger, producing bread riots, and the general depression of trade all serve to render it as impossible to stop emigration as it would be to dam up the Hudson [River] with bulrushes."[35] Troublesome exogenous factors that hastened the fulfillment of Mormonism's aims were often interpreted as expressions of divine will and approval.

External motivations for converting and emigrating, although convenient, were also problematic. Church leadership believed that only the most genuine of conversionary experiences could sustain the British Mormons in their arduous westward trek. Brigham Young, then president of the church, advised Franklin D. Richards to "[be] wary of assisting any of those who come into the Church now, during these troublesome times for Britain, whose chief aim and intention may be to get to America."[36]

No explanations of British Mormonism's success are more contrasting than those offered by E.P. Thompson and Malcolm Thorp. Thompson asserts that Mormon conversion in mid-nineteenth-century Britain was essentially a "reflex of despair" set off by the failure of social and political reform movements in the 1840s, especially Chartism.[37] In exploring a presumed causal relationship between Chartism's failure and Mormonism's success, Thompson contends that the movement's collapse in 1848 deepened the plight of the working class, which in turn precipitated a mild religious revival in certain sectors of industrialized Britain. This, he concludes, is evidenced by an increase in Mormon conversions in 1849.

Malcolm Thorp rejects the premise that there was any relationship between failed "agitation for political and social reform and outbreaks of chiliastic fervor."[38] Analyzing nearly three hundred personal accounts written by British Mormon converts of the period, Thorp asserts that there is no direct evidence supporting a Chartist/Mormon relationship, and that there were very few "former chartists, trade unionists, and participants in radical politics" among those baptized between 1837 and 1852. Thorp also discovered that the preponderance of these Latter-day Saints, although decidedly working class, were also reasonably prosperous. He notes that, of the total number of converts studied, only eight complained of being out of work when they joined the church.[39] Thorp's conclusion is consistent with the observation of the *Liverpool Albion* in 1842 that "in appearance and worldly circumstances" Mormon convert-emigrants appeared "above the ordinary men of steerage passengers."[40] Thorp claims the increase in British Mormon conversion in 1849 is attributable to endogenous factors alone. He highlights improved organization of the missionary program and the powerful personality of Orson Pratt, the new president of the British Mission, as primary determinants.[41]

Thompson attributes Mormonism's success to a failed political reform movement, while Thorp attributes it to the influence of a single man. This is a fascinating and revealing discrepancy. Indeed, the variables at play may be too numerous and interrelated to allow for a one-sided conclusion to the debate.[42] Certainly there is room in Mormon history for what Bertrand Russell termed "reciprocal causation," the notion that "the circumstances of men's lives do much to determine their philosophy, but conversely, their philosophy does much to determine their circumstances."[43]

Because this book is primarily concerned with Mormonism's endurance in Britain and not just its marked phases of growth, it builds on the position that internal factors were pivotal to the perpetuation of British Mormonism. Accordingly, it focuses on the impact of developments in Mormon doctrine on the religion's very endurance.

This book is not designed to argue against the significance of exogenous factors, nor does it assert the outright primacy of endogenous or spiritual factors within British Mormon history.[44] Rather, this book seeks to gauge the overall impact of a specific tenet of Mormonism—the doctrine of gathering (itself a distinct and powerful endogenous matter)—upon British church history. It does so through the identification of the gathering's corresponding manifestations and effects within congregations in Lancashire and the English North West.

The "exogenous versus endogenous" debate is limited if it regards growth as the primary factor by which "success" is defined and determined. The inherent restrictions of this dichotomy have prevented analysis of other important factors that helped ensure Mormonism's endurance in Britain. These factors include the perpetuation of the faith within non-emigrating families, the refining of the church's missionary program, and the development of lay leadership at the local level. Again, British Mormonism's true success is not its growth but its depth, manifested by its institutional maturation and enabled by the abiding commitment of its membership to the spiritual heartland of the English North West.

By favoring depth over growth, less-researched aspects of British Mormon history increase in relevance and compensate for the church's inconsistent conversionary success and minority status. Indeed, membership growth is but one of several means by which Latter-day Saints have increased their institutional exposure and impact throughout the British Isles.

Lancashire as Paradox

Regarding the history of Lancashire, John Walton writes, "It is easier to describe the divisions in the county, than to say what unites it."[45] In their own way, the Mormons have contributed to this divisiveness. They have also been impacted by it. From the establishment of the first congregation in Preston in 1837 to the completion of the Preston Temple in 1998, each succeeding generation of Latter-day Saints has had to come to terms with who they are in relation to their faith and their host culture. The terms of this relationship have never been static. Historically, the Lancashire Latter-day Saints did not have to grapple so much with their own religious identity as they did the identity of their homeland: a place that has at times seemed simultaneously blessed and cursed, holy and hellish.

Indeed, from the Latter-day Saint point of view, Lancashire is a place imbued with paradox. Although the region is laden with spiritual significance, the Latter-day Saint experience with it was not always positive. In spite of Joseph Smith's proclamation regarding the region's blessedness, missionaries throughout the nineteenth century reviled the industrialized north. They referenced its many social problems and increasing ecological squalor as evidence of its corruption and spiritual depravity, worthy of the cursing of God.[46] Apostle Orson Hyde proclaimed in Manchester in 1840 that the manifestation of God's "sore displeasure to this generation" would soon take the form of famine, warfare, and governmental collapse. "Earthquakes, strange things, and fearful sights," Hyde maintained, "together with the waves of the sea heaving themselves beyond their bounds, will cause men's hearts to fail them for fear."[47] Even Heber C. Kimball, whose affection for the people of the Ribble Valley was unbounded, later referred to their home as "wicked" and marveled that his converts from Chatburn and Downham remained faithful for the nearly twenty years between their baptism and emigration.[48]

Precisely how have the Latter-day Saints navigated their relationship with the British host culture? If the region is blessed, as both ancient and modern prophets proclaim, why leave? If it is cursed, why stay? This paradox, which is central to the history of British Mormonism, provides this book with its thematic structure. Cumulatively, the chapters of this book convey the transition of Mormonism's view of Britain as Babylon to Britain as Zion.

This transition is gradual—there is no precise point of demarcation that separates the saints' entrenchment in the first attitude from the emergence and fulfillment of the second. Though this line is blurred, the major changes in outlook hover around the end of the nineteenth century. Critical shifts in doctrinal interpretation, emigration policy, and property acquisition—all indicative of the church's interest in establishing a permanent presence in Britain—are conclusively twentieth-century developments.

To summarize, despite its importance to the global church, the history of British Mormonism has never been satisfactorily researched. While historians typically emphasize the nineteenth-century growth of the church in Britain, comparatively little attention is given to Mormonism's equally remarkable perpetuation, a gap in the historiography this book seeks to remedy. Endogenous factors suggest that British Mormonism's true success has not been its growth but its depth. From its establishment in 1837 to its maturation in 1998, the Mormon perspective of Britain has shifted dramatically. The following chapters chronicle that shift and reveal that the endurance of Mormonism in Britain has been enabled by doctrinal adaptation. From a nineteenth-century Babylon to a twentieth-century Zion, the history of British Mormonism is captured in a single word: change.

Chapter 2
The Gathering
Revelation and Adaptation

> This is the principle on which the government of heaven is conducted—by revelation adapted to the circumstances in which the children of the kingdom are placed. Whatever God requires is right, no matter what it is, although we may not see the reason thereof till long after the events transpire.
>
> —Joseph Smith, 1842

> Were I to live as long as Methuselah, and were I to learn every hour of my life something new from these books, and were I able to remember all that I had learnt, I should not after all know as much as I could learn in five minutes from revelation.
>
> —Brigham Young, 1861

Revelation is everything to Mormon history. It was through the medium of revelation—with Joseph Smith as revelator—that Mormonism positioned itself before the world as the restored Church of Jesus Christ, what Fawn Brodie describes as "a real religious creation, one intended to be to Christianity what Christianity was to Judaism: that is, a reform and a consummation."[1]

From Joseph Smith's first vision in 1820 until his death in 1844, Mormonism was a theological work in progress characterized by its ongoing organizational adaptation and doctrinal development. "Take away the Book of Mormon and the revelations and where is our religion?" asked Joseph Smith, "We have none."[2] Early members of the church found that the tenets of their belief shifted under their feet every few months as the prophet continued his perpetual and often unpredictable work of restoration.

For the Prophet Joseph Smith, the challenge was not receiving revelation so much as it was determining how to disseminate revealed truth appropriately. "It is my meditation all the day," wrote Smith, "and more than my meat and drink, to know how I shall make the Saints of God comprehend the visions that roll like an overflowing surge before my mind."[3] Ironically, the converts drawn to Mormonism because of its belief in an open canon and ongoing enlightenment through a living prophet were not always receptive to Smith's revelations. Regarding the hesitancy of some church members to acknowledge the authenticity of his revelations, Smith wrote, "I have tried for a number of years to get the minds of the Saints prepared to receive the things of God; but we frequently see some of them, after suffering all they have for the work of God, will fly to pieces like glass as soon as anything comes that is contrary to their traditions."[4]

For the young prophet, determining which revelations to disclose to the general membership—and when—were delicate and frustrating tasks laden with tremendous ramifications for the fledgling church. Many who found Smith's revelations at odds with the popular beliefs of the day were quick to apostatize.[5] The missionaries who sought to spread Mormonism throughout Britain had the difficult task of keeping the content of their preaching current with the latest doctrinal developments. Although ongoing revelation was presented to the world as proof of the divine authenticity of his call, Joseph Smith discovered the potential stumbling block his revelations were to the growth of the church he had founded. Deliberateness, selectivity, and caution were needed to keep the missionary zeal of the young church in check.

This chapter focuses on one of Joseph Smith's most enduring and influential revelations—the gathering of modern Israel. At the outset of the inaugural mission to England, Joseph Smith expressly forbade the teaching of the gathering. And yet, within three years, this doctrine would become central to the purposes of the British church. This chapter examines the gathering as it was explained, publicized, and adapted through the *Latter-day Saints' Millennial Star*—the official newspaper of the church in Britain published from 1840 until 1970. By examining the implementation and adaptation of this distinct doctrine, every other important aspect of British Mormon history is contextualized.

The *Millennial Star*

The doctrine of gathering is best understood as seen through the lens of the *Latter-day Saints' Millennial Star*—a Lancashire-based periodical through which the message of Mormonism pulsed to all of Britain.

From the beginning, the *Millennial Star* was intended to be an incomparable publication. In the prospectus of the first volume, the editor, Apostle Parley P. Pratt, noted that the *Millennial Star* was to "stand aloof from the common political and commercial news of the day" and be devoted strictly to "the spread of the fullness of the gospel, the restoration of the ancient principles of Christianity, the gathering of Israel, the rolling forth of the kingdom of God among the nations, the signs of the times, the fulfillment of prophecy . . . in short, whatever is shown forth indicative of the coming of the 'Son of Man,' and the ushering in of his universal reign on the earth."[6]

The gathering of modern Israel featured prominently in the *Millennial Star* throughout the remainder of the nineteenth century. Indeed, the *Star* published over five hundred articles concerning the gathering between 1840 and 1900.[7] Over four hundred of these articles dealt with emigration—the practical application of the doctrine of gathering.

Initially, the gathering was tied to the early Latter-day Saints' powerful millenarian expectations.[8] During the millennium, reported the editors of the *Star*, "all the political, and all the religious organizations that may previously exist, will be swallowed up in one entire union—one universal empire—having no laws but God's laws, and saints to administer them."[9] In preparation for this universal empire, Mormon teachings maintained that:

> God will set his hand a second time to restore the house of Israel and the house of Judah to their national rights, to the favor of God, and to their own land. They will gather out from every nation under heaven, with their silver and gold, &c., employing the ships, steam-boats, railroad carriages, canal-boats, litters, horses, mules, camels, and swift beasts, and every kind of conveyance which the nations can furnish. This gathering will be by a mighty hand, with a stretched-out arm, and with fury poured out; and in short, Jehovah's arm will be made bare in the eyes of all the nations, in signs, in wonders, in miracles, in revelations, in judgments, and in mercies.[10]

As evidence that the gathering of Israel was underway, the *Millennial Star* reported proudly in June 1840 that the first emigrant company, comprised primarily of converts from Preston and Manchester, had left Liverpool for New Orleans. The news of this voyage aimed to "give a new impulse to the spirit of emigration and put to shame those who have published falsehoods concerning this plan of deliverance."[11]

Before the close of the first volume of the *Millennial Star*, both the First Presidency and the Quorum of the Twelve Apostles addressed the British Latter-day Saints respecting the great gathering of scattered Israel. Joseph Smith, Sidney Rigdon, and Hyrum Smith wrote the gathering "cannot be too forcibly impressed in the minds of all . . . for this is according to the instructions we have received from the Lord."[12] Central to the First Presidency's endorsement of emigration was the construction of the temple at the saints' new settlement in Nauvoo, Illinois. The immediate association between the doctrine of gathering and the temple was established by Joseph Smith in 1843:

> What was the object of gathering the Jews, or the people of God in any age of the world? The main object was to build unto the Lord a house whereby He could reveal unto His people the ordinances of His house and the glories of His kingdom, and teach the people the way of salvation; for there are certain ordinances and principles that, when they are taught and practiced, must be done in a place or house built for that purpose.[13]

In the Nauvoo Temple, the First Presidency promised, "all the functions of the priesthood [would] be duly exercised and . . . instructions from the Most High [would] be received."[14] In addition to the spiritual powers and gifts the First Presidency promised, temporal blessings were assured to the gathering saints:

> [In Nauvoo] we may expect a scene of peace and prosperity, we have never before witnessed since the rise of our church, and the happiness and prosperity which now await us is . . . incalculably great. By a concentration of action, and a unity of effort, we can only accomplish the great work of the last days, which we could not do in our remote and scattered condition, while our interests both spiritual and temporal will be greatly enhanced, and the blessings of heaven must flow unto us in an uninterrupted stream; of this, we think there can be no question.[15]

Not wanting to mislead British converts into thinking the saints were without blemish, the First Presidency openly admitted that emigrants "must not expect to find perfection" in Nauvoo, but that through obedience to the commandments individual prejudices among converts "not only from different states, but from different nations" might be overcome, and the saints may dwell as the united, covenant people of God.[16]

While the vision of the gathering was dramatically portrayed by the Prophet Joseph Smith and his counselors, the challenging logistics of emigration were left to the Quorum of the Twelve. The British Mission had been in operation for three years when the doctrine of gathering was disclosed and emigration was adopted as official church policy. During that time the Twelve noted that the majority of converts in Britain were people of modest means, those of the "respectable working class" for whom self-funded emigration was unlikely. Consequently, the Twelve established a structured

FIGURES 2.1–2.2. These pen and ink portraits of Joseph and Hyrum Smith were produced by Sutcliffe Maudsley, a convert from Tottington, Lancashire, in early 1844, just a few months before Joseph's martyrdom in Carthage, Illinois. Courtesy L. Tom Perry Special Collections, Harold B. Lee Library, Brigham Young University, Provo, Utah.

and prioritized system of emigration intended to enable the converts to gather in Zion. In an epistle to the British saints, published at the conclusion of the first volume of the *Millennial Star*, the Twelve wrote:

> It will be necessary, in the first place for men of capital to go on first and make large purchases of land, and erect mills, machinery, manufactories, &c., so that the poor who go from this country can find employment. Therefore it is not wisdom of the poor to flock to that place extensively, until the necessary preparations are made. The brethren will recollect that they are not going to enter upon cities already built up, but are going to "build cities and inhabit them." Building cities cannot be done without *means* and *labor*.[17]

The combination of the vision of the Prophet Joseph and the pragmatism of the Twelve established the doctrine of gathering as a central tenet of Mormon belief by the end of 1840. The foundation laid, the saints had little idea how challenged their commitment to gather would be in the six years that followed, during which the work and life of Mormonism's founding prophet would reach its violent end.

Martyrdom and Aftermath

> We are afraid, at times, that some individuals suppose that if they could only get to Nauvoo their troubles would be ended; but we would wish to at once undeceive such. Trials and difficulties they will still have to encounter; Satanic agency will not be found slumbering, but will, while permitted, call into action every energy that can possibly be wielded to annoy and distress the people of God; therefore, while we urge upon the Saints the subject of gathering, we would also have them to bear in mind that the day of discipline is not yet past; but even in this reflection they may rejoice likewise, knowing that all things shall work together for their good.
>
> Thomas Ward, editor, *Millennial Star*, 1844[18]

On June 27, 1844, the gathered saints at Nauvoo learned of the murders of Joseph Smith and his brother Hyrum at a territorial jail in Carthage, Illinois. The news did not reach the lay membership in Britain until August of that year, in a special supplement inserted in the *Millennial Star*. Any remaining delusion that all was peaceful and prosperous in Zion was now abandoned. The "trials and difficulties" referenced by Thomas Ward on page forty-seven of the *Star* stood in paralyzing juxtaposition to the announcement of Joseph Smith's assassination two pages later.

In Lancashire, the saints demonstrated their grief at the loss of a prophet they had never met and in whom their hopes and expectations were centered. The congregation in Liverpool gathered to mourn at the rented music hall, where they decorated in black drapery the raised gallery whereon sat the officers of the local priesthood.[19] Latter-day Saints throughout Britain were advised to pay their respects publicly and in like manner.

Eagerly, converts awaited word as to how Smith's death had influenced the society of the members in Illinois, wondering how the impact of his murder would affect their own hopes of emigration. Richard Halewood, a convert from Liverpool, expressed his concerns in a letter to loved ones in Nauvoo. In what may be the earliest recorded description of a British Latter-day Saint's reaction to the news of the prophet's death, Halewood wrote:

> I am very anxious to hear from you and to know how you are situated in your affairs and what affect it has had in them since the deaths of Brother Joseph and Hyrum. When the news reached Liverpool and informed us of the horrible death they had met with from a blackhearted and ruthless mob I

assure you it caused a deep sensation amongst the Brothers and Sisters nearly the whole have put on the sable garb of mourning as well as decorated the churches in black in respect for our Beloved Brother Joseph and Hyrum.

Dear Brother and Sister send me every particular how you are situated and how you are going on. There have been some come back from Nauvoo and have stated that the people were starving to death there, with a deal more of such like tales. I hope that you will send me every particular as I should like to read your letter to the Saints in Liverpool to comfort their hearts. They have sorrow enough at present about the death of Joseph and Hyrum without such tales coming from there. I know that you will send me the true state of things.[20]

Church members and leaders on both sides of the Atlantic doubted the gathering could continue independent of the Prophet Joseph. The forced abandonment of the city of Nauvoo and its recently completed temple complicated matters for converts overseas. While the members in Nauvoo had no option but to flee, the saints in Britain worried that the gathering had ceased altogether.

The main body of Mormons in America was well acquainted with migration at the time of Smith's martyrdom. Since the doctrine of gathering was first revealed in 1831, church members had migrated from New York to Ohio and thence to Missouri. Smith taught that in Jackson County, Missouri, the city of Zion—or the New Jerusalem—would be built in preparation for Christ's return to the earth.[21] Even after the Mormons' expulsion from Missouri in 1838, the prophet maintained that Jackson County would remain a dedicated site for a future temple and would one day be the location of the "center stake" of Zion.[22]

Some British converts felt that the abandonment of Nauvoo was unacceptable—an unauthorized repeal of one of Joseph Smith's most significant and seemingly incontrovertible revelations. In response, the editors of the *Millennial Star* wrote:

> But again, others ask, "Where is there a revelation to leave Nauvoo?" which we would answer by asking another—"Where was the revelation for them to leave Jackson county, in the state of Missouri?" Every true-hearted Saint believes in the revelations given in reference to the building up of a great city and temple there, and yet the Saints have abandoned it.[23]

Further justifying the exodus from Nauvoo, the editors continued:

> Nauvoo has, as it were, served its purpose for the present time; it has been a central point for the Saints, to teach them the principle of the gathering;

> there they have acquired many a lesson of industry and wisdom in connexion [*sic*] with the kingdom of God; they have learned to estimate the capabilities of the Saints when united and under the blessing of the Lord; and though they have practiced the virtues of forbearance and long-suffering, they have discovered that they have a power and an energy at command, that will be called, at no distant day, into exercise at the will of God. Why then do the Saints leave Nauvoo? Why? Because reason, truth, humanity, the seed of Jacob, the furtherance of the great cause of truth, and the judgments of Almighty God demand it.[24]

By the end of 1844 Brigham Young and the Quorum of the Twelve had firmly established themselves as the governing body of the church. The transition in leadership from the prophet to the apostles, however, was far from seamless. In Nauvoo the Latter-day Saints were forced to deal with the disruptive fissures caused by the death of Joseph Smith. And potential successors who vied for the presidency deepened the division.

It was not long before the controversy concerning the succession of the church presidency became transatlantic in scope, affecting the remaining British membership. Disciplinary action administered by the leadership of the British Mission suggests how threatening the issue had become. In 1846 a handful of members in Liverpool were excommunicated for "receiving and acknowledging the authority of the imposter James J. Strang, and denying the lawful authority of the martyred Prophet Joseph Smith in the person of President Brigham Young and the Twelve Apostles."[25] In 1844 Strang had presented to the membership in Nauvoo a letter he claimed had been written by Joseph Smith. This letter designated him as successor to the office of church president and further designated Voree, Wisconsin, as the new site for the gathering. Although the Quorum of the Twelve Apostles exposed the letter as a forgery and advanced their plans for the westward trek, Strang persisted in his claims. He garnered a small but committed following, among whom were three former members of the Twelve. Each of these members had been excommunicated for apostasy—John E. Page, William McLellin, and William Smith, the prophet's younger brother.[26]

For some, the matter of succession remained an unresolved issue. In 1862 the Liverpool members were again cautioned against the influence of the various Mormon sects that spawned at the time of Smith's death. In particular, the Saints were urged to be wary of a certain Charles Derry, who busied himself recruiting membership into the Reorganized Church of Jesus Christ of Latter Day Saints, led by Joseph Smith III.[27] For the majority of church members, however, there was little question that the deaths of Joseph and Hyrum Smith had effectively dissolved the First Presidency, leaving the

Quorum of the Twelve Apostles as the governing body of the church. By February 1846 Brigham Young and the other members of the Twelve had led most of the Saints in Nauvoo across the Mississippi River and into Iowa for winter refuge.

For the British Mormons who wished to abide in the faith, there was no option but to divorce their understanding of Zion from the city of Nauvoo, and from the temple to which they had contributed tithes, and fix it upon the apostles as they looked westward in search of another home. This was no small thing. The Nauvoo Temple, with its endowments of spiritual power for the living and saving rites of the priesthood for the dead, was "the center not only of the world, but also of the universe."[28] For the saints it was, as Richard Bushman described, "the center of a global vortex."[29]

Notwithstanding Nauvoo's spiritual and social centrality, even Joseph Smith seemed confident that the saints' migration would continue. Two years before his death, Smith prophesied that the members "would continue to suffer much affliction and would be driven to the Rocky Mountains," where they would "build cities [and become] a mighty people."[30] Smith later directed the Twelve to "investigate the locations of California and Oregon, and hunt out a good location, where we can remove to after the temple is completed, . . . have a government of our own, get up into the mountains, where the devil cannot dig us out, and live . . . as old as we have a mind to."[31]

With these instructions still in mind, some Latter-day Saints speculated that Brigham Young and the Twelve would ultimately direct the members of the church to establish Zion on the West Coast. Elder Reuben Hedlock of the British Mission presidency addressed the Latter-day Saints from mission headquarters in Liverpool and urged them to take personally the travails and efforts of their fellow members in America. He also challenged them to remember that

> while our brethren [in America] are laboring and sacrificing their all, and going into the wilderness to prepare a home for us; I say, while they are in an unsettled state, let the Saints in Britain not slack their hand, but use double exertions to swell the amount of capital, and prepare every needful thing for a company of Saints to take with them next September to California, that they can take their weary brethren something to comfort their hearts in the wilderness.[32]

By April 1846 the remoteness of church leadership in Iowa had slowed communication with the British Mission to a near standstill. Lacking direction, the mission presidency issued a temporary halt on emigration, deepening fears among the members that the day of gathering was past.[33] In October of that year, Elder Orson Hyde of the Twelve arrived at Liverpool charged with the presidency of the church in Britain.

Assuming editorial control of the *Millennial Star*, Hyde concluded the October issue with the following notice:

> As there are many who wish counsel concerning going to America, we would say to them be not anxious to go this year. We have instructions for the Saints upon the subject, which we shall lay before them in due time. Be content, therefore, for the present, and your contentment to remain here a little longer will be for your benefit.[34]

Although the emigration of the British Latter-day Saints had ceased, local church authorities continued to teach the principle of gathering as a defining aspect of their religion. Notwithstanding the uncertain future of the program, Elder Wilford Woodruff urged the church members in Britain to "keep in view the gathering" and maintain a patient expectation of improved opportunity.[35]

Between 1844 and 1848 church leaders on both sides of the Atlantic used the *Millennial Star* to keep the gathering fresh in the minds of the British members. When the doctrine was challenged by critics, church leaders published an ardent defense, maintaining that the gathering was a divine mandate consistent with biblical precedent, and was a precise fulfillment of prophecies concerning Zion in the last days. In all things the gathering was portrayed as the only means whereby the faithful might be spared the sins of the world and plagues that would be poured out.[36] The point was clear: the quest to establish Zion would continue as Joseph Smith had directed. But only after a new destination was identified could the gathering find a renewed impetus.

The Valley

Unbeknown to the Latter-day Saints in Britain, Brigham Young and the first few companies of Mormon pioneers arrived in the Salt Lake Valley in late July 1847. Affirming that he had seen the valley's expanse in a vision months before, Young declared an end to the saints' westward trek.[37] After establishing a rudimentary infrastructure and successfully surviving their first winter, church authorities directed that the membership in Britain be informed. The February issue of the *Millennial Star* delivered the news in exultant tones:

> EMIGRATION!—the channel of Saints' emigration to the land of Zion, is now opened. The long-wished for time of gathering has come. Good tidings from Mount Zion! The resting place of Israel, for the last days, has been discovered. Beautiful for situation, and the ultimate joy of the whole earth is the Stake of Zion established in the mountains. . . . There vegetation flourishes with magic rapidity. And the food of man, or staff of life, leaps into maturity

> from the bowels of mother earth, with astonishing celerity. . . . The various timber of lofty mountains wait in proud readiness to bow at the signal of the axe, and to go forth to beautify the temple of our God. The box, the fir, the pine, and maple, have sprung up at the dictation of prophecy, just where they are needed. Mills, factories, hamlets, mansions, houses, and cities, can be supplied with building materials from the unculled forests of many ages.
>
> Now rejoice, and lift up your heads, O ye pure in heart, and let the laboring and heavy laden, that have been bowed down under the weight of accumulated oppressions, in every nation, prepare themselves to come to their inheritance in the land of promise. The day of release dawns, and the notes of millennial jubilee reverberate from the mountain heights of Zion. Let all that can, gather up their effects, and set their faces as a flint to go Zionward in due time and order. All things are now ready. The word of the Lord comes forth from Zion to the upright of all the earth, "gather yourselves to the place of your rest, for there is no time to be lost."[38]

While the excessively sanguine rhetoric generated unrealistic expectations about life in the harsh desert environment, it also fired anew the imagination of *Millennial Star* readers in Britain. Expectations began to mount. It was not long before manifestations of this became evident within British congregations. Compelling evidence of the powerful westward orientation of the British saints is found in the membership records of the Upholland Branch. Of the fifty recorded blessings given by local priesthood officers to the infants and young children in the congregation, over half directly reference the gathering. All such blessings promised their youthful recipients a successful and timely migration upon the conditions of individually proven faithfulness and the diligent moral instruction provided by parents.[39] Clearly, qualifying for the blessings of the gathering was a family affair.

With Zion's new destination fixed in place, church leaders in both Britain and America worked to restore the sense of urgency that had formerly characterized the Mormon emigration. The British saints responded with zeal and enthusiasm. *Millennial Star* year-end statistical reports indicate that emigration accelerated dramatically. Between 1849 and 1868, over five thousand Lancastrian Latter-day Saints had set sail for Zion.[40]

With funnel-like trajectory, church members throughout Britain gravitated toward Liverpool in anticipation of departure. The Liverpool congregation thus became, in microcosm, the commixture of British regional identities that later would characterize the blended constituency in Salt Lake City. The amalgamation of cultures and backgrounds tested the very fabric of the saints' Zion initiative. For the first time, the members' deeply rooted regional identities were necessarily subsumed by their shared religious identity.

Congregational unity, however, was tenuous, and the relationships between the diverse convert groupings in Liverpool were sometimes strained. Accordingly, the management of the Liverpool Branch during the peak years of emigration required diplomacy and ample administrative skill, as evidenced in the following anecdote. In 1854, the Liverpool Branch council concluded that the Welsh saints in Liverpool should be separated from the rest of the membership and gathered into their own autonomous congregation, presided over by Welsh priesthood leadership. Although the reasons for this division were not expressly recorded, a later statement by George Reynolds, who presided over the Liverpool Branch in 1864, hints at the cause. These members, Reynolds wrote, "were not so united as most branches, as they came from almost all parts of the Kingdom, English, Irish, Scotch and Welsh, and do not amalgamate as well as other Saints do."[41] Thus, the Zion ideal characterized in Mormon scripture as "one heart and one mind" appears to have had its practical limits in Britain, as the regional identities of the membership remained preeminent.[42]

There is a distinct relationship between the frequency with which the editors of the *Millennial Star* emphasized the doctrine of the gathering and the rate at which members actually emigrated. It is thus important to differentiate between the gathering as both doctrine and practice when relying on the *Millennial Star* as a primary historical source. Overall, the majority of *Millennial Star* references to the gathering deal with the pragmatic and logistical matters of emigration rather than the underlying religious significance and rationale—a numerical ratio of more than four to one. During the peak years of emigration, between 1853 and 1868, the practical applications of the gathering received overwhelming attention while the gathering as a religious doctrine was scarcely mentioned at all.

A striking example is 1855, in which 388 Latter-day Saints emigrated from the English North West. The *Millennial Star* that year published a total of twenty articles on emigration. These articles report on the journeys and experiences of particular emigrant groups, note the progress of parties en route, and extend caution, counsel, and advice to those anticipating departure. Only one article deals specifically with the gathering from a doctrinal perspective. Conversely, when emigration began to wane in 1858, the *Star* editors responded by increasing their emphasis on the doctrines sustaining the emigration program. In the two years that followed, the doctrinal and practical aspects of the gathering received almost equal emphasis in the *Star*, with fifteen articles teaching the religious principle and sixteen reporting on actual emigration. In 1870 and again in 1876, both comparatively weak emigration years, the *Millennial Star* heavily accented the religious—and specifically the eschatological—principle behind the gathering. The numbers of articles teaching the doctrine outnumbered the emigration reports more than two to one. The increased attention to doctrine was an effective encouragement to the saints, and the number of Lancashire emigrants tripled from 40 in 1876 to 121 in 1878.

Although the contest for control of the church following the murders of Joseph and Hyrum Smith temporarily interrupted emigration between 1844 and 1846, the gathering rebounded dramatically in the decade following the Saints' arrival in the Salt Lake Valley in 1847. Between 1849 and 1900, over seven thousand members of the church emigrated from over sixty congregations spread throughout the English North West. This success must be attributed, at least in part, to the editors of the *Millennial Star*, who promulgated the sustaining religious principles behind the migration whenever emigration slowed. The pattern of teaching the doctrine and monitoring and reporting its implementation sustained Mormon emigration from Britain for half a century.

Migration Problems

Conversion to Mormonism has always carried consequences. Nineteenth- and early twentieth-century conversion accounts reveal how wide-ranging and problematic these consequences were, and how they adversely impacted the lives of individual Latter-day Saints in Britain. Loss of employment and feelings of social and familial ostracism commonly attended conversion. The doctrine of gathering presented its own set of consequences, both unifying and divisive.

For the faithful gathered in America, Mormonism bound its adherents to one another in a powerful covenant society rooted in millenarian expectancy. The cohesion of this community was galvanized by ongoing persecution. In Britain as well as America, Mormonism was inherently divisive. Adherence to its tenets separated families, both geographically and denominationally. Mormonism's burgeoning emigration program cast a shadow of suspicion over the institutional intent of the church, which appeared to many as a peculiar and polygamous threat to staunch Victorian morality. For various reasons, including the above-mentioned pressures, some British Mormons resisted the call to gather.

Throughout the 1850s, church leadership used the *Millennial Star* both to urge the Saints westward and to unapologetically rebuke the sluggish. As one editor wrote in 1852:

> We know that the majority of the Saints in Britain, especially the poor ones, are filled with the spirit of gathering, and they are striving with all the energies of their souls to fulfill this great commandment, and make it honorable.

> We do not write to chide or reprove such Saints as these; but we know there are some who might gather, and who will not make the effort; they are engaged in business and say they cannot [give] it up, or they are partners in a firm, and cannot dissolve the partnership, or they are afraid when they get to Zion they will not obtain the social, literary, and scientific temporal comforts and luxuries which they enjoy in Babylon, or they cannot sacrifice them for the dangers of a sea voyage, the hardships of a journey over the plains, or the inconveniences of a new country. Now to such Saints as these, who lust after the luxuries of Babylon . . . we wish our remarks to apply as forcibly as cases may require and we shall not be displeased if our words fit as close as a huntsman's cap. If we may judge by their actions, these Saints think it is to their interest to delay their gathering until they can go a little more comfortably than they can now, or until Zion will be filled with comforts and luxuries for their especial convenience. Now this is folly, and perhaps, when it is too late, such persons will find they have made a woeful miscalculation. Every year passed in Babylon by a Saint who has the ways and means of going to Zion, unless he have special counsel to stay, is one year lost to him, and he will yet be conscious that such is the case.[43]

Although LDS membership records reveal that it was common for select members of a family to join the church together or within a few years of one other, rarely did an entire family unit convert en masse. Thus, conversion divided families spiritually and emigration separated them literally and, in many cases, permanently. This is an uncomfortable historical reality for a church that prizes the enduring nature of family relationships.

The letters of Jane Thornber provide an intimate perspective of the influence of Mormon emigration upon British family life. Jane was a cotton weaver from Downham, Lancashire, who likely converted during the initial mission to the upper Ribble Valley in 1837–38. At age sixteen, Jane emigrated, leaving almost all her family in the village. She married Matthew Ellison, a convert from Chipping, Lancashire, and the two of them settled in Nauvoo. Following the death of the Prophet Joseph, the Ellisons remained in Illinois. In time, Jane found herself struggling with feelings of isolation from both her family in England and the religion that had motivated her emigration.

By the early 1860s Jane's feelings of estrangement had peaked. Her letters to family in Lancashire bespeak her discouragement with a struggling American economy and concern for her two sons, who had been conscripted to fight in the U.S. Civil War—two consequences of conversion neither Jane nor her family could have anticipated when she joined the church twenty years earlier.[44]

The Spencer family is another striking example of the effects of the gathering upon families in rural England.[45] Hailing from Easington, Yorkshire, Richard and Mary Spencer moved to Lancashire as young adults and were married in the village of Slaidburn in 1819.[46] Over the ten years that followed, Richard farmed in various locations around the River Hodder until economic considerations forced him to relocate his growing family to the more promising Ribble Valley. With the expectation that their children would take up mill work, Richard and Mary moved into a small home in Waddington. Their oldest child, George, was then nineteen. An ambitious and hardworking young man, he opted to remain in the Hodder Valley where he worked a rented farm alone.

During a proselytizing tour of the upper Ribble Valley in 1839, Elder Joseph Fielding stopped to preach in Waddington. Among his interested listeners was the thirty-nine-year-old Mary Spencer. A mother of ten children, Mary was quickly convinced that her family's future lay in Mormonism and within days Fielding baptized her. Skeptical, Richard kept the foreign faith at arm's length and witnessed his wife's baptism with what must have been mixed emotions. Although Richard refused to join the church, he did not oppose Mary in her newfound religion. He supported his wife as she actively incorporated Mormonism into the lives of their children, who were each later baptized.

In 1840, as soon as the doctrine of gathering was preached openly to the saints, Mary Spencer began planning her family's emigration. Despite his lack of faith, Richard supported Mary in this profound decision. The Spencers moved again to Clitheroe, where each employable member of the family worked earnestly with the aim of funding their westward trek. Meanwhile, seemingly oblivious to the dramatic change within his family on the opposite side of Waddington Fell, George Spencer continued to farm in the Hodder Valley. As the missionaries' proselytizing efforts were centered largely upon the towns and villages of the Ribble Valley, it is conceivable that George heard nothing of Mormonism, and may not have known of his family's conversion.

With their plans to emigrate about to materialize, Richard Spencer walked the fifteen miles to his son's farm and broke the news. Richard's conveyance of the conversions of Mary and the other children mystified his oldest son, and the two of them discussed the prospect of emigration from their perspective as the two remaining non-Mormons in the family. Richard's plea was simple: if George would not join his family in their faith, as Richard himself had not done, then he could still be sympathetic toward their religion and accompany them to their new life in America. Stunned, George considered his own ambitions and refused the offer. The two parted ways amicably and saw each other for the last time. Shortly thereafter Richard and Mary Spencer removed to Liverpool. They sailed for New Orleans by the year's end.[47]

The Spencer family joined the saints at Nauvoo. Following Joseph Smith's death in 1844, they lingered for several years before trekking west in 1851. That same year, en route to the Salt Lake Valley, Richard died in an accident near Council Bluffs, Iowa. Although he had remained close to his family, Richard never converted. Mary and her eight surviving children pressed westward and settled in the Mormon community of Payson, Utah Territory. Meanwhile, in Lancashire, George Spencer farmed in the Hodder Valley for the following twenty-five years. He married twice, fathered six children, and finished out his life in the upper Ribble Valley, working a rented farm near Downham. There is no evidence suggesting he kept in touch with his family overseas.

Although they promptly developed roots in Utah, the Spencer family retained their sense of attachment to Lancashire and the Ribble Valley. In 1901 Richard Henry Spencer, a grandson of Richard and Mary, was called to serve as a missionary. He was sent from his home in Indianola, Utah, to proselytize in his family's ancestral home of Lancashire. Prior to his departure home, Richard Henry was urged by family members to seek out relations in the Pendle Hill region. He succeeded in locating his aged uncle George, then eighty-one years old. Richard Henry stayed with his uncle for several days and acquainted himself with his cousins in the area. He doubtless shared the message of Mormonism with his relations, perhaps with the hope that the same faith that had divided the family sixty years earlier would now reunite them. Although none of George's family gave Mormonism any serious consideration, they were thrilled to reconnect with a lost relation and eager to learn of the goings on in the lives of family members overseas. Shortly after this encounter, a grandson was born to George Spencer. He was given the name Richard Henry, in honor of his American namesake.[48]

Given the myriad strains associated with life on the American frontier, it is probable that at some point either the Ellisons or the Spencers contemplated a return to England. Although there is no record of their having done so, there is ample evidence that suggests, for other Latter-day Saint emigrants, the difficult realities of life in Zion proved disillusioning. Those who lost their faith and returned to England discovered they had to deal with another set of consequences in the form of disciplinary measures administered by church authorities back home.

The earliest recorded incident of this reverse migration occurs in the council meeting minutes of the Liverpool Branch in 1842. In September of that year the council decided that disciplinary action should be taken against two former members of their congregation, a Brother and Sister Parr, for "returning from America in defiance of the command of the Lord . . . speaking evil and giving a false report of the Church at Nauvoo, and . . . giving heed to the statements of enemies, and not conferring with the members of the Church."[49] Similarly, in 1857, Liverpool Conference President John M. Kay proposed that another high-profile local leader, Elder James Marsden, be excommunicated from the church for his refusal to emigrate when he was well positioned to do so.[50]

A particularly striking case of Latter-day Saints in Lancashire disregarding the command to gather occurred in the village of Upholland. In the summer of 1855 a member of the Upholland Branch discovered that the Baldwin, Marsh, and Rowbottom families, who had each emigrated the year before, were back in the village. Their return shocked the congregation's leadership and angered much of the membership, whose collective financial contributions had funded the families' emigration in 1854. As disciplinary proceedings ensued, the heads of the returned families each justified their return to England by citing a frustrating discovery. Life in Zion, they claimed, revealed a startling disparity between the teachings of Mormonism they had embraced in England and the character of the church's presiding authorities. Charged with apostasy by members of the branch council, Joseph Marsh insisted in his defense that the "principles [of Mormonism] are good but the men who teach them are bad" and asserted that he could "be as good a Saint" in Upholland as in Salt Lake City.[51]

Marsh continued his defense of the three returned families. Seeking theological recourse, he refuted the doctrine of the gathering and argued that "the [Salt Lake] Valley was not the place of gathering, but the mount of Olives" in Jerusalem.[52] The branch president saw matters differently. He revoked the men's priesthood and excommunicated them. Interestingly, within the following year, all three excommunicated men applied for rebaptism, were eventually admitted back into the branch, and were reinstated to their previously held priesthood office. Branch records indicate that all three men remained committed members of the church thereafter, although none ever returned to Zion.

In the face of the many questions and fears the scandal engendered among the local membership, the branch council was undeterred and resumed the business of facilitating emigration. In January 1856 the first agenda item was approved by the council: to revive the branch emigration fund and commence soliciting donations to fund the journeys of the Crandall and Paster families.[53]

Although incidents like the controversy at Upholland were rare, they did occur, and church leaders in Zion were mindful of their potential to disrupt the flow of incoming immigrants. Rumors of the harsh conditions in the Great Basin, the economic struggles facing the saints, and the fallibility of church authorities were difficult to quell, regardless of their validity. Members of the Quorum of the Twelve Apostles took a firm stance against disillusioned converts, whose tales of hardship and hypocrisy discouraged others from gathering. At a conference in Salt Lake City in 1856, Heber C. Kimball addressed the matter plainly: "When you hear false statements from disaffected characters, do not circulate them; do not send them back to England . . . to prevent those from coming here that otherwise would come."[54]

Ending the Gathering

Near the close of the nineteenth century, emigration became an unsustainable and unnecessary enterprise. The institutional survival of the church, once dependent upon converts, was secured through the successful transmission of faith to the next generation—through reproductive means as well as conversion. The millenarian fervor that once sustained the gathering gradually faded into abeyance, although many of the pioneer generation continued to pine for the much-anticipated return of Christ.

Over forty years of active immigration fueled the church's colonization efforts throughout much of western North America, resulting in the establishment of over five hundred settlements throughout the western United States, Mexico, and Canada.[55] At Mormonism's institutional core, the annual arrival of hundreds of poor British and European converts put strain on the public resources of Salt Lake City. Many immigrants depended upon the church and its local leaders for their temporal security.[56] Change was ineluctable.

Church leaders never formally rescinded the doctrine of gathering, nor could they. The matter was too integral to the doctrines of the Restoration. Nevertheless, the interpretation and implementation of the gathering doctrine were altered significantly within all levels of church operation. The *Millennial Star* evidences a crucial shift in church leaders' regard for the gathering, especially between 1891 and 1911. Fully adjusted, the new interpretation of the doctrine entirely altered the course of British Mormonism, changing quite literally the worldview of its membership.

Silence, not publicized announcement, signaled the change. Beginning in 1891, the number of articles concerning the gathering dropped precipitously. This baffled avid readers of the *Millennial Star*, who had grown accustomed to the ubiquity of the latest emigration report. There had been no hint at any change of policy on the gathering in the volumes of the preceding few years. To the contrary, in January 1890 the editors of the *Star* reflected on the previous year's emigration with satisfaction, noting that "two or three hundred more obeyed God's command to gather than did so in 1888."

The editors of the *Star* continued their active encouragement of emigration throughout the 1890 edition. However, in the following decade perceptive readers would have noticed a distinct decline in articles concerning migration. Between 1891 and 1900 the *Star* printed a total of only seven items on the gathering, the fewest in any ten-year span since the periodical first went to press in 1840.

The silence finally broke in 1893 with the authoritative voice of the First Presidency: Wilford Woodruff, George Q. Cannon, and Joseph F. Smith. Writing from Salt Lake City in February of that year, the presidency suspended all British and European convert emigration.[57] The moratorium pertained specifically to the current emigration season and did not signal an outright change in church policy. It did, however, send

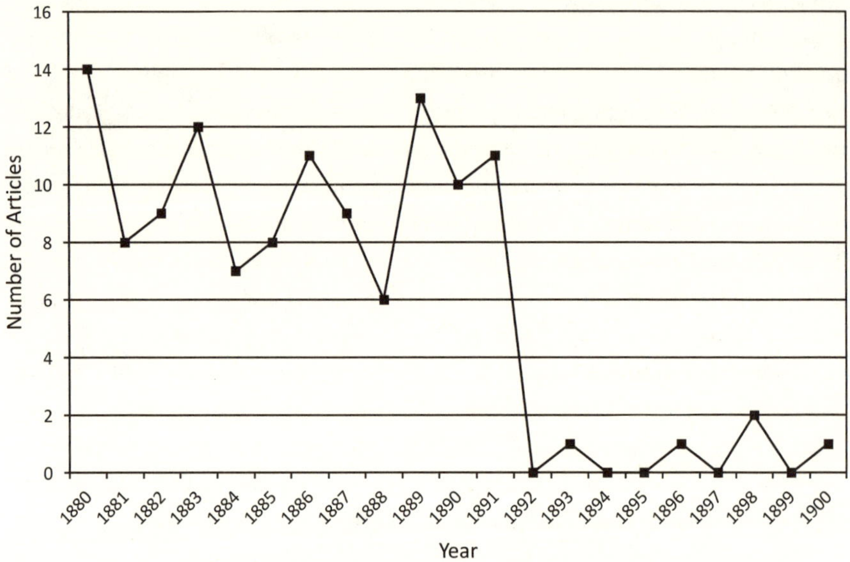

FIGURE 2.3. *Millennial Star* articles concerning emigration and the doctrine of gathering, 1880–1900.

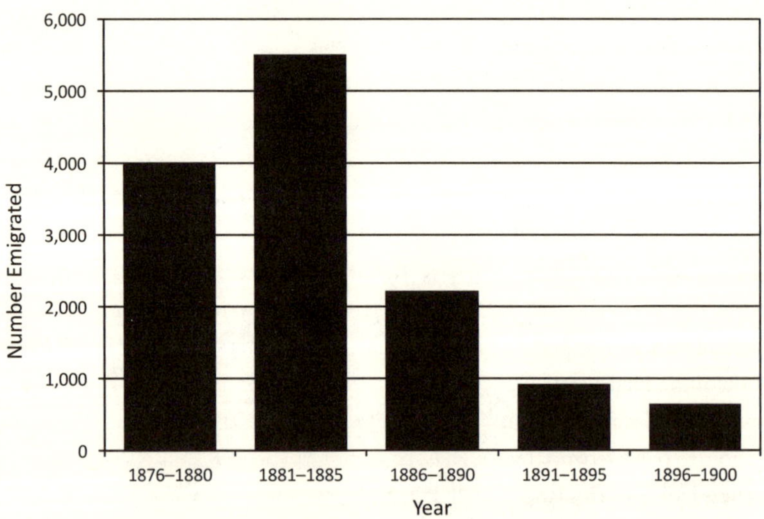

FIGURE 2.4. Membership emigration from Great Britain, 1876–1900.

the commanding message that the gates of Zion were kept by the First Presidency and would swing open only as wide as the prophet deemed fit. Emigration statistics from the Manchester and Liverpool Conferences indicate that the dictum was largely obeyed by the local saints, with only sixteen total members emigrating that year—a sharp decline from seventy-eight in 1892.

Beginning in 1893, British church members were requested to forestall emigration until they were "so advised by the proper authority."[58] The bearer of this difficult news to the saints in Britain, European Mission President Brigham Young Jr., was himself on the verge of returning to Salt Lake City, where the much-anticipated dedication of the Salt Lake Temple was about to occur. Young sought to soften matters with the following valediction:

> We part in this land to meet in Zion, we trust. Let no hearts fail, for the Lord is managing His affairs in His own way, and the most obscure Saint and active Elder are the objects of His especial care. Seek Him earnestly. He is a present help, and never will desert the righteous. We pray that the freedom of the Gospel may speedily come unto the oppressed of all nations, and every good and honest hearted person in the world, be gathered to that chosen land, Zion.[59]

All told, the message was a mixed one. At times upper church leadership in Utah and local church leadership sent contrasting signals regarding the gathering, resulting in some confusion among the general membership. True, the First Presidency had effectively closed emigration for the first time since Joseph Smith's death, yet local leadership continued to buttress the hopes of those still desiring to gather.

The vacillation continued to the end of the nineteenth century, as emigration was both decried and defended in the *Millennial Star*. In 1896 the editors unequivocally discouraged improperly motivated emigration, believing it would facilitate the spiritual weakening and eventual apostasy of many of the remaining saints in Britain. Those who supposed that life as a Latter-day Saint would be easier or more rewarding in Utah than in England were seen as particularly vulnerable.[60] In contrast, two years later George Q. Cannon of the First Presidency openly extolled the advantages of the gathering. Cannon maintained that it was "impossible for the human mind, unaided by the spirit of revelation, to comprehend the greatness of the future and the grandeur of the destiny of the people to whom this land has been given as an abiding place."[61] Regarding the saints who had gathered to the Great Basin, Cannon proclaimed that with "the advantage which they possess in the land where they reside, their future is assured, and every day will give us increased reason for thankfulness that the Lord has revealed the doctrine of gathering together of His Saints."[62]

As the twentieth century dawned, the church's stance regarding emigration seemed to hinge more on the attitude, preparation, and intent of the individual emigrant than on the program's doctrinal underpinnings. The doctrine itself remained incontrovertible—scattered Israel would be gathered and Zion would continue to be established. However, this no longer required that Israel be gathered to the same geographical destination, or that Zion's boundaries be restricted to the members in the Intermountain West. Given these adjustments, an approved and proper motive emerged as the ultimate filter through which prospective emigrants had to pass.

The longing to unite with already emigrated family members[63] and the desire to escape the "reproach and persecution" that attended the adoption of an "unpopular faith" remained valid justification for leaving Britain.[64] However, to the individual whose reasons for emigrating included anything other than building up the kingdom of God and supporting the church, rather than being supported by it, the gates of Zion remained closed.

By 1904 the adjusted interpretation of the gathering doctrine was nearly complete. The call to come to Zion had been central to the message imparted by missionaries throughout much of the nineteenth century. In the early twentieth century, however, under the direction of Apostle Heber J. Grant, the *Star* editors proclaimed, "emigration is not preached by the Elders of the Latter-day Saints." New converts who desired "to connect themselves with the body of the Church in Utah [were] positively counseled not to emigrate."[65]

Where emigration did occur, it was preceded by discussion with and authorization from local church officers. In the words of the *Star*: "No Saint should think of emigrating without consulting the president of the branch in which he has membership, and he will invariably be safe if he takes the advice of these men."[66]

Problematically, the editors of the *Millennial Star* continued to publish membership correspondence that celebrated the virtues of life in Zion even though general policy now discouraged the practice. Upon his arrival in Utah in 1909, John Cummard, a convert from Liverpool, wrote:

> I have been in the Church of Jesus Christ of Latter-day Saints a little over a year and a half, and at the end of that time I say, as I have often said, "Thank God I am a 'Mormon.'" . . . I shall never forget the first twenty-four hours I spent in Zion. One brother brought us over a sack of flour and two dozen eggs, as he thought we might need some assistance. He would not allow us to even thank him for them; said it is the duty of the saints to help one another. This is the sprit that pervades Zion. . . . I repeat that I am thankful to the Lord that I am in this land, where we can rear our children in the ways

> of righteousness, where they will not see drunken men rolling in the streets nor listen to foul language, nor live in crowded cities. We have not been in Utah a year, and yet our home is nicely furnished, and we enjoy many other blessings, among them good health. I know that "Mormonism" is true.[67]

In order to discourage further emigration, church leaders seized control of the overly idealized perception of Salt Lake City and called into question the spiritual maturity of those who retained the desire to gather. In the 1904 issue of the *Star,* the editors accused those British church members of clinging to a dangerous naiveté:

> They do not realize the hardships of a new country, and, in spite of the testimonies of those who know and have the welfare of the Saints at heart, they refuse to believe that the emissaries of evil, that vice and crime, Sabbath-breaking, envy and a host of other sins are to be found in Salt Lake, just as much as anywhere else on the face of the earth.[68]

The *Millennial Star* reported that in 1904 Salt Lake City's population was approximately seventy-five thousand, of which roughly half were not members of the church. At this time the city was hardly the scene of unified, communitarian prosperity and pervading religious commitment that its founders had envisioned in 1847. Furthering their point, the editors of the *Star* identified a difficult irony: the nearer a church member was to Salt Lake City, the more difficult it was for him or her to remain faithful. It was in Salt Lake City, they maintained, and not in Manchester, Liverpool, or London where "the temptations of Satan and his efforts to destroy the faith of the Saints reach their climax almost under the shadows of the Temple."[69]

The Babylon-like ills of the old world permeated the protective position of the saints in the Great Basin and even Zion's capital city was subject to compromise. The Saints understanding of Zion as an actual geographic location gradually gave way to a more abstract understanding. In its fullness, Zion was also an inward, spiritual condition—what Joseph Smith defined in 1833 as the "pure in heart."[70] Despite the transition from external geography to internal spirituality, the principle of Zion remained attached to the temple, which, even in Salt Lake City, had become Zion's only true refuge.

Access to the temple became the sole remaining reason for a British Latter-day Saint to justify emigration. Although the sacred rites of the temple were deemed necessary for exaltation in the afterlife, the preponderance of "temple work" centered on the performance of proxy ordinances for the deceased.[71] Crucially, all this work had to be preceded by the compilation of genealogies—an act that required much patience and ready access to historical records. In this, the saints in Britain found themselves in a crucial position regarding the furtherance of one of Mormonism's key aims: the redemption of the dead. To those British members still contemplating emigration, the editors of the *Millennial Star* directed the following admonition:

> There is a work to be done by every Saint before he is prepared to leave the land of his fathers. The work in the House of the Lord; the performing of its ordinances both for the living and for the dead should be primarily the great object of all gathering today. The principle of vicarious work for the dead is a most precious one to all the Saints, and we have no higher, nobler mission on earth than that of opening the doors of the prison-house for our loved ones who have passed into the spirit world. It rests with us, here in the fatherland, to carry on the great work of turning the heart of the fathers to the children, and the heart of the children to their fathers, and of connecting all of our kith and kin in the bonds of eternal salvation. The preparation for that work must be done here—the records obtained and the genealogies gathered. . . . The spirit of Temple work should be born here, not on the other side of the water.[72]

The saints throughout Britain were urged to make use of local records and temper their yearning for life in Zion with the understanding that the key genealogical resources at hand would be forever unavailable to them upon their arrival in Utah. Only when an individual's genealogy was completed and certified by local church authorities was emigration sanctioned freely. For the British Latter-day Saints of the new century, passage to Zion was earned, not granted.

The pursuit of exaltation for the living and the dead, and not the anticipation of Christ's Second Coming, was now the heart of the matter. The relationship between genealogical work and the timing of emigration was summarized in the *Millennial Star* as follows:

> When their [genealogical] labors here are completed the Spirit of the Lord will reveal it to them; and then, whether in the prime of life or in the feebleness of old age, whether in comparative poverty or blessed with this world's wealth, they may gather home with the people of God, bringing their sheaves with them, prepared to finish their work on earth and to stand as saviors on Mount Zion.[73]

For the saints who took this counsel seriously, compiling a thorough family history would have delayed their emigration significantly, possibly for years. Progress came slowly, but it did come. In the five years that followed the genealogical directive, 1905 through 1909, emigration from North West England rose to an average of sixty-three members per year, a marked increase from twenty-seven between 1895 and 1900.

The British Latter-day Saints of the 1890s were understandably concerned with temple ordinances, however little they may have understood them. The dedication of the Salt Lake Temple in 1893 was highly publicized among the saints in Britain. The moratorium placed on emigration that year only sharpened the growing intrigue stoked by the writings in the *Millennial Star*. Between 1892 and 1896 the *Star* printed seventeen articles about the temple and the place of temple ordinances within Latter-day Saint theology—a greater number than in any other five-year period in the publication's history. The temple was fast becoming the centerpiece of the Mormon experience.

Problematically, the abiding allure of the temple further enticed British saints to emigrate precisely when church officials were seeking to slow the westward migration. As means of encouraging the British saints to remain in their homeland, ecclesiastical leaders challenged them to consider more seriously their part in the growth and development of the church locally. Furthermore, they urged the British membership to expand their vision of the purpose of the church. They were to see it not as a self-isolating and self-preserving denomination that had withdrawn to the American West, but rather a divinely authorized catalyst for change, a great religious and revolutionary movement that would sweep the earth. The membership of every British Latter-day Saint was to be steeped in power and purpose.

In the beginning of the twentieth century, a shift in the institutional agenda of the church was becoming clear—Mormonism was going global. Any lasting expansion into Europe would depend upon a solid membership base in Britain. The British saints were asked to ponder their contribution to the global expansion of the church and become the bedrock upon which their local congregations could grow. To these members the editors of the *Star* queried:

> Do our people pause to consider the requirements of the Church in the world? Today it stands in need of faithful, prayerful Latter-day Saints, who live the principles of their religion, just as much as it needs the services of the traveling ministry. The world needs their example; the branch needs their services, their tithes, their influence. And it is because these Saints, who are of infinitely more use here than they are in America, are in such a hurry to get to Zion that our local branches and organizations are constantly depleted and are kept in a struggling condition. Too often those who are the best tithe-payers, the most faithful in the performance of their religious duties while they are striving to accumulate enough to take them to the Rocky mountains,

just as soon as this object is accomplished and prosperity begins to visit them in their new homes, commence to lose all interest in the Gospel.[74]

Just as the saints of the nineteenth century were urged to demonstrate their commitment to Mormonism by emigrating, the faithful of the early twentieth century were asked to manifest the same by staying put. The grand pioneering enterprise of traveling over sea and plain to colonize the Great Basin was, in the new century, complemented by the greater venture of spreading Zion's cause throughout the earth, beginning with Britain itself.

Before continental expansion could be pursued, local congregations required strengthening. Progress was quantifiably apparent. In 1892 the number of LDS congregations in Lancashire had dwindled to nine, with a total membership of 272. By 1909, the number of branches in the region had increased to twenty-four, with a membership of over 1,400.[75] Increased missionary activity and ongoing encouragement to forego emigration had begun to turn the tide of church affairs both in the English North West and throughout Britain at large.

The emphasis on growth required the abandonment of the British saints' westward orientation. In 1911 the editors of *Millennial Star* ceased reporting on emigration altogether. Although unsanctioned emigration continued, the *Star* no longer included emigration numbers in its year-end statistical reports. Between 1907 and 1911 the final few issues of the *Star* dealing with the topic of emigration did so defensively. These issues responded to increasingly lurid and sensationalized accusations in the popular press that the Mormons were actively recruiting young women to go to Utah for immoral purposes or to enter into polygamous relationships.[76] In time, the matter was addressed personally by Joseph F. Smith, then president of the church. President Smith denied the allegations and invited the press to correct its scandal-clad reporting of Mormonism and choose to see the Latter-day Saints as they saw themselves—members of the literally restored Church of Christ.

Despite the changes in policy and practice, the gathering retained significant, albeit altered, doctrinal status. In 1918 Charles W. Penrose, then a member of the First Presidency, published a brief article dealing with the gathering of Israel. He noted simply that the reemergence and "gathering-in" of Israel's tribes was "pre-ordained" by God, and ultimately would occur as anciently prophesied and would be a sign that Christ's return to the earth was imminent.[77] Interestingly, nowhere in his article did Penrose associate the emigration of Mormon converts with the fulfillment of the gathering doctrine. In one sense, this brought the entire matter full circle. Once again the gathering was associated with the millennial reign of Christ, just as it was during the time of Joseph Smith and Brigham Young, although now it had no literal migratory implications for church members. Rather, it placed the gathering into a certain theological abstraction. The fulfillment of the doctrine, it seemed, had passed from the hands of the First Presidency and the Twelve and back to God, who would, as President Penrose put it, accomplish the gathering "when the right time comes."[78]

Twentieth-Century Gathering

Despite the efforts of upper church leadership to dissuade the British Latter-day Saints from gathering, the only force that proved capable of halting migration altogether was war. During both the First and Second World Wars, British Latter-day Saints did not pursue emigration, although it resumed in the years immediately following each conflict. A mild resurgence of gathering occurred in the early 1920s and again in the early 1950s as several hundred British Latter-day Saints migrated to Utah and other North American destinations.[79]

A surge of British Mormon emigration following the armistice in 1918 drew a response from Elder Orson F. Whitney of the Quorum of the Twelve Apostles. Whitney acknowledged sympathetically that the appeal of emigration was "perfectly legitimate," adding further that "under ordinary circumstances, [it] would be a very proper course for Latter-day Saints to pursue." Although Whitney's stance on emigration was considerably softer than church leaders' views in the first decade of the 1900s, he nevertheless urged those contemplating emigration to remain in their homeland, cautioning them that their zeal, when carried to excess, would develop into misery-inducing fanaticism. "Stay where you are until further instructed," Whitney counseled. "There is a time for all things, and the Lord's time is the best time."[80] Time, however, was clearly running out.

While supervising the British Mission from its headquarters in Liverpool in 1923, Apostle David O. McKay further dissuaded the saints from emigrating. Unlike his predecessors, McKay openly acknowledged the conundrum church doctrine and policy presented to the British membership. While doctrine required the receipt of the ordinances of the temple, policy discouraged emigration to those locations with temples. McKay's solution was simple and ambitious. He urged the British members to build up the church locally and with haste, that there might be membership sufficient to justify the construction of a temple on British soil. When asked if the British saints of the 1920s should emigrate, McKay replied:

> No, it is important that the branches be built up, and members should remain and work toward that end. Some day we shall have temples built for them [in Britain] which will be accessible to all, so that the desired temple work can be done without uprooting families from their homelands.[81]

This great realization was the key to securing Mormonism's perpetuity as a British denomination. Fully ending the migratory flow of church members could be achieved only when a temple was built in the British Isles. Until that time, British Mormons would be caught in a theological crossfire: discouraged from emigrating because it diminished the viability of the British church and yet denied the opportunity to participate fully in the restored gospel through temple ordinances only available in the American West.

Expanding the British church to the point where temple construction was possible required greater missionary activity. As the Second World War loomed, however, the withdrawal of the American missionaries became inevitable. This withdrawal was problematic and demoralizing. In response to these concerns, Apostle Richard L. Evans assured the saints in 1937 that the future of the British church did not depend "upon the activities and continuance of its 'imported' missionaries" and there was "little or no relationship" between the number of American missionaries proselytizing and actual conversion rates.[82] Despite the growing prospect of war, Evans maintained that the saints should be undeterred in their commitment to building up their local congregations. As David O. McKay had done in the previous decade, Richard L. Evans again linked the cessation of emigration to the importing of Zion's qualities to the British Isles:

> Whether the traveling "Mormon" missionaries from America are called out of Great Britain tomorrow, or whether they remain there for the next hundred years, changes the fundamental situation not the least. The fact remains that unsettled world conditions and immigration restrictions mean that the Church must be built to flourish as a permanent institution in Great Britain. And every Latter-day Saint in the British Isles must strive toward that day when the Church of God shall be mighty in Britain, and when the spires of a Temple of the Lord shall pierce British skies, for "Zion is the pure in heart."[83]

At the end of the Second World War, David O. McKay, then a member of the First Presidency, again urged the British saints to remain in their war-ravaged homeland. The post-war agenda of British Mormonism mirrored that of the nation at large, and could be summarized in a single word: rebuild. In a letter from the First Presidency, the saints were urged to

> regard it as their moral and religious duty to do all they possibly can to assist the missionary Elders in building up branches and maintaining them with a view to the perpetuation of such organizations, so that peradventure, there

> may always be found some left ready to receive the missionaries and to render them the necessary assistance to enable them to still reach out and open up new fields of ministerial labor: and thus, by saints and missionaries working harmoniously together, branches may be continued in their organized capacity by constant additions to their rolls of membership, which otherwise might become broken up and cease to exist through unwise emigration.[84]

Surprisingly, despite increasing discouragement from the First Presidency, in 1947 the *Millennial Star* resumed its former practice of reporting member emigration. Such reporting appears to have been a courtesy to local membership and not an endorsement of gathering. A brief notation at the end of the December 1947 issue stated: "Mormon Church officials in England are desirous of building membership there and do not encourage emigration to Utah."[85] And yet, emigration continued. In Burnley, Lancashire, post-war emigration removed thirty saints from the faltering branch, reducing the congregation to five active members.[86]

In an effort to offset the steady drain of membership, in 1950 the *Millennial Star* began detailed reporting of convert baptisms. In 1949, the *Star* abandoned all emigration reporting, shifting readers' attention away from the lives of local members and toward the labors of the missionaries. Congregational replenishment and expansion became the greatest priority.

Importing Zion

In 1953 church authorities purchased a large parcel of land near Lingfield, Surrey, and designated it the location of the first Latter-day Saint temple to be built in Britain. Two years earlier, David O. McKay, whose service to the British church had spanned decades, was sustained as president of the church. Fittingly, he traveled to England to dedicate the temple site. The official groundbreaking ceremony was held in August 1955 and three years later the London Temple was completed.

At the temple dedication President McKay declared the church in Britain had entered a "new era." The president of the British Mission, T. Bowring Woodbury, seized the two-word phrase and adopted it as the mission motto. All efforts to grow the church took on a new intensity and zeal. In January 1959 Woodbury laid out a three-pronged prospectus for church development in Britain: first, the complete abandonment of emigration; second, the development of local ecclesiastical leadership; and third, the construction of purpose-built meeting houses.[87] Progress, development, and permanence were the watchwords of the "new era."

The construction of the London Temple eliminated the last-remaining justification for emigrating, although a deeply-rooted gathering ethos still lingered. This is represented in the following letter written by a teenage Latter-day Saint following her attendance at a three-day convention for church youths in 1959:

> Everyplace I turned I saw a smiling "Mormon" with hand outstretched in a warm greeting . . . and I had a wish in my heart that there could be a village where everyone was a "Mormon" and we could spend our time in the loving association of Saints. We could call it "Mormon Village," for everyone would be a "Mormon."[88]

Her "Mormon Village" never materialized, although other organizational developments were underway that would provide the British Latter-day Saints with a stronger sense of community. In 1960 the doctrine of gathering took on a fresh significance with the formation of the Manchester Stake—the first in Britain. "Stake" was a term unknown to new converts, derived from Old Testament prophecy regarding the expansion of Zion, which Isaiah likened to an unfurling tent: "Enlarge the place of thy tent, and let them stretch forth the curtains of thine habitations: spare not, lengthen thy cords, and strengthen thy stakes."[89] Grander in scale and purpose than the "Mormon Village," the stakes of Zion were to serve as the gathering place for local Latter-day Saints.[90]

In 1971, at the Belle Vue Exhibition Center and Free Trade Hall in Manchester, the church held its first British Area general conference. At this unprecedented gathering Joseph Fielding Smith, then president of the church, placed British Mormonism in a global context. "Thus the Church is not an American church except in America," President Smith explained, continuing, "In Canada it is a Canadian church; in Australia it is an Australian church; and in Great Britain it is a British church. It is a world church; the gospel is for all men."[91] President Smith also pointed out that, with the exception of Joseph Smith, every church president (including himself) had engaged in missionary service in Britain, thus establishing the ongoing association between Mormon prophets and the British Isles.[92]

When the leadership of the church designated the English North West as the site of the first stake of Zion in the British Isles, they deepened the region's significance to Mormonism's past and future. The formation of the Manchester Stake was formalized on March 17, 1960, a day the presiding apostle Harold B. Lee declared to be "the greatest day . . . in the development of the Church in England, a day which promises even greater days which lie ahead."[93] Over the next twenty-two years, four additional stakes were organized in the North West: Liverpool and Preston in 1976, and Ashton-under-Lyne and Chester 1982.[94]

The maturation of the church in Britain, as well as the designation of stakes as domestic gathering places for Latter-day Saints, is consistent with the direction given by Apostle Bruce R. McConkie in 1977:

> Israel shall be gathered one by one, family by family, unto the stakes of Zion established in all parts of the earth so that the whole earth shall be blessed with the fruits of the gospel. This then is the counsel of the Brethren: Build up Zion, but build it up in the area where God has given you birth and nationality. Build it up where he has given you citizenship, family, and friends.[95]

The call to build Zion at home was taken literally by Gertrude and Bessie Corless, sisters hailing from Preston, Lancashire. After joining the church as adolescents in the 1930s, the Corless sisters emigrated in the early 1950s, contrary to the prevailing counsel of church leaders. Their motivation was similar to the thousands who had gathered in the nineteenth century. They wanted to experience life in a location characterized by a high concentration of church members as well as reconnect with family members who had previously emigrated.

For over thirty years the Corless sisters lived in America, dividing their time between California and Utah. In 1987, just before the church celebrated its sesquicentenary in Britain, the sisters returned to Preston, eager to strengthen the local congregation and share their faith with the children of their non-Mormon relations who had remained in Lancashire. The same commitment to faith and family that had motivated their departure thirty years earlier ultimately led to their return.[96]

As illustrated by the Corless sisters, the adjusted interpretation of the gathering doctrine from westward to homeward required a concomitant adjustment to the British Mormons' desires, attitudes, and behaviors. Only when a total harmony existed between doctrine and practice could the British Latter-day Saints pursue the work of establishing Zion locally.

Conclusions

As Joseph Smith taught, it is through revelation "adapted to the circumstances in which the children of the kingdom are placed" that the church is governed. Indeed, it is through such adaptability that Mormonism has survived in Britain. The gradual adaptation of the doctrine of gathering guaranteed the successful perpetuation and maturation of Mormonism in the British Isles.

Historically, the English North West has been central to the gathering. During the years of sanctioned emigration, the British Mission offices in Liverpool coordinated the departure of tens of thousands of British and European Latter-day Saints. In the post-emigration church, the organization of the Manchester Stake signaled a domestic gathering of church members. While the construction of the London Temple eliminated the last remaining justification for emigration, the Preston Temple hastened a domestic gathering of saints unparalleled in concentration. This gathering has confirmed the English North West as the heartland of British Mormonism.

Church leadership adjusted their interpretation of the doctrine of gathering between 1891 and 1911, although it was not fully adopted by the British members until the middle of the twentieth century. This crucial adjustment divides British Mormon history into two parallel yet distinct periods—emigration and post-emigration—and contextualizes each remaining aspect. The several chapters that follow examine additional key elements of British Mormon history: missionaries and meetinghouses, converts and congregations, and opponents and apostates.

Chapter 3
Establishment and Expansion
1837–1853

> The news from all parts of the vineyard . . . is truly cheering. Here in Manchester some thirty persons were added to the Church in about three weeks, and are now rejoicing in the truth. In Rochdale, some twelve were being baptized and confirmed at once. In Stockport also there is a great increase in numbers, and in faith and love.
>
> —*Millennial Star*, 1841

Between July 1837 and April 1838, Mormonism took firm root in Preston, Lancashire, and throughout much of the Ribble Valley. Heber C. Kimball and Orson Hyde left Preston in early April 1838 and arrived in late May at the headquarters of the church in Kirtland, Ohio, where they reported their successes to the Prophet Joseph Smith. Prior to leaving the fledgling British mission, Kimball appointed one of his missionary associates, Joseph Fielding, to preside over the church in England, which then comprised twenty-six budding congregations, most of them in Lancashire.[1]

Although his ministerial duties were many and pressing, Fielding knew that expansion, not congregational maintenance, was the real goal. In the early spring of 1839, Fielding began prospecting for church growth beyond the Ribble Valley, most notably in the conurbations surrounding Manchester. Public curiosity and suspicion were beginning to mount. It was time to move. In a letter to his wife, Fielding invoked the writings of the New Testament gospels, declaring: "New doors are opening on all sides; truly the Harvest is great but the laborers are few; pray, therefore, the Lord of the Harvest to send forth Laborers unto his Harvest."[2]

For much of the 1840s, Joseph Fielding's assessment proved accurate: the harvest in England was great and the laborers relatively few. Initially, this personnel shortage appeared to be doctrinally induced: by design, there were only twelve apostles. The Twelve expanded the proselytizing program, consistent with Joseph Smith's 1838 revelation distinguishing them as the only body authorized to "open up the kingdom upon the four corners of the earth."[3] Their staggering achievements in the British Isles are still celebrated in the contemporary church.

British Mormon historiography is dominated by analysis of the powerful but brief "apostolic missions" of 1837–41. Consequently, comparatively little has been uncovered regarding the generations of missionaries that followed. A broader perspective reveals that the apostles were but the spearhead of a protracted and ambitious proselytizing thrust that was sustained by hundreds of local converts. Between 1842 and 1853 the crucial efforts of these homegrown emissaries spread Mormonism throughout the English North West and beyond, resulting in the greatest rates of numerical growth the British church would see in the nineteenth century.

While the previous chapter considered the impact of the Latter-day Saint doctrine of gathering, this chapter examines the gatherers themselves: the missionaries whose labors secured Mormonism's place as a British denomination. Although the vast fruits of their labors are evident, little is known about their identities. Simply stated, who were they? Where were they from? What methods did they employ? How effective were they in their efforts? Were the American apostles more or less successful at promulgating Mormonism in Britain than their local counterparts?

In an attempt to answer these questions, this chapter takes the form of an extended case study. Its purpose is to compare and contrast the proselytizing efforts of two nineteenth-century missionaries: the famed American apostle, Heber C. Kimball, and the relatively unknown Lancastrian convert, Henry Stocks. Each represents one of two early phases of Mormon proselytizing in Britain: the apostolic establishment of 1837–41 and the membership-driven expansion of 1842–53. Comparing the experiences of Kimball and Stocks will reveal the relationship between the respective missionaries' identities, methods, and effectiveness. This chapter will also feature an additional case study of early Mormon conversion in the upper Ribble Valley, and will identify the broader social and religious considerations that augmented Heber C. Kimball's oft-celebrated, but little understood, conversionary success. Uncovering British Mormonism's earliest missionary foundation is essential to understanding and explaining its institutional endurance.

Establishment: 1837–1841

From one perspective, British Mormonism is a religious enterprise born of an American economic crisis. As the saints gathered to Ohio in ever-increasing numbers, the beleaguered finances of the young church exacerbated distrust of the Prophet Joseph Smith. When Smith's petition to start a bank in Kirtland was refused by the state government, the prophet was instrumental in establishing an alternative—a joint-stock company named the Kirtland Safety Society. In 1837 the shock waves of a nationwide economic panic precipitated the society's failure, and many Latter-day Saints held Smith responsible. The disaster was debilitating to the church, carrying apostasy in its wake. The prophet saw the disruption in spiritual rather than temporal terms and later wrote: "No quorum in the Church was entirely exempt from the influence of those false spirits who are striving against me for the mastery; even some of the Twelve were so far lost to their high and responsible calling, as to begin to take sides, secretly, with the enemy."[4]

Within seven years of its organization, economic woes threatened to destroy the infant church. Reflecting on this period, Smith later wrote, "apostasy, persecution, confusion, and mobocracy strove hard to bear rule at Kirtland."[5] Although it seems likely that this internal strife and the resultant vulnerability of its upper leadership might have deterred Smith from thoughts of expansion, the opposite proved true. "In this state of things," Smith wrote, "God revealed to me that something new must be done for the salvation of His Church."[6]

This "something new" was the first overseas missionary endeavor of the church, over which Apostle Heber C. Kimball was called to preside. Of the original members of the Quorum of the Twelve Apostles, only two—Kimball and Brigham Young—remained unflagging in their devotion to the prophet. The fact that Smith would deny himself Kimball's support and association, when so few remained faithful to him, suggests the great importance with which the prophet viewed the prospect of expansion to England.[7]

Regarded as the father of British Mormonism, Heber C. Kimball is a compelling figure. No comprehensive history of British Mormonism can excuse itself from consideration of his contributions. Mormon historians have pored over Kimball's life, and his relatively brief but staggeringly successful missionary labors have been closely analyzed. Kimball has been eulogized and memorialized by his biographers, and the writings concerning him could properly be regarded as hagiographic.[8]

Heber C. Kimball personifies all that was effective about the American missionaries who labored in early-Victorian Britain. His apostolate ministry in the Ribble Valley in the late 1830s and early 1840s was central to the Mormons' sacralization of the region. The portrait of Kimball displayed in the missionary training center adjacent to the Preston Temple hangs as a constant reminder of the golden age of Mormon proselytizing in Britain, and seems intended to motivate modern-day missionaries to aspire to similar success.

What is most widely known about Kimball's Lancashire missions are his impressive numbers—approximately 1,500 converts between July 1837 and April 1838.[9] Far less clear are the root causes of his effectiveness. Attempting to explain his success requires the consideration of both his message and his methods—the doctrines he preached, and the fashion in which he preached them.

Kimball's well-documented capacity to raise congregations seemingly at will during his two missions to Lancashire in 1837–38 and 1840–41 has long captivated his biographers. Of all the historical sources that explain this phenomenon, the least insightful are Kimball's own writings. Kimball acknowledges his success, but neither marvels at it nor accounts for it. He speaks of winning converts as though it were a natural occurrence, no more startling or remarkable than a morning sunrise. Fortunately, other sources are more revealing. Kimball's personal correspondence with converts, and the several descriptions left by those who observed him at his proselytizing finest, portray him as naturally affectionate, benign, and effusive. Kimball's proficiency in winning converts seems bound up more in his personal demeanor and commitment to providing pastoral care than in the persuasiveness of his oration or the doctrines he taught.

An original member of the Quorum of the Twelve Apostles at the time of its organization in 1835, Heber C. Kimball never wanted for authority in the church. What he lacked, surprisingly, was confidence. Nowhere is this more apparent than in his reaction to Joseph Smith's revelation that he would oversee the commencement of missionary work in the British Isles. Invoking the Old Testament writings of Isaiah, Kimball wrote: "O, Lord, I am a man of stammering tongue, and altogether unfit for such a work; how can I go to preach in that land, which is so famed throughout Christendom for learning, knowledge and piety; the nursery of religion; and to a people whose intelligence is proverbial!"[10] With less ornate prose, Kimball later confessed, "the idea of such a mission was almost more than I could bear up under. I was almost ready to sink under the burden which was placed upon me."[11]

Kimball took solace in the prescient utterances of other church authorities, who spoke of the success he would encounter as if it was an inevitability. Hyrum Smith, brother of the Prophet Joseph and counselor in the First Presidency, said simply, "Go, and you shall prosper as not many have prospered."[12] Shortly before embarking, the First Presidency prophesied openly of what they regarded as Kimball's imminent success. Kimball later recorded that they promised "God would make me mighty in that nation in winning souls unto Him; angels should accompany me and bear me up, that my feet should never slip; [and] that I should be . . . blessed and prove a source of salvation to thousands."[13]

In contrast to Kimball's stifling self-doubt is the overwhelming confidence placed in him by the First Presidency. Kimball's ministerial certificate, composed and signed by the First Presidency two days before he was formally called to open the British mission, reveals their assurance that he was both qualified and capable:[14]

> For the long acquaintance we have had with this, our worthy brother, his integrity and zeal in the cause of truth, we do most cheerfully and confidently recommend him to all candid and upright people as a servant of God and a faithful minister of Jesus Christ. We do furthermore beseech all people who have an opportunity of hearing this, our brother declare the doctrine believed by us, to listen with attention to the words of his mouth.[15]

Notwithstanding the prophet's enthusiastic recommendation, Kimball remained daunted and sought additional help. Kimball appealed to the prophet to commission Brigham Young to join him in opening the British mission. Joseph Smith declined, insisting "he had something else for [Young] to do."[16] Kimball was thus left alone to come to terms with the frightening realities of his unprecedented appointment.

Reflecting years later on his feelings of inadequacy, Kimball articulated a moment of powerful self-realization. His misgivings were then supplanted by a growing conviction that he had a divine commission:

> [The] moment I understood the will of my Heavenly Father, I felt a determination to go at all hazards, believing that He would support me by His almighty power, and endow me with every qualification that I needed; and although my family was dear to me, and I should have to leave them almost destitute, I felt that the cause of truth, the gospel of Christ, outweighed every other consideration.[17]

Although Kimball attributed his success to the verities of the Restoration, he failed to recognize additional factors. First, Kimball was careful to align his efforts with Joseph Smith's directives. Second, he simplified the message of Mormonism to its fundamental Christian principles. Third, Kimball invested heavily in personal relationships with prospective converts. Brigham Young, who accompanied Kimball on his second mission in 1840, closely observed Kimball's proselytizing practices. Years later, Young recalled Kimball's uniquely personal preaching style, which he contrasted with the comparatively ineffective labors of others:

> But brother Kimball would say, "Come, my friend, sit down; do not be in a hurry;" and he would begin to preach the Gospel in a plain, familiar manner, and make his hearers believe everything he said, and make them testify to its truth, whether they believed it or not, asking them, "Now, ain't that so?" and they would say, "Yes." And he would make Scripture as he needed it, out of his own bible, and ask, "Now ain't that so?" and the reply would be

> "Yes." He would say, "Now, you believe this? You see how plain the Gospel is? Come along now;" and he would lead them to the waters of baptism. The people would want to come to see him early in the morning and stay with him until noon, and from that until night; and he would put his arm around their necks, and say, "Come, let us go down into the water."[18]

The "plain, familiar manner" in which Kimball preached endeared him to prospective converts and granted him an undeniable conversionary persuasion. It does not, however, clarify the content of his preaching. Indeed, the very message of Mormonism must not be discounted in seeking to explain Kimball's success.[19]

Analysis of Kimball's initial mission to Lancashire raises important questions about Mormonism's development and the timing with which its revelations were publicized by missionaries and embraced by converts. For the missionaries who first preached in England, determining what not to preach was of vital importance, and the Prophet Joseph was quick to define the boundaries: "My instructions to the brethren were, when they arrived in England, to adhere closely to those first principles of the Gospel, and remain silent concerning the gathering, the vision, and the Book of Doctrine and Covenants, until such time as the work was fully established, and it should be clearly made manifest by the Spirit to do otherwise."[20]

Clearly, the intricacies of Mormonism were not to be conveyed all at once, nor could they be. Much of the prophet's contributions to Mormon doctrine still lay ahead. Evidences of Joseph Smith's revelatory gifts abounded in 1837, and within a few years they were touted before British clerics as proofs of Mormonism's veracity. And yet, as the mission found its footings, these sensational matters were strictly off limits. A more tempered, ecumenical approach helped Mormonism take root and gain respectability. As directed, Kimball and his associates emphasized only the "first principles," defined by Joseph Smith as: "(1) Faith in the Lord Jesus Christ; (2) Repentance; (3) Baptism by immersion for the remission of sins; (4) Laying on of hands for the gift of the Holy Ghost."[21] These core tenets established a common ground between the missionaries and their audiences, which were comprised primarily of smaller, Christian nonconformist sects.

Kimball reinforced the prophet's call for restraint with his six missionary associates: Orson Hyde, Joseph Fielding, Willard Richards, John Goodson, John Snyder, and Isaac Russell. Simplicity of speech and purity of testimony was the only approved method. All other methods were otiose. However, some of the missionaries failed to conform. For John Goodson, who was dispatched from Preston to Bedford in August 1837, the temptation to divulge some of the prophet's revelations proved irresistible. Goodson disclosed to the Reverend Timothy Matthews "the Vision"—a detailed description of the post-mortal condition of man—against which Joseph Smith had specifically cautioned. The effect was devastating. Kimball recorded the aftermath as follows:

> Brother Goodson, contrary to my counsel and positive instructions, and without advising anyone, read to Mr. Matthews the vision seen by President Joseph Smith and Sidney Rigdon, which caused him to stumble, and darkness pervaded his mind, so much so, that at the time specified [for his baptism] he did not make his appearance, but went and baptized himself in the River Ouse; and from that time he began to preach baptism for the remission of sins.[22]

Dismayed, Joseph Smith noted that the violation of his instructions had "turned the current of feeling [toward Mormonism] generally, and nearly closed the door in all that region."[23] In contrast, Kimball submitted fully to the prophet's instructions and experienced protracted success. Centering his efforts within Preston and the Ribble Valley, Kimball facilitated the conversion of as many as 1,500 of the approximately 1,600 people baptized during the 1837–38 mission, nearly all of them from Lancashire.[24] Accounting for this achievement years later, Kimball explained, "I said but little, but what I did say went straight to the hearts of the honest."[25] Reliance on the prophet's direction focused Kimball's efforts, bolstered his confidence, and augmented his success. The anxiety that had vexed him in Kirtland was no more.

The simplification of the missionaries' message wasn't just an act of obedience—it was a pedagogical necessity. In encouragement to his fellow missionary Isaac Russell, who was then laboring in Alston, Cumberland, Kimball wrote: "The people of this country want simple things. The majority of them are illiterate, and know but little about the bible and the more simple things you can teach them the better."[26] Historical studies suggest that in the 1830s as many as two-thirds of rural Lancastrians were illiterate.[27] Kimball's recommendation that the missionaries teach the people "simple things" affirms this observation.[28] Adapting to and working within the educational limitations of prospective converts was more crucial to their success than Kimball and his associates realized. Simplification of their message proved especially important in the upper Ribble Valley, where the pervading lack of literacy threatened to undermine the proselytizing value of the Book of Mormon. This book was the most important evidence presented by the missionaries to those who questioned the authenticity of Joseph Smith's prophetic station.

Possessed of a rudimentary education himself, Kimball was acutely aware of the need to adjust his message to a people whose appreciation for scripture as written text was minimal. By basing his preaching upon the "first principles" delineated by Joseph Smith and proclaimed throughout the Book of Mormon, Kimball excused illiterate parties from careful examination of the critical yet controversial translated text.[29] In addition to these basic Christian teachings, Kimball emphasized the more general spiritual phenomenon the Book of Mormon evidenced.[30] To believers, the book's very existence signified matters of transcendent importance. The opening of the heavens and the establishment of Joseph Smith as a modern-day prophet were foundational matters. The fantastical story surrounding the book's emergence acquainted prospective converts with an unlikely cast of characters—mortal and immortal, angelic and demonic. It was captivating spiritual drama. More than mere show, it was a cohesive, unfolding revelation through which the mysteries of godliness were explained, priesthood authority was restored, and the ancient Christian faith was renewed. The Book of Mormon as a sacred symbol was as influential upon early converts as it was as text.

The Book of Mormon was minimally influential on the outcome of Kimball's initial missionary efforts, although it soon gained prominence within the broader proselytizing program.[31] By 1841 the distribution of the book became a matter of great urgency. In a letter to a convert at Oldham, Willard Richards, then a member of the Quorum of the Twelve Apostles, explained, "We are desirous the Saints should purchase and read the book as fast as they can, for it contains things which if followed, will make them wise unto salvation."[32]

Despite the theological innovations Mormonism's open canon enabled, it was ancient scripture and not modern revelation that provided the basis of Kimball's sermons. One observer of early Mormon proselytizing in Manchester remarked that the King James Version of the Bible was the preferred tool for preaching, of greater value than even the Book of Mormon: "With the Bible they are very expert, and, strange as it may appear to some persons, make more converts by that means than any other. [Taking] advantage of circumstances as they exist, they find the Bible most useful in this country."[33]

The Latter-day Saints' belief that they were literally the restored Church of Christ gave them a special claim on the Bible. This was particularly so with the New Testament, which chronicled the sacrifices and discipleship of their ancient counterparts, the "Former-day Saints," after whom they patterned their lives and ministries.

It may be that a paucity of printed volumes contributed to the lack of attention paid to the Book of Mormon in early proselytizing. Production of a British edition of the book became an important priority for the Quorum of the Twelve Apostles. British printing technology enabled an accelerated proliferation of the text on two continents. In July 1840, Apostle John Taylor reported to Brigham Young that one of his converts, a compositor in the printing office of the *Liverpool Mercury*, could be of great assistance in reviewing proof sheets of a British edition of the Book of Mormon.[34] Although the utility of the book as a proselytizing tool remained unproven, the better-quality, less expensive volumes produced in Liverpool were of tremendous value to the gathering saints in frontier America.

Advanced publishing techniques in England allowed early church leaders to produce more ornate and attractive editions of the Book of Mormon, projecting a sense of class and sophistication upon the text. Willard Richards wrote that these more expensive copies, complete with embossed binding and gilt pages, were intended to "please the eye a little." Justifying the additional expense, Richards noted that "the gold is the Lord's, some like to see some of it on his word.—& I do not know that there is any harm in putting two of the Lord's goods together when we have the opportunity."[35]

Gradually the Book of Mormon worked its way into the lives, beliefs, and traditions of the British saints. This internalization is uniquely expressed in the membership records of the congregations in Chatburn and Clitheroe. In 1844 two baby boys were born within one month of each other to the recently converted Richard and Mary Battersby of Chatburn and William and Betty Cottam of Clitheroe.[36] The Battersbys and Cottams each named their sons Moroni, in honor of the final ancient-American prophet who wrote in the Book of Mormon and, as a resurrected being, delivered the record to Joseph Smith for translation in 1827. This name is tantamount to the Mormon doctrine of restoration. Its adoption into the family nomenclature of rural Lancashire, verified by period census reports, bespeaks the significance of this doctrine to early converts. As neither the Cottams nor the Battersbys joined the main body of Latter-day Saints in America, their boys certainly received countless questions throughout their lives regarding the origin and significance of their highly peculiar name.[37]

Some historians mistakenly assume that the Mormonism first preached by Kimball and his associates in Lancashire in 1837 is identical to the Mormonism preached at any point throughout the nineteenth century. This assumption is flawed and makes no allowance for the doctrinal development known to have occurred throughout Joseph Smith's life.[38] An example of this incomplete perspective is W.H.G. Armytage's false summarization of Mormonism's "strange new gospel," purportedly preached by Kimball and his associates in Preston:

> Man, [the missionaries] proclaimed, was part of the substance of God and would become God. Man was not born in sin and was not accountable for offenses other than his own. The Earth was a colony of embodied spirits, one of many such settlements in space. God was president of Spirits, Men, Angels, and Gods. Spirits still waited to receive their fleshly tabernacle. Men were immortal beings with living souls and human bodies. Angels were immortal

> beings who had lived on earth in imperfect obedience to the law. Gods were immortal beings, the final state of men who have lived on earth in obedience to the law.[39]

The sensational theology Armytage recounts is a far cry from the simplicity of the "first principles" emphasized by Joseph Smith and preached by Heber C. Kimball. In fact, many of the theological aspects Armytage obliquely outlines were not even taught by Joseph Smith until nearer to his death in 1844. As such, they could not possibly have featured in the missionaries' preaching at the opening of the British Mission seven years earlier.[40]

In a similar strain, Mormonism's crucial doctrine of gathering, from which all emigration stemmed, was not taught openly in England until 1840.[41] Accordingly, there cannot have been a causal relationship between the prospect of a new life in America and the roughly two thousand conversions that occurred in Lancashire between the commencement of proselytizing in 1837 and the announcement of the gathering three years later.

We return to the primary question. To what, then, can Kimball's proselytizing success be attributed? Psychologists of religion recognize seven general stages of the conversion process: context, crisis, quest, encounter, interaction, commitment, and consequences.[42] The social turbulence for which early-Victorian Britain is known justifies historians who accentuate the importance of "context" and "crisis" in accounting for religious conversion. And yet, Heber C. Kimball's storied ministry in the upper Ribble Valley suggests the "encounter" and "interaction" stages were of equal if not greater significance. The abundance of conversion stories reinforces this view, particularly the autobiographical sketch penned by Mary Haskin Parker Richards of Chaigley, Lancashire. At some point between her conversion in 1838 and her emigration several years later, Richards wrote the following account of her introduction to Mormonism through its consummate messenger, Heber C. Kimball:

> In the spring of 1838 it was reported one Sunday that an American was to preach at Mr. Richards' chapel. Accordingly I went in the evening and heard a discourse delivered by H C Kimball on the first principles of the gospel. [He preached] again on Monday and Tuesday evenings. [He baptized] 6 persons of whom my Brother John was one. The [Reverend] Mr. Richards, then finding that he was losing all his members, forbid them preaching in his chapel. Soon after I heard that my father and brother Rodger was baptized the next Sunday after them. My mother and sister Alice was baptized also. After this they held their meetings in my father's house. Two months

> after this I went home to see my friends. It being on Sunday the house was filled. Mr. John Alston addressed the meeting followed by several others. I was much pleased with the meeting and returned back with determination to become one of their number.[43]

This passage alludes to several important aspects of Kimball's missionary efforts, all of which are congruent with the seven stages of conversion. Of note, Mary Richards's direct reference to the "first principles" certifies that Kimball's proselytizing efforts were indeed focused upon the basic Christian principles, as advised by Joseph Smith. This falls within the "encounter" stage of the conversion process, wherein dealings with both message and messenger forges a personal connection with a new system of meaning that is laden with emotional gratification. Consistent with the conversionary continuum, this leads to the "interaction" and "commitment" stages.

Second, Richards's interest in Kimball's nationality suggests that the presence of an American in the village was itself a noteworthy event, and one that added intrigue and persuasion to the "encounter" stage already experienced by several members of her family. Consistent with Mary Richards's observation, Kimball's own writings suggest that his nationality was indeed an influential matter:

> We were absent from Preston five days, during which time Brother Fielding and I baptized and confirmed about 110 persons; organized branches in Downham, Chatburn, Waddington, and Clitheroe; and ordained several to the lesser Priesthood, to preside. This was the first time the people in those villages ever heard our voices, or saw an American.[44]

It must be noted that Kimball was not the first American preacher to proselytize in the Ribble Valley. The famed American revivalist Asahel Nettleton preached extensively in Preston during the early 1830s, several years before Kimball's arrival.[45] Prior to this, the revivals staged by the eccentric Lorenzo Dow in 1805 and 1818 profoundly impacted the local Primitive Methodist tradition.[46] However, if Kimball's assessment is correct and he really was the first American to proselytize the upper Ribble Valley, the sensation this caused no doubt augmented his success. Even if Kimball's nationality bore no direct influence on conversionary outcomes, it certainly stoked local interest in Mormonism and helped him gain access to important social and religious networks. Through these networks he was able to ferret out those who were receptive to his message.

Early critics of Mormonism took issue with Kimball's nationality and the American origins of the newly arrived sect. This is evidenced in the following article taken from the *Preston Chronicle*, dated March 1838:

> The American "Saints" who profess to have discovered in the New World, a "new" revelation, and who have made this town the principal scene of their labours, have, singular to say, succeeded in making a great number of converts in the town and neighborhood. Their disciples, however, comprise only very ignorant persons, as the glaring absurdity of the "new revelation" on which their faith is founded, has caused it to be repudiated by those who are capable of judging for themselves.[47]

The Anglo-American tensions reflected in the *Preston Chronicle* bespeak a little-acknowledged aspect of early Mormon proselytizing in Britain. It hints at the wider cultural climate of early-Victorian Lancashire, what Lewis Rambo calls the "ecology of the conversion process," within which powerful "group proclivities result in either outright rejection of the new [religious] option, or mere apathy toward it."[48]

More influential than Kimball's nationality was the deep and conspicuous affection he developed for his converts. "Relationships," Rambo asserts, "are often the most potent avenues of connection to the new [religious] option."[49] To the converted, Kimball assumed an almost fatherly role. His letters, both to individual saints and congregations at large, represent his deep concern for their temporal well-being and spiritual development. To the Latter-day Saints in Chatburn and Downham Kimball wrote:

> I give you the gratitude of my heart for the kindness which you have bestowed upon me and my brethren; for when I was hungry you fed me, when I was naked ye clothed me, when my clothes were ragged ye mended them, when I was destitute ye gave me money, when I was a stranger ye took me in and lodged me; and, as ye have done these things to me and my brethren in our necessities, my heavenly Father shall minister unto you in your necessities; for I am not forgetful of these things, and I do ever remember you in my prayers, praying my heavenly Father to sustain you, and enable you to walk worthy of the holy vocation unto which ye have been called unto the end. [50]

To Edward Martin, the presiding elder of the Preston Branch in 1840, Kimball expressed his strong feelings for the local membership:

> I have a great desire for their welfare here and hereafter. I do not know that I shall be satisfied till I see them all safe in the kingdom of God. I feel to pray for them always that God will keep them in the hollow of his hand; that they may never stumble to bring a wound on the cause of Christ, or on their own persons. Our Father grant that their garments may be kept white and without spot.[51]

After emigration became church policy, Kimball directed his converts to gather to Nauvoo, Illinois. Upon arrival, they were received cordially by his wife, Vilate Kimball. She in turn wrote to her husband, informing him of his converts' condition and progress.[52] Mary Richards's autobiography further reveals that the tender attachment Kimball felt for his converts was not only powerful but also reciprocal. Richards noted that in 1840, shortly after returning to Lancashire for his second mission, Kimball hastened to visit his converts in the upper Ribble Valley. Having taken ill, he sought out the Richards family and convalesced with them for at least a week. Mary waited on him ceaselessly, noting that she "took much comfort washing his feet and administering to his wants." In exchange for her tireless service, Mary wrote that Kimball "often gave me good instructions and pronounced many blessings upon my head."[53]

Without question, the emotional closeness that developed between Kimball and the people of the upper Ribble Valley facilitated conversions still celebrated in the contemporary church. This did more than grow the church's numbers. It also forged some remarkably enduring relationships, which stabilized the converts in their new religious identity and altered their expectations for the future.

In September 1856 many of Kimball's converts from Chatburn and Downham finally arrived in Zion. Having made transatlantic passage on the ship *Enoch Train* and journeyed overland with the handcart company led by Edmund Ellsworth and Daniel McArthur, the converts of these two villages were welcomed by their beloved mentor miles before setting foot in the Salt Lake Valley. He celebrated their arrival in a public discourse he delivered almost immediately thereafter:

> I went out with brother Brigham [Young] to meet those companies, and when within a mile and a half of the foot of Little Mountain we left the company that was with us, and drove on until we met Captain Ellsworth's company. I did not shed any tears, though I could have done so, but they would have been tears of joy; my heart was so full that it was impossible for a tear to pass it; that is the way I felt. . . . I have prayed for those companies night and day, and I never was more pleased to see any persons than I was to see those brethren and sisters, and the Elders that have brought them here. I baptized several of them eighteen years ago in Chatburn and Downham, England, and I thank God that they have come here. It proves that they were good Saints, to stand so long in that wicked country, and sustain "Mormonism" eighteen or nineteen years.[54]

The ardor demonstrated by the villagers of the upper Ribble Valley is revealed further in the journal of Joseph Fielding, who accompanied Kimball during his first mission to the region in early 1838. Regarding their success in Downham and Chatburn, Fielding wrote:

> It appears as though the whole of the inhabitants were turning to the Lord from 10 to 90 years old. It is truly affecting to see them. While I was praying one day previous to baptizing 17, the little girls kneeled around me; some leaned against my back and some against my arm. They are full of love for us and each other.[55]

It is inaccurate to suppose that Heber C. Kimball's affability and homespun preaching style fully explain Mormonism's popularity in the upper Ribble Valley. Historians who overemphasize Kimball's role in the conversion of over one thousand rural Lancastrians fail to recognize important environmental considerations. Prevailing social attitudes and religious sensibilities likewise deserve attention. Elevating the impact of the missionary while ignoring the voluntary religious behavior of new members eliminates half the conversion equation. It must be acknowledged that the success Kimball experienced in the upper Ribble Valley had as much to do with the characteristics and attitudes of the villagers themselves as it did either the message of Mormonism or its persuasive messenger. The converts of Chatburn and Downham are a particularly compelling case-in-point.

From the outset, the villagers of the upper Ribble Valley captivated Kimball and his associates. "There is something peculiar in the people of this place," wrote Kimball in 1840. Concerning the residents of Chatburn, Kimball noted:

> Others had tried in vain to enlist them into their folds but on hearing the first preaching of the fulness of the gospel they were overwhelmed in tears of repentance, and more than twenty were immediately baptized. It is a small village, but the members soon increased to about ninety. We have never received anything like an insult all the time we visited the place, and we feel bound to bless them.[56]

The piousness of the people had deeper roots than Kimball could have recognized. In 1804, thirty-four years before Kimball arrived in the upper Ribble Valley, the Anglican cleric Thomas Wilson reported the residents of nearby Downham village as a "very orderly, decent and religious People."[57] This judgment placed the people in stark contrast with the growing numbers of irreligious parishioners in the faltering parish of Whalley, of whom the curate of Altham and Accrington wrote, "Profligacy, Drunkenness, and Sabbath-breaking . . . [were] greatly to be found."[58]

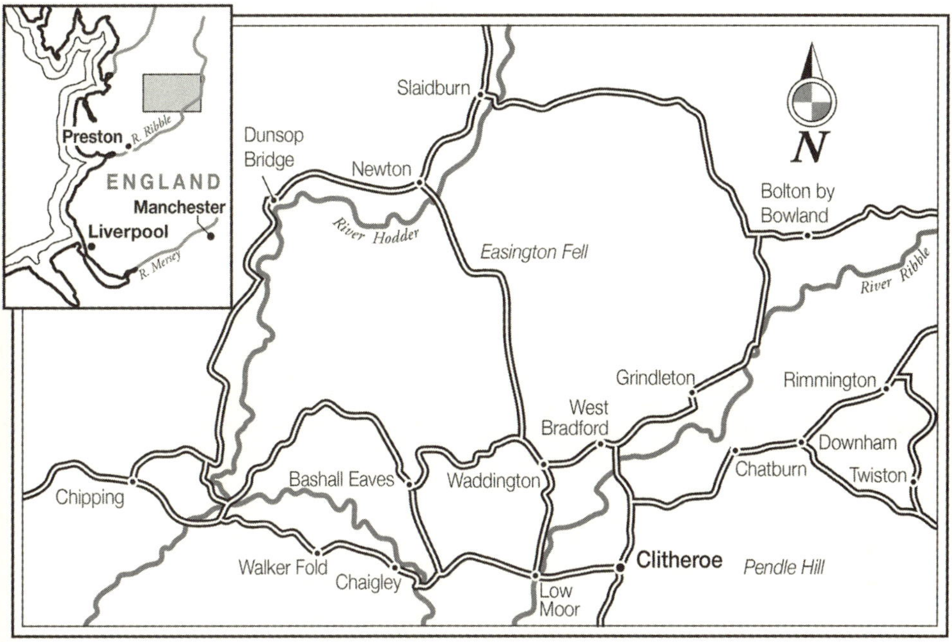

Map 3. Communities proselytized by Heber C. Kimball, 1838–1841. Map by Tom Child.

If, when Kimball first arrived in 1838, the people of Chatburn and Downham had indeed remained as religiously inclined as Wilson formerly described them, it was not their reputation elsewhere in the Ribble Valley. To the contrary, Kimball's converts nearer Preston cautioned him against even attempting to proselytize in Chatburn and Downham, which had gained the reputation of being altogether unreceptive to the convert-seeking sects of the time. In later years, Kimball recalled the warning as follows:

> Having mentioned my intention of going to Downham and Chatburn, . . . several of the brethren . . . endeavored to dissuade me from going, informing me there could be no prospect of success whatever, as several ministers of different denominations had endeavored in vain to raise churches in these places, and had frequently preached to them, but to no effect, as they had resisted all the efforts and withstood the attempts of all sects and parties for the last thirty years, who, seeing their attempts fail, had given them up to hardness of heart. I was also informed they were very wicked places.[59]

Thomas Wilson's 1804 observation of the high degree of religious observance in Chatburn and Downham is surprisingly at odds with the reputation of the villagers when Kimball arrived a generation later. And yet, the description rendered by Kimball and his associates presents the villagers as anything but obdurate, and far from hardened against religious influence. The only recorded opposition the missionaries met in these villages is a mild case indeed. The incident was recorded by Kimball in the first edition of the *Millennial Star:*

> [We] went to Chatburn, held meeting at evening—there was great joy in the place. The next day we went to Downham, held meeting at eve—many came to hear—we bore testimony of the gospel, and of the work of the Lord in these last days. The people were very attentive. When we had closed, a certain man wished to ask a few questions, he appeared much agitated; in fact we were reminded of the prediction in the Book of Mormon, that "men would anger and tremble because of the truth." He demanded some evidence of the truth of the gospel, or message, of which we testified; but would not tell us what evidence would satisfy him, so we could only repeat our testimony to him, and let him go, with no other evidence than ourselves and tens of thousands of others had believed and were satisfied with. The saints had a time of rejoicing. On Saturday we returned to Chatburn, held meeting at eve, after which three persons were baptized and added to the Church.[60]

Further investigation into the local history of the upper Ribble Valley reveals two additional players who enhanced Mormonism's popularity: the clerics of the Anglican parish of Whalley, and the Asshetons of Downham, the region's most powerful landowning family. There is no question that the Church of England's influence was waning throughout Lancashire's vast parish of Whalley during the first half of the nineteenth century.[61] Pastoral neglect, insufficient numbers of clergy, and the failure of ecclesiastical courts plagued the Church of England in both the rural and rapidly industrializing areas of North West England. In the upper Ribble Valley, a disregard for parishioners' needs was acutely manifest in matters of Sabbath worship. Surprisingly, despite the close proximity of the villages of Chatburn and Downham, Anglicans in Chatburn were expected to travel to the parochial chapel in the market town of Clitheroe each Sunday. Adding to the frustration was the fact that a "chapel-of-ease" had already been constructed in Downham. Difficult traveling conditions often prevented residents from making the three-mile walk, as noted by a visiting cleric: "The road from Chatburn to Clitheroe being often very difficult and troublesome to be passed, the inhabitants of the said village of Chatburn have generally repaired (in winter time especially) for conveniency's sake, to the said chapel of Downham and few or none to that of Clitheroe, which is at least four times further."[62]

The fact that Chatburn residents had to take matters concerning Sabbath worship into their own hands hints at the broader inability of local Anglican leadership to anticipate and eliminate temporal obstructions to even the most basic spiritual needs. The conspicuous friendship and abundant pastoral care offered by Heber C. Kimball in 1838 would have been a welcome contrast.

In his 1876 history of the parish of Whalley, area native Thomas Whitaker proposed a direct association between the "manners and morals" of rural parishioners and their nearness to a place of worship.[63] This hypothesis, easily defensible in Downham village, where the parish church of St. Leonard sits prominently upon the village hilltop, makes the administrative decision to send Chatburn's Anglicans to Clitheroe even more puzzling. Sponsored by Parliament and directed by its commissioners, the Church of England sought to combat growing disaffection in the early Victorian era by accelerating its church and chapel building program. The effort, however, was sluggish and outpaced easily by the rapidly moving, itinerant preachers of the many energized sects of the period. Christ Church, the parish church in Chatburn, was not completed until 1838—several months after Heber C. Kimball had converted nearly ninety of the village residents.

The administrative weaknesses evident within Anglicanism were easily exploited and capitalized upon by Nonconformist preachers in pursuit of new adherents, including the Mormons.[64] And yet, within Downham and Chatburn, the Assheton family's endorsement of the Church of England created an Anglican stronghold, making the villages atypical in their religiosity. In light of this, the caution Kimball received concerning the failure of other sects to raise congregations in these villages begins to make more sense. It is not that the people themselves were irreligious, but that the Church of England's broader failure to retain the affection and loyalty of parishioners was far less pronounced in Downham and Chatburn. The cooperation of the Asshetons and local Anglican officials contributed to this. Furthermore, it is interesting to note that the approximate thirty-year period to which Kimball referred, when the villagers were notoriously unresponsive to Nonconformist encroachment, coincides exactly with the decision of William Assheton II to make Downham Hall the family's primary residence.[65]

By early 1838, the year of Kimball's arrival in the upper Ribble Valley, the influence of the Asshetons on village life in Downham was never more pronounced. The family owned approximately ninety percent of the housing in the village, as well as the majority of the surrounding farmland.[66] In the years that followed, the Asshetons acquired every property in or adjacent to the village. This tenurial control manipulated nearly every aspect of village life, including matters of religious worship. It is unclear to what extent Kimball's conversionary successes in the village may have disrupted the Asshetons and the social and religious mores they propagated, although there is little doubt it caused considerable stir among the villagers and within individual families.

Mormon conversion and emigration influenced more than the religious life of the villagers at Downham. It also impacted the village socially and economically. The occupational profiles of Downham converts closely resembles that of the village at large. Comparative analysis of Latter-day Saint membership records and government census returns reveals that most of the converts in Chatburn and Downham were employed in textiles, primarily as handloom weavers. Farmers and agricultural laborers made up the second largest group of converts. The emigration of these converts would have had some impact upon the manor's finances, as nearly all of them rented either farms or homes from the Assheton family.[67] Records at Downham Hall suggest that the economic impact caused by the withdrawal of Mormon converts was temporary. There was already an increased turnover in residential rentals in the village due to the broader decline of handloom weaving.[68]

Interestingly, none of Kimball's early converts from Downham were employed directly by the Asshetons, either in the upkeep of the manor or the management of the estate. Social historians could argue that the displacement that attended the collapse of handloom weaving predisposed out-of-work villagers to convert, while those in the employ of the Asshetons were less receptive on account of their relative job security. The paternalistic controls in the village may have motivated those in the Assheton's employ to keep Mormonism at a distance for fear of dismissal. It has already been well documented that loss of employment was a common consequence for conversion to Mormonism. As one missionary laboring in England in 1843 noted: "The people here are bound down by their tyrannical employers. They are afraid of joining for their work's sake as their masters are much endowed with the Spirit of aristocracy and they have to crouch beneath their opinions as semislaves."[69]

In 1840 Heber C. Kimball returned to Lancashire in the company of two additional members of the Quorum of the Twelve Apostles, Brigham Young and Parley P. Pratt. Upon landing in Liverpool, Pratt wrote to his wife of his expectation that the British Mission would flourish and expand into Europe:

> So here we are in a new world to us, and yet the very world of our forefathers, and a world where we hope soon to have thousands of Children in the Gospel. . . . Here all the kingdoms of Europe are before us on every side. There is a boundless harvest for the next 15 or 20 years, or as long as God holds forth the arm of mercy.[70]

In all, nine members of the original quorum would proselytize in England between 1837 and 1841. Apostle John Taylor focused his efforts in Liverpool, which the initial group of missionaries had bypassed three years earlier on account of more promising opportunities in Preston.[71] In short order, Taylor began to have success among members of his wife's extended family. His growing network of converts in Liverpool led to additional preaching opportunities in the Isle of Man. Between October and December, Taylor baptized around forty converts in Douglas and organized them into the first congregation established on the island.[72]

For Heber C. Kimball, the first order of business was to return to his prized congregations in the upper Ribble Valley. Having visited the saints in Preston, Kimball pressed on to Clitheroe and the surrounding villages. In a letter to John Taylor dated November 9, 1840, Kimball wrote:

> The work is spreading in this part of the land there has been about 25 baptized here in Clitheroe of late. There seems to be an increase in this part of the land among all of the [congregations]. In Preston there is from 10 to 12 each week baptized here on the Sabbath. Their meeting house was full all day. Running over. The excitement is [as] great there as it was when the work first commenced. Last evening I preached in Waddington [to] more than one hundred . . . this is the case in these parts. While meeting was [in progress] one man called on a priest and went out and was baptized, when I got through he was confirmed. I am going to Chatburn tonight. They have the gift of tongues poured out upon them in this part of the vineyard. The need much teaching for some have become wild in some things, but they are like children ready to be taught.[73]

In Kimball's absence, some converts of the upper Ribble Valley engaged in spiritual experimentation. Although the so-called gifts of the spirit, including the gift of tongues, are still celebrated and sought after in contemporary Mormonism, their use is often restricted—as the *Encyclopedia of Mormonism* states—to "the privacy of home and heart."[74] In early Mormonism, however, they played a much more dominant role. The manifestation of spiritual gifts was regarded as confirming evidence of the Restoration's veracity. In this, the early saints took their cues from the New Testament gospel of Mark. For those looking for a renewal of the ancient faith, the gift of tongues was among the signs that "follow them that believe."[75] The mild disdain expressed by Heber C. Kimball for the undisciplined expression of this gift among the membership in Chatburn is likely an extension of Joseph Smith's effort to detach Mormonism from the spiritual extravagances of American frontier Christianity.[76] As the hierarchy within Mormonism developed, the presence and expression of spiritual gifts became less spontaneous among the general membership.

Having renewed his association with his treasured converts, Kimball journeyed south to London in August 1840. The success that abounded in the Ribble Valley eluded him in England's capital city. After six weeks of challenging preaching, primarily in public squares and markets, Kimball had baptized only eleven converts.[77] His proselytizing methods, which had proved so effective in the rural communities of Lancashire, were impossible to employ in London. His inability to tap into the city's competitive and interconnected social and religious networks stymied his efforts. Kimball's associate, Apostle Wilford Woodruff noted, "London is the hardest place I ever visited for establishing the gospel. . . . It is full of everything but righteousness."[78]

Before leaving England in 1841, the Twelve organized the rapidly growing British church into congregational groupings—branches and conferences—and ordained select individuals to the offices of the priesthood. By the mid-1840s, Mormonism in Britain was primarily overseen by the locally converted. Importantly, it was from among the ranks of these new converts that the church expanded its outreach into every notable population center in the United Kingdom.

Expansion: 1842–1853

Throughout the mid-nineteenth century, missionaries were both imported from North America and taken from among the newly established congregations. Church growth cannot be explored independent of the origins, identities, and labors of these local missionaries. Distinguishing the imported, North American missionaries from their native counterparts sheds interesting light upon the development of Mormon proselytizing between 1842 and 1853—the years when the British church achieved its highest rates of conversion in the nineteenth century.

In the late 1840s, there was little that distinguished church member from missionary. Conversion was consummated through facilitating the conversion of others. In the language of one of Joseph Smith's revelations, "it becometh every man who hath been warned to warn his neighbor."[79] This convert-turned-missionary was characterized by a great proselytizing zeal. Such was the case with William Clayton of Penwortham, near Preston. Refusing to wait for the apostles to preach in Manchester, Clayton assumed the pioneering role himself. His efforts were met with stunning success, and he raised a congregation of 240 in a matter of months.[80]

Less well known are the experiences of Henry Stocks, a native Lancastrian whose missionary experiences parallel those of Heber C. Kimball in several important ways. This case study of Henry Stocks begins with a review of his personal background and conversion. Thereafter, it traces his missionary labors in Upholland, Newton-le-Willows,

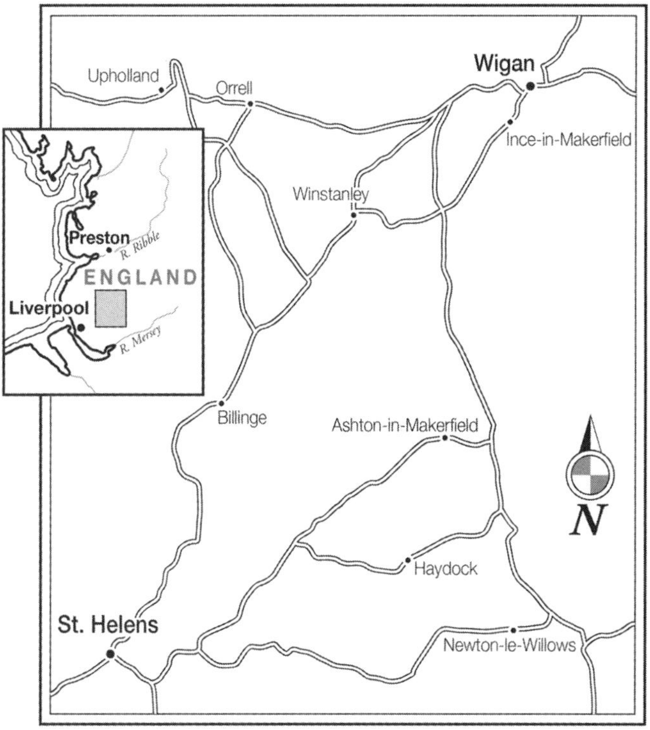

MAP 4. Communities proselytized by Henry Stocks, 1844–1850.
Map by Tom Child.

and Chester between his conversion in 1844 and his emigration in 1855. After describing and analyzing Stocks's extensive missionary service, the study concludes with a brief discussion of the similarities and differences between Heber C. Kimball and Henry Stocks.

Henry Stocks was a lapsed Methodist from Newton-le-Willows, employed at Vulcan Foundry. He converted to Mormonism in 1844, baptized by Charles Simpkins and confirmed by John Evans. At the time of his baptism he was twenty-three years old and had been married for just over a year.[81] Two years following his conversion, Stocks was ordained to the priesthood and occupied the office of teacher. Immediately thereafter, he began proselytizing. As a bearer of the Aaronic or "lesser" priesthood, Stocks's involvement in missionary work was subject to some restriction. His primary role was to assist those of higher priesthood office with their outdoor preaching.

Stocks was ordained a priest in 1846 and immediately took on more responsibility, which his personal journal indicates he took very seriously. Following his ordination, Stocks made weekly Sunday trips to surrounding communities and preached repeatedly in Warrington, Ashton-in-Makerfield, Golborne, Houghton Green, Vulcan Village, and Croft. He preferred to preach in the open air, unaided and alone.[82]

With increased experience and proven faithfulness, Henry Stocks was entrusted with more authority and responsibility. At a conference in Liverpool in December 1847, he received the Melchizedek or "higher" priesthood and was ordained to the office of elder by Simeon Carter. Stocks was emboldened by his new office, and his evangelizing became more frequent and broader reaching. To ease the demands of travel associated with his preaching circuit, Stocks rented a second home in Haydock, which gave him greater access to the outer limits of his expanding field of labor. In August 1848, Stocks ventured into the village of Upholland, where he formed powerful relationships with the local residents and experienced uncommon success.

Stocks was not the only preacher in Upholland. He noted in his journal the presence of another Latter-day Saint elder, John Holt, who had recently taken up residence in the village and was also engaged in spreading the word. Tersely summarizing their respective and complementary efforts, Stocks wrote, "I planted and he watered."[83] The cumulative effect of two months of preaching was a wave of conversions so large that its management surpassed both Stocks's organizational ability and his priesthood authority. Accordingly, in October 1848 Stocks summoned the Liverpool Conference president, Milo Andrus, who came to Upholland, officially organized a new branch, and appointed Henry Stocks as presiding elder.

Stocks's new duties were more administrative in nature than evangelical. Management of the burgeoning branch tied Stocks to Upholland village and effectively ended his four years of itinerancy. The Upholland Branch required almost daily attention. The ten-mile journey from Newton to Upholland, undertaken multiple times each week, exhausted Stocks and frustrated his family. "[It] was more than I could well stand," he wrote in 1849, "however I continued seeing that my labours were blest and I could rejoice."[84] Stocks's journal reveals he traveled over seven hundred miles on foot in thirteen months of service to the saints at Upholland.

Stocks could not long suppress his desire to engage in missionary work, although the management of the branch was his top priority. Because his many duties precluded his participation in his preferred activity, itinerant preaching, Stocks dispatched other local priesthood members into the surrounding villages to distribute tracts while he intensified his own proselytizing within the village.[85]

The congregation at Upholland flourished under Stocks's direction. Scores of village residents now called themselves Latter-day Saints and the cohesion of the membership was strong. The Newton Branch, however, which Stocks's wife and children attended, was in total disarray. Stocks's employment at Vulcan Foundry required that he retain residence at Newton and he agonized over the condition of the local branch, unable to assist in its strengthening.

Henry Stocks's life was stretched, at times painfully, between his three primary obligations: service to his church, maintaining his employment, and meeting the needs of his growing family. This strain was exacerbated by the demands of constant travel to and from Upholland. Near breaking point, his plight ended abruptly in the summer of 1849, when President Milo Andrus released Stocks from his stewardship over the Upholland Branch and commissioned him to take charge of the faltering congregation in Newton.

Although his transfer to Newton simplified many aspects of his life, and delighted his wife and children, Stocks found it difficult to part with the saints in Upholland. The powerful rapport he had developed with his converts is apparent in his personal journal. Concerning his final Sunday with them, he wrote:

> I addressed [the saints] in the a.m., showing them the necessity of doing every thing that was in accordance with the Gospel of Christ which they had received, that they must be humble and then they would be blessed. I expressed my mind before them in the afternoon, feeling sorry to [part] with them. They seemed to feel grieved and weeped. It was like separating Father and Children, as I was their tutorer. I left having the confidence of every member, I believe. I asked the Lord to bless them and gave them the parting hand. On the 26th August 1849 I went to Liverpool conference to represent the Branch for the last time. It numbered 58 members, 2 elders, 7 priests, 1 teacher, [and] 1 deacon. They enjoy the gifts of the spirit and know this to be the work of God.[86]

In Newton, Stocks engaged daily in ministerial work. His journal delineates the breadth of his duties and hints at the complex community formed by the Latter-day Saints in Newton in just five years. During his first month of service to the Newton Branch, Stocks listed his many activities, which, in addition to proselytizing, included: holding cottage meetings, visiting the saints, performing healings, baptizing converts, conducting singing practices, meeting in council with other branch officers, blessing children, settling disputes between members, excommunicating dissenters, and traveling to Liverpool to represent the branch at the quarterly conference. At the conclusion of his first month of service to the Newton Branch, Stocks wrote: "Held three meetings in Newton. The Spirit was powerfully poured out in the afternoon upon the Saints to speak in tongues and prophesy. Good day."[87] Stocks found his greatest satisfaction in the manifestation of spiritual gifts among the members he sought to serve.

Throughout this busy period, Stocks maintained employment at Vulcan Foundry, occasionally missing work on account of the pressing nature of his church service. Economic woes vexed many in the branch. Early in 1850, Stocks noted the increasing number of members who were out of work and contemplating emigration. That April, Stocks acknowledged with a growing sense of dread that poor trade had reduced his workload and the overall productivity of the foundry. One month later he was discharged.

Stocks had no prospects for continued employment in Newton, and it became likely that his search for work would necessitate leaving the area, perhaps permanently. Twice he solicited advice from members of the Liverpool Conference presidency. Twice he was urged to remain in Newton and continue leading the branch. "[It] seems right to go according to natural opinion," Stocks wrote, "but I am determined to abide by counsel and say the Lord's will be done."[88]

Evicted from their home, Stocks led his family to Haydock, where they lived rent-free with a friend. Unemployed, Stocks intensified his proselytizing efforts. For over a month he traveled and preached without ceasing, engaged fully in the ministry that had come to define him. After an unsuccessful attempt at finding work in Chester, Stocks visited his beloved Upholland, where he found spiritual rejuvenation and received financial donations from the members he had baptized two years earlier. Returning home, Stocks discovered a letter from the new Liverpool Conference president, Glaud Rodgers, which directed him to "prepare to go into the vineyard for a short time until [he] could go to Zion."[89] He was released as president of the Newton Branch and assigned to the city of Chester, where he was charged with replicating the success he had formerly enjoyed in Upholland.

The "short time" Stocks was expected to labor in Chester stretched into three difficult years marred by persecution and privation. Shortly after arriving, Stocks noted he "could not live upon the means that the Branch collects, being few and poor."[90] The conference presidency encouraged Stocks to move his family to Chester and pledged to support them financially and fund his family's emigration within a year. In addition to his responsibilities in Chester, Stocks was assigned to preside over the branches in Kinnerton, Cheshire, and Ewloe, Flintshire, which were "in a poor condition, all the best Saints [having] emigrated."[91]

The natural success Stocks experienced in Upholland and Newton proved evasive in Chester, and he struggled to expand the fledgling branch. "Chester is a hard place," he wrote in September 1850, "they will not hearken to the truth as I could wish."[92] After three months of active proselytizing, eight baptisms, and three excommunications, the branch numbered only twenty-five. Stocks urged the saints to engage in a monthly fast "that the Lord might prosper us in this branch and numbers join the Church . . . and

[that] the gifts of the Spirit be poured out in our midst."[93] In November, Stocks noted that the branch was beginning to prosper, but he maintained that Chester was "one of the hardest places in England" to proselytize.[94]

There is a noticeable shift in the tenor of Stocks's journal entries beginning in February 1851. The optimistic and faithful rhetoric that had characterized his writings in both Upholland and Newton was offset by despondency, as expressed in the following entry:

> The care of this branch in this old city . . . and so few coming forward to obey the gospel . . . has almost destroyed my body. My mind has sorrowed many times because of the condition of the people, being blinded by the priests of the day and is covered with gross darkness and superstition. . . . I hope the time will soon arrive when my wife and children with me will be gathered to Zion where they can live in peace.[95]

In addition to conveying his obvious frustration, the reference to emigration bespeaks his total dependence upon the Liverpool Conference, both for his daily means and for his future hopes of gathering to Zion. The Liverpool Conference had effectively replaced Vulcan Foundry as his employer and he was, in many respects, bound to its service.

Stocks's dedication to the ministry brought both benefits and challenges. Although it helped ensure his family's temporal welfare during his years of unemployment, it also kept him tied to the British Babylon he was urging other church members to forsake. The financial assistance Stocks received from the Liverpool Conference was insufficient and could hardly be subsidized by donations from the few saints at Chester. Lack of outside employment made self-funding his family's emigration impossible. If Stocks and his family were to emigrate, it would be at the conference's expense, and according to the conference's timetable. For reasons never explained to him, the conference presidency continually forestalled his family's emigration, adding to Stocks's anxiety. By 1853, he was at his wits' end with his work in Chester and was desperate for reprieve. Although communication from the conference presidency was regular, it increasingly avoided any discussion of emigration.

In the summer of 1853 Stocks was startled to learn he had been reassigned to the Manchester Conference and commissioned to preside over the branch at Bury. The needs of his family, coupled with a sense of duty and a desire to leave Chester, impelled Stocks to accept the position. The unanticipated move made the prospect of emigration seem more remote than ever. The presidency of the Liverpool Conference had not fulfilled their promise, and Stocks understandably regarded it as a personal affront.

After a few months in Bury, Stocks bypassed the officers of the Manchester Conference and appealed to the presidency of the British Mission directly. He urged them to do one of two things: either promote him to the office of conference president or facilitate his family's emigration to Zion without delay. The mission presidency did neither.

In July 1853, worn out and frustrated by the growing mission bureaucracy, Stocks resigned as the branch president of Bury. He led his family back to Newton-le-Willows, where their saga as Latter-day Saints had begun nine years earlier. Bringing the matter full circle, Stocks resumed employment at Vulcan Foundry. Unburdened by major duties for the first time since his ordination to the priesthood, Stocks spent his Sundays touring the region where he had formerly preached. The fruits of his labors were still evident, although the composition of the branches he helped raise had changed a great deal. While attending a Sabbath meeting in Hazel Grove, Stocks reminisced:

> I certainly felt much when standing before the Saints and could not help but weep when I came to reflect upon what had passed the few years that I had been [away] from them. Many changes has taken place, many that I have had sweet communion with has fled, some has gone to Zion, some to the world of spirits, some fallen away from the Church, and some stand to the truth and are still willing to go forward and obtain the blessings promised in the Gospel.[96]

In February 1854, nearly a decade after he joined the church, Henry Stocks undertook a valedictory tour of the congregations he had both built and strengthened in his years of dedicated service. The experience reached an emotional and spiritual climax in the company of those he had grown closest to—the saints in Upholland:

> I walked to Upholland and back [to] the branch that I raised, being assisted by some few others. Thomas Kendal [is now the] presiding elder. He is going to emigrate in March. I wished to see him, along with all the Saints. They was all very glad to see me. They as a branch are doing well. They enjoy the gifts and blessing of the Holy Spirit. We certainly had a time of rejoicing, I preached for them in the evening and felt well in their midst. I pray the Lord to bless them as a branch and preserve them from evil and save them along with me and my dear family in the Kingdom of God amen.[97]

In 1855, with the endorsement and assistance of British Mission president Franklin D. Richards, Henry Stocks and his family finally emigrated. His service to the Liverpool and Manchester Conferences was concluded, and Stocks never again engaged in full-time proselytizing. After arriving in the Salt Lake Valley, he was dispatched to the Mormon settlement in Manti. He later returned to Salt Lake City, where he died in 1873.

Henry Stocks's ten years of missionary service reveals some important themes regarding the mid-nineteenth century proselytizing efforts of British converts. First is the inescapable significance of priesthood authority within the missionary program. The unordained were not authorized to proselytize and could neither perform ordinances nor hold office in branch councils. Henry Stocks's journal suggests that priesthood ordination and council appointments were highly selective, and were tied inextricably to the privilege and obligation to proselytize.

Second, priesthood officers who proselytized effectively could be drafted into full-time missionary service. Although this was a position of honor within Latter-day Saint circles, and included financial compensation, it also complicated and delayed the pursuit of emigration—putting the missionary fundamentally at odds with his message. By the time the gathering doctrine was reoriented toward the building of Zion at home, it was no longer customary for the British Mission to employ its emissaries.

Finally, if Henry Stocks's experience is at all representative of other period converts, success in missionary work seemed more likely to occur closer to home than in more distant locations. It is interesting to note that Stocks's effectiveness decreased the further he got from Newton and Upholland. His frustrating and less-productive experiences in Chester and Bury seem partially attributable to his lack of personal ties to those communities.

Indeed, familiarity with a community seems to have streamlined the success of many of the British-born missionaries. The local converts intuitively capitalized on existing relationships. In many cases they already possessed valuable knowledge of and an influential place within their community. Accordingly, the imported American missionaries, devoid of such connections, should have been decidedly less effective than their British counterparts. However, this was not the case for Heber C. Kimball. Interestingly, in the last quarter of the nineteenth century, the relationship between the missionaries and their British host-culture again becomes an important factor in maintaining the proselytizing program, as we shall see in the next chapter.

Conclusions

Mormon missionary work in Britain underwent two general stages between 1837 and 1853. The first was defined by the relatively brief but phenomenally successful "apostolic missions," initially led by Heber C. Kimball. By the mid-1840s, when Henry Stocks joined the church, the missionary program was largely membership driven. It was during this second phase, when Mormon proselytizing was conducted largely by the recently converted, that the church experienced its greatest numerical growth.

Comparing the experiences of Henry Stocks with Heber C. Kimball elucidates a few facts about Mormon missionary work in Victorian Britain. First, the powerful rapport that developed between missionary and convert added great strength to the proselytizing program and contributed to the retention of converts. Second, a missionary's national or regional identity could positively impact his prospects for success. The novelty of Kimball's American origins captivated his earliest audience, though it also drew criticism from British Mormonism's earliest opponents. Through his own life experience, Henry Stocks understood the plight of the working class, and this common background helped him draw converts from among them.

Success in proselytizing was augmented by the individual missionary's capacity to connect spiritually and emotionally with prospective converts. Of equal value was the reciprocal investment from the converts themselves. The act of baptism, which officially admitted an individual into church membership, also consummated the close relationship between preacher and neophyte.[98] This verifies Douglas Davies's assertion that Mormon conversion is historically "grounded in persons and personalities" as much as in "sharply focused doctrine."[99]

Harmonious environmental circumstances, such as those present in the village of Downham and the Anglican parish of Whalley in the late 1830s, further enhanced the success of the missionaries. The absence of a harmonious environment, as illustrated by Stocks's frustrating experiences in Chester, could stifle the efforts of even the most persuasive of missionaries. It is important to recognize that some of the British-born missionaries were as effective as their American apostolic counterparts. This was especially the case when they enacted the same proselytizing pattern employed by Heber C. Kimball: heavy investment in human relationships, careful social networking, and simplified preaching. Henry Stocks's success in Upholland and Newton are in this sense comparable to Kimball's achievements in Chatburn and Downham.

There remains one additional point of comparison between Stocks and Kimball: neither found success in more populous areas, where proselytizing was far less intimate. As Stocks and Kimball preached in the cities of Chester and London, respectively, their preaching was conducted primarily in public venues. While this brought increased exposure to the Mormons and their message, it also restricted personal contact between the individual missionary and his prospective convert. Neither missionary found much success in cities where preaching was more closely associated with debate and argumentation than social networking and pastoral persuasion.

The first generation of missionaries in Britain understood that proselytizing and conversion was as much about human needs and relationships as religious doctrine. Early missionary work was a reflexive activity and conversionary growth was organic. Missionaries explored villages, neighborhoods, and family and social groupings, mining them like veins of ore. In time, proselytizing activities became increasingly structured and standardized, and the effort was always tied to priesthood ordination. The origins and traits of the individual missionary played an important role in the early establishment of British Mormonism.

Chapter 4
Consolidation and Decline
1854–1900

> The curtain . . . opens upon [the 1840s], and what is then seen? [Latter-day Saints] of many nations and kindreds; multitudes, in Europe and America, and the islands of the sea. . . . The scene again closes, and opens upon the 20th century. And what is then beheld? A great multitude which no man can number—peace smiles award them, and truth is shining in their midst. They are the Church, which 70 years before consisted of six members.
>
> —Parley P. Pratt, 1840

In the early 1840s, the British Latter-day Saints were brimming with confidence. From his Manchester office, Pratt penned his prognostication with the full conversionary impact of the apostolic missions still resounding. The growth of the church in the English North West had indeed been spectacular and, for the Mormons, without precedent.

What Pratt did not foresee were the myriad complications associated with maintaining congregational viability. The Mormons had an undisputed capacity to win converts in early Victorian Britain. As the nineteenth century advanced, however, social and cultural crosscurrents combined with growing suspicion of the saints to threaten the endurance of Mormonism as a British denomination.

The challenge facing the saints is reflected in membership statistics. By 1852 the number of members in the Manchester and Liverpool Conferences totaled just over five thousand. By 1892, the cumulative toll of forty years of emigration and disaffection reduced that number to fewer than three hundred. A comparable diminution occurred in every conference of the British Mission. As the twentieth century dawned, the "great multitude" of saints Pratt originally envisaged was, in the British Isles, far from reality.

Throughout British Mormonism's first decade, church leaders had good reason to suppose that growth would continue unabated. By the close of 1849, Mormonism in Lancashire was booming. Milo Andrus, then president of the Liverpool Conference, noted with satisfaction that four hundred people had been baptized in Liverpool alone since he began leading the conference in August 1848. "The Saints are at peace with one another," Andrus wrote, "and a spirit of union and love prevails."[1]

Approaching mid-century, members of the church understandably felt optimistic. Conversion rates had never been higher, the emigration program was gaining serious traction, and the main body of saints had finally established their permanent headquarters in the Salt Lake Valley. These achievements boosted the confidence of local missionaries and gave the region's converts a powerful sense of purpose and direction. The grand opportunities associated with the colonization of the Intermountain West beckoned and many British Latter-day Saints had their eyes firmly fixed upon Zion. With the gathering in full swing, British Mormonism was on the cusp of significant change.

This chapter chronicles and analyzes that change. It is a twofold examination. First, it considers the effects of Mormonism's steadily declining membership on the church's ecclesiastical structure. Second, it explores the experiences of the missionaries who sought to stem the tide of diminution through an ongoing and pertinacious proselytizing campaign.

The chapter begins by tracing the decline of the church's membership and the resultant consolidation of its congregational structure, both at the branch and conference level. The membership records of the Preston Conference and the statistical reports of the *Millennial Star* inform this analysis. Thereafter, the chapter considers the vital role played by three successive generations of missionaries, whose labors were central to Mormonism's perpetuation during a period characterized by decline. Twelve personal journals kept by missionaries who labored in the English North West between 1875 and 1900 sustain the latter portion of the study.

Diminution

The Clitheroe Conference, established in 1841, was the first of the conferences in the English North West to manifest signs of institutional weakness. Although the upper Ribble Valley had been a hub of Latter-day Saint activity for over a decade, by 1850 church growth in the region had slowed significantly. In fact, the region would never again see the dramatic rates of conversion that attended the initial missionary thrust. As convert emigration accelerated, local branches lost their priesthood leadership. Missionaries were imported from Zion to shore up the faltering congregations, but they were unable to replenish the membership.

At a conference held in Manchester in 1850, mission leadership determined that the Clitheroe Conference could no longer sustain itself as an ecclesiastically autonomous organization. The members were too scattered and the priesthood base was too weak. The agreed course of action was expedient, but disheartening: dissolve the conference, release its leadership, and restructure. The neighboring Preston Conference, then comprised of 450 members, annexed the remaining congregations, creating a new total of thirteen branches and over 700 saints.[2] The merger brought a refreshed vitality to the congregations in the Ribble Valley. Although some perceived the consolidation as evidence of the church's dwindling influence, others considered it a sign that the gathering of the Lord's covenant people was well underway.

The Preston Conference was faring reasonably well when the leadership of the British Mission announced its imminent fusion with the Clitheroe Conference. At that time the Preston Conference was led competently by George D. Watt, whose distinction as the first baptized Englishman made him something of a figurehead to the local saints. Watt was a living reminder to member and missionary alike of the successes of the apostolic missions and the zeal of the original convert generation.

When Watt was released from his duties as conference president in late 1850, the Preston Conference boasted nearly ninety priesthood members. The merger with Clitheroe changed the face of the Preston Conference significantly, expanding not only its geography but also its opportunities for renewed proselytizing and membership growth. Missionary work progressed well under the new conference president, Joseph W. Johnson, who happily reported seventy-nine baptisms during the first year of his presidency.[3]

The unification of the two conferences brought a sense of relief to the strained church leaders in Clitheroe. No longer solely responsible for the pastoral needs of the scattered membership, priesthood leaders in Clitheroe redirected their focus to strengthening the congregation at home. In early 1857 Charles Dana reported that the Clitheroe Branch was in excellent condition.[4]

In the first four years following the annexation of the Clitheroe Conference, the membership figures of the Preston Conference remained fairly static, hovering between 680 and 700. The emigration of the local saints had only a slight impact on the statistical profile of the conference, as the fruits of ongoing proselytizing largely offset the loss.

However, in early 1855 the trend began to change. The coming of spring ushered in a new emigration season and increasing numbers of saints positioned themselves for departure. By June, over 150 members of the Preston Conference had sailed for America, nearly one-fifth of the conference's total membership.[5] By the year's end, an additional thirty-six members had emigrated, reducing the members to 491. Although the missionaries enjoyed a reasonably productive year of proselytizing, thirty-nine total converts did little to replenish the conference.

The 1855 emigration season signaled a permanent change in the church in the English North West. At the October general conference in Salt Lake City, the First Presidency disclosed detailed instructions concerning handcart travel—an innovative approach intended to increase immigration at reduced cost.[6] The initiative was officially launched in 1856 and created an unusually productive emigration season. The commensurate depletion of the membership on the Isle of Man led to the closure of that conference in July 1856, and the branch in Douglas was placed under the supervision of the Liverpool Conference.[7]

On the mainland, the saints in Lancashire who had formerly been unable to finance their passage lunged at the opportunity. Hundreds emigrated over the following twelve months. By December 1857 emigration had reduced the numbers of branches in the Preston Conference by half, returning it to its pre-amalgamation stature of only six congregations. The total membership of the conference plummeted to an all-time low of 137 members—and only three converts were baptized during the year.[8] Although the sudden exodus damaged the viability of the Preston Conference, it was nevertheless celebrated by church members on both ends of the migration trail.

For many British Latter-day Saints, the promised day of gathering had finally come. The resultant diminution of the Preston Conference proved both steady and irreversible. Returning to his native Preston in 1867, George D. Watt observed that the "Preston Branch of the Church, whose congregation numbered hundreds in 1851, does not now have a congregation of over fifteen persons."[9] So in 1868, the presidency of the British Mission announced that the Preston Conference would be absorbed by the better developed and more secure Liverpool Conference.[10] The merger more than doubled the Liverpool Conference's total area. As regional membership plummeted, the geography of the Liverpool Conference continued to expand. In October 1868 the Liverpool Conference annexed the Bolton Branch from the Manchester Conference and in 1870 its boundaries expanded further to include the long-neglected Furness peninsula. Conference borders were extended yet again in 1874 when several congregations in North Wales were likewise annexed. By 1880 the boundaries of the Liverpool Conference had never been larger, and its membership had never been less concentrated. The scattered saints were becoming strangers to one another.

It did not take long for the leadership of the Liverpool Conference to recognize the challenges in providing adequate pastoral care to the membership. "The Liverpool Conference [covers] a very extensive tract of country," observed Conference President Henry Leigh in 1874, "and has needed constant traveling that the Saints might be visited."[11] The required effort had an exacting toll. By June both Henry Leigh and John

Quayle, who long had been the sole church representative on the Isle of Man, were released from their priesthood offices on account of ill health. Both returned to Utah. Leigh's successor, Bedson Eardley, was immediately struck with the immensity of the conference now under his care. His initial challenge was locating the far-flung membership. "I found it somewhat difficult in visiting the Saints to find their whereabouts and introduce myself," Eardley wrote, "however, by the aid of an old register I succeeded tolerably well in finding the presidents of the various branches, and am happy to say was very well received by them and the Saints."[12] By mid-October 1874 Eardley had, with the exception of the Isle of Man, successfully traversed the immense conference area, a preaching circuit of nearly 350 miles.

In the final quarter of the nineteenth century, Mormonism's profile in the English North West took on an uncanny resemblance to the beleaguered Anglican parish of Whalley in the 1830s and 40s.[13] Like the vast parish, the Liverpool Conference was plagued with a comparable host of administrative challenges, including insufficient leadership. Despite these setbacks, proselytizing continued. How the missionaries approached their work during this season of decline is representative of the Mormon's enduring commitment to maintaining a presence in the British Isles.

Missionary Origins and Identities

Missionary work in Britain has always been a transatlantic endeavor. Of the seven missionaries who first arrived in Lancashire in 1837, three were born in the United States, two in England, and two in Canada. Each converted to Mormonism in North America. The social and familial ties of the English-born missionaries hastened early church growth. The origins of the Preston and Alston Branches can be traced to Joseph Fielding's and Isaac Russell's abiding connections to those respective communities.

For British Mormon emigrants, the desire to return to their homeland to engage in proselytizing was fueled by their affection for the friends and relations they had left behind. However, North American missionaries who had no direct ties to Britain were motivated by a different set of influences. For them, missionary service was an adventure, a crusade, and a divinely commissioned duty. Their determination to forsake home and family in Zion in exchange for a ministry abroad bespeaks the depth of their commitment to Mormonism and their trust in its governing councils.

The membership register of the Preston Conference gives valuable insight into the origins and contributions of the missionaries—both British and North American—who served in Lancashire throughout the 1850s and 60s. The register was initially compiled in 1852, at which time the Preston Conference comprised nine congregations: Accrington, Blackburn, Burnley, Clitheroe, Kendal, Leyland, Longton, Preston, and Todmorden. The records, organized by branch, contain basic membership information: names, dates and places of birth, and dates and places of baptism into The Church of Jesus Christ of Latter-day Saints.[14] A vital clue concerning the identities of the North American missionaries is found in the baptism and confirmation records. Conference records indicate these ordinances were often performed by men whose names do not appear on the membership lists themselves. These ordinances were not conducted by local branch officers, but by traveling priesthood authorities who were responsible for overseeing the growth of the church within the geographic boundaries of a given conference.

Baptism and confirmation were the fruits of proselytizing, and the authorized means whereby an individual became a Latter-day Saint. There is an obvious association between those who performed these ordinances and those who engaged in missionary work. All missionaries were members of the priesthood, but not all members of the priesthood served as full-time missionaries. In either case, it is important to recognize the ongoing significance of priesthood authority within the church and its efforts to expand. Missionaries in this period did not receive formal training preparatory to engaging in proselytizing work. Rather, they were commissioned, ordained, and authorized by upper church leadership, and sent forth consistent with biblical precedent.

The membership records of the Preston Conference's nine congregations reveal that only a small portion of missionaries traveled widely throughout the region. The majority remained fairly local in their ministry. Of the 198 priesthood officers whose names appear in the Preston Conference records, only thirty-four served in three or more congregations. These missionaries were not tied to a particular town or branch by family or employment obligations. Rather, like Henry Stocks, they seem to have proselytized full-time. The fact that these missionaries were free to travel so extensively suggests they had no other responsibilities and were probably sent to the Preston Conference for that one purpose.

Their itinerancy does not, however, affirm their origins as North American. A noteworthy example is William A. McMaster, whose name appears on the registers of four congregations within the Preston Conference. Although his wide-ranging influence indicates he may have been among the more mobile North American missionaries, McMaster was actually of Scottish origin. He was recruited into full-time church service following several years of successful missionary work in the Edinburgh Conference.

McMaster's proselytizing path followed a southeasterly course, carrying him from Kendal to Clitheroe and then to Burnley, Accrington, and Preston. Interestingly, McMaster's personal journal indicates that his family accompanied him as he traveled from one branch to another. This was a rare luxury for traveling missionaries, made possible through the donations of members. McMaster's nearly six years of work in building up local congregations culminated in the Preston Conference presidency sponsoring his family's emigration in 1854.[15]

The majority of missionaries who proselytized in Lancashire had to travel from origins much more distant than Edinburgh. For missionaries sent to Britain from Utah Territory in pre-railroad America, the journey took months and was fraught with hazard and difficulty. Financially, the undertaking was a genuine leap of faith since the missionaries rarely had sufficient means to make the journey. These missionaries were characterized by a powerful devotion to their faith. Given their indigence, accepting the mission call was especially challenging. Each faced the agony of abandoning their family in a region that was still far from civilized.

The experience of Jesse Bigler Martin is one example. Martin left Salt Lake City bound for Liverpool in the spring of 1853. In his company were three other elders. With one tragic exception, each of these missionaries would soon occupy significant leadership positions among the saints in England. En route, David Roberts, one of Martin's companions, drowned in the Platte River in Nebraska. A hasty internment interrupted their eastward trek and caused them to briefly hesitate in pressing forward with their assignment.

After five months of overland travel, Martin and his companions stopped in Michigan and began preaching in the tiny settlements of Pulaski and Wolf Creek. As they journeyed, they solicited donations from the few church members in the area. By December, Martin's company was in Pennsylvania, still seeking the means to finance their transatlantic passage. In Albany, New York, Martin scoured the city "from morning till night but could not find one Mormon."[16] For weeks Martin roamed the various metropolises of the northeast United States in search of faithful saints to help fund his journey.

Thanks to the generosity of a non-Mormon benefactor in Boston, Martin ultimately succeeded in raising the needed money. He landed in Liverpool in mid-January 1854, nine months after leaving home. A few days after his arrival, Martin was assigned to labor in the Manchester, Preston, and Liverpool Conferences for the duration of his mission. Although he was struck by the "darkness and gloom that seemed to overshadow the land," Martin recorded that he "felt glad [to have] the privilege of bringing the light to them that dwell in it."[17]

Of the nearly two hundred known priesthood officers who proselytized in the Preston Conference between 1837 and 1868, very few were conclusively North American. Of these, most were high-profile leaders from the main body of the church in Utah, whose influence was both supervisory and temporary.

As the nineteenth century progressed, the number of North American missionaries serving in Britain increased significantly. The fulfillment of the church's emigration policy naturally depleted the number of local priesthood officers who could engage in missionary work. To offset this deficiency, church authorities in Zion dispatched an increasing number of elders. Some of these missionaries would serve multiple missions in Britain over the span of many years.

As the number of local priesthood officers diminished, the British saints became more reliant upon the elders from overseas. Liverpool Conference membership records reveal an effort to reduce this growing dependency. In the 1870s and 80s conference leaders initiated an abrupt increase in priesthood ordinations and office advancement among the local male membership in Preston.[18] Convert baptisms during this period had waned significantly, and conference leaders understood that long-term congregational viability required a sufficient priesthood base. If they could not increase the priesthood base through conversionary growth, they would have to strengthen the leadership capacity of those men already baptized.

Increased priesthood ordinations, it was thought, would empower the saints to become more self-directed in proselytizing, thereby reducing the need for imported missionaries. This move toward greater self-reliance is consistent with the relaxation of the emigration program and foreshadows the church's efforts to expand and reinvigorate the British congregations in the beginning of the twentieth century.

Despite the increased number of priesthood ordinations, there is no evidence that suggests the return to membership-driven missionary work was successful. In fact, the Liverpool Conference missionary register indicates that by 1898 every missionary then serving hailed from one of the many Mormon communities in Utah, Idaho, and Wyoming. The only exception was an unlikely companionship: Lorenzo and Mary Ellen Wilmot of Accrington, Lancashire, who were commissioned to engage in full-time proselytizing as husband and wife.[19] The Wilmots fulfilled their assignment without once leaving their hometown.

By the end of the nineteenth century, Mormonism's public face in Britain had become decidedly North American, an image that would become both stereotypical and problematic for the church in the early twentieth century. The initial place of the imported missionaries had been supplementary and supervisory. By the century's end, they had become the program's very mainstay.

Over the course of the nineteenth century, missionary work in Britain had shifted from being a spontaneous, reflexive, and membership-driven endeavor to a highly structured and adaptable program carried out primarily by men drawn from the stable ranks of the church in Utah. These missionaries typically served for one to five years and busied themselves distributing tracts, conducting cottage meetings, and shoring up Britain's dwindling congregations.

Missionary service was a profound highlight within the Latter-day Saint experience and always the foremost responsibility of the priesthood. By the end of the nineteenth century, it also had become somewhat of an anomaly. Missionary service was an intense but temporary season of one's membership in the church. By the end of the 1800s, missionary service had created its own class within the church. There were members and there were missionaries, and the identities and purposes of each group did not always coincide.

The British church in the second half of the nineteenth century was characterized by steady diminution and punctuated by seasons of sharp decline. Between 1853 and 1859, the membership of the church in the English North West plummeted from over 5,000 members to a little over 1,200. In all, the combined emigration of these seven years relocated nearly 2,000 Latter-day Saints to their American Zion. Even more damaging was excommunication, which depleted the nonemigrating membership by an additional 3,000. Were it not for the roughly 2,400 baptisms and rebaptisms that occurred during this same period, the net loss caused by emigration and excommunication could have devastated the church's viability and perpetuation in Lancashire.[20]

Emigration and excommunication diminished British congregations both in size and number. In 1853 there were sixty-five branches spread throughout the Liverpool and Manchester Conferences. By 1859 there were thirty-five. Loss of membership to emigration was not to be lamented, since it fulfilled the church's institutional agenda to gather to the American West. Similarly, among the faithful, excommunication was not regarded as overly problematic either. Rather, it was deemed a necessary purging of the uncommitted whose faithlessness was a hindrance to Mormonism's progress. As a general rule, the devoted saints emigrated, the uncommitted were cut off, and the indifferent faded into anonymity.

There were many profound consequences, organizational and otherwise, that attended British Mormonism's diminution. Church leadership may not have anticipated the way in which the emigration of the faithful and the elimination of the faithless challenged the effectiveness of the proselytizing program. As noted, the missionary force of the 1840s, 50s, and 60s was comprised of the locally converted. Their emigration left the British Mission woefully shorthanded. Not surprisingly, conversion rates experienced a commensurate drop. Between 1849 and 1859 there was an average of 516 convert baptisms per year in the English North West. Between 1860 and 1870, the annual average had fallen by over fifty percent to 253.[21] In time, quality of conversion supplanted quantity, the latter becoming indisputably unattainable. Septimus Sears, who presided over the Liverpool Conference in 1865, wrote:

> In the year 1864 we added 74 to our numbers by baptism, the greater number of whom, I believe, embraced the Gospel for the love they had for the truth. They were not those who came in through excitement, or because they had heard some Elder preach who could use very fine language, or deliver a

> discourse in a very systematic and eloquent manner, but many were brought in by the simple testimony of a humble brother or sister, and because they could see something in the Gospel worthy of their attention. I have noticed, in my experience, that those who come into the Church through temporary excitement require something of this nature all the time to keep them alive, and as soon as it ceases, they lose their desire to associate with the Saints. I have also noticed another class—those who have been persuaded by their friends to be baptized, and who, ever afterwards, have needed persuading in everything they have done for the kingdom of God, and have performed nothing willingly. I am thankful to say this is not the class of people who are embracing the Gospel at the present time in the Conference.[22]

The prospects for church growth in the second half of the nineteenth century were poor. All hopes for success depended upon the replenishment of the missionary force. Because the local members who could assume this responsibility were few, more missionaries were sent from the church's Utah base. Interestingly, the majority of those missionaries were either British-born or of immediate British descent.[23] Familiarity with the country, climate, people, and culture significantly influenced the motives and methods of this new generation of missionaries. They were returning home—not to enjoy it, but to change it.

Back to Babylon

For many of the missionaries who labored during the final decades of the nineteenth century, returning to Britain yielded a host of complicated and deeply emotional reactions. Invariably, their first sight of England was Liverpool, where the offices of the British and European missions had long been headquartered. The city itself provided an immediate point of contrast. Although England was their homeland, it was no longer their home. The missionaries had grown accustomed to life in the Mormon communities of Utah Territory, and had been shaped by the society of the saints. For many, reverting from Zion to Babylon was an alarming experience, even for those who were once familiar with the English North West's distinctive character. Upon returning to Liverpool in 1871, George Reynolds manifested his mixed feelings:

> I have said good bye to my wife and little ones, and am again bearing my testimony in my native land to the fact that God has established a Kingdom in these last days, and that by obedience to his words, by his prophets, all men can be saved. To me Zion is the dearest place on all the earth, and did not duty call me to be here I should not long remain; though how long I may be

> here I do not know, all I wish is to fulfill my mission honorably before the Lord and my brethren, and when I have finished, be it two years, be it more, or be it less, return joyously to my home in the Mountains.[24]

Reynolds's time away from Liverpool lent him a certain objectivity with which he examined the evolution of the city, its people, and their collective attitude toward Mormonism, all of which had shifted during his years in Utah. Reynolds identified evidence of both progress and stasis, noting promising improvements in Liverpool's public appearance as well as problems associated with its urban sprawl. To a fellow missionary, Reynolds wrote that Liverpool

> to outward appearances is much improved. During the last six years numerous new offices and magnificent railroad stations have been erected, its trade has greatly developed and its wealth increased, but is a whitened—no, blackened sepulcher, nothing is white here. The rich are richer and the poor are poorer, and the poorest still of Liverpool form a large percentage of its people. The indigent seem more haggard, unhealthy and diseased than ever. In fact the people entirely seem to be getting smaller. It is very noticeable that the youth of England are growing up a stunted, undeveloped race.[25]

Although Liverpool's differences were plainly apparent to Reynolds, the lack of them proved especially disturbing. "Other things are much the same," Reynolds later wrote, "the same old smell pervades the market, the usual amount of squalid children infest the streets, as numerous as ever are the girls, without covering for the feet or head, clad in a calico dress penned up behind, showing a short, dirty red skirt, with a small shawl over their ample shoulder.[26]"

The pitiable situation of the underprivileged and the stifling conditions in which they languished were abhorrent to Reynolds, even though he had been well acquainted with these problems before his emigration. Comparing the merits of life in Zion with the depravity and gritty realities of the long forgotten Babylon, of which Liverpool now seemed the capital, Reynolds concluded fatally, "I am thinking the time will soon come [in Liverpool] when right minded parents will scarcely know if it be a blessing or not to have children born unto them."[27]

For the returning missionaries, the contrasts between Liverpool and Salt Lake City could not have been starker. "The beauties of Liverpool are . . . , I think, few and far between," Reynolds wrote. "The leaden sky, the dirty sooty buildings, the narrow crowded streets, form a dull contrast to Salt Lake City when I left it, clad as it ever was, in the brightest hues the blossoms of peach, apple, apricot and currant could give."[28]

FIGURE 4.1. George Reynolds (seated) and Septimus Sears, Liverpool, circa 1865. Sears served as president of the Liverpool Conference and Reynolds served as president of the Liverpool Branch. Reynolds also clerked for two mission presidents, Elders George Q. Cannon and Daniel H. Wells of the Quorum of the Twelve Apostles. Courtesy LDS Church History Library.

Life in Zion had dimmed the missionaries' recollection of their homeland's social problems, resulting in a pronounced sense of reverse culture shock. Returning to Liverpool in 1890, Frederick Chappell noted that "the wretchedness and abject squalor of the inhabitants was something dreadful to behold." Chappell continued, "It made my heart bleed to see the little children running along at the side of their mothers barefooted, bareheaded, and without clothes sufficient to cover their nakedness. Their dull eyes staring vacantly from thin pinched and half-starved faces. I cannot find language neither could pen describe the wretchedness I beheld during that day in Liverpool."[29]

Though the nonnative missionaries' comparisons between Zion and Babylon—Salt Lake City and Liverpool—differed somewhat, their conclusions were the same and there was no mistaking their bias. Daniel Greene, a ninth-generation American and one of the few missionaries who had no ties at all to the English North West, first arrived at Liverpool in 1887. "No one can imagine my feelings to stand on foreign soil and view the sights of England," Greene recorded. "I think Liverpool a much nicer city than New York but none of them compare with Salt Lake City."[30]

The affection the missionaries held for Zion was made more acute by their comparisons. Contemplating a proselytizing sojourn in Britain for two years or more intensified a longing for home. This is evidenced in the following rhyme penned by Greene at the outset of his missionary service:

> And now to my friend for the present adieu
> Though my body is weak my heart is still true
> And when in old England my work is complete
> Far away in blest Utah oh give me a seat
> Where with friends and loved ones and saints I may stay
> And wait for our Savior, Oh welcome that day.[31]

In their private writings, the missionaries from Utah were highly critical of the social problems afflicting Britain's major cities. For those missionaries who were native Britons, however, returning to their homeland also carried a reminiscent sweetness. Even George Reynolds, who was so critical of the region he once called home, conceded to a colleague in Salt Lake City that "still, the scenery of England has its redeeming qualities in its smooth lines, its green fields, its noble oaks, and its lovely past."[32] William Barton, upon returning to his native town of St. Helens, noted simply, "I had many reflections and recollections of a pleasing character."[33]

Socially, economically, and environmentally, there were many points of contrast between the English North West and the American Intermountain West. Prevailing attitudes toward religion was yet another difference to which the missionaries struggled to adapt. Compared to the shared spiritual strivings of the Mormon communities in Utah, the relative indifference toward religion in England was both a disappointment and a trial. The religious fervor that had fueled the early progress of the British Mission was, a half-century later, eclipsed by a host of contemporary issues facing the British nation. Concerning his efforts to rekindle an interest in Mormonism, George Reynolds lamented:

> There is little enquiry . . . few baptisms and no interest manifested by the world at large. The excitements of the days, the war in France, social legislation, political turmoil and general corruption fill the minds of the people. Religion is becoming less and less respected, except with the Roman Catholics who are rapidly gaining ground. Protestantism is about played out. It has so slight a claim on its believers that most are either gliding toward atheism or sinking into infidelity . . . or some kindred phase of unbelief.[34]

Missionaries laboring in the outer reaches of the Liverpool Conference also noted a pervading indifference toward religion. Where intense feelings did exist, they often were negative. This was particularly evident on the Isle of Man. In 1875, the Manx-born missionary John Caine published in the *Millennial Star* his correspondence with the president of the British Mission, Joseph F. Smith. His account chronicled the many struggles he encountered while preaching in Douglas. "The pleasure of my visit to this Island, my native land, has not been unattended with pain," Caine wrote. "I seemed to be amongst a strange people, who had little or no knowledge respecting me."[35]

Caine's personal ties to the Isle of Man were useless in furthering his proselytizing efforts. A widespread disdain for Mormonism and a growing concern for secular matters proved insurmountable. Caine noted: "There is as much prejudice and bigotry among the people as ever, and they show little disposition to listen to anything relating to our faith. The love of money, and the fear of what the world will say, will prevent them, I fear, from opening their ears to the truth, until something stronger than preaching reminds them of their situation."[36]

Caine's frustration was deepened by the spiritual apathy he perceived among the local church members. "There are not many Latter-day Saints on the Island," he wrote. "I have only found three persons who acknowledged themselves members of the Church. When a boy I remember hearing of several quite large Branches of the Church being here, but they have gathered with the Saints, are dead, or worse than dead, lost their faith and given up the ship."[37]

Between 1875 and 1880 other missionaries serving on the Isle of Man complained of the public's growing obsession with economic matters, which were tied to the seasonal inundation of traveling holidaymakers. In 1880, Liverpool Conference President

George Crane described his visit to the isle. The town of Douglas, he wrote, "was all in a bustle, caused by the great influx of summer visitors, who appeared to be on pleasure bent, having escaped for a few days from the crowded towns of Lancashire."[38] Crane meticulously sought out every Latter-day Saint on the island, but lamented that "the nature of their business precluded the possibility of our enjoying much of their society, Douglas being supported almost entirely by its transient population [and] the natives must gather honey whilst the sun is shining."[39]

John Caine and George Crane each converted and emigrated during the 1850s—the peak years of popular religious fervor in Britain. The indifference that abounded when they returned left them feeling estranged from their former countrymen. Accordingly, the society of fellow Latter-day Saints became increasingly precious. Most of the missionaries who returned to the English North West in the 1870s and 80s had relatives scattered throughout the region, and there is ample evidence that suggests the renewal of familial ties was an important priority. The real kinship the missionaries enjoyed, however, was among the faithful. Missionaries devoted countless hours to visiting, encouraging, and worshipping with the scattered saints, upon whom they were also reliant for their temporal well-being.

The discovery of "lost" saints—those who had never migrated to Utah—was a rare and important occurrence. Missionaries often traveled great distances in search of missing members, manifesting an impressive commitment to those who had become disconnected from the main body of the church. George Parkinson's experience is noteworthy. In April 1883, while conducting an open-air meeting in Wigan town center, Parkinson encountered an elderly woman who professed before the assembled crowd her longstanding belief in Mormonism. Surprised, Parkinson closed the meeting at once and rushed to her side. He learned that she resided in the village of Adlington, six miles to the north, and was in Wigan temporarily on business. He was stunned to discover that she had been baptized by one of Heber C. Kimball's associates thirty-five years earlier. Impressed by her enduring devotion, Parkinson abandoned his daily responsibilities and walked to the woman's home in Adlington, where he spent several days familiarizing her with developments in the church.[40]

As part of their work, native-born British missionaries renewed relationships with their non-Mormon relatives. In many cases, these efforts were brief and emotionally taxing. Unfailingly, tension arose between the missionaries and their relatives on the subject of religion. Some missionaries preferred to avoid altogether any discussion of their faith with relatives, no doubt sensing the disruption it had already caused. And yet, other missionaries made their faith the basis of their dealings with their non-Mormon kin, refusing to dissociate themselves with their religion even when it jeopardized family relationships. In his journal, George Parkinson recalled rebuking his uncle for hypocritically welcoming both him and the discussion of his beliefs while later rejecting his missionary associates.[41] For Parkinson and other missionaries of this period, there was no compromise to be struck. Religion superseded all else, family relationships included.

It was common practice for missionaries returning to Britain to seek out relatives promptly after arrival and invest time in revitalizing these relationships. These efforts, though an obvious priority, were also secondary. Journals from this period suggest that, although reconnecting with family was important, the mission came first. Once a missionary received his formal appointment to a specific field of labor, heavy responsibilities often prevented ongoing contact with relatives. Toward the end of a missionary's term of service, it was again customary for him to seek out family before returning to America.

Not surprisingly, much of the time missionaries spent with relatives was dominated by the discussion of Mormonism—the faith that had motivated both their initial emigration and their eventual return. As the journals indicate, these discussions were often uncomfortable for both the missionaries and their relatives. Certain aspects of Mormonism—its past as well as its practices—seemed frustratingly incommunicable for the missionaries and altogether unbelievable for their non-Mormon relatives. These conversations reveal that, when pressed, the missionaries sided with their faith more than with their families. They were willing to argue in defense of their beliefs so much that they jeopardized the very relationships they had hoped to nurture.

Invariably, the missionaries' relatives took issue with the church's practice of plural marriage, a wildly controversial aspect of Mormonism still in effect in the 1870s and 80s. In the event that the missionary himself was engaged in this marital principle back at home, the issue was often personal, always delicate, and potentially explosive. In a letter to his brother in 1880, missionary Thomas Jackson defiantly wrote:

> I am ready to prove that God did sanction a plurality of wives or plural marriage [and] that the scriptures do not condemn it. You seem to think polygamy is all the principles of religion that we have and all we think about. You believe it to be a delusion. I know it to be true and knowing it to be true I speak of it in the streets . . . where ever a chance opens.[42]

Frederick Chappell's initially joyous reunion with his relatives in 1890 quickly soured after polygamy entered the conversation. Reflecting on the troublesome encounter, Chappell wrote:

> They seem to think that the Mormons are bad people. They can't understand that they might be good but take for truth everything they hear against us

> and always ask how many wives one has. I asked Agnes how she could think her own relations such bad people. In very deed does darkness cover the earth and gross darkness the minds of the people.[43]

Unwilling to repudiate this crucial element of Mormon life, missionaries in Britain continued to defend the religious principles that underpinned plural marriage even after President Wilford Woodruff called for an end to the practice in 1890. In 1893, while visiting his uncles and cousins in Stockport, the missionary George Rigby noted:

> All of the boys and their families came down and we had our debate and I proved to them that we had the same organized church as existed in the days of the Savior. Then they started on polygamy and I showed to them it was practiced in ancient times. And so the evening was passed until a very late hour when all parted with good feelings.[44]

Some British Latter-day Saints who returned to their homeland as missionaries were successful in facilitating the conversion of family members. These conversions, although rare, were pivotal in securing Mormonism's regional perpetuation. An important example began in Wigan in 1885 with the conversion of Joseph Eckersley. Following Eckersley's emigration and settlement in Loa, Utah, in 1900 he was called to return to his native Lancashire as a full-time missionary. Upon arrival, Eckersley wasted no time connecting with his immediate family in Wigan, and in short order had baptized his mother Ellen, his sister Hannah, and her husband, John Hayes. The three converts were a boon to the faltering Wigan Branch, and their enduring commitment to Mormonism helped guarantee the congregation's survival throughout the first half of the twentieth century.

A few years after his conversion, John Hayes was appointed president of the Wigan Branch, at a time when most of the region's congregations were totally dependent upon imported American missionaries for their leadership. The Hayes family was one of three Mormon families living in Wigan in the early twentieth century. Their activity and service sustained the branch throughout the precarious years of the First World War. In time, John Hayes's son, Horace, also presided over the Wigan Branch, and his leadership maintained the congregation's viability through the equally difficult years of the Second World War.[45] The perpetuation of the faith within families became the key to the endurance of British Mormonism itself.

For those few families who converted en masse, Mormonism was a remarkably unifying and stabilizing influence. For the many families who were divided by conversion and separated by emigration, Mormonism was unendingly contentious. The missionaries' ongoing efforts to convert their relatives suggests their abiding hope that reconciliation could be made. However, as the above examples illustrate, the terms were clearly one sided, and always conditional upon their relatives' conversion. How differently Latter-day Saints and their Protestant relations surely regarded the same words of Jesus: "For I am come to set a man at variance against his father . . . [and] a man's foes shall be they of his own household."[46]

Gospel or Scandal

Infrequent conversions toward the end of the nineteenth century motivated change in the missionary program. The leadership of the British Mission had to consider how to adapt their message to the wider interests of the public, maximizing Mormonism's appeal. What the public wanted very much, however, was not Mormonism as a source of salvation but Mormonism as a seedbed of scandal.

Curiosity, not spirituality, often drove the discourse. The Mormonism the missionaries intended to preach and the Mormonism the public desired were two very different things. This discrepancy was a common characteristic of the missionary journals of this period, and comparative analysis reveals interesting manifestations of both adaptation and stasis within the missionaries' message.

The sheer doctrinal breadth of the missionaries' preaching is staggering. Between December 1880 and September 1881, Thomas Jackson recorded preaching on the following topics: the Book of Mormon, the first principles (faith, repentance, baptism by immersion, and receiving the gift of the Holy Ghost), vicarious work for the dead, influence of evil spirits, defense of plural marriage, the fall of Adam and its consequences, the reality of Christ's resurrection, ancient Israel's deliverance, judgment, revelation, destruction incident to Christ's second coming, the gathering, and the celestial glory promised to the saints.[47] The titles of the tracts distributed in the early 1890s further hint at the core elements of Mormonism the missionaries desired to convey: "Only True Gospel"; "Is Baptism Essential to Salvation?"; "Is Belief Alone Sufficient?"; and "Glad Tidings of Great Joy."[48] Theologically, it seems there was something for everyone.

Despite the wide assortment of these topics, the message the missionaries imparted remained largely consistent with that of Heber C. Kimball's day. Roughly fifty years after the opening of the British Mission in 1837, missionaries continued to center their preaching on the first principles. Their preference notwithstanding, the missionaries found that keeping their message restricted to these fundamental tenets was no easy task. Variation from the basic tenets often aroused public animosity, especially if it conjured up suspicion of Mormonism's founding prophet. At a meeting at Islington Square in Liverpool in 1883, one missionary recorded:

> [We] had a very good attendance. . . . The congregation listened well until the name of Joseph Smith was mentioned and that was just like throwing cold water on the whole thing. Some turned with a sneer and walked away while others out of curiosity remained to hear more. However we gave them our testimonies by which some day they will perhaps have to be judged.[49]

What further complicated matters for the missionaries was the insatiable public appetite for the sensational. Few things seized the collective imagination more than the lurid reports of Mormon polygamy. A missionary's refusal to entertain questions about the controversial practice disappointed and even aggravated audiences. George Parkinson's journal recounts a public meeting conducted by the saints at the Masonic Hall in Douglas. There, the missionaries' unwillingness to indulge the audience's curiosity about Brigham Young's plural wives resulted in wild and unruly behavior. Despite the pressure to cave in, the missionaries kept their message on target, and Parkinson recalled congratulating his companion for his success "in confining his remarks to the first principles of the gospel, and in carrying his subject through very well."[50] Similarly, at a meeting in Salford in 1886, Thomas Sleight noted that his unyielding avoidance of the subject of polygamy so enraged the audience that a riot ensured that had to be broken up by the police.[51]

Fully sidestepping the issue was impossible. In order to capitalize on all proselytizing opportunities, missionaries had no choice but to address polygamy directly and repeatedly. While the most intrepid of missionaries did not shy away from the topic, they always tried to frame the discourse on their own terms. Some missionaries preferred to preemptively deal with the matter, before public curiosity demanded it. It was not uncommon for missionaries to sponsor public lectures focused on Latter-day Saint life in Utah, during which polygamy was placed in its biblical context and presented as a scripturally justifiable practice.[52] For a brief period, visiting church authorities from Utah presented lectures intended to demystify the society of the Latter-day Saints, including their marital customs.[53] Mormonism's controversial beliefs kept the church present in the public eye, however unflattering its image may have been.

Discouragement

As the missionaries' expectations of conversionary success diminished, their work ethic and sense of purpose flagged proportionately. Personal writings from the 1870s, 80s, and 90s feature a preponderance of journal entries that chronicle missionaries engaging in a wide array of leisure activities. In the mission's more productive years, this would have seemed shamefully self-serving, if not altogether negligent. In some cases, the missionaries invested more detail in recording personal pursuits—such as shopping, studying, and letter writing—than actual proselytizing activity.[54] Trips to local theaters, zoos, races, and parks pervade the records left by these missionaries, suggesting that their feelings of frustration were appeased, but not eliminated, by amusements and recreational pursuits.

Despair was difficult for many missionaries to avoid. Homesickness in particular proved a very real impediment. Not long after his return to Lancashire in 1890, Frederick Chappell recorded: "[I] went to meeting in Liverpool, was called by Brother Teasdale to speak and broke down completely. I think it was the thoughts of home coupled with the effect of the music of the organ."[55] After two months of service, Chappell still had not come to terms with the challenges and disappointments that attended his new life as a missionary. "I don't know how it is," Chappell wrote, "but whenever I sing the songs of home they make me very sad. I have to pray constantly to God to take homesickness away from me."[56] An additional manifestation of homesickness is found in the journal of Brigham Davies, whose troubled emotions haunted him even in his sleep:

> I [dreamed] I just picked up and went home without saying a word to anybody. After getting home people asked me how I liked it in England. I told them I did not like it and [in response] they treated me cold. . . . They thought I ought to have [remained] and not come back. While I write this I felt bad so I got down and prayed to God to help me that I might be able to overcome this feeling.[57]

It is important to remember that missionary service in the 1840s and 50s was a natural outgrowth of conversion. It was a reflexive, almost spontaneous, movement fueled by the religious zeal of the converts themselves. Subsequent generations of missionaries, who had only known life in the Mormon colonies, struggled to adjust to the rigors of missionary life in a foreign field.

As difficult as missionary work was in late nineteenth-century Britain, the consequences of giving up and returning home were even worse. The prospect of returning to Zion prematurely would not have been well received by the members at home. The main body of the church, seasoned by fifty years of ardent missionary activity, maintained the cultural expectation that those sent from their midst would labor well, labor long, and return honorably when released by the mission presidency.

The temptation to abandon the mission haunted those missionaries who struggled to adapt to the challenges of representing an unpopular faith. As Frederick Chappell languished in the early months of his mission, he seriously considered resignation. However, various internal and societal pressures prevented him from enacting his desires. "I felt very bad," he recorded, "and wrote a letter to [the conference president asking] to be released but did not post it for which I feel very thankful."[58]

The abiding emotional struggles the missionaries of the later nineteenth century faced had but one approved antidote—work. After finally coming to terms with the agonies associated with his appointment, Chappell noted, "I find that only in his labors can a missionary find relief."[59] The peace of conscience that attended a missionary performing his expected duties did as much to assuage feelings of inadequacy and loneliness as did actual productivity and conversionary success.

At its best, missionary work was demanding. At its worst, it was nearly intolerable. Following his first full day of proselytizing in Liverpool, Chappell noted in his journal, "I went with Brother A.B. Wilson distributing tracts and I can say that I did not like it and unless God my Heavenly Father strengthens me I cannot stand it."[60] And yet for some, the rigors of the work produced a religious euphoria. Henry Whittaker Lunt's first experience with preaching on the street in Preston ran the gamut of human emotions:

> We had made up our minds to hold an outdoor meeting. We had prayer and asked the Lord for help as we all felt very weak. We started but soon came to a street where seemed to be quite a number of people. By this time I was feeling bad (that is I was very scared) as I had never done any outdoor speaking. We stepped out into the street, Brother Boyce took charge. We sang [a] hymn. . . . Prayer was offered. . . . Brother Charles Murdock then spoke on the first principles of the Gospel. By this time there were quite a number of children around us and some grown people. I then spoke for a short time. It being my first attempt at speaking on the street I was full of fear. I depended on the Lord for help and received it. I felt very well. . . . After giving tracts to all on the street we went on our way rejoicing.[61]

The proselytizing methods these missionaries employed were few, lacked variety, and were dependent largely upon the distribution of printed tracts. Door-to-door "tracting" was useful in that it enabled missionaries to detect the general receptivity of a given community. Where there appeared to be adequate promise, a missionary might rent a hall, publicly advertise a meeting with printed broadsides, occasionally engage the service of a town crier, and present his message to interested parties.[62] Despite such efforts, public meetings were often sparsely attended, and the bulk of those present generally comprised church members.

As public interest in Mormonism waned, missionaries sought any audience, which increasingly became the local members. With few remaining options, many missionaries devoted their time to reaching out to indifferent and estranged members. Even these efforts bore little fruit. After going to great lengths to restore the wayward saints in Liverpool to activity, one missionary noted, "[They] seem to have lost all light and desire to live according to the requirements of the Gospel."[63]

Frustrated with the general lack of progress, mission leaders throughout Britain converged at the church's headquarters in Liverpool in 1883 to discuss the way forward. Liverpool Conference President George Parkinson noted the outcome:

> [It is] the opinion of all . . . that very little more can be done in the ruts that have been worn deep by reason of so much tramping in years gone by and that the only source now to acquaint ourselves [with the public] is to get out amongst strangers and warn them by preaching in halls, holding meeting in the open air and distributing tracts in every village and neighborhood.[64]

Although mission leaders recognized their current proselytizing methods were ineffective, there appeared to be no option but to carry on with even greater resolve in doing those things that had worn the very "ruts" they were seeking to escape. A new audience, and not a new method, was the only variable that could conceivably be changed.

The diminished prospect of success was chief among the painful realities that attended the British missionaries in the final quarter of the nineteenth century. Although the religious climate in Britain had changed significantly since Heber C. Kimball opened the mission in 1837, the missionaries could not avoid comparing their present failings with the oft-celebrated and widely documented successes of the past. This was particularly so in Preston and the Ribble Valley, where stories of sweeping conversions had become legendary. No one recalled British Mormonism's golden age more clearly than the members themselves, some of whom were the direct products of the more fruitful years of proselytizing. In 1874, Elders Bedson Eardley and William Barton reported: "We have in the Conference some very old members of the Church—some are the fruits of the labors of President [Brigham] Young, Heber C. Kimball, Willard Richards and Orson Hyde; they tell with pleasure the success that attended the labors of these brethren in the early days of the mission in this part of the vineyard."[65]

Outside the church, Mormonism's diminishing influence threatened to reduce the movement to mere memory. Communities that once had been meaningfully impacted by Mormonism now saw little evidence that the saints had ever been present. George Parkinson noted this as he sought to regenerate interest in Mormonism in the rural communities of west Cheshire:

> [We] walked out through the [villages] calling on a house occasionally and enquiring as to whether there were any old Saints in the place but we failed

> to find one. We were treated with the utmost kindness by the people but none cared to hear anything about the "Mormons" or their doctrine. Still we found some who had heard nothing about Latter-day Saints, with these we conversed as long as our time would allow us.[66]

While some communities had become oblivious to Mormonism, others continued to bear the conspicuous imprint of its former influence and conversionary growth. Such was the case with the village of Ewloe in Flintshire, North Wales, which Parkinson stumbled into in 1883. Following a thorough trawling of the village, Parkinson was surprised to discover that, nearly fifty years after Mormonism was first preached there, "the names of Heber C. Kimball, Orson Hyde and other veterans in Israel are familiar in almost every household."[67] Although the missionaries of the 1880s marveled at the enduring impact of the early apostolic missions, they also contended with feelings of comparative inadequacy, having been commissioned to preach the same message in the same region but achieving different and disappointing results.

For some missionaries, the pervading reminders of the glory days of Mormon proselytizing were motivation to strive for similar success, however unrealistic their chances. George Parkinson tried to replicate former achievements by deliberately seeking preaching opportunities in locations where Kimball was known to have labored. In May 1883 Parkinson visited the villages of the upper Ribble Valley and spent several days preaching in Chatburn and Downham. Parkinson's visit was motivated at least in part by the fact that he was descended from converts Kimball had won in the Pendle area in 1838. Although Parkinson's proselytizing efforts in the region yielded no conversions, he boasted in his journal that he successfully conducted "two good meetings" in Downham and that his efforts constituted "the first time the Gospel has been preached in these villages for many years."[68]

Proportionately, these efforts to recreate a Kimball-like campaign in Lancashire never amounted to much. In 1888, after nine months of active proselytizing, Daniel Greene performed his first, and only, convert baptism.[69] Although Greene did not draw a direct comparison in his journal, it is impossible to overlook the fact that Heber C. Kimball's nine months of preaching in the same region resulted in a wave of conversions numbering nearly 1,500.

Some British missionaries of the 1880s and 90s manifested an almost obsessive tendency to compare their circumstances and experiences with those of Kimball's generation. Many recounted embellished anecdotes concerning Heber C. Kimball and his associates, citing exaggerated statistics associated with the fabled apostolic missions. The journals of missionaries who served in Preston all reference the many historically significant names and dates associated with the town's Mormon past. The constant retelling and ongoing comparison revealed one fact only—British Mormonism was not what it once had been.

The sites associated with Kimball's ministry in Preston and the Ribble Valley became important destinations for missionaries serving in Britain. Touring these locations became something of a religious pilgrimage. In December 1893 Henry Whittaker Lunt, who had been proselytizing in Preston since April, contemplated his own faith and church service at the sites made famous by Kimball and his associates. After visiting Kimball's lodgings on the corner of Fox and St. Wilfred Streets, Lunt repaired to the banks of the River Ribble and gazed into the water where the first nine baptisms were performed in July 1837. From there Lunt walked to the derelict Vauxhall Chapel, where Mormonism was first preached to the Nonconformist congregation of the unsuspecting Reverend James Fielding. "I stood in the pulpit and looked around the building," Lunt wrote, "my mind going back to the time when the servants of God delivered their first message in this country and how they were received with open arms by many thousands of the people and what a change has taken place. Today it is hard work to get to talk to anyone about the faith of the Latter-day Saints."[70] Lunt's pilgrimage concluded at the site of the old "Cock Pit," the building used as a meeting place for the local temperance society. The Mormons first occupied it for their conferences between 1837 and 1841. "Now [it is] in ruins," Lunt noted, "nothing standing but three sides of the old wall."[71]

In a sense, the building's dilapidation is an apt metaphor for the church in the Britain at the end of the nineteenth century. The 1880s in particular could justly be termed the "decade of decay" for British Mormonism. Similar to the Cock Pit, the church was, in many ways, crumbling. The members were few and far flung. Latter-day Saint parents struggled to pass on their faith to their children. Reliance on missionaries from America stifled the development of priesthood leadership at the local level. A climate of religious indifference prevailed, and hostility continued to mount against the saints on account of inflammatory reports of polygamy in Utah. The challenges were significant, and the church was, in many respects, ill equipped to deal with them. And yet, as with the Cock Pit, important evidences of former strength remained. The reminder of earlier days and apostolic underpinnings provided a foundation upon which missionaries sought to rebuild in the beginning of the twentieth century.

Conclusions

Throughout the second half of the nineteenth century, British Mormonism was in clear decline. Emigration took an enormous toll on the Latter-day Saint congregations, and the burden of replenishing the depleted membership fell upon the missionaries. Mormon proselytizing was undertaken by three general groups, all with ties to Britain.

The first group comprised the locally converted. Their labors spanned the 1850s and bolstered the membership of the British church. Their emigration was a boon to the main body of the church in America, but a profound disadvantage to the viability of the British congregations. The second group comprised returned convert-emigrants, many of whom had labored as missionaries in Britain before their departure for Zion. Their service spanned the 1860s and 70s. The reverse migration of these missionaries, although difficult, was pivotal to the proselytizing program and the maintenance of the diminishing branches and conferences. Their enduring ties to their native land, as well as their relationships with non-Mormon friends and relatives, added motivation and complexity to their efforts. Proselytizing in the 1880s and 90s was undertaken by the third group of missionaries—those sent from the Intermountain West. Although the majority of these missionaries were American by birth, most were of immediate British extraction. Thus, in an era characterized by religious decline, the enduring relationship between the missionary and his homeland, whether immediate or ancestral, was an important source of motivation needed to offset the frustrations and meager prospects for growth.

The second half of the nineteenth century saw a gap develop between the British membership of the church and the American missionary force attempting to spread the word. While early generations of converts often engaged in reflexive proselytizing, by the 1890s the general membership had relatively little to do with missionary work. In time, the British church became increasingly dependent upon imported missionaries for support and direction. This reliance reduced membership involvement in missionary work, increased congregational vulnerability, and cost the church its Britishness. When disruptions in the twentieth century interrupted the flow of imported missionaries, the local saints were left bereft of representation, protection, and leadership. The manner in which the church navigated the resultant reversals will be considered in the next chapter.

Chapter 5
Opponents, Apostates, and Dissenters

> The Elders [should] go forth . . . in all meekness, in sobriety, and preach Jesus Christ and Him crucified; not to contend with others on account of their faith, or systems of religion, but pursue a steady course. This I delivered by way of commandment; and all who observe it not, will pull down persecution upon their heads, while those who do, shall always be filled with the Holy Ghost; this I pronounced as a prophecy.
>
> —Joseph Smith, 1836

> Every time you kick "Mormonism" you kick it upstairs; you never kick it downstairs. The Lord Almighty so orders it.
>
> —Brigham Young, 1859

Mormonism has never been without its opponents. While believers regarded it as the restored church of Christ and a wellspring of powerful spiritual gifts, many outside the fold viewed Mormonism as controversial and divisive—a social menace and a theological sham.[1] Critics took issue with Mormonism's doctrinal departures from traditional Christianity and bridled at its claim to be the "only true and living church" on earth.[2] Conversely, early Mormon leadership decried the myriad Protestant sects of the day. They regarded the many contending denominations as the false fruits of a great apostasy by which the primitive church "lost its power, authority, and graces as a divine institution, and degenerated into an earthly organization only."[3]

The theological tensions between Mormonism and British Christianity intensified as the nineteenth century progressed. In his 1869 account of the religious groups of Preston, Anthony Hewitson dismissed Mormonism as "a mass of 'abysmal nonsense,' an olla-podrida of theological whimsicalities, a saintly jumble of pious stuff made up."

Of all the creeds in the world (or, at least, of all the creeds then operating in Preston), Hewitson generalized, "there is not one more energetic, more mysterious, or more wit-shaken than Mormonism."[4]

Efforts to discredit the Mormon movement became increasingly sophisticated throughout the nineteenth century. Official anti-Mormon societies were organized throughout Britain, and at least one operated in the English North West.[5] The varying points of view concerning the "Mormon problem" resulted in a protracted war of words, with battles fought both in person and in print. Public lecture halls and the popular press were the theaters of this unique conflict.[6] As LDS historian Leonard Arrington notes, the history of Mormonism "is largely a story of creative plot and counterplot."[7] Thus, the antagonistic publications intended to tarnish the church's public image also emboldened the British Latter-day Saints, many of whom responded to the slander as they would a call to arms. In response to the derision leveled at the saints in 1857, one rather pugilistic editor of the *Millennial Star* replied:

> For heaven's sake, gentlemen, quit such nonsense, drop your toys, throw away your pop-guns, tin swords, and sixpenny bows and arrows, and arm yourselves with the manly weapons of truth and reason—come boldly up to the fight, meet the issue fearlessly, bring forth your strong reasons, show us our errors, and logically prove our doctrines to be false, or else admit their truth and keep silence. You surely cannot be afraid of investigation. If you have the truth on your side, you are sure to conquer. For once, then, for the sake of your credit, cease to be children, think and speak like men.[8]

Historically, Mormon proselytizing in Britain resulted in the growth of both converts and detractors. As determined in chapter three, the successful proselytizing methods modeled by Heber C. Kimball in the 1830s and Henry Stocks in the 1840s were based on committed personal contact, careful and intimate social networking, and proven pastoral care. By the 1850s, however, Mormon proselytizing became noticeably more combative, which in turn engendered active refutation from opponents. In time, the interplay between the missionaries and their critics became more reminiscent of a blood sport than a worship service. The private persuasion and steady Christian exhortation that characterized Kimball's proselytizing had, within a generation, been supplanted by public confrontation, and the contest for men's souls was an event at which spectators were frequently present.

For the Mormons, the audience could never be large enough. In 1856 the president of the British Mission, Orson Pratt, who had grown impatient with the sluggishness of the proselytizing program, hatched an ambitious proposal to pronounce Mormonism's doctrines to all of Britain's inhabitants within a single year.[9] Although the plan proved unrealistic, it represents the urgency with which church leaders wished to engage in public discourse and reveals the universal breadth of their intended audience. It was a nationwide effort to expedite the fulfillment of Joseph Smith's 1842 declaration that "the truth of God will go forth boldly, nobly, and independent, till it has penetrated every continent, visited every clime, swept every country, and sounded in every ear."[10]

Not all who listened appreciated what they heard. Clerics of other faiths who regarded Mormonism as preposterous were nevertheless forced to deal with both the reality and the consequences of the deep inroads the saints were making in the broader Nonconformist community. Concerning the reception of Mormonism in Longton, a stronghold of Wesleyan Methodism when the Mormons first preached in the village in 1838, one observer remarked:

> [Nearly] everybody went into raptures over the "new doctrine;" Mormonism fairly took the place by storm; it caught up and entranced old and young, married and single, pious and godless; it even spread . . . amongst the Wesleyans, who at that time were very strong in Longton—captivating leaders, members, and some of the scholars in fine style; and the chapel of this body was so emptied by the Mormon crusade, that it was found expedient to reduce it internally and set apart some of it for school purposes. To this day the village has not entirely recovered the shock which Mormonism gave it 30 years ago.[11]

Leaders of the particularly vulnerable splinter groups, such as the Primitive Methodists in Preston and the United Brethren in Herefordshire, found their congregations threatened by Mormonism's persistent encroachment.[12] The reaction of the Reverend James Fielding to the decimation of his Preston congregation is illustrative. To his brother, Joseph Fielding, one of Heber C. Kimball's missionary associates, the minister wrote: "With regard to your robbing me of my flock . . . I do not believe at all that you were sent of God to rend my little church to pieces—Were I to speak as 'plain' as you do I should boldly declare that it was not God but Satan as an angel of light [who] sent you here."[13]

Clearly, the history of British Mormonism is incomplete until it considers the points of view of those who denounced it. The superstitions, attitudes, and efforts of those who pursued Mormonism's expulsion impacted the development of British Mormonism in important ways. There are several acute manifestations of regional anti-Mormonism, which reveal important themes pertaining to the endurance of the British church.

The pages that follow note the transatlantic origins of British anti-Mormonism. They feature a comparative analysis of three punctuated instances of Mormon persecution within the Liverpool and Manchester Conferences in the second half of the nineteenth century. Thereafter, the chapter considers how the efforts of disaffected and excommunicated members augmented British anti-Mormonism. The chapter concludes with a discussion of the toll exacted by decades of persecution and explores the ways in which this opposition both damaged and strengthened the British church in the decades leading up to the twentieth century.

Transatlantic Anti-Mormonism

The earliest anti-Mormon pamphlet known to have circulated in Britain was composed by the Reverend Richard Livesey, a native of West Bradford, near Clitheroe. During his years as a preacher in Massachusetts, Livesey was exposed firsthand to the sensation Mormonism had become in America. Learning that it was taking root at home, Livesey published his first tract, *An Exposure of Mormonism.* It went on sale in the spring of 1838—precisely when Heber C. Kimball was enjoying success in Livesey's native region.[14]

Livesey's pamphlet was the first to counterbalance an earlier American tract circulated in Britain that propagated the Latter-day Saints' restorationist doctrines and eschatological ethos. Orson Hyde's *A Timely Warning to the People of England*, which was widely distributed during the apostolic missions, was first printed in Preston in August 1837. The tract was actually a reprint of Hyde's *A Prophetic Warning*, formerly produced in Toronto and distributed in New York City before Hyde's arrival in England.[15] The tract underwent several notable revisions and, by 1840, was mass produced in Manchester.[16] *A Timely Warning* had a remarkable print run in Britain—over sixty years—and missionary journals verify it was still in active distribution as late as 1895.[17] Moreover, oral histories indicate the pamphlet was in use by the general membership of the church in Britain throughout the first decade of the twentieth century.[18] The pamphlet's staying power suggests its enduring utility in reaffirming the church's religious position in the face of its many opponents, both in North America as well as Britain.[19]

The transatlantic nature of early British anti-Mormonism is further evidenced in the personal correspondence of the Iowa land speculator David Wells Kilbourne and the Reverend Thomas Dent, an Anglican parson in Lancashire's parish of Whalley.[20] Concerned by the incursion of the Mormons among his parishioners in the upper Ribble Valley, Dent sought further information about the Latter-day Saints from American correspondents. Dent developed a relationship with Kilbourne, whose position as a prominent developer and businessman in Montrose, Iowa, put him in close contact (and repeated conflict) with the gathering saints in Nauvoo, Illinois, on the opposite shore of the Mississippi River.[21] Kilbourne's preserved correspondence is vitriolic and highly critical of the Latter-day Saints. It reveals Dent's and Kilbourne's shared antipathy for Mormonism's growing influence. The celebratory tone with which Kilbourne informed Dent of the murder of Joseph Smith is particularly revealing:

> I hasten to inform you of the wonderful events which have taken place at Nauvoo since my letter to you a few days since. The work of death has commenced. The Mormon Prophet Joe Smith & his brother Hyrum are no more. I have just returned from Nauvoo & I this day looked upon the lifeless remains of these two men—the great heads & leaders of Mormonism. Their work of infamy is finished & their dupes about two hours since committed their remains to the silent grave.[22]

After rehearsing to Dent the particulars of the murders and lamenting the survival of several Mormon leaders, Kilbourne expressed his fear that the saints would now claim the moral high ground of the martyr, unwittingly created by the perpetrators' lawlessness: "at the same time all regret that it happened while he was a prisoner & had a right to expect protection. It is regretted because his followers will now claim that he died a martyr when if he could have been tried on charges & convicted he would have died a felon."[23]

Bringing the events in Nauvoo into greater relevance to the concerned clergyman, Kilbourne notified Dent of his chance meeting with some of Dent's former parishioners. The Longstroth family, who hailed from Clitheroe, Lancashire, converted to Mormonism in 1841 and emigrated shortly thereafter. Kilbourne described them as "an interesting family" and noted that the head of the family, Stephen Longstroth, admitted to having "heard [Dent] preach many a time."[24] Reports of this nature deepened Dent's awareness that, although the center of Mormonism was thousands of miles away, their persuasive proselytizing activities were very close to home.

There is no clearer expression of early anti-Mormonism than the murders of Joseph and Hyrum Smith: a dual assassination regarded by Mormonism's opponents as a *coup de grâce* that freed them from the social, economic, and political menace they perceived in Joseph Smith's religious enterprise. While critics such as Kilbourne reveled in Joseph Smith's death and the concomitant displacement of the saints in Nauvoo, the members in Lancashire assuaged their grief with hopes of just and swift retribution. Writing to their recently emigrated children in Nauvoo, who arrived just before the prophet's death, William and Ann Parry of Toxteth Park, Liverpool wrote: "We were pleased to hear that your faith of Joseph Smith being a Prophet of the Most [High] God was what you anticipated. We are sorry to hear that he was so soon snatched from you by base and cruel assassins [and] we hope they will find no rest for the soles of their feet until their atrocious deeds are brought to light and punished accordingly."[25] With surprising optimism, the Parrys assured their children that, even though Mormonism's founder was now dead, "the same God is able to raise another Prophet which he will do if they only keep faithful."[26]

While opponents hoped the death of the prophet would end Mormonism as a movement, the reverse turned out to be true. Richard Halewood, an early member of the Liverpool Branch, said the martyrdom actually increased public interest in Mormonism, and that the fascination with Smith's murder proved a boon to local proselytizing efforts. To Richard Moon, a fellow Lancashire Latter-day Saint, Halewood wrote:

> Dear Brother, the news of their death [has] greatly strengthened the cause of Christ. It has been the means of bringing hundreds to come and hear for themselves and learn the principles of the Gospel. It has caused great numbers to be baptized which perhaps would not have heard the fulness of the Gospel in this world. This event shows to the world at large that we don't build our faith upon Joseph Smith but upon the pure principles of the gospel as taught by our Lord and his apostles eighteen hundred years ago.[27]

The violent extremes of early anti-Mormonism, represented in the murders of Joseph and Hyrum Smith, generated a curiosity in Britain that ultimately favored the growth of the church. As Smith himself noted in the years preceding his death, "Persecution has not stopped the progress of truth, but has only added fuel to the flame, it has spread with increasing rapidity."[28]

Persecution

Despite the wealth of documentary and manuscript sources that portray the history of British anti-Mormonism, the topic has gone relatively unexamined by historians. A noteworthy exception is found in the work of historian Malcolm Thorp, whose useful treatment of the subject concerns Mormonism's earliest years in Britain, 1837–1860.[29] Thorp argues British anti-Mormonism in this period was predominantly a regional phenomenon, concentrated mainly within smaller population centers in South Wales and the West Midlands.[30] Based on Kenneth Inglis's analysis of patterns of religious worship in 1851, Thorp notes that anti-Mormon activity was most likely to turn violent in medium-sized towns where religious attendance exceeded the national average (between two and twelve percent).[31] Higher levels of religious observance, it seems, also meant lower levels of religious tolerance, an ideal prized but not necessarily practiced by the early Victorians.[32]

Conversely, Thorp asserts that anti-Mormon violence in the industrialized North of England was, by comparison, far less pronounced. This he attributes to the generally lower levels of worship, which also suggests the region's relative indifference toward religious matters. Although Thorp's study implies that the opposition in the English North West was comparatively less extreme, abundant primary sources indicate it was by no means uncommon. Indeed, by virtue of Mormonism's sheer longevity in the region, no other area of Britain saw more consecutive years of anti-Mormon expression. This makes the English North West an ideal setting in which to examine the evolution of British anti-Mormonism.

The manifestations of persecution that follow are a sampling of a much broader, even transatlantic, phenomenon. In an effort to identify the enduring themes that characterize the opposition directed at the British saints, this section examines three specific occurrences at different locations and at different points in time. The first instance occurred in Chester in the early 1850s. It was recorded in the journal of Henry Stocks, whose successful labors in Upholland and Newton were discussed in chapter three. The second manifestation happened in Douglas on the Isle of Man in the mid-1870s. Correspondence from missionaries Henry Leigh and John Quayle to the president of the British Mission, Joseph F. Smith, informs the examination of this case. The third instance occurred in Castleton, near Rochdale, in the late 1880s. This example is brought to light through the personal diary of William George Phillips, who served as a missionary in several villages north and west of Manchester.

Chester

Mormonism was first established in Chester in 1842. Two years later, the still-evolving public image of the church in the area was tarnished when a Mrs. Cartwright accidentally drowned in the River Dee while attempting to be baptized. The officiating elder, Jonathan Pugmire, and Mrs. Cartwright's husband were both tried for manslaughter and were detained in Chester Castle.[33] Although the legal proceedings resulted in acquittal, the incident shocked the local religious community and cast a pall of suspicion on the fledgling Mormon congregation. The consequences of the scandal quickly faded, however, and by the end of the decade the local opinion of the saints was largely characterized by indifference. In fact, after eight years of active proselytizing, Mormonism in Chester had hardly taken hold. By 1850, the number of Latter-day Saints in the city had stagnated at around twenty.[34]

As noted in chapter three, the success Henry Stocks enjoyed in Lancashire eluded him in Cheshire's county town. Devoid of personal connections in the city, Stocks's proselytizing efforts were dominated by house-to-house tract distribution and seeking to elicit doorstep discussion. The work was time-consuming and largely ineffective. Printed materials were in short supply, and Stocks had to travel to the *Millennial Star* office in Liverpool to obtain tracts, which he lent out or sold to the relatively few interested parties he encountered. Stocks was shocked to learn that a family to whom he had lent several valuable tracts had burned them in protest against the Mormon presence in Chester. A journal entry from September 1850 hints at the growing suspicion: "Was distributing tracts, met with many insults saying we want no more of them, we are church people."[35] All told, the affront was mild in comparison with the antagonism that broke out shortly thereafter.

Frustrated with the lack of progress in Chester, Stocks sought alternative preaching venues. By late autumn he was preaching regularly in the village of Holt on the Welsh border. At a meeting in late October, Stocks encountered a different type of opponent: an apostate member who challenged him to public debate. Stocks energetically embraced the opportunity and solicited help from two other missionaries from Liverpool. The contest was held in the town hall, which, Stocks recorded, "was crowded to excess—the Mayor and other respectable gentleman present." The debate was brief and Stocks ensured it remained centered on the first principles, which had long been established as his preferred talking points. Regarding the apostate's efforts, Stocks wrote, "He could bring nothing against these principles, though he tried but was defeated. So the truth prevailed."[36] On the basis of this singular encounter, Henry Stocks mistakenly supposed that disaffected members posed little threat to his proselytizing efforts.

In March 1851, Henry Stocks learned that a coalition of clergymen had sought out and brought to Chester a former Latter-day Saint named Andrew Hepburn, who was "lecturing against the Saints with all the power that is about him, telling the most abominable lies and tales . . . [putting] the whole town in a complete stir about Mormonism."[37] In response to this new threat, Stocks printed one hundred placards and posted them throughout the city. These bulletins promoted Mormonism and invited the public to attend the saints' weekly meetings, through which they might come to their own conclusions.[38] Ironically, Stocks's attempts to defend the credibility of the church only intensified the opposition. The advertising campaign brought a host of opponents and curious spectators into the meeting hall, whose influence changed the tenor of the Mormon meetings from worship to vehement debate.

At a Sunday evening meeting in mid-March 1851, Stocks was alarmed to discover that Hepburn was in attendance. Before the meeting closed he incited much argument against the elders' preaching. "Hepburn rose up," Stocks recorded, and "said he could not stand it any longer. He [Hepburn] was like a Fiend of Hell. The congregation was all up and the powers of darkness raged in the most wildest fury. We expected to be either killed or lamed but providentially was [*sic*] not harmed. I never saw such a scene in my life like as if the whole place would be torn up and us killed."[39] The protest so alarmed Stocks that he immediately filed for a preaching license and registered the meeting hall with the local authorities in order to obtain legal redress in the event of future disturbances.

Each week for the following four months Henry Stocks was unable to conduct worship services undisturbed on account of the crowds of detractors that swarmed the meeting hall. Twice he went before the local magistrates seeking defense and protection, but his journal suggests these efforts proved futile. The apostate Hepburn, whose lecturing was catalytic to the chaos, was ultimately abandoned by his clergyman sponsors after his teetotalism was discovered to be a guise.[40] To Stocks's dismay, Hepburn's withdrawal from Chester did not diminish the developing mobocracy that had begun to take on a life of its own.

The antagonism peaked in late June 1851. Following yet another disruption during a mid-week lecture at the meeting hall, Henry Stocks summoned the police and demanded that the man responsible for the disturbance be removed. The request incited a riot. Stocks's journal vividly portrays the violent outcome:

> The people rushed round, and said the man should not be taken. It appeared as if we should be beaten or killed, however with great perseverance of the police we [were] all [escorted] out of the room. We then proceeded upon the main street followed by hundreds of men, women, and children [who were] shouting, howling, throwing horse dung, like as if all Hell had been let loose. We wished the police to go with us home to guard us but [they] would not. We started [and the crowd] immediately began to shout and hurrah, and to throw stones, brick ends, more horse dung, etc. There [were] hundreds to witness this usage. I was struck with a large stone on the back of the neck, on my elbow, on my arm, and all over my body. My hat was three or four times furiously knocked off my head. I was pasted from head to feet with miry dirt from some convenient places by the wayside, and was hurt or pained. [I was] not seriously wounded but was every moment in danger of being killed and can say that by an unseen power I was preserved for it is a miracle that I was not killed. We all walked together to my house and entered. The door was struck and the chamber window was smashed in by throwing stones at it. Nine large panes broke. The shutters [were] closed at the bottom, else they would have been broke also. We all stripped and washed four or five [times] in order to be free from the dirt which was on us. We [were] frightful to look at. Many of the brethren and sisters [were] awaiting our return

> inside and the wicked multitude outside round the house. The whole city is in a complete uproar.[41]

Four days following the attack, Stocks went to Liverpool to represent the Chester Branch at the quarterly conference. He relayed the abuses he and other church members had suffered to Franklin D. Richards, then president of the British Mission. Stocks noted in his journal that Richards invited him and his associates to "wash our feet against them, bearing witness to God that we had done our duty."[42] The minutes from the quarterly conference confirm this decision: "it was decided that the gospel be taken from Chester for a season."[43] Regarding themselves as representatives of the restored Church of Christ, both Stocks and Liverpool Conference President Glaud Rodgers literally invoked the New Testament injunction: "And whosoever will not receive you, when you go out of that city, shake off the very dust from your feet for a testimony against them."[44] In late July, Stocks and Rogers repaired to the River Dee at night, where they "attended to this ordinance . . . witnessing to God in prayer what we had done."[45]

This initial example of anti-Mormonism in Chester reveals that missionaries were deemed a common foe by clerics of various Protestant faiths whose respective denominations had become temporarily united against the Latter-day Saints. Although in this case the local heads of faith instigated the resistance, the opposition itself, or at least its violent expression, was decidedly mobocratic. The once-pervasive indifference toward Mormonism in Chester escalated to active antagonism following the public testimonials of an excommunicated member. Early efforts to undermine Mormonism were carefully developed, cooperative, and multifaceted. Once the campaign against the saints was launched, public opinion soon embraced the notion that Mormonism was more than a mere curiosity, but an actual threat.

Isle of Man

Mormon proselytizing on the Isle of Man commenced in September 1840. The first representatives of the church on the island were Elders John Taylor and Hiram Clark.[46] Mormonism took root in Douglas in much the same way as it did in Preston—through the missionaries' familial connections and social networking. Within weeks, Taylor had baptized a cluster of associates and relatives of his wife, Leonora, herself a native of Douglas.[47] Shortly thereafter, the elders expanded their audience significantly, and began renting the Wellington Rooms as a venue for their preaching. Early antagonism accompanied these public lectures, as Taylor noted on October 2:

> I have taken a large room in Douglas, capable of containing 1000 persons and have preached in it a number of times, to a large concourse of people

> of all ranks, who have assembled from the first until the present time. I have had a controversy with a Primitive Methodist preacher, but of all the lame attempts to oppose the truth that ever I heard, I think his was the weakest and the worst, and the people were disgusted with him. I baptized six today and many more are believing.[48]

After several weeks of preaching, Taylor returned to Liverpool. His successor on the Isle of Man, James Blakeslee, continued to preach to large audiences in public settings. According to his own writings, the novelty of Mormonism drew hundreds of listeners away from their customary places of worship. The Manx clergy, Blakeslee wrote:

> were complaining bitterly, and had few or no hearers at present. One priest complained to the high bailiff, saying that he on the previous Sunday had had no hearers, that he knew not what it meant, but after his meeting had concluded to go to the Saints' meeting in New Market, and on arriving there he could not get in, the room being full, and he had found his whole congregation there. He insisted that something be done to drive the Saints out of town, but had received no encouragement.[49]

Although interest in Mormonism was intensifying, conversions remained rare. In all, it is unlikely that the number of saints on the Isle of Man ever exceeded two hundred. The conversionary successes of the saints, however modest, were fiercely opposed by local Wesleyan Methodists. Articles in the *Manx Liberal* condemned Mormonism and chastised local town officials in Douglas for "abetting such a cause" through their inaction.[50] The saints retaliated through a series of pamphlets authored by John Taylor, which decried the corruption of the Wesleyan ministry and reiterated the needfulness and truthfulness of the latter-day restoration.[51]

Although Mormonism on the Isle of Man was once sufficiently developed to operate as an autonomous conference, its strength was unsustainable. By 1856 the branch in Peel had closed, emigration having depleted the congregations on the island. Elders John M. Kay and Charles Dana, president and pastor of the Liverpool Conference respectively, visited Douglas in June of that year to ascertain the condition of the members now under their jurisdiction. What they saw was pathetic—a smattering of scattered, defenseless saints, wounded by widespread calumny and prejudice. Proselytizing had ground to a halt and the few remaining members on the island were floundering and without leadership.

Although the strength of the Liverpool Conference sustained the faltering membership for a time, continued persecution obstructed several attempts to rejuvenate proselytizing. In August 1857 visiting elders from the Liverpool Conference delivered two lectures on the Book of Mormon at a meeting hall in Douglas. The meetings attracted a good deal of attention, and opponents turned out in numbers. The threat of mob violence closed the meeting prematurely and a jeering crowd followed the missionaries to their lodgings.[52] There was not a single baptism on the island for the next six years.

In November 1863, a visit from the president of the Liverpool Conference, Thomas Taylor, reinvigorated the local saints. Taylor extended his stay for several weeks, preaching in both public and private settings. Soon four converts were baptized.[53] Although Taylor's efforts provided a much-needed boost to membership morale and missionary work, the effects were short-lived. Nevertheless, his visit illustrates the concern of upper church leadership for the often-overlooked Douglas Branch and signifies the commitment of the Liverpool Conference to provide pastoral support. When compared with the enduring persecution suffered by the saints, however, such support must have seemed episodic, irregular, and disproportionate to the severity of the pressures at play. The suspicion and antipathy toward Mormonism was too pervasive to be countered effectively by the handful of remaining saints. Any efforts to improve the church's standing on the island had to be undertaken by visiting missionaries.

By 1874 the number of Latter-day Saints on the Isle of Man had dwindled to seven. In April of that year Liverpool Conference President Henry Leigh traveled to the island with John Quayle, a native of Douglas who had returned from Salt Lake City hoping to convert his relations. "Elder Quayle has labored indefatigably among the people," Leigh recorded, "visiting them at their homes and striving to impart unto them correct information with regard to the doctrines of our faith. [Quayle] has succeeded in gaining the good-will and respect of a large number of persons and in disabusing their minds of many false impressions and prejudices respecting the Latter-day Saints. Whether any material good will result from his labours remains yet to be seen."[54]

To test the receptivity of the Manx to a refreshed proselytizing effort, Leigh and Quayle advertised and conducted a series of public meetings at a hired hall in Douglas. Any remaining hope that the population's former disdain for Mormonism had dissipated was quickly dashed. Within the first few minutes of the meeting, a mob of fifty detractors swarmed the seats in front of the rostrum and manipulated the lecture into a debate. The disruption curtailed the elders' efforts, and they dismissed the audience with the understanding that the meeting would reconvene that evening. Between sessions, the hall agent indicated he would not permit an additional meeting until advance payment had been made to cover the cost of damages the hall and its furnishings would inevitably sustain when the mob returned. Additionally, the agent urged Leigh and Quayle to secure police protection to reduce the probability of a violent outcome. The missionaries' efforts to enlist local law enforcement proved fruitless and they returned to the hall at the appointed hour.

Upon arrival, the elders were shocked to discover that a mob numbering nearly two hundred had already overwhelmed the entrance to the meeting hall. Again the hall agent intervened, and, fearing the onset of chaos, pleaded with Leigh and Quayle to desist. Although the missionaries agreed to his request, the mob refused to let the evening pass without incident. The following scene described by Leigh illustrates the intensity of the opposition:

> We had gone but a very short distance when the crowd, who had been consulting together and were doubtless disappointed at the turn affairs were taking, came rushing after us like a band of wild Indians. The crowd kept augmenting as we proceeded on our way—men, women, and children rushing first to their windows and doors and then out of their houses and joining the mob, and joining in the most unearthly and fiendish yells that it is possible for human beings to give utterance to.[55]

Incensed at the indignities suffered by the elders, Leigh decried the "rough element of the populace" on the island, whose formidable efforts to oppose the saints had negated all of Quayle's earlier progress. "Such has been the reception that our efforts to preach the Gospel have met with," Leigh wrote. "The Manx," he continued, "[are] a bigoted and priest-ridden people, and the opposition we [have] met with . . . was at the instigation of the priests, parsons and the press."[56] The police, it seemed, were either unable or unwilling to intervene.

These instances of persecution on the Isle of Man reveal how quickly anti-Mormon expression could flare-up, even after several years of quiet. Anti-Mormonism was, at least on the Isle of Man, a largely latent but deep-rooted sentiment that was easily recalled and rekindled. The conspicuous mobocracy in Douglas is comparable to the aggression in Chester, though there is little evidence that suggests it extended from a collaborative and well-structured campaign initiated by local clergy. Rather, opposition directed at the saints on the Isle of Man seemed to extend from a more pervasive suspicion of the Latter-day Saints that, when sufficiently encouraged, became explosive. By the 1870s, Mormonism appeared to be little more than a peculiar religious influence, resented for its tendency to conduct periodic proselytizing raids upon an otherwise settled and insular community. Several decades of emigration cost the saints their identity as a local congregation comprised of indigenous adherents. Throughout the remainder of the nineteenth century, the Mormons remained a foreign, if not an unwelcome, guest.

Rochdale

Mormonism in Rochdale first became controversial in 1854. In March of that year, Elders John S. Fullmer and David B. Dille baptized the Marsden family. Among the members of the family was eighteen-year-old Alston, who had been born both deaf and mute. Shortly after joining the church, select members of the Marsden family claimed that Alston's hearing and capacity for speech had suddenly and remarkably improved after his baptism and confirmation. Fullmer and Dille counted it a miracle, and publicized it as such in the next edition of the *Millennial Star*.

The "Miracle at Rochdale," as it came to be known among the local saints, was presented by missionaries throughout Britain as evidence of the restored priesthood authority exclusive to the elders of The Church of Jesus Christ of Latter-day Saints.[57] Writers for the *Manchester Examiner and Times* ardently opposed the missionaries' story and over the next several months both the *Examiner* and the *Millennial Star* published a series of contradicting depositions purportedly written by acquaintances of the Marsden family. Eventually, the editors of the *Star* abandoned their defense of the miracle, although they never rescinded their claim to its authenticity. For several years thereafter, critics of British Mormonism referred to the Alston Marsden story as a falsified case of healing promoted by desperate church authorities.[58]

While sensational reporting of the Mormons' activities often generated public interest, useful in advancing the missionaries' cause, the reverse proved true in Rochdale. Their reputation smeared, the Mormons struggled to establish a congregation in the town, though they did so quite easily throughout nearby Bury, Middleton, and greater Manchester.

Although positive interest in Rochdale remained low for decades thereafter, suspicion of the Mormons gradually neared a fever pitch. In early summer 1887 William George Phillips was preaching in nearby Castleton when he recorded the following disturbance:

> A mole broke up our meeting in this place and the streets were lined with hundreds of people this evening making all manner of threats such as this: that if we attempted to preach they would throw us into the canal or they would stone us out of the town or they would get us down and stamp us to death. Before we commenced our meeting I told the people what we had heard in town through the day. I said we were not here for fun but to preach the Gospel of the Son of God and if they were willing to give us a peaceful hearing, we were perfectly willing to preach to them and if they did not wish to listen we did not wish to talk.[59]

The audience permitted Phillips and his associates to preach on the conditions prescribed, but the orderliness did not last long. Phillips continued:

> [We] went on with our meeting. Brother Quigley spoke about 20 minutes when one [cried] out "What about Joe Smith's bank account?" another "You said that a man would go to hell if he was not baptized." At this stage of the proceedings a well dressed man commenced crowding the people and asked the following question: "Are you willing to meet an escaped elder from Utah?" I asked him who [he] was he said [his] name was Jarman and he had to escape from Utah and leave his wife and daughter to be ravished by the cruel Mormons.[60]

The "escaped elder" was the apostate William Jarman, who gained notoriety throughout Britain following his return to England from Utah in 1883, having left behind his estranged wife and several children. For at least fifteen years Jarman terrorized the British Latter-day Saints. He traveled extensively in England and Wales and preached against Mormonism with the intent of exposing the controversial practices he alleged were carried out at the church's remote Utah base. His perspective as a former insider made his presentations especially persuasive, and thousands flocked to hear his sensational lectures. Although Jarman's critics continually called his mental health into question and the leadership of the British Mission derided him openly, his irrepressible campaign made him the most virulent, most effective opponent of the saints in nineteenth-century Britain. The *Millennial Star* editors found him a formidable foe, and they denounced him in over fifteen articles spanning as many years.

George Phillips's firsthand account of encountering Jarman in Castleton is noteworthy for two reasons. The first is that the majority of Jarman's efforts were directed at Latter-day Saint congregations further south—Birmingham,[61] Swansea,[62] Wolverhampton,[63] Exeter,[64] and London.[65] The second is that Jarman, who customarily lectured on his own terms in rented facilities of his own choosing, had come to one of the saints' meetings where he did not have the upper hand. Regardless, Jarman's disruptive influence was still powerful enough to turn the meeting on its head. Scrambling to regain control of the meeting, Phillips noted:

> I said we would not meet him because he was too low and I knew this man and [his] statement . . . to be false. With this, the crowd commenced to hoot, yell, howl, and push till we had to get away from there. They followed us all over town making all manner of noises. I have seen wolves upon the plains by

> the hundreds and in the mountain gorges and heard their horrible yells but never before have I seen Fiends in human shape. It seemed that every imp of the infernal pit was turned loose upon us, but the Spirit of the Lord rested down upon us and we did not fear them.[66]

The crowd's violent reaction to Phillips's refusal to engage Jarman in open debate is similar to the derision Henry Stocks encountered in Chester when he sought to deny detractors the opportunity to rebut his preaching. These cases suggest that the missionaries' avoidance of debate was contrary to the rules of engagement and sense of "fair play" upon which, at least in Rochdale and Chester, the public had come to insist.

Phillips's reticence to engage Jarman is even more understandable in light of the harassment Jarman had incited against the Latter-day Saints elsewhere in Britain. In Birmingham, Jarman's followers had developed such a singular sense of identity as to be called "Jarmanites" by observers.[67] As a band of organized rioters, they distinguished themselves as anti-Mormon and were known to haunt the saints' meetings, armed and wearing uniforms. Unlike the earlier instances of mobocracy chronicled in this chapter, where the preaching missionary bore the brunt of persecution, the Jarmanites in Birmingham targeted the rank and file membership. The saints most often encountered harassment when entering and exiting their meeting hall, as the following *Millennial Star* report reveals:

> As some of the Saints were leaving the chapel they were surrounded by the mob, who hooted, threw fowls' heads, stones and mud at them. The crowd followed Mr. Mererdith, using vulgar and abusive language, calling him an old "Mormon," shouting "there goes old Brigham Young! He has got about thirty-five wives," and threatening to murder him. He was struck in the face with a stone, and several other missiles struck him in various parts of the body.[68]

The fact that church members persevered in their meeting attendance amidst such persecution is a wonder, although not without explanation. The *Millennial Star* rewarded the faithful for their heroics and did not hesitate to include in their weekly editions vivid depictions of endured persecutions. Rather than frightening the membership, these tales imbued them with a martyr's dignity.

In Lancashire, Jarman found an especially receptive audience among men and boys, to whom he directed a series of lectures focused on a highly sensationalized and sexually charged analysis of polygamy in Utah. The lectures, which culminated in the sale of literature deemed pornographic by local presses, occurred in the late 1880s in both Bolton and Eccles. In Bolton, the Victorian standards of morality benefitted the saints, who found backhanded support through an article in the *Bolton Weekly Guardian*: "To expose the evils of Mormonism may be a commendable object, but to revel in pictures of indecency, and to enter into a graphic description of unrestrained lust is surely not the way to promote the moral improvement of either boys or men."[69]

Eager to capitalize on the *Guardian*'s criticism of Jarman, the editors of the *Millennial Star* responded, "We honor an honest, respectable opponent; but when our enemies descend to measures which corrupt public morals, they should be dealt with according to law." The *Eccles Advertiser* also decried the sexually orientated lectures and offered interesting insight into the particulars of the meetings and their audiences. Jarman kept admission to his meetings inexpensive, preferring instead to seek profit by marketing salacious literature. The publications he sold were described by the *Advertiser* as "a library . . . of compilations from ALL THE LITERARY SEWAGE that ever found outlet in the midst of a decent community." The *Advertiser* described the patrons themselves as being comprised of "a large percentage of gaping saucer-eyed lads, who sat for an hour drinking in crapulous beastliness and odoriferous anecdotes, the reeling off of which for the modest sake of the popular pence is evidently the real business of that latest development of platform enterprise, the 'anti-Mormon' impostor."[70]

Indeed, the money that could be made opposing the Latter-day Saints attracted several impostors who masqueraded as excommunicated or disaffected members. The most well known was a Jarmanite from Swansea named Adolphus Bolitho, who had considerable success mimicking his mentor's methods. Bolitho posed as a disaffected convert-emigrant who, like Jarman, had returned to England to expose the church and its leaders as perpetrators of sexual crimes. In time, the competition between Jarman and Bolitho escalated to the point that they nearly destroyed one another's enterprise in a series of drawn-out lawsuits that defamed them both.[71]

The anti-Mormon riot in Castleton confirms the threat disaffected members posed to the church's reputation in Britain and identifies polygamy as a particularly damaging point of criticism. Jarman's disturbance of the meeting in Castleton was part of a broader strategy intended to stoke suspicion of the saints and increase the marketability of his lectures. By the close of the nineteenth century, British anti-Mormonism had become a profitable game indeed—a pursuit for the cleric, a practice for the paid lecture, and a pastime for the masses.

Dissent

As noted, British anti-Mormonism drew its strength largely from attacks made by disaffected former members.[72] Attitudes concerning Mormon dissent were deeply polarized. From the members' point of view, it was outright apostasy—a despicable

FIGURE 5.1. Missionaries of the Manchester Conference, Oldham, 1898. Seated on the front row (fifth and seventh from right) are Rulon S. Wells and Joseph W. McMurrin of the European Mission presidency. McMurrin petitioned President Wilford Woodruff for female representation in the British Mission, hoping to counter the negative claims made by William Jarman concerning the condition of women in Utah. In response, Amanda Inez Knight and Lucy Jane Brimhall (second row, fifth and sixth from right) were called as the first women missionaries in the church. Courtesy LDS Church History Library.

denunciation of a former commitment; a breaking of a sacred and everlasting covenant.[73] Formal writings produced by church leadership regarded the dissenter with pity (mingled with opprobrium), urged the general membership to greater faithfulness, and warned against the apostate's doom.

From the dissenter's perspective, abandoning the church was regarded as emancipation from a superficially appealing yet fundamentally deceitful practice—an awakening from a terrible and costly delusion. Writings produced by apostates also resonated with pity (mixed with reproach) for the believing Latter-day Saint who had not yet seen the error of his or her ways. This section argues that beneath the feigned benevolence of both parties seethed a reciprocated contempt that fueled the antagonism between the saints and their opponents. The points of view of both the disaffected and the faithful deserve consideration in the analysis of British Mormonism's battle for survival.

In 1864, an excommunicated Latter-day Saint named J. Benjamin Franklin went before the mayors of Liverpool and Manchester with an urgent caution. "Do not run away with the idea that Mormonism has done its work here in England," Franklin warned. "There are thousands of good, honest souls that have embraced Mormonism, and will go to the Salt Lake yet, if not saved in time."[74] The missionary zeal that had long characterized British Mormonism found its counterpart in the work of disillusioned former members. Of these, many regarded their disenchantment as providential, and their efforts to discredit the church as a noble and redemptive crusade.

In his address to the mayors, Franklin expressed regret in joining the church and lamented the injury he caused to his countrymen by promulgating Mormonism among them. While a believing Latter-day Saint, Franklin's missionary efforts resulted in the baptism of roughly thirty converts in Whetstone north of London. Franklin conceded, "I am sorry to say [that] most of these are Mormons to this day."

As penance for converting to Mormonism in the first place, many dissenters felt obliged to persuade other Latter-day Saints to likewise part with the church. Regarding his effort to reclaim his former converts, Franklin said:

> I have tried to gain their hearts back to that position which I found them in when I first went there; but I have failed. They now believe I am a devil, and that when I was amongst them I was a servant of God. However, leaving these on one side, I have been the means of converting over from Mormonism to the God of Truth above seven hundred precious souls, by my lectures throughout the country.[75]

The dissenter's intent to extricate other Mormon converts from their beliefs was manifested earlier by Samuel Hawthornthwaite of Hulme, Manchester, in 1857. To the leadership of the Manchester Anti-Mormon Committee, Hawthornthwaite advised:

> Gentlemen, your object is a good one, and if energetically carried out, with a Christian spirit, you may be enabled to save from the grasp of a desperate combination of villains, thousands of your deceived fellow-countrymen. The course I would suggest is, to spread a knowledge of facts among the Saints themselves, and at all times to offer them a friendly hand, inasmuch as they are taught to believe that the Gentiles hate them.[76]

Viewed together, there are several striking similarities between Franklin's and Hawthornthwaite's criticisms of the church, though seven years separate the publication of their respective pamphlets. Apparent is their shared disdain for upper church leadership in America, expressed in abundant and logically fallacious ad hominem attacks. Both Franklin and Hawthornthwaite devoted much of their respective writings to the character defamation of those regarded within the church as prophets and apostles. Concerning Joseph Smith, Hawthornthwaite wrote that "from a boy, [Smith] was a perfect brute;—a degraded low animal, whose desires groveled only in the filth and mud of the worst of human imperfections. He was calculating and crafty, but not to any great extent, as he never ascended above the gratification of his own immediate lusts."[77] Similarly, J. Benjamin Franklin openly reviled Heber C. Kimball, revered among the local saints as the father of British Mormonism. In an effort to summarize Kimball's allegedly corrupt character, and using his many polygamous marriages as evidence, Franklin stated simply, "[a] more disgusting man never lived."[78]

Both Franklin and Hawthornthwaite were highly critical of what they perceived as the moral duplicity of the upper church leadership in America. "Mormonism in England and Mormonism in Utah are two very different systems," Franklin wrote. "In England all its objectionable principles are denied; its apostles and elders utter [many] falsehoods, in order to induce belief."[79] As evidence, Franklin pointed to the saints' stringent code of health, the Word of Wisdom.[80] Akin to teetotalism, the Word of Wisdom condemned all alcoholic consumption and discouraged both tobacco use and the drinking of tea and coffee. This standard was taught as gospel law in England, but Franklin claimed he observed the elders in Utah imbibe freely. Franklin spent several years among the saints in Salt Lake City, and even lived for a time in the home of Brigham Young. His insider's perspective added strength to his many criticisms, and he knew it.[81]

Samuel Hawthornthwaite also scrutinized the church and its membership for discrepancies between doctrine and practice—inconsistencies he touted as Mormonism's unforgivable hypocrisy. He claimed that several major elements of Mormonism—including the practice of plural marriage and the performance of sacred temple rites, which were the foundation of society in Utah—were either ignored or denied by the American elders directing the church in England. Describing the esotericism of the Utah church, Hawthornthwaite wrote, "There is a wheel within a wheel, which you know nothing about!"[82] "Mormonism," he concluded, "is not what it appears to be."[83]

In reality, Hawthornthwaite had no firsthand knowledge of the Utah church. He never emigrated, and he never visited the Salt Lake Valley. To compensate for this deficiency, Hawthornthwaite cited his own observations of radical adaptations within British Mormonism during his eight years of membership. What most disturbed him was the admission of the British Mission presidency in 1852 that polygamy was indeed a reality in Utah Territory. While many British saints accepted the matrimonial form as divinely inspired doctrine, Hawthornthwaite perceived it as evidence of Mormonism's corruption. Summarizing his many criticisms, Hawthornthwaite wrote:

> Mormonism has been on a continual change ever since its introduction into this country, and there is no Latter-day Saint will deny that there is not the slightest similarity between Mormonism now [in 1857] and the Mormonism of eight years ago; indeed, the authorities are not backward to acknowledge

> it, for they say that Mormonism was then a child, but it has now grown up to manhood.[84]

Hawthornthwaite was equally critical of the converts themselves, whose motives for joining the church, he maintained, were far from sincere. He claimed that many of Mormonism's new adherents were gleaned from among the displaced and dissatisfied—those who were drawn to the church as means to self-serving ends. "The chartists, communists, and disappointed politicians, fall an easy prey," Hawthornthwaite wrote, continuing:

> Many who have struggled for "the five points,"[85] "equalization," and "political reform," for years, begin to feel discontented with their circumstances and country, and any change—especially one in which there is a chance of bringing forth their darling idea,—is a temptation not to be resisted. The elder steps in, and represents Mormonism as an infant world—just born; and men who have studied the rights and wrongs of mankind, are the very men required to form and fashion its future existence. All those hopes, which have long since been buried in disappointment, revive, under the idea of a vast system of Christian communism. There could not be a more miserable swindle. Thousands have emigrated to Utah with this notion, and, in their disappointment, have complained to Brigham [Young], but they receive no redress.[86]

Although Hawthornthwaite and Franklin were outspoken critics of British Mormonism, they were once faithful, and fairly prominent, Latter-day Saints. Both men realized they had to account for their former religious conviction and the authenticity of their conversionary experience without appearing either gullible or mad. Both Hawthornthwaite and Franklin broached the matter carefully in their writings, attempting to contextualize their dissent and place their arguments against the church in bolder relief.

Their efforts to account for conversion while explaining and justifying their disaffection each produced a treatise laden with puzzling inconsistencies. For example, in his examination of the various factors that precipitated his ill-fated conversion, Franklin was surprisingly generous in his praise of Mormonism. He extolled its religious virtues to such an extent as to render dissent utterly preposterous. Regarding the character of the apostles he later denounced, Franklin wrote:

> The illustrious examples of such inspired apostles were industriously imitated by similarly inspired elders. From the lips of such inspired men did I first hear Mormonism; the character of Smith; his many mighty miracles; his

> profound sagacity; his inspired teachings; the love of the saints; the purity of their Zion; their frequent tribulations and sufferings came forth resplendent from their testimonies. Such statements, repeated constantly and by different individuals induced me to embrace it. That I was sincere in my faith and conscientious in my conduct I believe no one will attempt to dispute.[87]

Unlike Franklin, Hawthornthwaite refused to directly address his conversion. Although he left the topic largely unattended, he did offer a detailed description of his baptism and confirmation—the ordinances, or "rituals of incorporation," that signified the maturation of his conversion and formal admission into the church.[88] Hawthornthwaite described these events with obvious cynicism and disdain, leaving the reader to puzzle over the fact that he seemed to have joined the church in spite of his own better judgment. Conversely, the sincerity of Franklin's conversion account, and his description of the powerful influences that underpinned it, lends his disaffection an almost tragic air. These emotional qualities notwithstanding, neither dissenter was seeking sympathy. As Hawthornthwaite was quick to point out, "I may be termed an apostate, but such an epithet will not apply in my case . . . I resigned—I was not turned out."[89]

Historically, conversion and dissent are comparable in that each led to the fellowship of the likeminded—whether believing or critical. Transitioning from one body to the other was an experience laden with confrontation and strife. As former church members, Franklin and Hawthornthwaite knew their writings would be reviewed by Mormons and anti-Mormons alike. Accordingly, each employed rhetorical tactics suited to their deeply polarized readership. Franklin struck a decidedly defensive tone when he described the saints as covertly violent and retaliatory toward dissenters. Citing a *Deseret News* article purportedly published in Utah concerning his apostasy, Franklin attributed to Brigham Young the following proclamation: "It will be the duty of my brethren to secure this man [Franklin] . . . on his way across the mountains, so that his lying tongue should not reach the saints in England. By the consent of my brethren, I shall move, that this man be cut off from the church, and that he be delivered over to Satan to be buffeted in the flesh."[90]

The need for defensiveness, Hawthornthwaite explained, stemmed from "the invariable custom of the Mormon authorities, when a work appears against them, to vilify the character of the writers, so as to blind the minds of the Saints, and invalidate the evidences brought forth."[91] From the point of view of the faithful, however, the character of the apostate was the only evidence worth considering. The flaw, they argued, was not with the doctrines but with those who failed to embrace them.

While the pamphlets published by J. Benjamin Franklin and Samuel Hawthornthwaite were being circulated widely in Britain, another commentary from a very different perspective was in development. "Apostasy, its Cause and Effect" was prepared in Salt Lake City by British convert Robert Aveson, who had arrived in Utah in 1866.[92] Although it was never published, Aveson's manuscript survives as an interesting counterpoint to the polemical works of British Mormonism's opponents.

Aveson's examination of the causes of dissent is limited, but keen. It centered on his observation of a friend's gradual departure from the church in the two years following his emigration. Aveson claimed the adverse economic conditions then pervading the Great Basin were the primary cause of the disaffection. Unanticipated temporal concerns were particularly threatening to the spiritual convictions of British converts in Utah, and many members either returned to the eastern United States or pressed on to California in search of more promising opportunities. Such pursuit, Aveson noted, came at the expense of life in the covenant community—the interpersonal side of Mormonism that, by its nature, required the fusion of life and worship within its society.

Though Aveson acknowledged that temporal difficulties contributed to disaffection, he asserted that spiritual matters were ultimately preeminent. Concerning his disaffected friend, Aveson wrote, "And now his mind had become darkened. Why? Because he had grieved the Spirit—neglected his duties, prayers and sacrament meetings."[93] From Aveson's perspective, apostasy was a joint function of avarice and apathy. The effect was a complete reversal in religious outlook, which proved problematic for those who remained faithful: "Oh what a change! For years he had been one of the most faithful workers of the Gospel of Christ, and now one of the most bitter opponents."[94]

The dissent Aveson sought to account for concerned those who had grown disillusioned with Mormonism following their arrival in the Great Basin. There is, however, ample evidence that suggests many British Latter-day Saints lost faith having never laid eyes on Zion. Regional membership registers indicate that dissent ravaged many British congregations in the 1850s and 60s. Nowhere is this more apparent than in the Ashton-under-Lyne Branch. Of the 516 converts known to have belonged to the branch between 1837 and 1857, at least 124 were excommunicated.[95] More dramatic still was the branch in Middlewich, Cheshire, where 60 of the congregation's 110 total members were cut off from the church by June 1855.[96]

Although the reasons for excommunication varied, the most common causes were behavioral. In the Ashton register, adultery was the most frequently stated cause, followed by "conduct unbecoming of a Latter-day Saint." The record indicates this included drunkenness, dishonesty, and even dancing. Of particular relevance are those whose cause for excommunication was identified as "neglect of duty," "apostasy," "rebellion," or "individual request." Thus, not all who left the fold were forced out.

There was a sizable contingent of former members whose behavior and lifestyle may have been well suited to the moral rigors of Mormonism, but who left the church for other reasons. The membership records of the Chatburn Branch have no apparent pattern regarding excommunications, nor is there any similarity of status among those cut off from the church. The excommunicated included roughly as many women as men, both early and recent converts, and even the presiding elder of the branch.[97] Notably, the majority of excommunications occurred after 1852—the year polygamy was first preached in Britain. That many who requested excommunication did so in protest against this controversial tenet is indisputable.

Church authorities were uncompromising in their perspective that transgression was the root cause of all dissent. From their point of view, no individual would willfully leave the church or speak out against its leaders except for the cause of sin. As one *Millennial Star* editor wrote in 1869:

> Experience has proved that the indulgence in whoredom, adultery, and lust is fatal to the faith in the Gospel. This practice is so antagonistic to the spirit of the Gospel that the two cannot co-exist in the same individual. Experience has also proved that opposing or speaking out against the priesthood of the authority which God has placed in His Church to govern it, is inevitably followed . . . by a loss of faith and by complete apostasy.[98]

As critics both within and without the church raged against Mormonism in the 1850s and 60s, the leaders of the British Mission responded by urging the saints to attain higher levels of diligence, obedience, and faithfulness. Because the most common causes of excommunication were behavioral, it was assumed that only increased devoutness could stem the tide of rebellion. In time, the aim was not to fight against the church's many detractors but to heighten the commitment and moral uprightness of the membership.

Not all who parted with the church remained permanently estranged. Rebaptism was encouraged by the mission leadership and sought after by contrite former members, of whom there were seemingly few. Paul Harrison, an excommunicated member from Middleton, proved his penitence in a letter published in the *Millennial Star*. Making himself a cautionary tale to all would-be dissenters, Harrison wrote hyperbolically:

> Oh, my God, why was not my spirit forced, by the monster death, from its tenement, ere I was permitted to breathe a breath of slander against [the Latter-day Saints,] a virtuous, a holy, and the best people on the globe. Would to God I had been more humble and more obedient, then I had not at the

> present been by all forsaken, but now I am cheerless. I forsook the church, and in return, am forsaken. Since I have begun my hellish course, I have not had one hour's comfort; troublesome days and nights have been my portion. I would rather sweep Zion's streets than reign in Babylon's palaces. Let me say . . . that if I were denied re-admission into the church, that I would, could it be one, make my fingers into pens, and with my heart's blood write in the dwelling of every Saint, Beware—oh, beware, of the doomed Apostate's fate.[99]

Conclusions

Throughout the nineteenth century, anti-Mormon expression included various forms of retribution, misrepresentation, and abuse. Early anti-Mormonism in Britain was an emotionally and spiritually charged campaign driven initially by survival instinct. The sectarian violence directed at the British Latter-day Saints in the 1830s, 40s, and 50s represents a more general concern with congregational preservation during an era characterized by intense religious competition. As the century wore on, however, and as pervading religious attitudes shifted from competitiveness and zeal to apathy and indifference, anti-Mormonism became less conspicuous in some quarters and more apparent in others. This provided many challenges for the missionaries seeking to spread the faith, and for the membership striving to keep it.

Throughout the second half of the nineteenth century, the motives of those who opposed the church evolved significantly. What began in the 1830s as yet another manifestation of sectarian rivalry had, by the mid-1880s, developed into a potentially lucrative and carnival-like spectacle in which the Mormons were center stage. The examples of persecution in Chester, Douglas, and Rochdale reveal that British anti-Mormonism was a product of at least three factors: initial sponsorship from rival heads of faith, inflammatory endorsement from disaffected former members, and widespread public regard for Mormonism as a societal threat. The influential role of the popular press in the latter category cannot be stressed too heavily.

Church leaders hoped that this interdenominational strife would strengthen the Latter-day Saints in their cause. In 1854 Andrew Ferguson, then president of the Preston Conference, noted:

> There is such a spirit of inquiry in some places, that the priests and parsons, fearing their craft is in danger, come out and oppose the brethren; but the more they oppose, and cry "impostors," the more people seem to investigate, and this opposition is the means of increasing our meetings. The brethren seldom discuss with these opponents. When they have done so, the power of God has rested upon them, so that they have been enabled to completely

> show up their opponents, to the satisfaction of the people, and it appears that priestly influence is losing ground with them.[100]

As the ensuing contest pitted many denominations against the saints, missionaries perceived both advantage and opportunity. The leadership of the British Mission touted their number of opponents as evidence of the truthfulness of their claims and the singularity of their position as the Lord's covenant people. And they stated their independence from the myriad Christian sects whose combativeness, they maintained, signified both their vulnerability and their corruption.

The only influence capable of fracturing the saints' solidarity was opposition from within. Disaffected and excommunicated members were central to the increase in anti-Mormon attitudes. Dissenters from within the main body of the church in Utah were especially effective in fostering public suspicion of the Latter-day Saints. Depicting themselves as survived escapees from the alleged moral atrocities of the Mormon colonies, former members—both actual and fabricated—were more damaging to the British church than the host of sectarian rivals. When the allegations of impropriety became popularly accepted, and the perception of Mormonism as a societal threat was embraced, public protest and mob violence ensued. At this stage, anti-Mormonism became endemic, and there was relatively little the saints could do to defend themselves. While the Mormons found periodic recourse in the laws guaranteeing free worship, legal right alone lacked the clout needed to outmuscle popular opinion.

Whenever and wherever anti-Mormonism had fully matured, the saints were left with two choices: weather the storm and outlast their persecutors, or withdraw altogether from the hostile host community. The itinerant missionaries frequently resorted to the latter option, although neither they nor the expansionist doctrines that drove them would permit an enduring absence. The local membership, however, could not always easily relocate. Thus, the real damage caused by regional anti-Mormonism was not the quelling of conversion rates, but the stifling of membership confidence. Understandably, gathering to Utah remained a welcome solution for the highly stigmatized saints—even after upper church leadership reversed the emigration policy. The enduring opposition that pervaded the second half of the nineteenth century no doubt reinforced the saints' perspective that Britain was Babylon indeed.

Chapter 6
Revivals and Reversals
The Struggle for Stability in the Twentieth Century

> As soon as we seem to get up, we go down. And usually we were down. It seems like Satan's just waiting for us to build up and then he kicks us down again.
>
> —Jeanie and Albert Pickup, Burnley Branch, 1987

The closing years of the nineteenth century comprised a period of uncertainty for the British Latter-day Saints. Church membership was in steady decline, with over 5,000 members in 1877 and little more than half that in 1892.[1] In the English North West, the saints experienced a similar waning, as the combined membership of the Liverpool and Manchester Conferences dwindled from 790 to 272. Not surprisingly, the number of congregations in the region diminished rapidly, plummeting from 25 to 9. The persecution-laden 1880s exhausted members and missionaries alike, and within the decade over 800 members had sought refuge in Zion.[2] Although the 1890s saw a mild resurgence of conversionary success, British Mormonism was still in desperate need of revitalization.[3]

By the century's end, the cessation of the global gathering and the call to build up Zion in Britain marked a clear directional shift for British Mormonism.[4] Nevertheless, ongoing emigration revealed the divergence between the ambitions of church leadership in Salt Lake City and the yearnings of the British members.[5] The turn of a new century was a convenient time for mission leaders to imbue the British saints with the new vision and its local purpose. Aligning the perspectives of the membership with the Utah-based church's institutional agenda proved an enormously difficult task—one that would ultimately require intervention from the leading councils of the church.

In June 1901 Elder Francis M. Lyman, a senior member of the Quorum of the Twelve Apostles, assumed the presidency of the British and European Missions. He relieved his brother Platte, who had presided over the missions since 1898.[6] As with his predecessors, Elder Lyman oversaw the entirety of the European church from its well-established Lancashire base. With the mission office still headquartered in Liverpool, it was not surprising that Lyman's first act as president was to meet with the dwindling local membership then scattered throughout the English North West.

Curiously, rather than assemble the saints at the customary gathering places in Liverpool or Manchester, or even historically significant Preston, Lyman set his sights on the nondescript mill town of Chorley. On June 19, 1901, members and missionaries gathered at a hired hall to receive instruction from their new president. Between meetings, Lyman and his entourage inspected Chorley, which the mission secretary described as a "clean, little town." Capturing Lyman's assessment of the place, the secretary noted: "[In] the streets we noted an unusual number of clean-looking, well-dressed and non-smoking sons of men. We fancied we saw a fertile field for evangelism if there was faith enough and patience in breaking that shell which is over men generally, and at times over even the Elders in the field of the world."[7]

At a glance, Lyman's stopover in Chorley appears incidental when compared to the broader concerns then facing the European church. Regardless, his visit to the town and his anticipation that Mormonism would flourish there reflects the abiding optimism displayed by visiting church authorities in the early years of the new century. Lyman's words are also strikingly prescient considering the vital role Chorley would yet play within the maturation of British Mormonism toward the end of the twentieth century.

Lyman's expectation that Mormonism would thrive in Chorley no doubt struck the assembled missionaries as a touch unrealistic. Circumstances had changed little in the early twentieth century, and conversions remained a rarity. Nevertheless, the tone struck by church leaders was one of growing, positive regard for British Mormonism's rejuvenation. This refreshed optimism, embraced by Lyman and his immediate successors, developed into an enduring and persuasive ethos that aided members and missionaries as they persevered in their quest for congregational stability.

This chapter is devoted to the examination of Mormonism's early twentieth-century revival in the English North West and the long-term consequences it engendered. This chapter reveals that a remarkable phase of growth between 1901 and 1909 both strengthened and threatened the British church for much of the century's remainder. This brief yet stunning conversionary upswing ensured Mormonism's survival. It produced a new generation of believers whose commitment outlasted the strains of two world wars and an economic depression—a generation upon whom the church would rebuild in the second half of the twentieth century. And yet, this resurgence also created unforeseen challenges for the church as new growth revived old societal fears concerning the perceived threat of Mormonism. The return of these anxieties led to the development of a troublesome and enduring social stigma, which manifested itself in the personal and family lives of subsequent generations of Latter-day Saints.

Between 1892 and 1911 church membership in the English North West experienced a sixfold increase—the most accelerated rate of growth in over fifty years.[8] Within that time, the years 1901–1909 stand out as an anomalous phase of rapid expansion. This punctuated period of growth is scarcely noticeable when the statistical contours of British Mormonism are examined as a whole.[9] However, the importance of this episode does not concern numerical growth as much as it does the key adjustments it engendered within British Mormonism—adjustments which shaped the development of the church in Britain in the twentieth century.

Setting the Stage

Elder Francis M. Lyman's purposes as mission president were revealed clearly in his letter of appointment, issued in the spring of 1901 by Lorenzo Snow, fifth president of the church, and his counselor Joseph F. Smith. Upon arrival in Liverpool, Lyman used the *Millennial Star* to disclose the contents of the letter to the British membership, making it known that he had been instructed to

> see that the Gospel is preached, as far as possible, throughout the nations where new opportunities which may present themselves for the introduction of the Gospel to regions where it has not yet been preached [and to] make such changes and appointments as may in your judgment, under the direction of the Spirit of the Lord, be necessary for the welfare, spread and prosperity of the work of the Lord and the warning of the people in the field where you labor, and over whom you are appointed to preside.[10]

Lyman trusted the membership to sustain him in his appointment and urged them to recommit themselves to the covenant life intended to characterize Mormons on both sides of the Atlantic. "I hope to become acquainted with many of the Saints," Lyman stated, "and to find them diligent, faithful, obedient and progressive; they will have my faith, prayers and blessings; I hope to have theirs."[11] Lyman encouraged the members to aid in missionary work, each within his own sphere of influence, "by inviting to our meetings their kindred and friends." As Lyman surveyed the breadth of Europe for opportunities to fulfill his charge, he trusted that the conference presidents throughout the British Mission would do likewise. Expectations of growth were beginning to mount.

Lorenzo Snow's injunction to proselytize in "regions where [Mormonism] has not yet been preached" was a difficult proposition for the missionaries of the Liverpool and Manchester Conferences. No part of the British Mission had been worked more comprehensively and relentlessly than the English North West, particularly within the triangular region between Liverpool, Preston, and Manchester. Local missionaries had long understood the need to find new venues for preaching, although their efforts amounted to little. In 1883 the president of the Liverpool Conference noted with dismay the restrictive "ruts that have been worn deep by reason of so much tramping in years gone by."[12] Progress accompanied persistence. The organization of the Lancaster Branch in 1884 was a direct consequence of the missionaries' efforts to break out of decades-old proselytizing patterns, which formerly had kept them bound to Lancashire's major, but decidedly unproductive, population centers.

In the years that followed, mission leadership became determined to pursue growth in communities outside the long-established strongholds in Preston, Liverpool, and Manchester, where the once-thriving congregations had become nearly defunct. This new resolve is evidenced in the journal of Brigham Davies, who noted in July 1893 that he and a companion were "appointed to go and open a new field at a place called Chorley," adding that "there are no saints there so if we get any we will have to make them."[13]

During Lyman's administration, raising new congregations became a mission-wide priority—one that energized the missionaries and emboldened them in their work. Throughout the first decade of the twentieth century, concentrations of newly converted Latter-day Saints began to form in the long-neglected outlying areas, where nineteenth-century Mormonism had never taken lasting root. Instead of continuing to seek converts in Liverpool, missionaries pursued growth in Birkenhead, Bootle, and Southport; in place of Preston, missionaries turned to Chorley; Nelson and Colne superseded Burnley; and Barrow-in-Furness surpassed Lancaster as a promising area of new growth.

Although the new fields of labor were beginning to take the place of the old seats of Lancashire Mormonism, both in prominence and opportunity, major population centers remained too important to abandon altogether. Liverpool retained its significance by virtue of its administrative centrality—both as mission headquarters and as an embarkation point for those who were, contrary to counsel, still intent on emigrating. Indeed, the viability of the Liverpool Branch was secured largely through the presence of the mission office and its resident leadership and staff. Because of Preston's deep spiritual and historical importance to the saints, members and missionaries doggedly maintained the congregation's viability. Through these efforts the local branch clung to its status as the oldest continuously operating congregation anywhere in the transatlantic church.[14] Conversely, by the end of the nineteenth century, Mormonism in Manchester had experienced almost total collapse. The cost of pursuing growth in the county's periphery, it seems, came at the expense of maintaining the historic congregations at its core.

An interesting note left by the Manchester Branch clerk in the 1902 membership register suggests a general detachment of the converts of the new century from the membership of generations past, of whom very few remained. "No historical record has ever been kept of [the Manchester] branch" the clerk claimed, "therefore little is known of what has been done in past years. We gather some information from some of the older members, that this was one of the largest branches in the European Mission, having a membership of over nine hundred."[15]

The clerk's observation of an apparent paucity of historical records reflects the condition of Mormonism in Manchester in the early twentieth century more than it does actual fact. In truth, an abundance of records existed on Manchester's Latter-day Saints, although there were few among the new generation of converts who could have known this. Of the thirty-three total members who comprised the slowly reviving branch in 1902, only one—eighty-one-year-old Sarah Cook Mycock, baptized by Apostle Parley P. Pratt in 1841—would have been able to remember the former glory of the Manchester congregation. The majority of the remaining membership converted between 1895 and 1902 and averaged thirty years of age or younger.[16] To them, Mormonism was a brand new enterprise, driven forward by the membership of what was predominantly a first-generation church. Largely unaware of the history that preceded them, it was the promise of Mormonism's future and not the knowledge of its storied past that informed the religious identity of the new converts of the early twentieth century.

As Mormonism gradually revived, the ties between the new and the old generations of Latter-day Saints grew increasingly tenuous. In Barrow-in-Furness, vigorous proselytizing resulted in twenty-eight convert baptisms between 1904 and 1909, justifying the formation of a new congregation.[17] At its core was the aged Mary Sheperd Gregson, who had joined the church in Preston in 1839 during the height of religious fervor in the Ribble Valley.[18] Having long been the sole Latter-day Saint in Barrow, Gregson suddenly found herself surrounded by a growing cluster of new and inexperienced converts. Her death in 1909 completely severed the new branch from Mormonism's original convert generation, whose enduring religious commitment had helped ensure Mormonism's perpetuation in Britain for over half a century. Despite the steady growth of the church in Barrow from 1900 to 1907, inexperience made the congregation susceptible to weakness. In 1909 the Barrow Branch was closed and its membership placed under the jurisdiction of the congregation in Lancaster.[19]

The foundations laid by Elder Lyman were crucial to early twentieth-century developments in British Mormonism and the revival of church growth in Lancashire. Among Lyman's chief contributions were his renewed emphasis on accurate and

FIGURE 6.1. Mission President Francis M. Lyman (second row, fourth from left) with missionaries of the Manchester Conference, Oldham, 1903. Lyman was serving as a member of the Quorum of the Twelve Apostles during his presidency. Courtesy LDS Church History Library.

consistent recordkeeping and his careful realignment of the boundaries of the eleven English conferences. This latter improvement was especially crucial to twentieth-century growth: it encouraged missionaries to focus their efforts within a clearly defined area, resulted in increased coordination of efforts, and added additional structure to the proselytizing program.[20]

In 1902, British convert baptisms peaked at 581—the mission's highest attainment in over 20 years.[21] Lyman's immediate successor, Heber J. Grant, expanded on these foundations and drove mission-wide conversions to a new high of over 600 converts per year in both 1904 and 1905.[22]

Reaping the Harvest

Turn-of-the-century growth, though gratifying, was but a harbinger of future attainments. The true revival of British Mormonism occurred during the administration of Elder Charles W. Penrose, another member of the Quorum of the Twelve Apostles, who presided over the British and European Missions between 1906 and 1909. Penrose's impassioned ministry stemmed from a deeply personal set of motivations. Unlike his immediate predecessors, Penrose was English born and well acquainted with missionary service among his countrymen. His own conversion in London in 1850 was followed by ten years of missionary service throughout the British Isles. Following his emigration in 1861, he returned to England twice for additional church service.[23]

As president, Penrose's enduring missionary zeal was apparent to all within his jurisdiction. Early in his tenure, Elder Penrose proclaimed to the growing membership, "There is a great and glorious work to be done and we are the ones to do it."[24] To the full-time missionaries, Penrose's instruction was even more emphatic. He argued missionary service was an active ministry, intended to consume the totality of one's time and attention:

> There is no time for us to waste. Every moment is precious. We are engaged, all of us, in the Lord's work, and our recompense will be in proportion to our diligence and devotion. The evenings of the missionaries should not be spent in idleness, either at their lodgings or elsewhere, but visits should be made either to the Saints that they may be strengthened and encouraged in the faith, or to non-members of the Church that they may be instructed in the things of the kingdom. The regret which will come to those Elders who have not employed their time to the best advantage will be deep and poignant, while the satisfaction that will come to their souls from the sense of activity and perseverance in the work of the Lord, will buoy them up for future labors and fill them with happiness and contentment in time and eternity. Wake up, brethren! Labor while the day shall last, for "the night cometh in which no man can work." Nothing can give so much joy and satisfaction as fervent, vigorous and continuous labor in the great cause of human salvation.[25]

In addition to bolstering the missionaries, Penrose made a second contribution to the proselytizing program, which augmented conversion rates throughout Britain. In 1898, six years prior to his service as mission president, Penrose produced a series of twelve printed tracts that organized the tenets of Mormonism and presented them in a logical and persuasive way.[26] These tracts, collectively entitled "Rays of Living Light," were distributed in Britain prior to Penrose's term of service (though their dissemination increased greatly during his presidency).[27] The purpose of the tracts, as described by one mission leader, was to point out "for the benefit of mankind and the glory of the Supreme and Eternal God" the "one everlasting way of life and plan of salvation."[28] Thus, a repackaging of the Mormon message at the turn of the century matched the reenergized mindset of the modern Mormon missionary.

The effectiveness of Penrose's tracts was celebrated in the *Millennial Star*. On February 7, 1907, Robert Price, a missionary serving in Liverpool, noted how the

FIGURE 6.2. Mission President Charles A. Penrose and his wife Romania (front row, center) with missionaries outside the Oldham chapel. Presumably, the photograph was taken on the occasion of the Oldham chapel's dedication in 1909. Penrose was serving as a member of the Quorum of the Twelve Apostles during his presidency. Seated on the front row, second from left, is Richard R. Lyman, who was ordained an apostle in 1918. Courtesy LDS Church History Library.

distribution of the pamphlets at an open-air meeting had facilitated the conversion of several attendees.[29] In March, another issue of the *Star* featured the testimonial of Walter Douglas, also of Liverpool, who said his wife's incidental purchase of the collected tracts was instrumental in bringing about the conversion of them both. "Before I had finished the first chapter," Douglas wrote, "I was convinced that the truths which it set forth were the truths of the everlasting Gospel . . . which I had sought for so long but had not been able to find. No theological work ever appealed to my reason and understanding as did that little book."[30]

Given the tracts' proven utility, the mere distribution of them appeared to some missionaries as an end in itself: a proselytizing panacea. Fearing that he had fostered a dependency on the printed material, Penrose reminded the missionaries that the purpose of the pamphlets was to obtain "access to inquiring persons," preparatory to "bringing them into the Church of Christ by the door of baptism."[31] Balancing this caution, Penrose counseled the missionaries that tract distribution

> should be kept up with fidelity and diligence. It is one of the best ways of obtaining introduction to inquiring minds. It should be pursued, not merely

> to see how many tracts can be distributed or books sold within a given period; not for the mere purpose of vieing [*sic*] with each other as to the quantity disposed of; not, indeed, as a race to outrun each other; but with the purpose of opening the way for the preaching of the Gospel in the homes of the people, and of drawing them to our public meetings that they may hear the word of the Lord spoken in the power and demonstration of the Holy Spirit.[32]

The success of the "Rays of Living Light" was gratifying to Penrose, who witnessed firsthand the impact of his printed testimony on conversion rates. Their effectiveness notwithstanding, the tracts remained no substitute for open and inspired discourse, passionately and persuasively portrayed by the missionaries. The doctrines of Mormonism had retained their compelling qualities in the new century. Conversion rates proved this. Less certain was the capacity of the missionaries to preach these doctrines effectively and independently.

Compensating for their own lack of doctrinal knowledge and oratorical skill, many missionaries relied too much upon the distribution of tracts and pamphlets. In some cases, proselytizing ceased altogether once supplies were exhausted. Through the distribution of the printed testimonies of others, the missionaries acquainted prospective converts with a theology that they themselves were unable to properly elucidate.

What the missionaries lacked in knowledge they made up for in zeal. Mormonism's revival in Britain was characterized by the expectant optimism displayed by its young emissaries. In 1907 missionary Jesse Owens wrote, "We are making much progress in Oldham, and the Lord is surely blessing our labors. Since February last fourteen homes have been opened to us."[33] From Liverpool, Robert Price reported, "The Lord is pouring out His Spirit upon many people in this city. Our meetings are attended by a number of strangers who are earnestly seeking for the truth, and it is believed that the labors of the Elders and Saints in this branch will be rewarded before long with a rich harvest."[34] Reveling in the high growth rates, the likes of which the saints in Lancashire had not seen since the 1860s, missionaries in Preston resumed the practice of performing baptisms in the River Ribble, the fabled site of the earliest Mormon baptisms in 1837.[35] It was as though the former glory of the apostolic missions had been restored.

Conversion rates throughout Britain validated the missionaries' sanguine outlook. The success in Lancashire was particularly pronounced, especially within the Liverpool Conference, where the number of converts in 1908 was nearly two and a half times greater than the national average. In all, the 290 converts in the combined conferences of the North West accounted for fully one quarter of the British Mission's total growth for the year.[36] Charles Penrose exulted in the impressive statistical reports, regarding

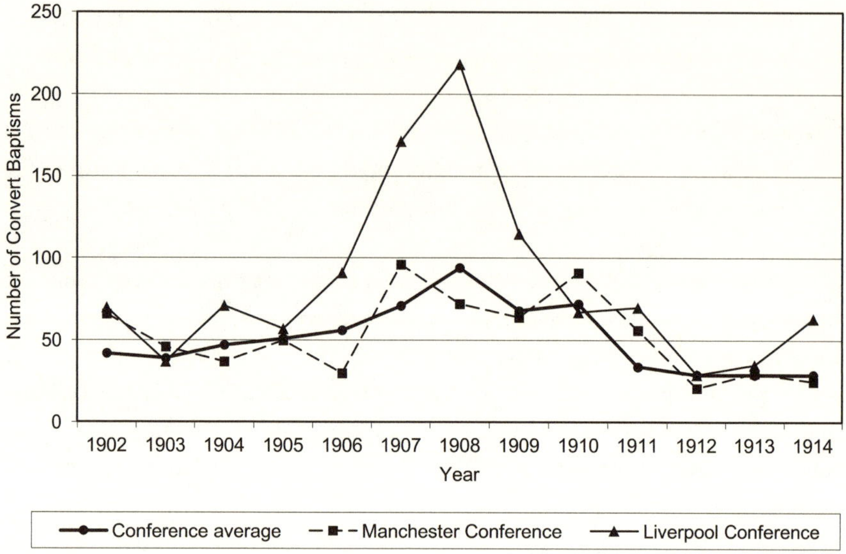

FIGURE 6.3. Convert baptisms in the Liverpool and Manchester Conferences, 1902–1914.

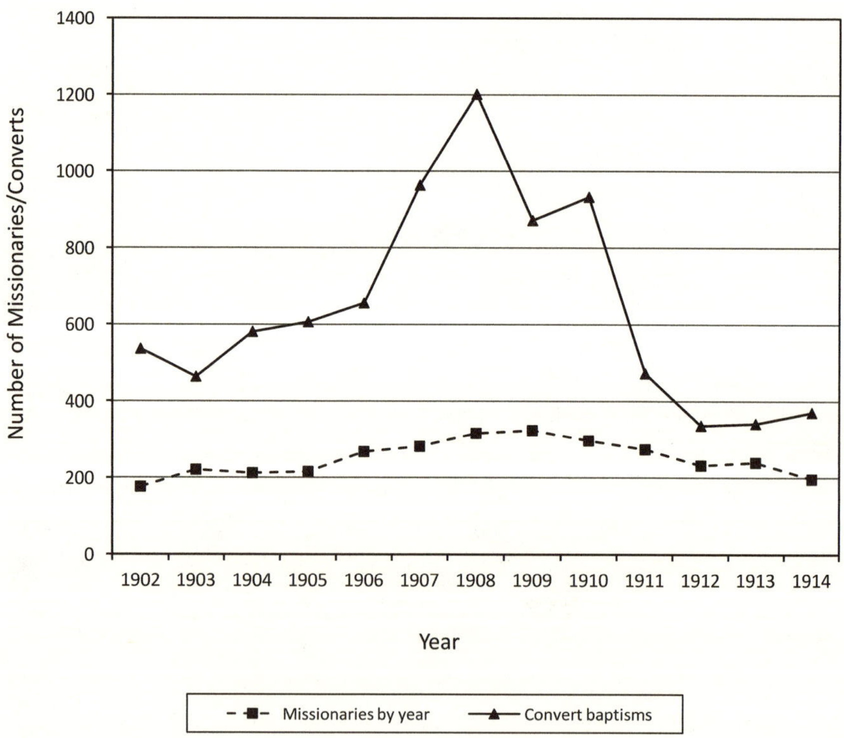

FIGURE 6.4. Missionaries and converts in Great Britain, 1902–1914.

them as "indications of the diligence of the missionaries and evidences that the Lord had greatly blessed their endeavors."[37] Although he accepted the 1908 baptismal record as "a grand testimony to the work performed by the elders, aided by many of the saints," Penrose was far from satisfied. He asserted that 1909 "should go some steps beyond that, because of our experiences and increased opportunities."[38]

Agitation

Newspapers throughout Lancashire and beyond regarded the Mormon revival as an irresistible story. Initial reports treated the saints respectfully, even with high esteem. Following a well-attended meeting at the Philanthropic Hall in Hyde in 1907, the *Cheshire Post* remarked, "Hyde has recently been invaded by a band of 'Mormon' missionaries direct from Salt Lake City. The preachers of the doctrines of Joseph Smith are certainly a smart set of men, and they appear to be very much in earnest over their work."[39] Outside the North West, observations were similar. The *Gloucestershire Echo* reported, "Not the least interesting amongst the religious movements of the day is the renewed activity of the Mormons, or, as they style themselves, Latter-day Saints, who are certainly second to none in the zeal with which they profess the faith that is in them and make personal sacrifices for its promotion."[40]

Between 1907 and 1908, as the Mormon revival gained strength, the media's favorable treatment of the saints was counterbalanced by a number of critiques. Critiques quickly became complaints; complaints soon devolved into propaganda. In August 1907, a London paper revived former tales of supposed moral atrocities in Utah, claiming "twelve hundred girls had been sent from England to Utah this year by Mormon missionaries." The allure of this claim was fueled by anti-Mormon societies, who displayed their paranoia on public billboards. The matter received widespread attention in the North West, which was still the operational center of British Mormonism. Both the *Liverpool Daily Post and Mercury* and the *Manchester Chronicle* added intrigue with their sensational reporting. Indignant, Charles Penrose proved the allegation's falsity and demanded the newspapers acknowledge the inaccuracy of the story.[41] Although the editors of the *Mercury* and the *Chronicle* each complied, neither paper could long forbear printing material about the Mormons, even though much of it was patently scurrilous.

By 1908 an obvious rivalry had developed between the editors of the *Mercury* and those of the *Millennial Star*, which kept mission leadership on the alert.[42] Penrose gratefully acknowledged the sense of fair play exhibited by the editors of the *Liverpool Courier*. Their coverage of the Mormons, although no more accurate or sympathetic than that published by the *Mercury*, at least included a place for rebuttal from church authorities.[43]

Antagonism from the print media was just the beginning. Other venues of creative expression also put the saints in a negative light. Novels, live theater, and motion pictures each featured fictionalized portrayals of the "Mormon Menace."[44] Between 1908 and 1924 novelist Winifred Graham proved a tireless crusader against the saints. Her lurid fictional works—such as *Eve and the Elders* and *The Love Story of a Mormon*—were widely read, even outside of Britain.[45] Graham's most popular novel, *Ezra the Mormon,* is believed to have been translated into twelve languages, suggesting how international anti-Mormonism had become.[46]

Domestically, contemporary social fears in Britain were attached to the already suspicious-looking saints. The melding of misfortune and misunderstanding fueled the efforts of a growing number of anti-Mormon writers, many of whom falsely associated Mormonism with stories of human trafficking and white slavery, a widespread concern then receiving parliamentary attention.[47] However, the antipathy directed at the Latter-day Saints is surprisingly disproportionate to the number of church members who lived in Britain. Between 1908 and 1924, the peak years of Winifred Graham's influence, the average number of Latter-day Saints in Britain hovered around 7,700.[48] Efforts by the British missionaries to swell their numbers created a backlash of such severity that few could have expected it.

Understanding that sensationalism underscored all discussion of Mormonism, the missionaries temporarily abandoned Penrose's "Rays of Living Light" pamphlets in favor of a more eye-catching tract titled "£200 Reward." This pamphlet promised two hundred pounds to the individual who succeeded in presenting actual evidence of Mormon elders abducting and exporting young women through the ports at Liverpool.[49] Missionaries perceived opportunity amidst opposition, and many distributed tracts outside those theaters that played anti-Mormon entertainment. Following one performance of "At the Mercy of the Mormons" at the Royal Court Theatre in Wigan in 1913, missionary Raymond Wells noted, "we tracted the first house as they were coming out and the second house as they were [going] in."[50] According to Wells, the only challenge associated with this method involved working with such large crowds. "[We] couldn't pass [out] tracts fast enough to get them all," he lamented.[51]

The anti-Mormon film industry embraced the resistance proffered by the saints as means of promoting the marketability of their product. Public protest made for effective advertising. In areas where the church members' quiescence threatened to sap the Mormon controversy of its sensationalism, resistance was fabricated. For example, in 1911 a mock protest was staged at a cinema in Garston, near Liverpool. Individuals posing as Latter-day Saints were forcibly escorted from the theater after causing a disturbance just prior to the screening of an anti-Mormon film. The *Liverpool Daily*

Post and Mercury attributed the agitation to the local "Mormon Brotherhood," which the new mission president, Rudger Clawson, vehemently denied.[52]

Though Clawson's administration was dominated by the public relations nightmare unwittingly brought on by Penrose's revival, he tried to remain hopeful. Seemingly of the opinion that all publicity is good publicity, Clawson wrote to the First Presidency:

> Our enemies are trying to stir up trouble for us with moving picture shows and theatrical performances, but usually the offering is so rank and abominable, that the mark is over-reached and the shaft falls harmless at our feet.[53]
>
> Just enough interest has been aroused in the subject to create a good demand for our literature and doubtless good results will follow.[54]

Despite Clawson's optimism, the anti-Mormon crusade stifled both church growth and the confidence of the membership. The former is illustrated in the numbers of regional conversions. As noted, convert baptisms in the Liverpool Conference in 1908 peaked at 218. In 1912, the last year of Rudger Clawson's presidency, that number had fallen to 29.[55]

The treatment of the Mormons in the years leading up to World War I contradict the claims of English historian R.C.K. Ensor, who maintained that "outside the churches in this period—and to some extent inside most of them—the religious attitude regarding creeds was one of growing tolerance."[56] Arguably, had the missionaries not been so active in their pursuit of growth between 1901 and 1909, the crusade against the saints might never have occurred. However, the expansionist nature of Mormonism would not have allowed permanent abandonment of its proselytizing program. In the face of many rumors defaming them, American missionaries persisted in their work while the British members dealt with the social consequences of belonging to a wildly unpopular denomination.

Aftermath

Malcolm Thorp argues that the abuse directed at the saints during the anti-Mormon campaign of 1910–1914 adversely affected popular attitudes concerning the church for many years thereafter.[57] Numerous oral histories of second-generation church members hailing from the English North West, whose parents converted to Mormonism during the revival period of 1901–1909, validate Thorp's claim. These histories suggest that an enduring anti-Mormon bias was a major burden borne by local membership throughout the mid-twentieth century. In many respects, it was the local church members who paid the price for the missionaries' success, which had emboldened Mormonism's opponents and deepened public suspicion of the saints. The price these members paid was both great and perpetual, as second and third generations of church members were forced to deal with the social consequences that attended Mormonism's negative image.

Both faith and fear comprised the dual inheritance of the next generation of Latter-day Saints: faith that Mormonism was all that it purported to be, and fear that a conspicuous commitment to it would carry an inescapable burden of prejudice. Accordingly, the second and third generations of British Latter-day Saints were encouraged to be both devoted to the practice of their religion and defensive of its reputation. The ongoing threat of persecution strengthened relationships among Mormon families and galvanized a shared sense of commitment within congregations. Nevertheless, the fears that accompanied membership in the church remained perplexing and at times seemed insurmountable. These high social costs encouraged a sense of escapism, which preserved the allure of emigration to Utah through the middle of the twentieth century.

Among the striking features of the British Latter-day Saint oral histories is the frequency with which the immediate posterity of the revival generation refer to the anti-Mormon prejudice endured by their parents. Many second-generation Mormons were raised with stories of bigotry and abuse, making it impossible to forget how difficult life as a Latter-day Saint had once been. The recollections of hard times, however, were more than just stories. They were also a type of social inoculation that, in addition to promoting resistance to future persecutions, generated an expectation that life would be laced with challenges stemming from their fixed, yet peculiar, religious conviction.

Many of these second-generation Mormons, when interviewed later in life, reflected passionately on the agonizing discrimination their parents withstood, almost as though they themselves had shared in the persecutions. This is demonstrated in the oral history interviews of Adelaide Tope and Sylvia Mills Whalley. Adelaide Tope was born in Liverpool in 1908 to recently converted parents. At age eight, consistent with the typical upbringing of Mormon children, Tope was baptized and confirmed as a member of the church. Her Mormon identity spanned her entire life.

Although Tope was too young to recall firsthand the abuses her parents suffered when she was a child, her deep sensitivity to their plight remained with her into old age. In 1987 she recalled: "To be a Mormon in those days was something terrible. Dad used to tell us of when he first joined the Church. Halfway through the [Sunday] meeting a brick would come through the window. Every Sunday night they'd come in at the back of the church and disrupt the meetings. It was a pretty hard time because it was a terrible thing to be a Mormon."[58] The stories of her parents' maltreatment imbued

Tope with a strong sensitivity to religious-based abuses. This sensitivity haunted her in early adolescence: "I wasn't very popular because I was Mormon," Tope remembered. "My school days [were] a very unhappy time."[59]

Sylvia Mills Whalley was a third-generation church member from Oldham. Her grandparents joined the church around the same time as Adelaide Tope's parents. Whalley's recollections of the sufferings her grandparents endured are nearly identical to those described by Tope: "My grandma used to tell me that people threw stones at them when they were going to church. At one time they had to get a policeman to come and guard the meetinghouse, because people would just throw stones at the windows and at the church and generally cause a riot that they couldn't hold the meeting."[60]

Unlike Adelaide Tope, Sylvia Whalley's insecurities about her Mormon identity never proved overly disruptive. As a third-generation church member, her sensitivity to these matters was noticeably less acute—time dulled the pain of persecutions past. The anti-Mormon prejudice of the 1920s and 30s was indeed less present in the years following World War II, when Whalley reached adolescence. What anti-Mormon bias she encountered was comparatively minor and stifled neither her social development nor her pursuit of education and employment. However, as with Adelaide Tope's interview, Whalley's oral history outlines several instances of emotional stress in early childhood associated with her belonging to a misunderstood religious minority.

Oral histories suggest that the pervading negative image of the Latter-day Saints yielded troublesome consequences for the lives of British Mormon children. Later in life, many of them admitted being the target of jokes, regarded with suspicion by neighbors, and excluded socially by peers. Remembering his boyhood as a Latter-day Saint in Wigan, Horace Hayes recalled:

> I was never chosen to play on the football team. Oh, they'd let me practice, and I could play on the team that was playing against our team for practice, but I could never play on the first team to compete with these other schools, because I was a Mormon.[61]
>
> When I was growing up as a little boy, [up to] seventeen years of age, all my friends, most of whom were either Baptist or Methodist, would have their little social evenings together, but Horace Hayes was never invited.[62]

Hayes discovered that, even in twentieth-century Britain, the controversy surrounding the church's polygamous past persisted. Much of the criticism centered on Mormonism's most eminent polygamist, Brigham Young. Suggesting how completely his religion shaped his identity, Hayes interpreted any derisive remarks directed at the former church president as a personal affront: "They used to call [Brigham Young] some terrible, terrible names, and it was real difficult. That was where most of the prejudice came from as I remember as a boy. And that was my prejudice in school."[63] Outside school, Hayes observed that the anti-Mormon sentiment he witnessed among his peers was actively encouraged by their parents, whose suspicion was also rooted in the church's former, but still notorious, marriage practices: "[We] used to play all kinds of [neighborhood] games. Tick and hide and seek and rope around the lamppost. But whenever the womenfolks would come out, and if ever the girls were joining in with the boys playing and I happened to be amongst them, they'd all take their girls in. I wasn't allowed to associate with them because I was one of those Mormons. They were very prejudiced."[64]

In addition to social exclusion, church members were generally regarded with suspicion. Horace Hayes remembered receiving blame for all sorts of mishaps that occurred in the neighborhood: "Anything that went wrong, if somebody's window got broke, Horace Hayes did it. When I was traveling, nowhere even in the neighborhood, [it was still] Horace Hayes [that] broke that window. It was always me. This continued right all the way through."[65] Such suspicion also surfaced within individual homes where families were divided by Mormon conversion. One adolescent convert complained that "when anything happened, if any sickness came, [father] thought it was because we'd joined the Church. He got quite bitter at times."[66]

For other Latter-day Saint youths, the social complications associated with their faith enticed them to mask their membership. Elsie Rickard, also from Wigan, described her fears that her religion would be discovered as she exited the branch meeting hall: "I can remember when we used to come down we'd be at the door peeping to see if anyone was watching us and them we'd make a dive out for fear anybody saw us."[67] Fear of discrimination was nearly powerful enough to drive some second-generation saints underground.

As the children of the revival generation matured, married, and started families of their own, they faced difficult decisions concerning their futures. Many were understandably reluctant to see their children subjected to the same stresses that had attended their own adolescent years. Accordingly, some of these second-generation saints disregarded church policy and emigrated, hoping that life in Utah would be less punishing for their children than it was likely to be in Britain. Horace and Edna Hayes reached this conclusion after World War II, emigrating in 1947. The maltreatment they feared their children would receive was one of their primary causes for leaving. "Our children had, more or less, the same antagonism aimed at them that Edna and I did," Hayes remembered in 1988, continuing, "And this is one of the main reasons [why] we came to America. This is why Edna said, 'We cannot let it go any further.

If we're going to make this move, we'd better do it now.' And there was a great deal of antagonism; yes, very much so."[68]

Expectations that anti-Mormon expression might return to its former levels of violence diminished with each successive generation. Although new converts in the mid-twentieth century recognized that social prejudice did exist, this was regarded as a function of misunderstanding rather than calculated opposition. Reflecting on his conversion in 1957, Derek Plumbley, a convert from the Manchester suburb of Wythenshawe, declared: "So there was a lot of prejudice to overcome, among people I knew [as well as] in my own self, and certainly in my folks. They weren't antagonistic, but they were concerned that [I was] being sucked into something quite evil and wrong. And that was true of workmates and all sorts of associates, quite a common attitude. So that was a hard time."[69]

Although the challenges of Latter-day Saint life may have persuaded some of those raised in the faith to abandon it in adulthood, the reverse was also true. Elsie Rickard reflected on the toll of anti-Mormon bias in surprisingly positive terms: "We had to watch what we were doing, I'll tell you, because we knew we were being watched. It made us perhaps more aware of our responsibility than it would have done if there hadn't been this persecution. As I think, persecution did a lot of good."[70]

Among the more troublesome consequences of church membership were reduced courtship opportunities and frustratingly slim marriage prospects, particularly for women. Because of their beliefs concerning the afterlife, faithful Mormons pursued marriage within the faith. Although romantic relationships between Mormons and non-Mormons were not uncommon, many members refused to compromise regarding marriage. Oral histories are replete with incidents of Latter-day Saint women urging beaus to convert to Mormonism as a condition of marriage. Despite such insistence, in the cases of Elsie Rickard of Wigan, Gertrude Corless of Preston, and Adelaide Tope of Liverpool, marriage remained unattainable. Rickard remembered:

> I did have a boyfriend at one time and I really liked him, but I never could get him to join the Church. Now I had to make a choice, either him or the Church. I've seen too many that promised and then they left so I said, "No, you either join the Church first [or we won't marry]," but he never did. Then he got killed on a motorbike, so I've never bothered since. The Lord's blessed me. I've never gone short in anything and I know I never will. I would never leave [this] Church for any man.[71]

Gertrude Corless had a different experience, as she was not yet a Latter-day Saint when the opportunity to marry first arose. Her hopes for joining the church, as her mother had already done, were pitted against an imminent marriage proposal. After informing her suitor of her intent to join her mother in the Mormon faith, negotiations ensued. As Corless later recalled:

> He told me what the alternative was. If I [married] him, I wouldn't have any association with the Church or anybody connected. . . . After a lot of talking and arguing he said, "I give you two weeks to make up your mind." I said, "I don't need those two weeks. I'm going to join the Church." This was in April [1930]. When he came again, I told him I was still going to be in the Church. I made the decision. I [was baptized] on May 2.[72]

Adelaide Tope's opportunity for marriage met an equally abrupt end. Her oral history evidences both the abiding societal disdain for Mormonism following the anti-Mormon campaign of the early twentieth century, as well as the social stigma associated with claiming church membership. "I had two chances of getting married," Tope explained:

> One used to live next door. I went with him. I took him to church once. When we came home we were talking. I said, "If we ever had any children I would want them to go to [the Mormon] church and be brought up in that." He said, "I'd murder them first." He said it with a sort of venom. That put me up right away. I couldn't marry a man that would be feeling like that against the Church.[73]

Although the religious commitment demonstrated by Rickard, Corless, and Tope denied them the opportunity to marry, the satisfaction and security they derived from their religious convictions was, according to them, sufficient compensation.

The quest for marriage prospects encouraged the emigration of many Mormon women throughout the first half of the twentieth century, some of whom pursued relationships with American missionaries who had labored within their congregations. A former president of the Rochdale Branch remembered that there were "a lot of girls that had what we used to call 'elderitis'—they were in love with the elders. They'd go to [missionary] ballgames . . . mainly to see if they could get an elder and get married and get to America."[74]

Although missionary standards prohibited the development of such relationships, Mormon GIs did not face the same restrictions. During wartime, Latter-day Saint servicemen from America swarmed the congregations near the Burtonwood military base outside Warrington. One member of the Wigan Branch recalled, "It wasn't an unusual thing for us to have between twenty and thirty GIs at our meetings on Sunday."[75] The oral histories of local members—particularly those from Wigan, Preston, and Liverpool—indicate that many marriages resulted therefrom.[76] Invariably, these couples settled in America, further discouraging the perpetuation of British congregations.

For Horace and Edna Hayes of Wigan, emigration was the only way to ensure the blessings of covenant marriage and eternal family. Justifying his family's emigration, Hayes explained:

> We didn't leave England to come [to Utah] because of money. We didn't come here for better work. We didn't come here for better pay. The only reason we came here was so Edna and I could go to the temple, and be married in the temple, and have our children sealed to us, and give our children a better opportunity, as we thought, to marry in the Church and live the gospel here than we could in England.[77]

Beyond matters of marriage, church members found it difficult to maintain friendships with those not of their faith. Derek Plumbley described the social transition he underwent following his conversion in 1957:

> You lose friends. There's no doubt about that. I mean, they still talk with you, but your social life so changes that you can't really keep [old friendships] up. There wasn't a breakdown in friendships, but it just happened. We just diverged if you like. [Church members] just didn't have outside lives. You couldn't do it. We were a separate little group.[78]

In an effort to offset the social costs of membership, church leadership encouraged the organization of special programs, associations, and societies that hastened the development of a powerful sense of community among the saints. As Douglas Alder points out, "though there are individual moments of mediation, of prayer, of worship, that are private among Mormons, the faith is mostly experienced in groups."[79] Of particular importance to the members in Britain were the development of the Relief Society and the Mutual Improvement Association (MIA). The Relief Society, a women's charity organization, was established initially by Joseph Smith in 1842. This society was instituted in Britain by Romania Penrose, wife of Charles Penrose, during her husband's presidency of the British and European Missions. MIA provided social activities and supplemental gospel instruction for the "mutual improvement" of both young men and young women.[80] The implementation of these programs contributed

FIGURE 6.5. Various social and educational programs helped the British saints withstand the opposition they faced in the early twentieth century. Here the Sunday school of the Liverpool Branch poses for a photograph in 1919. Courtesy LDS Church History Library.

to the formation of a tightknit community of believers, which provided the British Latter-day Saints with a sense of security, company, and identity.

Church leaders hoped that these programs would satisfy members' social and spiritual needs and increase their capacity to withstand opposition, whatever its form. While full participation in church programs did encourage an enduring faithfulness, it also required a tremendous time commitment. Derek Plumbley remembered:

> The Church in those days took up an enormous amount of your time, even as a new member. You were there all day on Sunday. Everybody went to MIA. You were eventually involved in [other] things, your wife [helped] in Primary and this kind of thing, or you were taking your children to Primary, which was an evening as well. It was sort of three evenings a week, I suppose, as well as Sunday, as well as all the other events that were going on. It was a very, very active church.[81]

The work of the church was demanding, and there was plenty to go around. For some, the degree of service required was a hardship in itself. When the British church faced situations of extreme need—particularly during wartime—positions of leadership were filled by anyone available. Beyond mere availability, it seemed qualifications were few. Sarah Cookman, a member of the Preston Branch, recalled that her husband was not even attending Sunday worship services when he was called to serve as president of the Preston District at the beginning of World War II. Notwithstanding his former lack of commitment, he accepted the position and was nearly overwhelmed by the responsibilities and pressures. "He was the district president for years," Cookman remembered. "He traveled all over. He never had a night home, you might say. He was always out on church duties. We never had any social life, only church work. We had to keep at it night after night besides doing our daily work. We didn't talk about anything except the Church. That was the only recreation, as you might say, that I got."[82]

Albert Pickup recalled the breadth of church duties he was asked to fulfill, which, by necessity, went well beyond his role as a counselor in the presidency of the Burnley Branch:

> I was the [organ] accompanist. We had no chorister, [and] I couldn't [both] sing and play. But we had the organist, myself, or alternatively I conducted and we didn't have [accompaniment]. On occasions I conducted the meeting, opened with prayer, administered the sacrament, passed the sacrament, was the main speaker, and played the organ. So, that was a rather marathon situation that—all at the same meeting.[83]

Bessie Morrill's recollections of the exhausting nature of church service are very similar. She reminisced on the many services she, her mother, and her sister Gertrude rendered to the Preston Branch:

> I think we've held all the positions possible. Mother was Relief Society president before she died. She worked a lot helping to finance things. Gertrude took so many positions. [At one point] the branch was so small that I held eleven positions, all different ones. We had to do that. There was nobody anymore to do it. I was Sunday School president, Sunday School chorister, Relief Society chorister, Relief Society teacher, [youth] teacher, and Sunday School teacher. Gertrude was the Sunday School organist. Everything possible I think we were doing, weren't we?[84]

Although church service placed extreme demands on the members' time and resources, it also offered important rewards. Reflecting on his years of service in Burnley, Albert Pickup stated:

> I feel satisfied, in spite of everything, with my work in the Church. I think we've done a good job here in Burnley, and I think that's some satisfaction in itself. The frustrations have been many, and there's been much hard work, but we've thrived on it and we've developed because of it. All I have and all I am I owe to the Church. The Church has really been good for us.[85]

Growth, Means, and Ends

In the second half of the twentieth century, Latter-day Saint leaders spoke twice of the church entering a "new era" as a way of sparking higher expectations for accelerated growth. First was President David O. McKay, who used the term in 1958 at the dedication of the London Temple. Second was Kenneth Johnson, president of the church's Europe North Area, who invoked the phrase at the groundbreaking of the Preston Temple in 1994. Johnson proclaimed, "I foresee a new era. I see thousands of people accepting the truth and coming to this temple to take upon themselves covenants. This is a glorious day."[86] Both 1958 and 1994 saw significant growth, which suggests an association between temple construction and membership increases. A mid-century surge in convert baptisms justified the creation of the North British Mission in 1960 and the Southwest British Mission in 1962.[87] In the mid-1990s, growth was concentrated primarily within the boundaries of what had, since 1976, become known as the England Manchester Mission.

In the "new era" of the mid-twentieth century, the methods employed to achieve growth represented the eagerness and inventiveness of the missionaries more than a heightened receptivity of the public. Beginning in 1959, missionaries throughout Britain sponsored informal athletic programs that attracted vast numbers of youths, thousands of whom were baptized. This was not the first time British Mormonism had utilized organized athletics in its missionary efforts. In the mid-1930s, frustrated by their lack of progress and dismayed at the church's negative reputation in British society, a group of missionaries organized the Rochdale Greys, a predominantly LDS baseball team. The Greys quickly gained a following, and the team was included in John Moores's Northern Professional Baseball League. Although the purpose of the Greys was to stimulate additional proselytizing opportunities, its real success was improving the church's public image. Missionaries sought to replicate this success elsewhere, and additional teams were organized in Oldham, Catford, and London.

As a public relations maneuver, the baseball program of the 1930s was remarkably effective. When the saints celebrated the centennial of the British church in 1937, the festivities were conducted not in Preston, but in Rochdale, largely because of the favorable image the church had secured there through its involvement in competitive baseball. After World War II LDS baseball was revived with the formation of the Nottingham Seagulls in 1948, of which Elder M. Russell Ballard, a future member of the Quorum of the Twelve Apostles, was a founding member.[88]

For a brief season, swinging bats, not knocking doors, became the preferred proselytizing method in the British and North British Missions. The resulting conversions were swift, abundant, and wildly controversial. In Burnley alone an estimated three hundred youths were baptized in the early 1960s. Two and a half decades later, only two of these converts were thought to have remained active members.[89] It was becoming clear that baptisms alone, even in great numbers, couldn't guarantee the vitality of the British church on the congregational level. Membership retention, not transitory conversion, became the elusive goal.

It is important to remember that the missionaries were a highly mobile contingent of church members, primarily American, who were eager to experience success in the few months they labored in a given location. A strong sense of urgency characterized their efforts, high expectations added pressure, and various incentive programs sponsored by mission leadership offered rewards to those with the highest statistical attainments. Complicating matters, as one missionary from this period observed, proselytizing success was often viewed as proportionate to spirituality.[90] Thus, in a mission subculture that celebrated the presence and priority of spiritual gifts, the stakes were quite high for those whose performance was below standard.

The motives and methods of many mid-twentieth-century missionaries were distinctly modern, consistent with the corporate meritocracy of the 1950s. These ideals and the efforts they engendered are markedly different from the millenarian impulse that fueled Mormon proselytizing in the days of Heber C. Kimball. Richard Mavin, who served at the height of the "baseball baptism" craze of the early 1960s, reflected years later that "zealotry [within the British Mission] resulted in the rationalization that the end justified the means; and aspiration affected almost everyone from mission leadership to ordinary missionaries."[91]

Few of these missionaries, it seemed, understood how burdensome the rapid growth became for local church units, none of which were prepared to receive the sudden influx of new youths. In Colne, for example, local ministers accused the missionaries of baptizing children without first acquiring parental permission. This negative attention created lasting difficulties for local branch members. Though the signed permission forms surfaced ten years later, the damage to the congregation's reputation had already been done.[92] Oral histories suggest that many youths who were baptized in Britain during this period experienced a superficial conversion. In the years that followed, many either were excommunicated or requested that their names be removed

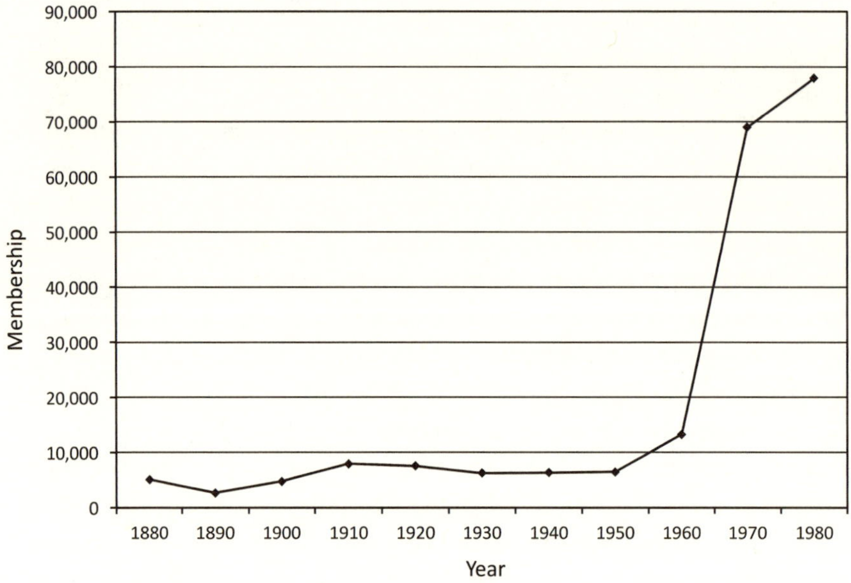

FIGURE 6.6. Membership in Great Britain, 1880–1980.

from church records.[93] Mavin believed the most unfortunate aspect of this was that "the majority of these baptized children never gleaned the valuable, positive benefits of the religion they joined."[94]

Many contemporary members regard the "baseball baptisms" as a blemish on the twentieth-century history of British Mormonism. The matter has perhaps received undue attention—it overshadows the sustained growth of the church in the twenty years that followed. In 1960 church membership in Britain barely exceeded thirteen thousand. In 1980 it approached seventy-eight thousand.[95] Although missionary activity accounts for part of the increase, this exponential growth cannot be attributed solely to a short-lived proselytizing gimmick. Rather, reproductive growth of member families represented a much more notable attainment—British Mormonism was on the cusp of becoming multigenerational.

By the 1980s the presidencies of the seven missions in Britain acknowledged that the lasting security of the British church would be assured only through the conversion and retention of entire families, not just individuals. In 1985 the term "real growth" was adopted by mission leaders to represent an expanded emphasis on progressing converts beyond baptism and into the fullness of a covenant life.[96] This ideal called for a deepened commitment from new members, signaled by ongoing meeting attendance, ordination of male converts to the Melchizedek Priesthood, and qualification for temple ordinances. These were precisely the same priorities maintained throughout the international church. In scope and purpose, the agendas of British Mormonism and global Mormonism were identical. Although missionaries continued to regard baptism as the desired end, for converts, congregations, and their leaders it was the beginning of what was intended to be a lifetime of total devotion.

In the English North West, the number of conversions in the 1980s and 1990s fluctuated significantly. In 1986 the England Manchester Mission reported 675 convert baptisms. The number diminished each year thereafter, with 538 baptisms in 1987, 434 in 1988, and 230 in 1989.[97] Perplexed by the decrease, mission leaders urged introspection among the missionary force. All missionaries were invited to strive for a greater degree of spirituality through exact obedience to gospel teachings. They were also encouraged to increase their effectiveness through strict adherence to the mission rules, which regulated nearly every aspect of missionary life. Unable to influence the receptivity of the society around them, the missionaries strove to master the only thing within their control—themselves.

In the 1990s there was a marked increase of convert baptisms in the English North West. Much of this stemmed from the optimistic expectancy associated with the construction of the Preston Temple. In 1997, under the direction of mission presidents H. Bryan Richards and H. Bruce Stucki, mission-wide baptisms surpassed one thousand.[98] Although after its dedication the temple would be used for the performance of vicarious ordinances for the dead, its construction made it an influential missionary tool among the living. The temple, in a very real sense, became both a means and an end. It was an edifice capable of encouraging conversionary growth among limited numbers of non-members, and was a wellspring of spiritual strength and commitment to believing Latter-day Saints and their families.

Conclusions

British Mormonism's revival between 1901 and 1909 represented the church's institutional intent to abandon the gathering ethos of the previous century and reestablish the British church. The number of converts during this period successfully rejuvenated many faltering congregations. The converts and their posterity secured British Mormonism's perpetuation throughout the following four decades. These members maintained a sufficient foundation from which the faith would expand after World War II.[99]

While the revival of the early twentieth century bolstered church membership numerically and reinvigorated Mormonism regionally, it also brought about unanticipated and difficult consequences. Rapid growth reawakened old suspicions concerning Mormonism and spawned a new generation of opponents. This anti-Mormon movement yoked the persuasive powers of modern media to undermine Mormonism's respectability and reduce it from a Christian denomination to a social menace.

As the spiritual and administrative center of British Mormonism, the English North West was a continual hotbed of opposition. Between 1910 and 1914, a once-mild antagonism escalated into a highly organized and virulent anti-Mormon crusade, which rocked the foundations of the British church. Although the campaign did not last beyond the First World War, vestiges of it remained for decades thereafter. A subtle yet persistent bias against the saints complicated the personal lives of subsequent generations of church members. In response, the church turned inward and invested heavily in congregational life. Through the implementation of various social and educational programs, the saints increased in resilience and withstood the pressures of church membership.

A cross-examination of membership records and oral history reports reveals that the revival generation of the early twentieth-century was the first non-emigrating group of British Latter-day Saints to successfully perpetuate their Mormon faith to their children and grandchildren. The abundance of oral interviews conducted with their posterity is clear evidence of this achievement.[100]

The stunning revival that opened the new century was offset by a nearly debilitating reversal: a deepened anti-Mormon sentiment that threatened the church's regional stability and escalated the social costs of membership. These consequences, though trying, were also laden with opportunity. The endemic bias galvanized the social and spiritual strivings of the British Latter-day Saints and hastened a transformation of mere congregations into tightknit religious communities. This communitarian ethos prepared local leadership to assume increased autonomy and reduced dependency upon the American church. These twentieth-century developments comprise a subtle but clear tipping point in the history of the British church. They signify the church's shifting view of Britain as a corrupt Babylon to a new and promising extension of Zion.

Chapter 7
A Home for the Saints
Developments in Worship Accommodation

We dedicate ourselves as well as this building, unto Thee, the Lord our God.

—Charles W. Penrose, 1908

In October 1992, President Gordon B. Hinckley, then a member of the First Presidency, visited Lingfield, Surrey, to rededicate the renovated London Temple. There Hinckley announced that the construction of the church's second temple in England would soon commence near Preston, Lancashire.[1] The construction site at Hartwood Green, on the northern outskirts of Chorley, had been selected in 1991 by Elder Jeffrey R. Holland, a general authority who was then overseeing church affairs in Britain.[2] Although the search for a suitable location was not deliberately limited to the Preston area, Holland could not help but note the significance of the site to the history of British Mormonism: "It just seemed to ring all the bells," he later stated. "What a way to celebrate the work of the early missionaries."[3]

Since its completion in June 1998, contemporary Mormonism in northern England has been dominated by the presence and influence of the Preston Temple. The true impact of the temple on LDS congregational dynamics throughout the region is just beginning to emerge.[4] Although the temple is the definitive symbol of British Mormonism's presence, promise, and institutional maturity, it is hardly suggestive of its local past—especially when compared to the history of the many other places of worship scattered throughout the British Isles.

The Preston Temple is the capstone of a multi-generational pursuit to secure the availability of the sacred rites of the church in Britain. It occupies a place of such prominence within British Mormonism as to overshadow what little is known about the saints' other meeting places. The identification and examination of places of worship is one of the least-researched aspects of British Mormon history. Such is the focus of this chapter.

Within Mormonism, the chapel or meetinghouse plays a fundamentally different role from the temple. This is not to suggest that the two structures are altogether unrelated in purpose and form. The chapel is a space devoted to the gospel's daily practices, the performance of baptisms and confirmations, and the renewal of the baptismal covenant. These comprise the ordinances of salvation, which serve as an introduction to the covenant life of the Latter-day Saint. Chapel ordinances, although essential, are also clearly preparatory within Mormon theology. It is the temple, with its sealing ordinances and endowment system, where the covenant life of the Latter-day Saint is fulfilled. Whereas the chapel's primary orientation is the mortal realm, the temple concerns itself with the afterlife. Chapel rites are linked to the pursuit of salvation, while temple rites are essential to salvation's fullness: in a word, exaltation.

In his phenomenological analysis of developments in Christian worship accommodation, Harold Turner classifies meeting places into two general categories: *domus ecclesiae*, the house of an assembled group of worshipers, and *domus dei*, the house of God.[5] Turner focuses on the theological tensions between these two categories and notes how the construction of each type, irrespective of denomination, bespeaks the wide spectrum of Judeo-Christian thought, dissonance, and practice in contemporary religion. Douglas Davies clarifies the difference between *domus ecclesiase* and *domus dei* within Mormon thought and architecture. He explains that the temple "is a place where the divine is believed to be present," and that "the deity dwells there in some particularly special way" irrespective of the worshipper being present. By contrast, the chapel "is simply a meeting place, an assembly hall, a mere container for a designated congregation, and when that group is absent, its status as *domus ecclesiae* ceases and it may serve other purposes."[6] In this chapter, examination of worship accommodation within the British church will be restricted to variants of the *domus ecclesiae*.

In October 1903, at the 74th Semiannual General Conference in Salt Lake City, President Joseph F. Smith addressed the needs, opportunities, and global agenda of the church at the dawn of the twentieth century. In his sweeping assessment of the church's condition, both domestically and abroad, Smith announced his intent to expand the church's investment in worship accommodation overseas. Demonstrative of his hopes for Mormonism's expansion and permanence on the international stage, Smith explained:

> Other meetinghouses for our people in other missions [abroad] are in contemplation, and, perhaps in the near future we may have headquarters for our Elders, and a meetinghouse, or church, if you please to call it that, in other mission fields, where we can advertise our name and our principles, and where we can have a permanent foothold and exhibit our works to those who are inquiring after the truth, and not leave the people, as in years gone by, under

> the impression that we are constantly on the wing in these distant lands, having no permanent abiding places there.[7]

Curiously, the construction of meetinghouses abroad was not motivated by convenience for the established international church membership, then being urged by church leaders to remain in their respective homelands. The twentieth-century reinterpretation of the gathering doctrine, discussed in chapter two, seemed to offer sufficient justification for constructing meetinghouses wherever the saints resided. However, President Smith's announcement suggests the development of permanent meeting places was intended to primarily benefit the missionaries and not the members—to give them an advantage in their efforts to spread the word. The acquisition and development of meetinghouses, it seemed, had more to do with growing the worldwide flock than accommodating those already in it.

Later in his address, Smith turned his attention specifically to the British Mission, where the need for worship accommodation had been apparent the longest. Smith continued:

> Our mission in Great Britain, for instance, has continued for the last sixty years or more, and yet we have never attempted to build houses of worship there, and many of the people have supposed that our work there was only temporary. But we desire it [to be] distinctly understood that "Mormonism," as it is called, has come to the world to stay.[8]

Mormonism's policy of permanence now hinged upon the construction of meetinghouses. Britain would be Babylon to the saints no longer. It would, through the establishment of dedicated places of worship, become home.

British Mormonism's various meetinghouses have evolved over time. They can be organized into a four-tier structure by accommodation type that, conveniently, follows a general chronological sequence. The first tier is made up of the earliest and humblest worship settings used at the beginning of the British Mission—individual homes, barns, and open-air gathering places. Also of note are several Nonconformist chapels in which Heber C. Kimball and his associates were invited to preach as guests. The second tier includes the numerous rented rooms and halls used during the second half of the nineteenth century, typically on an ad hoc basis. Third are the existing properties the church acquired in the early twentieth century and then repurposed as needed into chapels and offices. The fourth tier, and indeed the climactic one, includes Mormonism's purpose-built chapels constructed in the mid-twentieth century by missionaries and local church members under the direction of visiting American supervisors.

For organizational ease, the four tiers may be grouped into two broader categories: temporary rented facilities and permanent church-owned structures. The scope of this analysis will both precede and follow Joseph F. Smith's landmark 1903 announcement, when the acquisition and development of properties became official, and seemingly irreversible, church policy.

Early Worship Sites

British Mormonism's earliest use of space was a reflection of the priorities established by the Prophet Joseph Smith. Although he clearly anticipated the globalization of the church, Joseph Smith's primary intention—and indeed his life's work—was not the creation of an empire, but the establishment of an exultant city-state.[9] He envisioned Zion at its most elemental: a people, their prophet, and their God—whose presence was both symbolized and realized through the existence of a centrally located temple, or house of the Lord. It is important to note that, in addition to those facilities necessary for economic wellbeing and cultural refinement, Smith never directed his followers to build any structures other than homes and temples.[10] Chapel building was simply not part of the early program. Even when church membership in Nauvoo surpassed ten thousand, the prophet was reluctant to direct building resources toward anything other than the temple.[11]

The early members in Britain were captivated by the temple, although they scarcely understood its sacred purposes. Fired with millenarian expectations, they recognized the temple's spiritual centrality and invested eagerly in its development.[12] Throughout the English North West, individual members and entire congregations contributed funds to the temple's construction. For some, donations to the temple fund rivaled even the financing of emigration. For example, in September 1844 John Druce of Salford instructed John Snider, a fellow convert who already had emigrated, to redirect the six pounds he had formerly sent to purchase a plot of land in Nauvoo and "give it over as tithing to the Temple, on my account that the house of the Lord may be built."[13] Similarly, the members of the Liverpool Branch, eager to improve the design of the temple awaiting them in Zion, challenged the architects to incorporate a large clock on its single tower, and pledged to do their part to finance it.[14]

As he opened the British Mission, Heber C. Kimball expressed no concern for the establishment of places of worship. The missionaries were a people on the move, inviting their converts to follow. The destination was Zion and her temple. This is not to suggest, however, that houses of worship had no place in early British Mormonism. The first sermons preached by the missionaries were delivered in Nonconformist chapels in the Ribble Valley. Two local clerics, the Reverend James Fielding of Preston and the Reverend John Richards of Walker Fold, invited the missionaries to preach

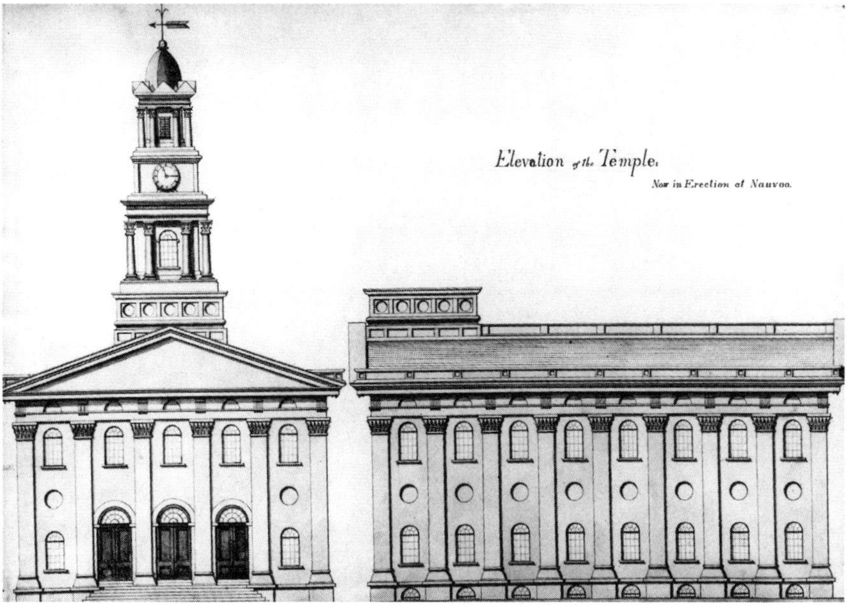

FIGURE 7.1. This architectural elevation of the Nauvoo Temple was produced in 1842 by James McCord, a convert from the Isle of Man. McCord's drawing appears to have been based on an earlier drawing by William Weeks, whom Joseph Smith had appointed chief architect. It is likely that McCord's rendering gave the British members their first picture of the edifice to which many contributed donations. Courtesy LDS Church History Library.

from their own pulpits: a fatal decision that devastated the viability of their respective congregations.[15]

In Preston, the now-demolished Vauxhall Chapel was the original forum for the sounding of the restored gospel.[16] To this day, Latter-day Saints reflect on it as the hallowed site of British Mormonism's inception. A brick from the demolished structure remains on display in the current LDS chapel in Preston. It is an enduring reminder of the church's Ribble Valley roots and apostolic origins. In the village of Walker Fold, Lancashire, the Independent Methodist chapel was the scene of several conversions that were crucial to Mormonism's early development in the upper Ribble Valley.[17] Reflecting on his work in Walker Fold and the utility of the local chapel in his proselytizing success, Kimball recalled:

> After Mr. Richards let me preach in his chapel, I baptized all of his young members, as I had before baptized his daughter. He then reflected upon himself for letting me have the privilege of his chapel; told me that I had ruined

FIGURE 7.2. This engraving depicts the Vauxhall Chapel in Preston as it would have appeared in 1837. When Heber C. Kimball preached here, the chapel was occupied by a congregation of Primitive Methodists led by the Reverend James Fielding. Courtesy LDS Church History Library.

> his church, and had taken away all his young members. I could not but feel pity for the old gentleman, but I had a duty to perform which outweighed all other considerations.[18]

Although the missionaries were comfortable preaching in formal chapels, and derived much benefit from the unsuspecting and ready-made congregations, they had no intention of creating similar places to worship and preach.

As the missionaries began baptizing new adherents, gleaned from these smaller Nonconformist sects, chapel doors were closed to them. This was of little consequence. Within weeks of their arrival, the missionaries' rapidly growing base of converts exceeded the capacity of these smaller chapels, and they sought alternative meeting places. The missionaries had virtually no financial resources at their disposal, and converts' homes became a popular gathering place. The size restrictions inherent to cottage meetings prevented the saints from gathering on a larger scale. However, this more

FIGURE 7.3. This home and chapel (right) is situated between the villages of Walkerfold and Chaigley, Lancashire. The chapel was the site of several crucial conversions in 1837–38, including Jenetta Richards, who later married Apostle Willard Richards. The chapel was used as a school at the time of the photograph in 1890. It is now a private residence. Courtesy LDS Church History Library.

intimate setting lent Mormonism a distinct and novel informality, which encouraged growth within close-knit social and familial networks.

The early missionaries relished the practicality of their religious iconoclasm and used their casual meeting style to further distance themselves from the clerical conventions of the day, which were decidedly more formal and restrictive. As Kimball remembered:

> We had to speak in small and very crowded houses, and to large assemblies in the open air. Consequently our lungs were often very sore, and our bodies worn down with fatigue. Sometimes I was guilty of breaking the priestly rules. I pulled off my coat and rolled up my sleeves and went at my duty with my whole soul, like a man reaping and binding wheat, which caused the hireling priests to be very much surprised. They found much fault with us, and threatened us continually, because we got all of their best members.[19]

The transience of early British Mormonism yielded several important advantages, particularly concerning missionary work. Unfettered by the restrictions of a stationary place of worship, missionaries were able to respond promptly to preaching invitations, focus their efforts, and maximize their impact. Rather than demand the people go to the Mormons, the Mormons went to the people. Although this approach augmented proselytizing success, it did not fully provide for the needs of the recently converted, particularly the important familial and social functions such as marriages and funerals.

Several key illustrations of the challenges associated with the Mormons' lack of formal worship accommodations are found in the experiences of the early members of the Clitheroe and Chatburn Branches. John Ormerod converted to Mormonism in the village of Waddington in 1841, and his wife Ellen was baptized in nearby West Bradford in 1848.[20] In 1850, despite their conversion, the two were married in Clitheroe under the auspices of the Methodists and not the Latter-day Saints.[21] Membership records certify the full activity of the Ormerods within the Mormon congregation in Clitheroe at the time of their marriage, eliminating the possibility of lapsed membership as a cause for marrying outside the purview of their own church leadership.[22]

Arguably, the Ormerod's marriage at the local Wesleyan chapel would have been deemed both acceptable and necessary by Latter-day Saints of the day. At a time when Mormonism was striving for legal recognition and protection in Britain, the Ormerod's Methodist wedding ensured marital respectability attainable only by complying with local custom. It is probable that other British Latter-day Saints pursued marriage in like fashion, with the understanding that after arriving in Utah their union would be solemnized—or "sealed"—by Mormon priesthood authority.[23] The compromise demonstrated by the Ormerods was thus temporary. Conveniently, it also satisfied the saints' marriage regulations on both temporal and spiritual fronts: temporally in the sense that it complied with the law of the land, and spiritually in that it legitimized their cohabitation, preserved their personal worthiness, and kept them eligible for the sealing ordinance then available only in Utah. In the case of the Ormerods, however, the promise of eternal marriage in the temple was not an eventuality. John's leadership of the Clitheroe Branch extended nearly until his death in 1901, and his commitment to serving the congregation appears to have precluded his family's hopes for emigration.[24]

For the early British saints, the lack of worship facilities proved especially problematic regarding infant mortality, as the absence of both church and churchyard complicated matters of burial. Mormon doctrines concerning baptism were at odds with the highly mobile nature of Mormon membership, influenced by the church's gathering doctrine. Infant baptism, derided in the Book of Mormon as a "solemn mockery before God," was a keen source of anguish for James and Nancy Smithies, early converts from

Bashall Eaves village.[25] Converted by Heber C. Kimball, the couple defied the tenets of their new religion by insisting that their daughter Mary be christened by the local Anglican vicar. Unaware of their motivations, Kimball urged the Smithies to desist. He later recalled: "I used every kind of persuasion to convince them of their folly; it being contrary to the scriptures and the will of God; the parents wept bitterly, and it seemed as though I could not prevail on them to omit it. I wanted to know of them why there were so tenacious. The answer was, 'if she dies, she cannot have a burial in the churchyard.'"[26] Kimball then allayed the Smithies's fears by blessing Mary himself—a theologically acceptable alternative. Although her infancy was fraught with illness, Mary survived, emigrated with her parents, and in adulthood became one of Kimball's plural wives.[27]

The blessing of infants quickly became commonplace among the members in the Ribble Valley and, indeed, throughout Britain. Conveniently, it was one of the few crucial Mormon sacraments that required no facilities at all. The practice helped assuage parents concerned about the afterlife, although it never resolved the problem of burial. A compelling example of this conflict is found in the lives of Isaac and Lucy Dacre, also of the Clitheroe Branch. Unlike the Ormerods, the Dacres were married in October 1840, before either of them had joined the church. Lucy was the first to convert, baptized in Clitheroe in August 1841. Isaac joined one month later. Lucy was baptized toward the end of her first pregnancy, only two weeks before the birth of her daughter, also named Mary. Mary was born on October 10, was blessed by Stephen Longstroth (the same man who baptized Lucy and Isaac), and died on Christmas Day. In the years that followed, an additional seven children were born to the Dacres, but only two survived.[28]

With the Dacre family setting the unfortunate example, every growing family within the Clitheroe Branch had questions surrounding infant mortality and burial. Membership records indicate that seventy children were born to branch members between 1841 and 1861, of which thirteen died at or near birth. The Ormerods confronted burial in the same way they had approached marriage—through carefully employed compromise. Between 1851 and 1862, John and Ellen Ormerod bore four children at their home in Low Moor, Clitheroe. Like the Dacre children, each was blessed by a priesthood leader from the branch approximately one month after birth. The Ormerod's youngest child, Mary Ellen, was born on February 15, 1862. Mary Ellen was particularly frail at birth. Her parents, fearing her imminent death, had her christened the following day. Although the location of her christening was not recorded, one must wonder if it was performed in the same Methodist chapel where John and Ellen were married twelve years earlier. Despite their fears, Mary Ellen lived and was blessed a month later by local Mormon elder Thomas Dugdale.[29]

The role of denominational allegiance in burial matters takes on further significance when one considers the experiences of William and Nancy Barton. Also of Low Moor, Clitheroe, the Bartons lost two children, Mary and Isaac Heber. Mary was buried in 1846 at a Methodist churchyard in town while Isaac Heber was interred at the cemetery adjacent to the Anglican chapel of St. James in 1854. It is possible that William and Nancy, who had been Latter-day Saints since 1838, professed some form of allegiance to both the Methodists and the Anglicans long enough to secure burial plots for their deceased children. If they did so, it was clearly not at the expense of their Mormon faith, since membership records certify that the Bartons eventually immigrated to Ogden, Utah.[30] Thus, for the earliest saints in Lancashire, the lack of accommodation was a source of perpetual frustration, both in life and in death.

From Homes to Halls

Despite the benefits associated with the informal accommodation types examined above, the need to establish and maintain denominational identity required facilities that were both more spacious and more reputable. When larger convocations were called for, such as quarterly conferences, church leadership adapted their meeting practices to suit their temporary needs. In 1837, the saints in Preston made use of the old Cockpit, which could accommodate up to eight hundred people.[31]

When the saints first engaged the Cockpit for worship, it had been converted into a temperance hall. Mormonism's likeminded avoidance of intoxicants likely helped missionaries secure accommodation with temperance societies elsewhere in Lancashire. The 1851 religious census reveals Latter-day Saints in Clitheroe held regular services in the upper room of the Temperance Hotel on Moor Lane.[32] A harmonious association between the saints and various temperance societies appears to have existed as late as 1908, when the Oldham Branch occupied the temperance hall on Horsedge Street.[33]

Overall, the desired qualities of the properties hired by the British members were few. Sufficient space in which to gather for instruction and the administration of key sacraments was the primary criterion during the second half of the nineteenth century. Storage space was obviously a low priority, as the saints retained very little property. An 1844 inventory of the assets of the Liverpool Branch reveals just how meager the belongings of the congregation were, even though it had nearly four hundred members: "9 forms, 2 temple boxes, 4 collection boxes, 3 wine cups, 2 sacrament bread baskets, and 1 sacrament wine urn."[34]

Of greater concern to local leadership was the extent to which the status of their rented facilities influenced the reputation of the church. In Liverpool, the saints found accommodation initially at the music hall on Bold Street. Although the hall was spacious and convenient, local leaders worried that its location would tarnish Mormonism's still-developing public image. This concern is reflected in the following correspondence between James Linforth of Liverpool and John Davis of Merthyr Tydfil. In April 1852, Linforth wrote:

> I have just returned from meeting, having had the privilege of preaching the last discourse in the Music Hall. Next Sunday we open our new chapel. . . . I have been over it today and am much pleased with it. It will be opened with prayer and fasting and instruction from Brothers [Franklin D.] Richards and [Lorenzo] Snow and others. On the day after we have a Festival and if it was not so far I should be tempted to invite you. We anticipate much good from the change of our place of meeting for the discreditable character of the Music Hall was a great injury to us.[35]

The rented accommodations used by the saints fluctuated in size and description, proportionate to the ebb and flow of membership numbers. Because the cost of renting meeting halls was met by the members, there was an obvious relationship between the numbers of saints in any one location and the quality of their accommodation. Lancastrians who converted to Mormonism during the peak years in the mid-nineteenth century, and later returned to the region when the church was in obvious decline, analyzed the saints' meetinghouses to ascertain the relative size and welfare of local church units. After returning to his native Lancashire from Utah in 1867, George D. Watt rendered the following comparison:

> In 1851 I attended a meeting of the Saints in Liverpool, which was held in one of the finest halls in the city and addressed a congregation of nearly one thousand people. In the month of March, 1867, I again attended a meeting of the Saints in Liverpool, and spoke to a congregation of not more than twenty persons, in a room or garret situated in the back streets of the city, measuring about ten feet wide and twenty-five feet long, being lighted by skylights from the roof.[36]

The substandard accommodation Watt observed became the norm for the British saints throughout the remainder of the nineteenth century and well into the twentieth. Although Joseph F. Smith's 1903 announcement that the church would establish permanent worship facilities was indeed promising, progress was slow to materialize. Throughout Britain, local members and missionaries combined their meager resources to maintain even the most basic and unadorned places of worship. The halls they rented were often in undesirable and inconvenient locations, such as above railway stations or in the upper stories of commercial buildings. When asked to recall the many settings in which the Latter-day Saints in Wigan worshipped in the early twentieth century, Elsie Rickard summarized the situation nicely: "I can remember climbing the stairs."[37]

Another member of the Wigan Branch noted how the saints' lowly accommodation was both an embarrassment and a point of ridicule:

> We used to meet in a little hall right at the top of a building. The bottom of the building, it was a wine shop where they sold all kinds of liquors. And then over them, there were some attorneys, and over them there was a pawnbroker, and then on the top floor [were] the Mormons. We used to climb these [four] stories up to the top of the building and [onlookers] used to laugh and say, "the Latter-day Saints like to get as close to heaven as possible while they're on earth," because about the only places that we could afford in those days were little tiny rooms that nobody else wanted on top of the building.[38]

Investigators in the early twentieth century found the saints' places of worship to be peculiar, if not off-putting. One convert in Preston, Gertrude Corless, said when she began attending meetings the members were gathering "just in a little room behind some boards and up some stairs. It seemed kind of strange after going to the Church of England building."[39] Horace Hayes of Wigan found the comparative splendor of the meeting places of neighboring faiths a continual and painful reminder of the Mormons' indigence:

> Across the street from [our meeting hall] was a beautiful Methodist church, and on the corner further down there was a beautiful Baptist church. And then on the opposite corner of the street across there was a lovely Catholic church. People would come to [our] little meeting hall stuck on the top of those stairs, and they [felt] they just about didn't belong to a church.[40]

Insufficient accommodation was a significant obstruction to Mormonism's growth in the early decades of the twentieth century. Although church members were continually urged to invite friends and acquaintances to worship services, their humble facilities caused considerable hesitation. Hayes remembered, "Sometimes I'd feel a little uncomfortable inviting my friends there and then having them comment, you know, 'is this where you go to church? What a place this is. I wouldn't go to church there.' You know comments like that. So I think this played a big part in not being able to have converts."[41] After worshipping with the members of the Burnley Branch in their rented rooms above the Cooperative Society on Trafalgar Street, one visiting church leader observed that the saints "had to have real faith" to worship therein. He concluded that it "was useless to expect investigators to come to such a place."[42]

Due to the discreditable nature of individual meeting places and the deterrent they proved to missionary work, the membership often avoided inviting acquaintances to worship services until opportunities arose for larger, regional gatherings of Latter-day Saints. In the 1920s, annual and semiannual district conferences served two valuable purposes. First, they gave the scattered members of the various congregations the rare opportunity to associate with one another. Second, they gave the missionaries the chance to put on a production of such scale as to portray Mormonism as a locally thriving denomination, both large in membership and of impressive means. Throughout the 1920s the Liverpool District gathered every six months, usually in Blackburn, where they hired the Independent Labour Party rooms at a reasonable price. Compared to the usual impoverished settings in which they met, the rooms in Blackburn were spacious, well lit, and finely furnished. Members from throughout the region flocked to these meetings, and attendance usually peaked at around five hundred. Horace Hayes remembered, "Investigators would come to something like that where they wouldn't come to some little meeting hall."[43]

In addition to giving the illusion of both size and strength, the impressive meeting place also falsely suggested the church's wealth. In reality, the saints' weekly meeting places were a more accurate representation of their small membership and modest means. One Latter-day Saint in the 1920s described the dimensions of their meeting hall as "about thirty by twenty [feet]," heated by "a little potbellied stove" with "no carpets or anything down" to cover "a plain pine board floor."[44] In Wigan the members could barely meet the financial obligations associated with their lowly meeting hall, which included a weekly payment of six shillings for rent and two shillings for light. The cost of heating the hall was offset by revolving donations from the members' personal stores of coal.[45] On the basis of accommodation alone, British Mormonism appeared to be a denomination on the brink of demise.

Property Acquisition

James and Susan Howarth of Oldham joined the church in 1908 and immediately became engrossed in fundraising for a new chapel on Neville Street: the first purpose-built meetinghouse of the church in northern England.[46] Inadequate meeting places had indeed been detrimental to missionary work, and the prospect of improved accommodations motivated even the newest convert to sacrifice. The property acquisition program of the twentieth century was an ambitious undertaking that incrementally redesigned Mormonism's outward appearance and imbued the local membership with a refreshed sense of purpose. It impacted the regional membership of the church on all levels, from the individual member to the president of the British Mission.

Although it was receiving more attention than ever before, property acquisition in the twentieth century was not without precedent. In Lancashire, administrative necessity kept upper church authorities resident in a series of office locations, which often doubled as chapels used by local congregations. The first formal office of the British Mission was established at 47 Oxford Street in Manchester. In the early 1840s, mission headquarters were established in Liverpool, with accommodation first secured at 36 Chapel Street. In 1845 mission offices were moved to the Stanley Buildings on Bath Street, Liverpool, which were later demolished to make way for a new thoroughfare. When Apostle Orson Hyde took charge of the British Mission in 1846, the mission and *Millennial Star* offices were temporarily located at 135 Duke Street, but were soon moved to 6 Goree Piazza, where they remained until June 1847. They were then removed again to 39 Torbock Street. The next relocation occurred in August 1848, this time to 15 Wilton Street, where the office remained until April 1855. Mission headquarters then took up more permanent residence at 36 Islington, not far from the Liverpool town center. Shortly after establishing themselves at this site, the municipal government adjusted the street's number configuration, which changed the office's mailing address to 42 Islington.[47] For nearly fifty years the British Mission was headquartered at this address.

At the dawn of the twentieth century the mission office was again relocated. In 1903 Francis Lyman attempted to purchase a stately end terrace house on the corner of Princes Road and Pomfret Street, but the restrictive deed covenants prevented the sale.[48] In 1904 Heber J. Grant, then president of the British Mission, acquired a large home at 10 Holly Road in Fairfield, Liverpool, where headquarters remained until January 1907. Then a superior property was purchased on the adjoining street at 295 Edge Lane, a site better known as Durham House. The offices of the British and European Missions were divided in 1929, the former relocating to 23 Booth Street in Birmingham.[49] In 1932, the British Mission office again relocated, this time to 43 Tavistock Square in Bloomsbury, London.[50] The headquarters of the European Mission and the printing office of the *Millennial Star* remained at Edge Lane until March 1933, when it was moved to 5 Gordon Square, London, never to return to the English North West.[51]

The relocation of the British Mission office from Liverpool to London was an important statement of institutional intent, intended to secure Mormonism's place as a British denomination.[52] Liverpool represented emigration: since 1847, the port city served as the administrative center of British Mormonism. In abandoning Liverpool, mission leadership attempted to divest the British church of its problematic American orientation. By stationing itself near the nation's seat of government, Mormonism was claiming a greater degree of "Britishness" than ever before.

FIGURE 7.4. This building at 42 Islington, Liverpool, was the center of administration for the British and European Missions between 1855 and 1904. "Old 42," as it was called, was also the printing site of the *Latter-day Saints Millennial Star*. The photograph was taken in 1885. Courtesy LDS Church History Library.

Of the many locations listed above, 42 Islington and Durham House possess a historical significance unrivalled by any other church property in Britain, the only clear exceptions being the London and Preston Temples. This is no doubt attributable, at least in part, to their combined length of use—a total of seventy-five years of service between them. Considering Mormonism had been in Britain fewer than one hundred years when its headquarters moved to London in 1932, the prominence of these two properties is apparent. For the succeeding generations of British members and American missionaries who made use of these facilities, 42 Islington and Durham House were valued places of refuge—veritable embassies of their American Zion in the midst of a British Babylon. For those hailing from Utah, each property was an extension of home. The saints' affection for the Islington property was expressed in the *Millennial Star* on the eve of its closure:

> For half a century, lacking but a few months, "42" has been the old world mission home of Elders and Saints, and the sacred memories that are connected

FIGURE 7.5. Durham House, 295 Edge Lane Liverpool. This house replaced the offices at 42 Islington and was the center of LDS operations for nearly twenty-five years. The photograph was taken by George Easter in 1930. Courtesy LDS Church History Library.

FIGURE 7.6. Missionaries and local church members pose for a photograph behind Durham House in 1921. Seated on the second row, fifth and sixth from right, are Elders Orson F. Whitney and George Albert Smith of the Quorum of the Twelve Apostles. Courtesy LDS Church History Library.

> with the historic building will be awakened in tens of thousands of hearts, the wide world over, when they realize that the dear old place is, for us, a thing of the past. From the "prayer room" of "42" has every Elder who has labored in Great Britain or on the continent of Europe been sent forth to his work with the counsel and blessing of the servants of the Lord, and in the same room have they received parting instructions and a blessing for their faithfulness ere they set sail homeward. Here, too, have the Saints assembled, time and time again, preparatory to gathering with the people of God in the distant valleys of [Utah]. These little incidents of life are treasured upon the hearts of those who have helped to make the history of this mission, no matter how small or apparently insignificant the part that they have taken. To them the mere mention "42" will bring a sense of joy and happiness—a testimony of duty done, a knowledge of approbation won.[53]

For the saints in Liverpool, the society at Durham House was Zion in microcosm: a practical representation of the communal harmony and purpose of Latter-day Saint life in Utah. In the post-emigration church, this was little more than an abstraction to many local members. Adelaide Tope, who was employed as the mission secretary at Durham House in the early 1920s, described the property's Zion-like qualities: "when you went to Durham House, you were going from home to home. You were mixing with these people that you were mixing with on Sundays. All week you were with the missionaries that worked in the office. [The mission president and his wife] were always there. People treated us so nicely. It was lovely because it was Durham House."[54]

Following the sale of the property in 1933, the *Millennial Star* announced the departure of mission headquarters from the site. Mournful, the editors wrote:

> Durham House, the Liverpool home of the European Mission and British Mission Office Staffs for more than a quarter of a century, has become, by name at least, almost an integral part of the Church in Europe. Within its walls, hospitality and goodwill have garnished intense industry and devotion to the latter-day cause in Europe. But, the mission of Durham House was finished. In location and size it no longer met the new demands; and the tooth of time threatened expenditures which could more profitably be expended elsewhere.[55]

Acquired by the University of Liverpool, Durham House met the same fate as the previous headquarters at 42 Islington: demolition. In 1936 the structure was razed, further obscuring the historical imprint of the British Latter-day Saints.[56]

Although the purchase of fixed places of worship finally gave the saints a home, it also made them a stationary target to their growing numbers of opponents. Durham House was attacked repeatedly by antagonists, particularly during the years of acute anti-Mormonism examined in the previous chapter.[57] The most extreme example occurred in 1911, when nineteen-year-old John Lowry led a small mob on a midnight attack on the house, resulting in extensive property damage and mild personal injury to the resident office staff.[58] That same year, the saints in Oldham listed several instances of mobs stoning their newly constructed chapel during worship services.[59] The members in Burnley, then meeting in the Piccadilly Rooms, regularly had their meetings disrupted "by children and adults opening doors and throwing in stones, clumps of earth, etc."[60] Thus, while early twentieth-century property acquisition gave the members a desired sense of permanence, it did not offer an equally valued sense of security. The stationary meetinghouses occasionally made battlegrounds out of dedicated worship sites.

As the church's collective financial resources became increasingly accessible to the British saints, mission leadership began purchasing existing structures to replace the inadequate rented meeting halls. While this policy signaled the church's institutional commitment to improve its places of worship, the newly purchased properties were, in some cases, frustratingly on par with the previous dismal sites. For example, in 1934 the Burnley saints acquired a former Baptist chapel on Liverpool Road. Although the local members appreciated having a structure that, by outward appearance, was unmistakably a place of religious worship, the inside of the chapel was no more comfortable than the meeting halls of the past. One member of the branch referred to it as "a very big barn of a place," while its offices, "which were in a tiny enclosed yard at the back of the building . . . were dirty and they were crumbling and they were smelly." The kitchen "was in a terrible state. It was a dump there."[61]

Although the Burnley chapel had been nicely fitted with pews and curtains by the Christian Scientists, who were using the building when the sale was initially agreed upon, the saints were disappointed to discover that, upon assuming occupancy, it had been "stripped clean to the church door."[62] Albert Pickup, a Burnley resident who joined the church during this time, described his first impressions of Mormonism as "a very strange one," on account of the building's inadequate interior. "The floor was not carpeted or polished," he remembered. "It was a rough wood floor. When I say rough, it was rough . . . the splinters of the wood were sticking up like spikes. And the walls were color-washed a pale green, and not a very good finish."[63]

Elsewhere the state of these newly acquired properties was equally poor. In Wythenshawe, Derek Plumbley described their accommodation as "a very difficult environment," in which teaching would occur "in a room which sat about a hundred

FIGURE 7.7. This chapel on Liverpool Road, Burnley, was constructed by the Baptists, subsequently occupied by the Christian Scientists, and acquired in the 1930s by the Latter-day Saints. It was dedicated by President Heber J. Grant in 1937, in conjunction with the British church's centennial celebration. Courtesy LDS Church History Library.

people at the most, and there would be four classes in there without partitions, without anything." Most of the other meeting places, he recalled, "were worse than that, meeting in dingy sort of premises, in unpleasant areas."[64] Plumbley, serving as a circuit speaker, had the opportunity to examine each of the meeting places used by the various branches within the Liverpool District.[65] In Rochdale, Plumbley remembered, the saints:

> had an old hall. It belonged to the Church, but it was a real ancient place. They had a big stand. I stood up to speak . . . and the branch clerk, who sat at a table on the stand, actually disappeared through the floor when I stood up, because the floor [had rotted] through! And it was also [an urgent] matter of getting your words in quickly before the carbon monoxide from the gas heaters in the winter put everybody to sleep. That was the sort of thing that happened. That's how the Saints survived.[66]

Where possible, various congregations attempted to update their new places of worship with adornments that were distinctly Latter-day Saint in style and significance. Upon the wall above the small rostrum in the Burnley chapel, the saints stenciled the words "the glory of God is intelligence," a canonical maxim taken from one of Joseph Smith's early revelations.[67] In time, the members of the Burnley Branch refitted the chapel with new pews, carpets, curtains, and a wooden proscenium for dramatic performances and the recreation of scenes from church history. Horace Mills, a convert from Oldham, was commissioned by the Manchester District to paint small murals on the walls of the local chapels, each depicting Joseph Smith's 1820 vision in the woods in upstate New York.[68] Beyond these few improvements there was little about the purchased properties that indicated their Latter-day Saint affiliation.

No adaptations made to these properties were of greater significance than those pertaining to the administration of priesthood ordinances, especially baptism. Full immersion was the standard practice, and missionaries had long repaired to the Irish Sea and various rivers to baptize. For a time, even public swimming baths doubled as fonts. Despite their proven adaptability, the Mormons preferred to baptize in settings reserved, if not created, for that purpose.[69] Early evidence is found in the manuscript history of the Liverpool Branch, which indicates that in 1849 the saints constructed a wooden baptismal font inside their rented meeting place on Bold Street. Upon completion, Milo Andrus, then Liverpool Conference president, formally dedicated the font to God "for the ordinance of baptism for the remission of sins and for the healing of the bodies of Thy Saints."[70] Andrus prized the newly erected font, and in his dedicatory prayer he petitioned God that "those [who] shall attempt to pollute [it] may be cursed before Thy face."[71]

Oral histories suggest that in the early decades of the twentieth century, meeting places outfitted for the performance of baptisms were more highly prized than those that were not. The above-mentioned chapel in Burnley, constructed by the Baptists, had the most comfortable baptismal facilities of any church-owned structure in the region. Converts were known to travel from as far as Liverpool for the privilege of being baptized in a font that was owned and maintained by the church.[72]

Throughout the first half of the twentieth century, church members constructed makeshift baptismal fonts throughout Britain in meeting places of sufficient size. These fonts were of simple yet adequate construction, although rarely plumbed. Phillip Ambrose, whose parents joined the church in Lancaster in the early 1900s, remembered the laborious process of pumping water into and out of the font at Durham House.[73] Despite these inconveniences, missionaries did their best to establish a suitable environment. Describing her baptism at Durham House, May Gartland recalled:

> [The] baptismal font was in the middle of the meeting room. All the congregation was sitting there. I can remember the hymn they sang was "Lo, On the Water's Brink We Stand." As we were walking down into the waters, all the congregation was singing this hymn. It was a lovely sensation, that. I can remember coming out of the water. Some of the sisters wrapped us up in big towels and took us into another room with a big blazing fire.[74]

Not all baptisms were as comfortably executed. One male convert from Oldham said the font beneath the floorboards of a meeting hall in Manchester "was so small that they banged his head three times before they managed to baptize him [properly]," resulting in him nearly being knocked unconscious.[75] Embarrassments of this nature detracted from the dignity and significance of the baptismal ordinance. They justified the British saints' desire for facilities of a much higher standard, purpose-built to accommodate all activities associated with church membership, especially the sacred rites.

Chapel Building

One of the earliest proposals for a purpose-built chapel was issued by council members of the Liverpool Branch in 1862. This gesture of permanence was poorly timed and clearly at odds with the institutional agenda of the church. The great gathering to Zion was in full operation and all focus was westward. An emigration office, not a house of worship, was the only facility deemed necessary in mid-nineteenth century Liverpool. The branch council persisted in their request and ultimately the measure was taken before the First Presidency, where it was not approved.[76] A century would pass before the saints in Liverpool would see their chapel hopes realized.

Although the development of purpose-built places of worship in Britain was anticipated by Joseph F. Smith in 1903, it was not until the middle of the century that the church made actual progress. Prior to the organization of the Manchester Stake in 1960, individual congregations desiring meetinghouses of their own were left to pursue the matter themselves, largely unaided by church authorities in Utah. This independence extends to the very roots of British Mormonism. In 1840 Apostle Wilford Woodruff facilitated the near-total conversion of a group of Primitive Methodists (called the United Brethren) in rural Worcestershire and Herefordshire. Their modest chapel, built in the now-extinct hamlet of Gadfield Elm in 1836, became the first church-owned meeting place in Britain. Between 1994 and 2004, the dilapidated structure was restored by a private trust and ownership was again deeded to the church.[77]

Since 2004, historians of British Mormonism have drawn much attention to the Gadfield Elm chapel, and for good reason. It is one of few existing church structures

FIGURE 7.8. Four missionaries pose outside the first purpose-built chapel in the English North West. Neville Street, Oldham, circa 1913. Courtesy LDS Church History Library.

that can boast undisputed provenance—a stone-on-stone monument that marks one of the most celebrated communities of converts in the international church. As with many other aspects of British Mormon history, the chapel is renowned for its connection with the famed apostolic missions of the early 1840s. Much less discussed is the small Mormon chapel in Llanelli, South Wales, which was dedicated in January 1849 and is now thought to be the first purpose-built structure of the church anywhere in the British Isles.[78] Although each is an important structure in its own right, neither chapel can be seen as anything but aberrant in relation to the principles and practices of early Mormonism. The fact that Brigham Young urged the newly converted United Brethren to sell the Gadfield Elm chapel to fund their emigration reveals how contrary property ownership in Britain once was to Mormonism's aims.[79]

Property acquisition and chapel building are decidedly twentieth-century features of British Mormon history. They are also perhaps the most obvious manifestation of the Latter-day Saints' reinterpretation of the gathering doctrine. One of the first building projects undertaken by the British Latter-day Saints occurred in Oldham, where between 1907 and 1909 the branch membership constructed the region's first purpose-built chapel. Fashioned out of corrugated iron and lined with lumber, the original Oldham chapel stood on Neville Street and was modest both in size and appearance.[80] Its main gathering room was no larger than many of the meeting halls occupied by other congregations throughout Britain, covering an area of twenty-five by thirty-two feet

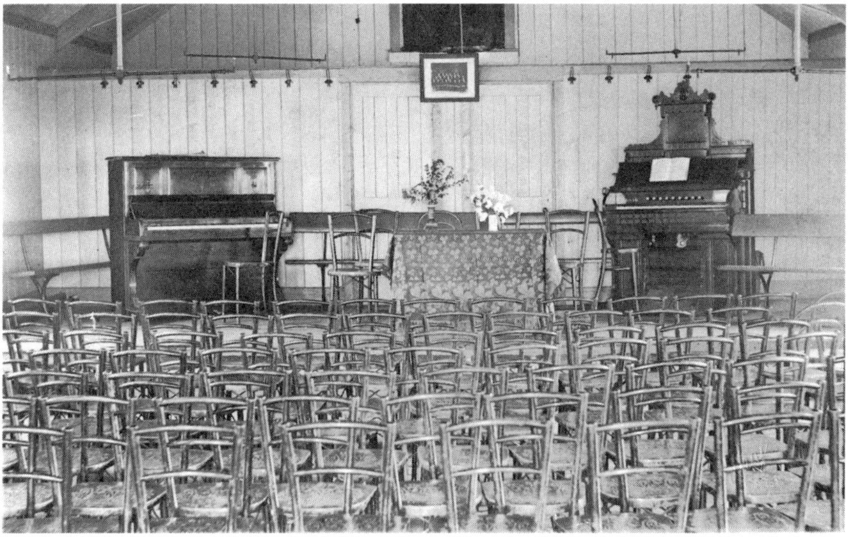

FIGURE 7.9. Interior view of the original Oldham chapel, 1909. Courtesy LDS Church History Library.

with two separate classrooms at the rear of the building.[81] The austerity of the chapel's appearance was an appropriate reflection of the unadorned nature of the saints' weekly worship services.[82]

Notwithstanding its diminutive dimensions, the editors of the *Millennial Star* described the Oldham chapel with pride. They gloried in its modern amenities such as gas lighting and a self-contained water heater.[83] The chapel itself, constructed for £110, was home to Oldham's Latter-day Saints for nearly fifty years. This first attempt at chapel building is an important representation of the British membership's growing capacity to meet the great task of the twentieth-century: to construct Zion at home.

More common than the building of chapels was the acquisition of existing structures, an effort that continued throughout the early decades of the twentieth century. It was not until the years following the Second World War that the chapel building program, pioneered by the saints in Oldham, began in earnest.

An obstacle faced by congregations throughout Britain was the identification of sufficiently sized lots on which to build. The acquisition of land proved enormously difficult for local branch leadership—exacerbated by the fact that church administration in Utah required each building site occupy a minimum of one acre.[84] The difficulties the British saints encountered in meeting this criterion are evident in the histories of both the Burnley and Oldham Branches. In Burnley, the branch obtained a suitable building site only after a member who belonged to the local town council used his political connections to drive down the price of the land.[85] In 1958, when the Oldham Branch leadership determined that the Neville Street chapel was unfit for further use, the membership attempted and failed to find a new building site in town. Lacking alternatives, the congregation engaged a public dance hall for their weekly services. There they faced the inconvenience of having to delay their Sunday meetings until the abundant evidence of the building's Saturday night festivities (both material and olfactory) had been cleared out.[86]

Frustrated with the lack of progress, the members in Oldham appealed to upper church leadership for help. In doing so, the local congregation surrendered control of the project. Consequently, they were chagrined when church authorities in Utah secured a building plot four miles away in Ashton-under-Lyne, a move some members felt undermined their congregational identity.[87] Despite their protests, work on the chapel in Ashton commenced in 1962. The members in Oldham watched with mixed feelings as their spiritual center of gravity transitioned from their own community to a place where, by comparison, the numbers of Latter-day Saints were relatively few.[88] The Oldham Branch would not occupy a new chapel in the town until 1987.[89]

Relationships between the members in Britain and the leaders in Utah were occasionally strained. Matters of local importance, such as the placement of new chapel, were determined by administrators at the distant church headquarters in Salt Lake City. This was an unavoidable reality, as the local congregations had neither the labor force nor the financial resources to bring about their own desires.

By the late 1950s and early 1960s it became clear that the acquisition of undeveloped land on which to build would remain unlikely. Fortunately, the demands of the postwar housing market reduced the value of once-popular Victorian villas, and the First Presidency approved the purchase of such estates in areas where larger congregations had formed. Thus, in Blackburn the saints acquired "Oman Brae," in Stockport they purchased "Beaconfield," and in Radcliffe they obtained "Wilton House." In Liverpool, following the sale of Durham House in the early 1930s, the church purchased "Devonia," another spacious estate on Edge Lane. This mansion served as the meeting place for the Liverpool Branch following the relocation of the British and European Mission personnel to their new London headquarters. In 1952, the Liverpool Branch occupied "Summerfield" in the suburb of West Derby—the site where the Mormons' modern chapel presently stands.

Although these new villas were spacious, attractive, and much appreciated by the local members, church administration in Utah regarded the properties in strictly utilitarian and forward-thinking terms. One by one, the estates were either sold or, more often, demolished in favor of capitalizing on what church administration saw as the properties' primary value: acreage. In time, the villas' manicured gardens were replaced by ample car parks; where the homes themselves once stood, new chapels were constructed. These meetinghouses gave British Mormonism its modern, standardized, and, some would say, American architectural image by which it is so easily recognized today. Although the architecture of LDS chapels in Britain has undergone several revisions, it has essentially remained the same in its blend of functionality and sanctity—a marriage of purposes Terryl Givens describes as a "premeditated porousness between the secular and the sacred."[90]

Paul Anderson explores the amalgamations of Mormon chapel architecture and interprets the church's stylistic preferences as an effort to distinguish itself from other Christian denominations. For the Mormons, Anderson notes, the process of creating an architectural style was "at times a delicate balancing act, wanting to be different, but not different enough to be marginalized."[91] In Britain, many members were aware of how incongruous the new structures appeared within their surrounding environs. In addition to looking out of place, many of the new chapels were also poorly adapted to the local climate. Derek Plumbley of Wythenshawe referred to the modern churches, each of which had been designed by an American architect, as "California buildings, not built for rain and cold, and . . . not cost-effective for us to operate."[92] These problems and idiosyncrasies notwithstanding, the new meetinghouses were undeniably more comfortable than anything the saints had before experienced. Concerning the new chapel on Ribbleton Avenue in Preston, Gertrude Corless noted that the members "were so proud of it after all the terrible halls we'd met in. They were just awful. After getting a new chapel all of our own, it was wonderful. That was a very wonderful day when we [got] our own chapel. It was quite small, but it was good."[93]

The church's building program advanced rapidly in the 1960s and 1970s and garnered much attention from the local press. In some cases, the increased publicity came with revived suspicion and various forms of protest. This was not without precedent. Concerning the original Oldham chapel, constructed at the height of Mormonism's early twentieth-century revival, it was rumored that the large floor mat installed in the building's entrance was a carefully disguised trapdoor through which attractive young women would vanish.[94] While the Liverpool chapel was under construction in the early 1960s, local youths believed the building was a portal to a transatlantic tunnel through which unsuspecting converts, and perhaps overly curious children, were abducted. Local lore maintained that the tunnel terminated at Salt Lake City; Atlantic seawater explained the salinity of the land-locked Great Salt Lake.[95] The rapid and simultaneous construction of so many Mormon chapels spawned a new generation of urban legends concerning the seemingly sinister saints. For the hordes of youths attracted to the church through its missionary-sponsored athletic programs in the late 1950s and early 1960s, entering the newly built chapels for the first (and often only) time must have been disappointing—neither tunnels nor trapdoors were anywhere to be found.

As with other instances of British anti-Mormonism, much of the opposition faced by the saints in response to their chapel building originated with other Christian denominations. Gertrude Corless remembered being invited to attend Pentecostal services while the new chapel in Preston was under construction. There she observed that the worshippers prayed aloud that the "the Lord would stop the Mormons from building their church." Corless further recalled, "It just got to us in the end that each one would say that. Though they were Christian people, yet they were talking about another Christian group and hoping they wouldn't be able to complete their building. We were going to complete our chapel. It was the Lord's work."[96]

Advancement of the building program was interpreted by many British saints as the work of divine providence. Robert Larsen, the first president of the Manchester Stake and a native of Ephraim, Utah, reflected joyously on the chapel-building efforts and proclaimed that "the hand of the Lord has been in all of these happenings, and the way has been opened up for this great building program to get underway in our stake in a way that can only be described as a miracle."[97]

Perhaps the miracle was that the local members, many of whom were fairly recent converts, were able to endure the building program's myriad hardships. Significant financial sacrifice and protracted physical labor, both of which were provided by the members themselves, sustained the program's progress. This was not an idle or effortless fulfillment of prophecy; this was hard work. An honest acknowledgement of these difficulties was expressed by Albert Pickup of the Burnley Branch, who described the years in which the local saints built their chapel as "terrible" and "a very hard period." Pickup continued:

> The digging, the actual manual work was very, very hard. We didn't have the current advantage of contractors. The members did the building under the supervisor's eyes. I organized a building committee in accordance with the Church's requirements. I think we had four members on it, who were doubling up or trebling up on several things. The time when we "lost ground" in the Church as a whole, the time when we lost people, was always during the building of a chapel. People couldn't stay the pace. The hard work, the money, the sacrifice, and the displacement, really, was very killing.[98]

These strains, Pickup remembered, "decimated the branch" and precipitated a tragic loss of membership. By the time the Burnley chapel was completed, only six of the many families belonging to the branch had remained active.[99]

Elsewhere in Britain, these membership-driven building projects rejuvenated the saints and unified the prewar members with the new converts of the 1950s and 60s. The sacrifices inherent to the program took on a profound religious significance, which deepened the spirituality of members young and old. In the Manchester area, the necessary financial donations rallied the saints and appealed to their sense of covenant consecration. As the Manchester Stake sought to pay down its enormous building debt, the stake presidency challenged each gainfully employed member to donate a full week's pay within a three-month period. Remarkably, most of these members participated. The blending of spiritual and temporal matters is reminiscent of the collective strivings of the nineteenth-century British saints, whose economic sacrifices enabled the emigration of one another. For the modern British members, the sacrifices required by the building program imbued entire congregations with a tremendous sense of urgency and purpose. The result was a shared religious euphoria. Concerning the members' involvement in the Manchester Stake's debt-relief program, Derek Plumbley recalled:

> Oh, they [the members] were fantastic. [The debt-relief program] did more for the members than anything I've ever seen done in my administration in the Church. You could see it build up. . . . We talked about nothing else for three months, and you could see the spirit and the dedication and the sacrifice build up. And when [the deadline] came and the members queued up at the bishop's office to pile a week's wages, usually in cash, on this table and then went into a fast [and testimony] meeting, that was something.[100]

Perhaps of greatest significance, the saints' involvement in chapel construction diverted their attention away from the enticing Salt Lake Valley and fixed it firmly upon their own communities. Zion, through permanent places of worship, had become a reality for the saints in Britain. Importantly, as with so many other aspects of Mormon life, the chapel building program was a family affair—women and children engaged in the work alongside the men.

To the faithful, every aspect of the building process had its spiritual counterpart. For President Martin A. Cook of the Ashton Stake, the completed chapels were divinely allegorical.[101] In the dedicatory prayer of Oldham's second chapel, completed in 1987, Cook invoked divine favor upon the building and delineated the sacred purposes of its components. The chapel's walls, Cook prayed, would "surround the spiritual vagrants of society"; the roof would withstand "the hail . . . of the disfavor of the world," and "deflect the ignorance of criticism." The doors would be "hinged upon the principle of love," while its locks would forbid entrance of "vandals and not the visitor," and "be closed . . . against inclemency and not the investigator."[102]

The chief lesson learned from the building program was that Zion and Britain were not just compatible, but synonymous. As Rodney Fullwood, a convert from Liverpool, recalled:

FIGURE 7.10. The chapel building program began in earnest in the late 1950s and directly involved the membership. Here, John Jones of the Liverpool Branch assists with bricklaying. Mill Bank, West Derby, Liverpool, 1963. Courtesy LDS Church History Library.

> A lot of families . . . started to get involved in the excitement of helping [lay] the bricks and [dig] the trenches and all these other things. We were getting involved in something that was our own. That I'm sure, must have contributed to some people thinking, "Well maybe we don't have to emigrate" . . . Because when you invest in something with your own labor, you tend to value it. It becomes a part of you. Those men and women and kids were all involved in something that was a part of them, rather than looking to the Salt Lake Temple and general conference and all these other things as being the most exciting things in the Church.[103]

In a similar strain, Derek Plumbley asserted the chapel building program filled a need formerly associated with the allure of the Utah Zion. "I don't think the Saints have that need now," Plumbley maintained. "You don't today see people saying, 'I must go to Salt Lake. It's Mecca.' They feel they have the Church. Although there's always a curiosity and everybody would like to go, there's no great desire."[104]

FIGURE 7.11. The building program involved church members of all ages. Here a young member totes a wheelbarrow on the building site of the Liverpool chapel in 1963. Courtesy LDS Church History Library.

Conclusions

The various types of worship accommodation sought and maintained by the British Latter-day Saints was an outgrowth of the church's changing regard for matters of migration. Again the primacy of Mormon doctrine within and upon the denomination's British history and development is evident. Throughout the nineteenth century, when Zion was associated primarily with the American West, worship accommodation in Britain was consistently poor and always temporary. For decades, British Mormonism's westward orientation reinforced the central role of the temple and the "city of Zion." The rented rooms and halls occupied by church members throughout Britain were regarded as local way stations—momentary places of gathering intended to accommodate clusters of saints anticipating emigration.

In regards to broader developments within worship accommodation, the English North West remains anomalous within the history of British Mormonism. This is

FIGURE 7.12. Beginning in the 1970s, meetinghouse development was overseen by the church's physical facilities department and construction was no longer undertaken by local congregations. Here the members of the Barrow-in-Furness Branch stand outside their newly completed chapel in December 1997. Courtesy *North West Evening Mail*.

primarily because of its long-established role as the administrative center of the British and European Missions. The facilities in Liverpool were always more elaborate and spacious than those maintained by other British congregations, and the offices at 42 Islington and Durham House are enduring cases in point. Following President Joseph F. Smith's announcement that property acquisition would commence in the British Mission, the saints began purchasing and occupying existing properties. This move both strengthened the denomination's local identity and yielded the first impressions of Mormonism's permanence within Britain's variegated, and often competitive, religious landscape.

The steady acquisition of properties in the first half of the twentieth century sent a clear message to both the British members and the wider public. Each group needed convincing that Mormonism was no longer equated with Utah. Consistent with President Smith's declaration, church leaders in Britain demonstrated their permanence by investing heavily in the purchase and refurbishment of fixed places of worship. Beginning with the construction of the Oldham chapel in 1909, church members throughout Britain increased their commitment to the development of meetinghouses. Progress reduced the saints' preoccupation with the Zion of the American West. Every brick laid and each shingle hung gradually diminished the desire to emigrate. Since the 1890s the British members had struggled to find a personal reason to remain in their homeland—they found that reason in the chapels they built themselves.

By the 1970s the membership-driven building program had become defunct. Contractors, not converts, populated the building sites of the later twentieth century. At its peak, the program built Latter-day Saints as well as chapels. It helped galvanize the religious commitment of the new generation of postwar converts—the first generation in a century to divest British Mormonism of its reliance upon American missionaries. For the first time since the 1850s, full operational independence at the congregational level was within grasp. Ironically, as self-sufficiency increased, the saints' involvement in property acquisition and chapel building decreased. By the 1980s, all such projects were managed strictly by upper church administration and overseen by representatives from the church's European headquarters in Solihull, Warwickshire.

Historically, all church developments regarding worship accommodation are united by one common priority: the creation of a sacred, or dedicated, space within a specific locale. Accordingly, the chapel building program may be the single most important development within British Mormon history. The members' shared undertaking of the enormous project, fraught with difficulty and sacrifice, effectively bound a generation of modern British Latter-day Saints both to one another and to the location wherein their labors were expended. The cumulative result of these "works of consecration" made Mormonism's Zion ideal immediately proximate for the converts, their families, and future generations of church members.[105] From the Vauxhall Chapel to the Preston Temple, the creation of a spiritual heartland or center place was vital to the endurance of British Mormonism and secured the foundations upon which modern church leaders clearly anticipate future growth.

Chapter 8
"In England's Green and Pleasant Land"
Britain as Zion

> Liverpool has now attained a notoriety for the worst feature of depravity, which a thinking mind cannot contemplate without a shudder. She is the most criminal town, perhaps, in the United Kingdom. She is the most drunken town, perhaps, in the world.
>
> —*Millennial Star*, 1866

> Liverpool is a kindly, wholesome, forward-looking city. The European Mission Office Staff leave "Mersey-side" with regret. . . . We are grateful for the protection and assistance that Liverpool has given the Latter-day Saints for nearly three generations of time, and pray that it may be rewarded therefore with blessings from on high.
>
> —*Millennial Star*, 1933

The history of British Mormonism is the story of the gradual formation of a sacred place and an enduring commitment to that place. The success of British Mormonism has not been its membership growth, but its institutional and cultural depth—an attainment it has achieved through doctrinal adaptation and concomitant changes in its perspective of and regard for its British host culture. Ongoing doctrinal refinement and organizational development have secured British Mormonism's endurance throughout the contrasting seasons of religious revival and decline that have spanned the Victorian and contemporary periods of British history.

The Church of Jesus Christ of Latter-day Saints has successfully maintained its presence in Britain in much the same way as it has throughout the rest of the world—through the incremental application of the Zion ideals that have been central to Mormon theology since the days of Joseph Smith. And yet, despite this similarity, the church's expanded theological and geographical interpretations of Zion have been central to the history of the British Latter-day Saints in several compelling and distinctive ways, which I shall now review.

As discussed in chapter two, the doctrine of gathering impacted the destiny of the British members for most of the nineteenth century. Indeed, as P.A.M. Taylor asserts, emigration must be regarded as the dominant contributor to British Mormonism's general diminution in the later decades of the 1800s.[1] Unsanctioned emigration, discouraged strongly by church leaders, hindered British congregations until as recently as the 1950s. Even in the modern British church, the appeal of life in Utah persisted—a particularly tormenting reality for many Latter-day Saint youths and young adults. One member from Liverpool said,

> [The] Church is almost a self-defeating organization because it teaches people to look for better things. So they want to get out of this dirty city that they grew up in. They see these . . . missionaries with nice white collars and ties, and so they want to go to Utah. The young people that I grew up with in [the Church] saw this . . . kind of bright, shiny image of excitement and of church involvement [and it] just caught the imagination of many, many young people.[2]

It is vital to remember that the gathering of converts in the nineteenth century was in fulfillment of the church's institutional agenda, while twentieth-century emigration was in direct opposition to it. Thus, the years 1892–1911 comprise a crucial transitional period when church leaders divested Mormonism of its westward orientation, permitted its millenarian expectations to wane, and encouraged its development as a British denomination. The paucity of Mormon conversions in the later 1880s and the dramatic increase of the same between 1906 and 1909 further highlight these intervening years as a genuine tipping point in the history of British Mormonism. Further examination of these pivotal years, rich in change and adaptation, is certainly merited.

The defining characteristic of these years is the dramatic shift in Mormonism's eschatological ethos. With the realization that the Second Coming of Jesus Christ would not occur within the timeframe popularly supposed, a new orientation emerged that enabled the development of a more positive worldview.[3] Reduced negativity enabled twentieth-century Mormons to abandon the perspective of Britain as Babylon and accept more fully the notion of Britain as Zion—a realization that helped the British saints embrace their place within the global church. Heber C. Kimball and Joseph Smith's 1838 pronouncement of the blessedness of the upper Ribble Valley took on added significance in the twentieth century, encouraging the formation of a religious heritage that was both proximate and native. Culturally, this allows contemporary British Mormonism to be less reliant on the nineteenth-century pioneer mythos that still dominates American Mormon history. The American-centric approach to LDS history continues to be a compelling point of tension between Mormonism in Utah and Mormonism in Western Europe.[4]

Beyond matters of migration, internal dissent (explored in chapter five) is an additional factor that complicated the church's operations in Britain. This opposition was paradoxically both self-defeating and self-strengthening. When anti-Mormonism was not arising from within the ranks of disaffected Latter-day Saints, it was forcibly expressed from without. The anti-Mormon crusade of 1911–1914, considered in chapter six, was the zenith of over seventy years of opposition faced by the British saints. Although these years comprise the most pointed manifestation of anti-Mormonism in British church history, it was preceded by several concerted attempts by heads of rival faiths to vilify and expel Mormonism from the religious landscape. Growing societal fears of human trafficking, perpetration of sexual crimes, and of foreigners generally—all linked to the Latter-day Saints in some way by the popular press—fueled the anti-Mormon crusade. Although anti-Mormon agitation was evident throughout all parts of Britain, much of it was concentrated within the English North West: the historical center of church administration. Ironically, but not surprisingly, this opposition was a catalyst to the regional strengthening of Mormonism. The many reactionary adjustments within LDS ecclesiology and congregational life, although initially a defensive measure, also added increased structure and purpose to the church, thus deepening the membership's commitment. The abundance of opposition the British saints had to endure could be regarded as one of the keys to Mormonism's regional endurance.

Since the beginning of Mormonism in Britain, relentless proselytizing offset membership loss, be it from emigration or excommunication. Without question, missionary work was central to the survival of British Mormonism and, as chapters three and four suggest, a dominant aspect of the Latter-day Saint experience. Missionary service is also tied to and strengthened by the powerful emotions associated with personal and family history. Particularly in the nineteenth century, missionaries drew motivation from the fact that they were returning to their ancestral homeland. They were laboring in a place that was central to their families' religious heritage, cultural identity, and hope for salvation. This iron-willed commitment to family, faith, and homeland sustained the faltering congregations during the second half of the nineteenth century, especially as conversions dwindled to a near standstill. Generation after generation, British Mormonism's pertinacious proselytizing provided a small but enduringly-committed base of converts, with sufficient size and doctrinal orthodoxy to maintain viability. The massive surge of membership growth in the late 1950s and early 1960s secured the foundation of the modern church. Further comparison of the origins and methods of nineteenth-century missionaries with their modern, twentieth- and twenty-first-century counterparts would illuminate the underlying and evolving motivations that continue to sustain Mormon proselytizing in Britain.

Family, Faith, and Temple

Because of British Mormonism's impressive longevity, its contrasting seasons of strength and weakness are readily apparent. Reviewing the condition of the Burnley Branch from the 1950s through the 1970s, one member remarked, "As soon as we seem to get up, we go down. And usually we were down."[5] Historically, British Mormonism's membership base was comprised of successive groupings of first-generation converts. One of the challenges this produced, particularly in the first half of the twentieth century, was securing the perpetuation of individual congregations. This was exacerbated by an ongoing need to identify and train new leadership drawn from the ranks of local converts. Later in the twentieth century, consistent with a renewed emphasis on conversionary growth, the perpetuation of the faith within families became a dominant priority. The converts who joined the church during Mormonism's revival in the early twentieth century were the first non-emigrating group of British Latter-day Saints to successfully transmit their faith to their children.[6] Although there are some third and fourth-generation Latter-day Saints in Britain, contemporary Mormonism remains predominantly first-generation.[7] Thus, the main challenge to the stability of British Mormonism in the twenty-first century will not concern its proven capacity to attract converts, but the willingness of LDS youth to remain active in their religion.[8] Accordingly, a sociological examination of the religious habits of British Mormon families may be the most useful study that could extend from this book. The above-mentioned converts of the early twentieth century would serve as an excellent basis for comparison.

Until British Mormonism genuinely and comprehensively becomes multigenerational, its future will never be assured and the viability of its congregations will remain reliant on conversionary growth. Assuming that this demographic shift is both attainable and imminent, it seems that Mormonism in Britain is on the verge of entering into a new and distinct era—a probability of which future researchers should take note. Of course, it must be remembered that the full institutional maturity of British Mormonism occurred only very recently, perhaps too recently to legitimize much conjecture.

Suffice it to say, British Mormonism's coming-of-age is evidenced by at least two things: first, the ongoing establishment of wards and stakes—the organizational hallmark of Zion—and second, the development of a core community of temple-attending believers whose service and covenant adherence sustains the church on the congregational level. Combined, these relatively recent attainments fitted British Mormonism for its third, distinct phase of operation, wherein the Latter-day Saint experience with the British host culture will be determined largely by the influence of the ordinances and covenants of the temple. Having built a British Zion, the Mormons of the twenty-first century must ensure its multigenerational prosperity. The temple, where family and faith are melded spiritually and permanently, will be at the center of this pursuit.

As this book demonstrates, the first phase of British Mormon history was governed by the great transatlantic quest to the build Zion in America, as envisaged by Joseph Smith. The second phase globalized the Zion initiative, a priority initiated by Smith's successor and nephew, Joseph F. Smith. Viewed together, these first two phases concern the institutional history of British Mormonism, signaled by the "Babylon to Zion" transition. The third and forthcoming phase will necessarily concern Mormonism as the center of family life, with the temple and the home occupying stations of equal prominence: *Domus dei* and *domus familiae*.

Further research must consider the impact of the Preston and London Temples on Latter-day Saint families and congregational dynamics. A most profitable study would compare the congregations assembled near Chorley, Lancashire, and East Grinstead, Sussex—the communities adjacent to both temples. For example, the dedication of the Preston Temple in 1998 triggered a domestic migration of church members throughout Britain to the North West region.[9] This modern-day migration is comparable to the gathering of the nineteenth-century saints to Nauvoo and Salt Lake City. It swelled Latter-day Saint membership in Chorley and Preston dramatically, resulting in the formation of three new wards and a new stake.

There are several compelling similarities between the nineteenth-century gathering to the American West and the contemporary, domestic migration of British saints to the English North West. Thematically, the history of British Mormonism runs parallel to the history of Mormonism in the American West, but in an opposite direction. In the nineteenth century, the objective of church leaders was to gather converts from Britain and establish a community of worshipers capable of constructing a temple. In short, the gathering, by necessity, preceded the temple. In twentieth-century Britain, the reverse was true. The London and Preston Temples, planned by upper church leadership and financed by general church funds, required minimal involvement and sacrifice from the British members. While westward migration in the nineteenth century was encouraged and even required, modern-day migration to Chorley, Preston, and the Ribble Valley has occurred spontaneously, unbidden by church leaders.

The Mormon tendency to gather is integral to its cultural fabric. It occurs irrespective of the church's official doctrines and direction provided by its living prophets. Discerning the motives of these modern-day migrants will not be possible without extensive surveying. This book should provide researchers with sufficient context to enable comparison with historical models. Within contemporary British Mormonism, Latter-day Saints can now reap the benefits of life in Zion without toiling and sacrificing for its physical establishment. Early church leaders would have interpreted this ease as morally hazardous.

There is one additional comparison between the historical gathering to the American Zion and the contemporary gathering to the British Zion that deserves mention. Just as nineteenth-century westward migration decimated British congregations, the recent domestic migration of British members to the English North West appears to have adversely affected the viability of congregations further afield. Anecdotal evidence suggests that the formation of a burgeoning community of Latter-day Saints in Chorley, Preston, and the Ribble Valley may be weakening congregations elsewhere in Britain. Various wards and branches continue to lose membership to this expanding center of strength. For example, it seems more than coincidental that membership growth in Chorley and Preston following the temple's dedication has coincided with a decrease in membership in Liverpool—a reduction that seems to have precipitated the merger of the city's two wards. The culture of gathering, which historians have long associated with the church in the nineteenth century, has found its contemporary counterpart in the British Isles.

The influx of membership to Lancashire and the English North West has created an organizational paradox for modern British Mormonism. The attractiveness of living near the Preston Temple and within a large community of Latter-day Saints has spurred the domestic migration of church members. This, in turn, has weakened congregations elsewhere. Accordingly, compensatory growth must be pursued, both immediately and indefinitely. Indeed, it may be that only through the establishment of additional strongholds of church membership can the weakening of congregations elsewhere be sufficiently offset. What remains to be seen is whether or not future centers of strength can be formed in Britain, independent of the construction of additional temples.

Global Comparisons

In many locations across the world, Mormonism has flared into existence and—due to emigration, persecution, and restrictive legislation—disappeared almost as abruptly. Internationally, the church recaptured in the twentieth century the many toeholds it secured abroad in the nineteenth century. Thus, much of the history of global Mormonism is characterized by a simple pattern: an initial advance, a subsequent retreat, and an eventual regrouping and reassertion. By and large, it is a history characterized by pertinacity, not uninterrupted continuity. Given its longevity, the British church is the most notable exception to this pattern.

Comparing the history of British Mormonism with church history elsewhere in the northern hemisphere yields surprisingly few similarities, notwithstanding Britain's cultural ties to North America and the European continent. In New England, the Ohio Valley, and Upper Canada, most of the early LDS congregations opened and closed within a generation. Converts in New York and Pennsylvania were more concerned with following their prophet to Zion than maintaining a stationary congregation. Their zeal for Zion fueled an ongoing migration, which bolstered and then diminished the LDS presence in Ohio, Missouri, and Illinois.

Despite the success of the church in Upper Canada in the 1830s, by 1861 the Canadian census reported fewer than seventy-five Latter-day Saints in all of Ontario. The Northern States Mission, established in 1889, mildly revived church activity in parts of Ontario, where Mormonism had been defunct for roughly a quarter century. During this same time, Latter-day Saint colonies were being established in Alberta, where church members fleeing federal persecution for their polygamous marriages sought refuge. Church operations throughout Canada were not regularized until the establishment of the Canadian Mission in 1919.[10]

As religious pluralism gained traction in Scandinavia in the early 1850s, missionaries rushed in to convert those who were particularly excited by the freedom of religious expression and its many new and novel alternatives. Conversions peaked in the 1860s, and the Danish Mission was particularly productive. In the 1870s and 80s enthusiasm waned, as did the numbers of Latter-day Saint congregations. It was not until 1905 that the church resumed active proselyting in the nations of Denmark, Sweden, and Norway.[11]

In China and Hong Kong, the Latter-day Saint mission opened and closed after just a few challenging months in 1853.[12] Missionary work in Japan commenced in 1901 and was disbanded in 1924, during which time a total of 166 converts were baptized. The Japanese Mission remained closed until 1948.[13] This is not dissimilar to the course the church has taken in South America. In late 1851 Elder Parley P. Pratt became the first representative of the church to preach in Latin America, and he based his efforts in Valparaiso, Chile. Unable to develop a proficiency in the Spanish language, Pratt sailed home four months later. It was not until 1925, after receiving a request for missionaries from two LDS German families then living in Argentina, that the church created a mission in South America.[14]

Surprisingly, the history of Mormonism in French Polynesia has much more in common with British Mormon history. In both locations, institutional perpetuation has continued uninterrupted. It is well known that the congregation in Preston, Lancashire, established in 1837, is the oldest continuously operating unit of the church worldwide. It is lesser known that the second oldest congregation is on Tubuai, established in 1844. There a mariner-turned-missionary named Addison Pratt built a congregation with as much natural ease and rapidity as Heber C. Kimball in the Ribble Valley. The similarities between these two men are striking: both initially served for approximately nine months, both were called and commissioned while the Prophet Joseph Smith was still living, each later returned to his respective field for additional missionary service, and both men had a deep affection for the local inhabitants, reciprocated by their converts.[15]

As with Pratt and Kimball, the congregations in Tubuai and Preston also have similarities. Despite the endurance of each, neither congregation effortlessly endured into the twentieth century. In Tubuai, government control of religion in 1852 forced the withdrawal of American missionaries. When these restrictions were eased twenty years later, representatives of the Reorganized Church of Jesus Christ of Latter Day Saints (RLDS) arrived and claimed the allegiance of most of the island's 1,500 members. Consequently, the branch nearly collapsed, and only one member is believed to have remained committed until the church again sent missionaries in the early 1890s.[16] Although the RLDS were quite active in England in the second half of the nineteenth century, their efforts never put them in serious competition with the British church. Rather, it was because of emigration and excommunication that the branch in Preston dwindled to fifteen members, with only three actually living within the city itself in 1890.[17] By 1893, the total branch membership was down to nine.[18] A note in the Preston Branch manuscript history states that the congregation was "reorganized" on January 8, 1899, suggesting that if the branch hadn't momentarily dissolved, it had come perilously close.[19]

Utility of Britain as Sacred Space

Following the interpretive shift of the gathering doctrine between 1892 and 1904, church leaders encouraged the global membership to develop a dual-commitment to the practice and the proliferation of their faith. Indeed, Mormonism's endurance in Britain has hinged upon the establishment of a community of worshipers bound equally to their beliefs, their families, and the notion that their homeland is, as Heber C. Kimball maintained, "holy ground." The importance of these three considerations within British Mormonism in the twenty-first century cannot be stressed too heavily. The British Latter-day Saints' sacralization of Lancashire's Ribble Valley illustrates the utility of sacred space within Mormonism.

It is impossible to overstate the influence of doctrine, tradition, and even lore on the history of British Mormonism, particularly as it pertains to the sense of sacredness church leaders have projected upon the Ribble Valley—a status long prized by the local members. Joseph Smith's proclamation that Lancashire's Ribble Valley was dedicated and blessed by ancient prophets created a defining lens through which subsequent generations of British Latter-day Saints have viewed the English North West. The region continues to resonate with spiritual significance, to a degree perhaps unrivaled by any other location outside the United States. The Ribble Valley is to the British church what the Hill Cumorah is to the American church—an interdispensational marker, and a specific place that binds Mormonism to the previous gospel epoch.

On the local level, this interpretation of place has helped the membership negotiate the troublesome circumstances associated with the host culture. No more interesting example exists than in wartime Preston. Throughout World War II, local members maintained that their town was divinely protected from the extensive bomb damage that devastated much of Liverpool and Manchester. Some members attributed this protection to the Ribble Valley's enduring blessedness and Preston's singular status as the first community in Britain to embrace the restored gospel.[20] Mormonism was their shield as well as their salvation.

Because Joseph Smith directly associated the Ribble Valley with the ancient Christian church, Lancashire became a religious symbol for the British Latter-day Saints. The villages adjacent to Pendle Hill can be interpreted within Mormon thought as a defined and validating link to Christianity's primitive past. An apt comparison is the hilltop in the central Utah town of Manti, upon which local Latter-day Saints constructed a temple between 1877 and 1888. When the leaders were determining the precise location where the edifice would stand, local lore holds that the site was predetermined by the ancient-American prophet Moroni, who dedicated the spot for a latter-day temple.[21] When the prophets of the past leave their imprint, the believers of the present follow suit.

The affiliation between the Pendle area of the Ribble Valley and the prophets of the original Christian church (who Latter-day Saints believe ministered in ancient Britain) has provided British Mormonism with an ancient and spiritually significant focal point. This unique interpretation of place, inspired by belief and secured through covenant, allows even the most recent British Mormon convert to locate himself or herself within a grand and unfolding story—a Christian epic spanning two millennia in which he or she has become a player on its modern-day, climactic stage. This is, quite literally, a dramatic theology that produces for its adherents a sense of religious identity that is both timeless and immanent.[22] From this perspective, Mormonism is hardly a "new religious movement"—a rather unimaginative and limiting description bestowed by social scientists.

Given its significance, it is not surprising that Lancashire's upper Ribble Valley receives many LDS visitors. The visitor registers at the Anglican chapel of St. Leonard's in Downham village abound with entries written by church members from both sides of the Atlantic. Their writings bespeak their reflective and near-worshipful intent, making their visits more akin to pilgrimage than tourism.[23] Local missionaries tour the area annually, where they receive instruction from mission leaders and seek inspiration regarding their proselytizing efforts.

In contemporary British Mormonism, missionaries pursue their aims with a total disregard for the myriad exogenous factors that limit their chances for success—limitations that make replicating the many conversions seen in Heber C. Kimball's day improbable. The memory of these conversions, and the hope that a grand harvest of souls may again be achieved, is what the modern missionary goes to the Ribble Valley to celebrate.[24] For each missionary in Britain, history is either a tutor or a taskmaster; an inspiration or a burden. Either way, the pressures of the precedent set by Kimball and his associates are inescapable.

The Mormons' interpretation of the Ribble Valley is brimming with theological significance. As the only location outside North America to be identified by Joseph Smith as "holy ground," blessed by the ancient prophets with whom he claimed to share identical authority, this corner of rural Lancashire justifies the local saints' restorationist beliefs. This viewpoint establishes the region as a center place, or spiritual heartland, of the British Latter-day Saints. The presence of the nearby Preston Temple secures this perspective and ensures its transmission to future generations of church members.

Mormonism took root in Britain at a time when the social ills attending its industrialization were at their most pronounced, thus making the English North West an unlikely candidate for the sacred status Mormonism has projected upon it. After all, it is in Glastonbury in Somerset, not Manchester, where tradition says a youthful Jesus visited ancient Britain. Invoking William Blake's imagery, it was not upon the "pleasant pastures" of the rural West Country where Mormonism took root, but among Lancashire's "dark Satanic mills." The depravity and moral decay of the northern industrial districts, although abhorrent to the Latter-day Saints, were also harmonious with early Mormonism's eschatological sensibilities. These feelings motivated the first few generations of missionaries to try and gather Israel's elect from among the corrupted constituency of a British Babylon.

The Latter-day Saints' conflicting perspectives of the British host culture took approximately 130 years to reconcile. This reconciliation extended primarily from the influence of two Kimballs—Apostle Heber C. Kimball and his grandson Spencer W. Kimball, the twelfth president of the church. According to Heber C. Kimball, the blessing pronounced upon Britain by ancient prophets was intended to facilitate a latter-day harvest of souls: a distinct group of believers whose purpose would be to build up the kingdom of God in the last days. This perspective was consistent with the gathering initiated by Joseph Smith in the 1840s. At the Manchester England Area Conference in 1976, President Spencer W. Kimball reflected on his grandfather's missionary success in the Ribble Valley. After noting the Prophet Joseph's proclamation concerning the region's blessedness, Kimball invoked this same interpretation of Lancashire as sacred space. President Kimball insisted that the region's longstanding blessedness was "another reason why I think we can expect great things from you people. The Church will be strong and powerful in this area. Many, many missionaries have been sent here from Zion to bring the gospel to these nations and this area has always been an important part of the Church."[25]

From Spencer W. Kimball's perspective, the "great things" expected of Lancashire's Latter-day Saints included preaching the gospel to a wider, even international, audience. With zeal comparable to that shown by his grandfather in 1837, Kimball urged these modern-day members to promulgate Mormonism throughout the North West and beyond:

> You can preach the gospel not only to this country, but also to Ireland and Scotland and England and Wales. You can preach the gospel across the water. You could form a bridge over to France and Holland and Scandinavia; you could form a bridge down to Iraq and Iran and Egypt and to numerous other places where the gospel has not yet touched. And we expect you to do that.[26]

President Kimball's proclamations illustrate that the Mormon interpretation of Lancashire as holy ground has remained consistent throughout British Mormon history. It also is clear that this perspective has been utilized periodically and, at times, overtly, to encourage the members to assist in fulfilling the church's institutional aims, particularly regarding proselytizing and congregational expansion.

The nineteenth-century notion of Lancashire as holy ground was consistent with Joseph Smith's quest to gather Israel's elect in one and establish the prophesied *city* of Zion on the American frontier. Following the reinterpretation of the gathering doctrine at the end of the century, Britain's "blessedness" was put forward by Spencer W. Kimball as a key to the global *empire* of Zion. This evidences the adaptability of Mormonism, the enormous influence of its prophets, and the enduring utility of its sacred spaces. The concept of Lancashire as holy ground helped ensure British Mormonism's continuity and encouraged its expansion in a place far from its American core, yet of comparable significance. Britain certainly may be regarded as Mormonism's most important subsidiary headquarters in the northern hemisphere.

This book examines the British Latter-day Saints' conflicting views of their host culture—views that pitted the evils of industrialization against the promises of enduring blessedness. Historically, these disparate perspectives challenged missionaries in their labors and complicated the formation of converts' new religious identities. In the post-emigration church, the British saints struggled to accept their place within a religion that had, for generations, placed the Zion of the American West at the center of its orientation. At stake was the cohesion of an increasingly global church.

To thrive, the British church needed to establish its own sense of identity—one that was related to, but not restricted by, Mormonism at its American core. An interesting expression of this identity development is found in a rather short-lived attempt to create an indigenous hymnody. In 1933, Leah D. Widtsoe, wife of the British and European Mission president John A. Widtsoe, challenged the British members to apply their talents to the production of a new and uniquely British hymn, which "must extol the beauties and virtues of the mother country, and should be written in a meter so as to be sung to a well-known [Latter-day Saint] tune."[27] Widtsoe called for "an inspirational hymn that will live forever." The contest winner was Joseph Orton Bettridge of Hucknall, Nottinghamshire. Bettridge's hymn, "O Britain, Dear Britain," was an adaptation of "O Ye Mountains High," written by Charles Penrose in 1853. Bettridge's version included some subtle but important variation to the lyrics. Most notably, wherever the chorus said "Zion," Bettridge inserted "Britain" in its place. This one-word substitution captures the inculcation imparted by church leaders since the beginning of the twentieth century. Britain and Zion were to be as one. Bettridge's lyrics idealize the virtues of the British Isles, its partnership with the church, and its mission with such zeal and adoration as to make the very prospect of emigrating absurd:

O my island home, where the billows roam
Clean and fresh with the breeze from the sea;
With her fields green and gold, beauty favors the bold,
In the land of the brave and the free.

O Britain! Dear Britain! Home of the brave!
Thy fair sons will defend, truth and justice extend
Over earth, while our colors shall wave.

Here the true Church of God found a fertile sod
On the shores of our bright little isle;
May her sons ever shine in a light so divine,
And our nation shall prosper the while.

O Britain! Dear Britain! Home of the brave!
May the Gospel of peace 'mong thy people increase,
For the Gospel is mighty to save.

Then ye saints now arise, for your power ever lies
In the influence for good that ye wield;
May our country be blessed and be freed of distress,
And the Gospel a rich harvest yield.

O Britain! Dear Britain! Land of the brave!
Of thy praises we'll sing, to thy just laws we'll cling
And assist thee thy glory to save![28]

The second place prize in Widtsoe's hymn contest went to Nora Hollinrake, a member of the Burnley Branch in Lancashire. Hollinrake's composition was set to the tune of "High on the Mountain Top," a favorite of the saints in Utah. The new Anglo-centric lyrics likewise lauded the relationship between England's "green and pleasant land" and Mormonism's restored gospel:

O'er England's leafy dells,
O'er England's grassy plains,
Hark, truth and wisdom swells
In clear triumphant strains.

The voice of God again is heard;
Come saints and hearken unto His word.

For lo! within your land
The truth is now restored,
As Jesus did command,
According to His word.

And England's shores shall ring with praise,
For truth restored in latter days.[29]

Hollinrake's decision to conform her hymn to the melody of "High on the Mountain Top" was more significant thematically than she could have realized. The central image of the original hymn is Ensign Peak, the promontory on the northern edge of the Salt Lake Valley from which Brigham Young and his associates planned the city that would become the church's global headquarters. The biblical literalism that pervaded early Mormonism inspired Brigham Young to regard the peak as the very location from which Isaiah's ancient prophecy would be fulfilled: "And he shall set up an ensign to the nations, and shall assemble the outcasts of Israel . . . from the four corners of the earth."[30] And so it was that the name Ensign Peak was bestowed. Here the historical parallel between Mormonism in the American West and Mormonism the English North West continues. Ensign Peak is to Salt Lake City what Pendle Hill is to Hollinrake's Burnley and Heber C. Kimball's beloved upper Ribble Valley—a monument to the gathering of Israel in the last days, crafted by the very hand of God. Indeed, for the Latter-day Saints, it was as though nature itself had endorsed the denomination's outright claim upon the British Isles as one of the most distinguished and significant provinces of Mormondom.

"How shall we sing the Lord's song in a strange land?" asks the psalmist. For the British Latter-day Saints who participated in the evolution from Britain as Babylon to Britain as Zion, the answer was at once simple, inspiring, and imaginative: through the composition of a new song, their own song, set to an enduringly sacred refrain.

Appendix A
Correspondence
Heber C. Kimball's Valedictory Address to the Members of the Upper Ribble Valley

WHAT FOLLOWS MAY be the most accurate representation preserved in print of Heber C. Kimball's early preaching style. It gives some hint as to what Kimball may have taught, and how, during his successful proselytizing campaign in the upper Ribble Valley. The text is taken directly from the first issue of *The Latter-Day Saints' Millennial Star*, page 103. The reader will note that the letter, presented as an apostolic epistle comparable to those of the New Testament, was dictated by Kimball and transcribed by his associate Willard Richards. Abundant allusions to the New Testament underscore the primacy of the Bible in early Latter-day Saint proselytizing. This suggests that the language and teachings of the Book of Mormon had not yet become embedded within Mormon religious discourse.

FAREWELL OF ELDER KIMBALL AS HE WAS ABOUT TO SAIL FOR AMERICA.

Liverpool, April 15, 1840.

To the Church of Latter-day Saints in Chatburn and Downham

Greeting:

Beloved Brethren,—Having given all diligence to make known unto you the common salvation of our Lord Jesus Christ, which ye have so joyfully received from my lips,—I feel now to write you a few words for your consolation, and the confirming of that hope which is possessed by you, that ye may be stedfast, immoveable, always abounding in the work of the Lord, that it may be made manifest unto all men that our labours have not been in vain.

Be kind and affectionate one towards the other, manifesting your faith by your works—doing as well as saying. If there is any one among you destitute of daily food, feed him; if any be naked, clothe him; if any one be cast down, raise him up; if any among you are sick, send for the Elders, or Priests, that they may come and pray for you, and lay their hands upon you, and the prayer of faith shall save the sick;—Therefore, brethren, let your faith be centred in God, for he is able to do all things, to forgive sins, and heal the sick, for you know this, that God has said that *these signs shall follow them that believe.*

Now, brethren, I exhort you, in the name of my master, for once to contend for that faith which was once delivered to the Saints; for the same faith will produce the same effect: for God has not changed, neither has his word changed; heaven and earth shall not pass away, but there shall not one jot or tittle of his word fail; all shall be fulfilled, whether it be by his own voice or the voice of his servants it is all the same; therefore, brethren, do not live by bread alone, but by every word that proceedeth forth from the mouth of God.

Dear brethren and sisters, be patient, be humble, be prayerful, visit your secret places. Pray in your families morning and evening, ye who are heads of families, and neglect not the assembling of yourselves together, but speak often one to another concerning the things of the kingdom, and diligently follow after every good thing, remembering that the diligent hand maketh rich.

Now, dear brethren and sisters, let these things be and about in you, and ye shall be neither barren nor unfruitful in the knowledge of God. Let your eyes be single, and your bodies shall be filled with light.

Now, to you, brethren, who have been ordained to watch over the flock, I would say, Stand in your places, and magnify the office which ye have received of the Lord Jesus to feed his sheep. Feed the lambs, watch over the flock in all things, be not partial to any one: remember these things, brethren, and the blessings of God shall attend you in all things.

Dear brethren and sisters, I give you the gratitude of my heart for the kindness which you have bestowed upon me and my brethren; for when I was hungry you fed me, when I was naked ye clothed me, when my clothes were ragged ye mended them, when I was destitute ye gave me money, when I was a stranger ye took me in and lodged me; and, as ye have done these things to me and my brethren in our necessities, my heavenly Father shall minister unto you in your necessities; for I am not forgetful of these things, and I do ever remember you in my prayers, praying my heavenly Father to sustain you, and enable you to walk worthy of the holy vocation unto which ye have been called unto the end. Amen.

Finally, brethren and sisters, farewell. Pray for me and my brethren; and may the God of all grace sanctify you wholly, and bring you into my Father's kingdom.

Adieu. This from your beloved brother in Christ,

Heber C. Kimball

I, Willard, wrote this Epistle.

Appendix B
Tract
Orson Hyde's "A Timely Warning to the People of England"

The text below is taken from a broadside tract authored by Apostle Orson Hyde in Toronto in 1836, adapted to an English audience in Preston in 1837 and reprinted in Manchester in 1840. As noted in chapter five, various editions of this document circulated in the English North West throughout the remainder of the nineteenth century. This suggests a certain degree of stasis within the Mormon message, at least until its millenarian expectations were supplanted by the reinterpretation of the gathering doctrine, as discussed in chapters two and seven.

The reader will observe several interesting similarities and differences between this document and Heber C. Kimball's epistle presented in appendix A. Renowned for his powerful, if not pugnacious, oratory, Hyde's literary capacity far exceed Kimball's. Moreover, Hyde's argumentative tone contrasts sharply with the tender Christian exhortation rendered by Kimball. A compelling consistency between the documents is found in the respective authors' heavy biblical allusions, with particular emphasis on the New Testament. Interestingly, Hyde hints only briefly at Mormonism's restorationist claims and makes little mention of the various supernatural phenomena that precipitated the full organization and authorization of The Church of Jesus Christ of Latter-day Saints—events now celebrated openly within contemporary Mormonism. Curiously, Hyde does not explicitly reference either Joseph Smith or the Book of Mormon, although he does cite one of Smith's 1832 revelations, later canonized as Section 84 of the Doctrine and Covenants. Hyde's writings accentuate the eschatological orientation of early Mormonism and dwell heavily upon the apostasy he believed was afflicting Christendom generally. He predicted the Western world would be severely punished for this. The transcription below is an accurate reproduction of the original broadside, faithful to the original spelling, grammar, and punctuation.

A TIMELY WARNING TO THE PEOPLE OF ENGLAND

Of every Sect and Denomination, and to every Individual into whose hands it may fall,

BY AN ELDER OF THE CHURCH OF LATTER DAY SAINTS, LATE FROM AMERICA

Preston, 19th August, 1837

Forasmuch as many have taken in hand to set forth in order, a declaration of those things which are most assuredly believed among us, and which must shortly come to pass: It seemeth good unto me and also unto the Holy Spirit, to write unto you, that you may know of a certainty your standing and relation to God; and also of the times and seasons for the fulfilment of the words of his servants the Prophets.

After our Lord had completed the work which his Father had given him to do, he led forth his disciples as far as Bethany, and lifted his hands towards heaven and blessed them. While in the act of performing this kind office upon his disciples, he was received up to heaven in a cloud. As the disciples stood gazing upon his exit, two men, (angels) stood by them, clad in white apparel, and said: "Ye men of Galilee, why stand ye gazing up into heaven? This same Jesus who is taken up from you into heaven, shall so come in like manner as you have seen him go into heaven.

Some have laboured to show that this promise of Christ's second coming was fulfilled at the destruction of Jerusalem; but such was not the fact. Jerusalem was destroyed during the reign of Vespasian, the roman Emperor, by Titus, his son. Vespasian began to reign in the 70th year of the Christian era, and reigned nine years. He was then succeeded by his son, Titus, who reigned two years; and Titus was succeeded by his younger brother Domitian, in whose reign, and by whose order, the Apostle John was banished upon the Isle of Patmos, in the 95th year of the Christian era; being somewhere between sixteen and twenty-five years after the destruction of that city. The Saviour, who appeared to John while in banishment, said unto Him: "Behold I come quickly, and my reward is with me to give unto every man according as his works shall be." It is plain, therefore, that Christ represented to John, that his coming was yet in the future, even sixteen or twenty-five years after Jerusalem was destroyed. Therefore, so far from that promise being fulfilled at that time, it yet remains to be fulfilled. And we may look with certainty for the Son of God yet to appear in the clouds of heaven with great power and glory. The question now arises: Is the Christian world prepared to behold the day of the coming of the Lord from heaven? The day that shall burn as an oven, when all the proud, and they that do wickedly, shall be as stubble. This is a question of no ordinary moment.

The Jews rejected the Messiah when he came to them, and the Gentiles received him; but when he comes the second time, the Gentiles will be entirely unprepared to enjoy his glory; but the Jews will be brought in by virtue of the promise and covenant which God made with their fathers, which I shall attempt to prove from the Scriptures.

There was a cause of the Jews rejecting the Redeemer; and what was the cause? It was their previous departure from the law which God gave them by Moses. The law was given them as a schoolmaster to bring them to Christ; and had they not made it void through the tradition of their elders, they would not have disowned their King. The Lord said to them, himself, "If you had believed Moses, you would have believed me, for Moses wrote of me. But if you believe not his writings, how can you believe my words?" The fate which this people met, some thirty years after they rejected the counsel of God, is entirely without a parallel in the history of the world. The wretched few that escaped destruction at that time only seem to have been spared to perpetuate their shame and misery until the day of their redemption, which now is near at hand.

The gospel was committed to the Gentiles for the express purpose of preparing them for the second coming of Christ, as the law was given to the Jews to prepare them for his first coming. But the Gentiles have made void the gospel through the tradition of their elders, which now becomes my painful duty to show; and may the great Shepherd of Israel inspire my heart with a clear view of the fallen state of the Christian world at this period, and enable me to declare it with all that sympathy, plainness, and Christian love, which ever were the characteristics of a servant of the Most High.

In the first place, let me ask: Have the founders of the Christian system foretold an apostacy of the church from the true order of worship? They certainly have. Paul says, 2 Thess. 2.3. "Let no man deceive you by any means for *that day* shall not come except there come a falling away first, and that man of sin be revealed, the son of perdition, &c." Again, 1 Tim. 4.1. "Now the Spirit speaketh expressly, that in the latter times some shall depart from the faith, giving heed to seducing spirits and doctrines of devils." Also 2 Tim 4.3. and 4. "For the time will come when they will not endure sound doctrine, but after their own lusts shall they heap to themselves teachers having itching ears; and they shall turn away their ears from the truth, and be turned unto fables." These passages clearly show what the churches would do when left to act upon their agency, viz: that they would forsake the truths of God and be turned unto fables and traditions of men.

I will now present the Gentile churches before the glass of the holy scriptures, and see if they possess the same form and beauty now that they did eighteen hundred years ago. When Jesus gave his disciples their last commission to go forth into all the world to preach the gospel, he said unto them: "These signs shall follow them that believe. In my name shall they cast out devils; they shall speak with new tongues; they shall take up serpents: and if they drink any deadly thing, it shall not hurt them: they shall lay their hands upon the sick, and they shall recover." It appears that this miraculous power did, and ever will continue with true believers: for the same Being who said, "These signs shall follow them that believe:" also said, "Though the heavens and the earth pass away, yet my words shall not fail." It is very readily discovered why the above signs do not follow pretended believers; because Jesus never said they should. There is a difference between the spurious and true coin; although the spurious contains some genuine silver, yet it will not lawfully pass; and is, comparatively speaking, of no real value. By a chemical process, we can very readily discover the difference between the pure and the base: so, by an application of the word of God to any religious body, we may soon determine whether they are believers in the scriptural sense of the word; or according to the notions and opinions of uninspired men. Some pretends to say that the promise of Christ to his disciples, that miraculous signs shall follow them that believe, was limited to the apostles. But I think that no honest man who understands the English language sufficiently to tell the difference between the second and third person, will contend for any such thing. For Jesus did not say, these signs shall follow you, (Apostles) but he said: "These signs shall follow them that believe."

Again: Paul said, God sent some in the church, first apostles; secondly, prophets; thirdly, teachers; after that, miracles; then gifts of healing, helps, governments, diversities of tongues. To one is given by the spirit, the word of wisdom; to another, faith by the same spirit; to another the word of knowledge, by the same spirit; to another the gifts of healing; to another the workings of miracles; to another prophecy; to another discerning of spirits; to another divers kinds of tongues; and to another the interpretation of tongues." This seems to have been the gospel and order of worship which Paul advocated and established; and said: "Though we, or an angel from heaven, preach any other gospel unto you than that which we have preached unto you, let him be accursed." Do the Gentile churches of this day, preach and practice the above order? or have they lost it? They certainly have lost it. And have they not great reason to fear that a curse instead of a blessing will rest upon them. If the Jews were broken off because of unbelief, what must the Gentiles expect, who have not continued in the goodness of the Lord? It really appears to me that every person who is not biased by most unhallowed prejudice, can see that the churches of this day bear but a faint resemblance to those which existed in the days of the Apostles. Whence arises this difference? Do we live under a different dispensation from what they did? If we do, when was the dispensation changed and by whose authority? If we do not, why not preach and practice the same things which they did? Because thou art fallen! fallen! from thy first love. But those who are determined to support their peculiar creeds at the expense of truth, and the most plain declarations of holy writ, which are found written, as with a sun-beam upon almost every page, will deny the possibility of these precious and heavenly blessings being enjoyed by mortals now. But let me ask: Has God changed so much during the last eighteen hundred years? The language of the Bible is, "I am the Lord, I change not; therefore, ye sons of Jacob are not consumed."

I am aware that there are many who preach for hire, and love to be called of men, Rabbi, &c. who will seek refuge from the arrows of truth behind the bulwarks of affected sanctity, and put the unhallowed influence in operation which they exercise over the hearts and consciences of their deluded followers, to prevent them from hearing, investigating, or receiving the truth. Such hiding places may screen iniquity for a time. But when the trump of God shall sound, such bulwarks shall fall to the earth like the walls of Jericho, leaving those who have taken shelter behind them, exposed to the sword of God's indignation which will proceed out of his mouth, saying: Depart ye cursed, &c.

How plain it is, therefore, that a great apostacy, from the true apostolic order of worship, has taken place; and it now becomes my duty to show the awful consequences of this apostacy, however painful may be the task. But

Shall I behold the nations doomed
To sword and famine, blood and fire?
And not the least exertion make,
But from the scene in peace retire?
No. While kind heaven shall lend me breath,
I'll sound repentance far and broad;
And tell the nations to prepare
For Jesus Christ, their coming Lord.

The Jews were the natural branches of the good olive tree, but were broken off in consequence of unbelief. The Gentiles were the branches of a wild olive; but were grafted in where the natural branches had been broken off, and received of the root and fatness of the pure stock. The apostle, Paul, gave the Gentiles a very solemn warning after they had been grafted into the good olive. See Romans 11.22. "Behold the goodness and severity of God; on them which fell, severity; but towards thee, goodness, if thou continue in his goodness; otherwise thou shalt be cut off. Nothing is more plain than that the Gentiles have not continued in the goodness of God; but have departed from the faith and purity of the gospel. Query: Must they now be cut off? Jer. 4.7. will answer this question. "The lion is come up from his thicket; and the destroyer of the Gentiles is on his way; he is gone forth from his place to make thy land desolate; and thy cities shall be laid waste without an inhabitant. Also, Isa. 24th chap. is a striking exhibition of the fate of the Gentiles in the last days. But the Jews will be grafted back into their own olive tree. Read Romans, 11.23–28.

Many are flattering themselves with the expectation that all the world is going to be converted and brought into the ark of safety. Thus the great millennium, in their opinion, is to be established. Vain delusive expectation! The Saviour said to his disciples; that, "As it was in the days of Noah, so shall it be also in the days of the coming of the Son of Man." Again, he said: "As it was in the days of Lot, so shall it be in the days of the coming of the Son of Man." Query. Were all people converted in the days of Noah, or mostly destroyed? Were the cities of Sodom and Gomorrah saved or destroyed in the days of Lot? The answers to these questions are familiar to almost every person, and further comment is necessary.

God will soon begin to manifest his sore displeasure to this generation, and to your own country by distressing famine; for the season will henceforth be more irregular and uncertain in causing the earth to yield her bounty for the sustenance of her inhabitants. The trade and commerce of nations which have hitherto been a source of great wealth and pride, already begin to feel the withering touch of the Almighty, and must fade and sink to rise no more. Your nation is now, probably, at peace; and so are most nations. The sun of prosperity has shone upon them for some length of time, with scarcely a cloud to obstruct its rays. But the golden luminary of peace is now fast reclining behind the western waters; and then comes a night darkened by war-clouds, arising from almost every quarter, and filling the political horizon with terror and dismay. The hearts of kings, rulers, and nobles, will then faint because they know not the time of their visitation; and will know not what measures to adopt to avert the calamites of war.

O ye shepherds! ye teachers! ye rulers in Israel! hear the word of the Lord concerning you—The Lord who shall suddenly come to his temple—The Lord who shall come down upon the world with a curse to judgment, and upon all the ungodly among you. Wo! Wo!! unto them, saith the Lord, who preach for hire and *pervert* the ways of *truth*. Wo unto them who suffer themselves to be led by the precepts of men, contrary to that which they know to be written in the oracles of truth, for they shall perish. Wo! unto him who drinketh strong drink, and taketh the name of his God in vain! Wo! be unto all the wicked ones of the earth; for the fire of God's jealousy will consume them, root and branch, except they speedily repent.

Earthquakes, strange things, and fearful sights, together with the waves of the sea heaving themselves beyond their bounds, will cause men's hearts to fail them for fear. This is the Lord's recompence for the controversy of Zion, whose innocent blood, unavenged, cries to him from the ground. The Lord has looked down from heaven and beheld all your scenes of revelling and drunkenness. He has seen all your frauds—all your evil designs, and all the snares you have laid to take advantage of your neighbor. He has, also, seen the sterling virtues of many of the fairest portion of his creation sacrificed upon the altar of infamy and prostitution; all of which have a tendency to increase the displeasure of the Almighty, and draw down upon the world the storm of his indignation.

The apostacy of the church is the prime cause of the earth being visited by the judgments of God. Had the church remained in a stedfast, upright, and righteous course, it would have saved the nations from destruction. But, alas! the salt has lost its savour. "They have transgressed the laws, changed the ordinances, and broken the everlasting covenant."

The wicked will behold these judgments, and know not what they mean; yet the servants of God will view them as tokens of the coming of the Son of Man, as messengers sent before his face to execute vengeance. They will continue the work of destruction until the Saviour comes; for,

> Lo! he comes with truth and vengeance,
> With his garments dyed in blood;
> To redeem his chosen people,
> Favour'd children, sons of God.

When Jesus appears in the clouds of heaven, the saints who have slept will arise from their graves; and those who are living will be changed speedily, and all be caught up to meet the Lord in the air. Then shall all the wicked who have escaped the former judgments be consumed root and branch. Then shall the earth be cleansed from pollution, and the Lord descend upon it, and all the saints with him, to reign a thousand years, while Satan is bound. Then will the saints inherit this promise:—"Blessed are the meek, for they shall inherit the earth." Then one need not say to the other, Know ye the Lord? for they shall all know him, from the least to the greatest. Then the earth shall be full of the knowledge of God, as the waters cover the great deep. Then shall the saints unite in singing this new song; saying,

The Lord hath brought again Zion;
The Lord hath redeemed his people, Israel,
According to the election of grace,
Which was brought to pass by the faith
And covenant of their fathers.
The Lord hath redeemed his people,
And Satan is bound, and time is no longer:
The Lord hath gathered all things in one:
The Lord hath brought down Zion from above.
The Lord hath brought up Zion from beneath.
The earth hath travailed and brought forth her strength;
And truth is established in her bowels;
And the heavens have smiled upon her;
And she is clothed with the glory of her God:
For he stands in the midst of his people:
Glory, and honour, and power, and might,
Be ascribed to our God, for he is full of mercy,
Justice, grace and truth, and peace,
For ever and ever. Amen.

I am unwilling to dismiss this subject without telling you what the Lord has done for his creatures in these latter times, and, also, what he requires of you, that my garments may be clean of your blood in a coming day. The Lord has been pleased to send his holy angel from heaven to announce the joyful tidings to witnesses now living, that the time has come for him to set his hand the second and last time to gather in the remnants of Israel; and with them the fullness of the Gentiles—to establish permanent peace on earth for one thousand years. The everlasting gospel must go forth to the nations once more, to seal up the righteous, and to prepare them for the hour of judgment and desolation that awaiteth the inhabitants of the earth; and, also, for the coming of the Son of Man, which will be witnessed by this generation, according to the testimony of the angel of the Lord.

As John was sent before the face of the Lord to prepare the way for his first coming, even so has the Lord now sent forth his servants for the last time, to labour in his vineyard at the eleventh hour, to prepare the way for his second coming, by the preaching of repentance and baptism for the remission of sins, that they may be ready to go forth to meet the Bridegroom.

I am quite surprised that the clergy of this day pursue the course which they do in relation to this message which God has sent to man. They appear to feel themselves perfectly justifiable in raising the cry of false teachers and false prophets against the servants of God; but have no fears whatever that they may offend the Lord by so doing. Christ once said that offences must come: but wo! unto him by whom they come, &c. They are very ready to close their doors against what they are pleased to call delusion and deception: but they have no fears that they may close their doors against good by so doing, and shut out Christ and his servants from them.

Jesus was once grieved and wounded in the house of his friends because he testified against their iniquities, corruptions, and gross departure from the truth of heaven; so when he sends forth his servants to do the same they may ever expect to meet with a similar reception. If we had come to you declaring that an angel had come from heaven and testified that your works and your ways were all accepted of the Lord; and that he had pronounced his benediction upon you: you, no doubt, would have acknowledged that the ministration of angels in these days, was a scriptural doctrine: but because he testified against your departure from the truth, your errors and your traditions, you are now ready to cry, "False prophets, and false teachers."

But we are determined to preach the doctrine of Jesus Christ and to contend for the faith once delivered to the saints, though every priest on Babel's towers should oppose us.

Therefore, go forth, little sheet, and tell the people of England, and all people into whose hands you may fall, that the Lord has spoken from the heavens—that he hath sent forth his servants to them, preaching repentance, and baptizing for the remission of sins, to prepare them for the coming of the Son of Man, which is drawing near.

August 22nd, 1840.

Preaching every Sabbath in the Carpenters' Hall, Manchester, at Half-past Ten o'clock; Sacrament Meeting at Half-past Two; and Preaching at Half-past Six.

REPRINTED BY W.R. THOMAS,
SPRING-GARDENS, MANCHESTER.

Appendix C
Dedicatory Prayers
Six Examples, 1849–1998

The Latter-day Saints have solemnized their relationship to the British Isles through the occasional utterance of dedicatory prayers. Without exception, these prayers accompany the opening of a new place of worship, whether chapel or temple. Examples of each are featured below. Beyond the dedication of physical structures, entire regions can be similarly dedicated by priesthood authority. Each nation the church proselytizes in is formally dedicated at the commencement of missionary labors. Dedicatory prayers are customarily offered by a member of the Quorum of the Twelve Apostles. Prayers of rededication can and have occurred in Britain at the discretion of local priesthood leadership. One such example occurred at the summit of Hartshead Pike in 1980, the transcription of which is given below.

Locations where dedicatory prayers are offered become sacred sites to the Latter-day Saints and have abiding significance within their spiritual geography. For example, Apostle Orson Pratt dedicated Scotland for the preaching of the gospel in 1840 from the summit of Arthur's Seat in Edinburgh. The act imbued the site with spiritual meaning for the saints, who have ever since called it "Pratt's Hill." Interestingly, there is no record of Heber C. Kimball formally dedicating England in like manner. However, the blessing Mormons believe was left upon the upper Ribble Valley by prophets of Christ's original church appears to have served a similar purpose.

The five prayers featured in this appendix are presented in chronological order, beginning with the dedication of the baptismal font constructed by the saints in Liverpool in 1849 and culminating with the dedicatory prayer of the Preston England Temple, written and delivered by President Gordon B. Hinckley in 1998. The transcriptions of the prayers in Liverpool, Hartshead Pike, and Oldham are from the LDS Church Archives. The transcriptions of the prayers offered by Charles Penrose are from the *Millennial Star*, and the *LDS Church News* published the text of Hinckley's prayer.

Example 1: Dedicatory prayer of the baptismal font erected in the LDS meeting hall in Liverpool, Sunday, July 13, 1849. The prayer was offered by Milo Andrus, president of the Liverpool Conference.

> O God, the Eternal Father, we the Elders of this Church have assembled in this place to offer up our prayers before Thee at this time. We pray that we may lift up holy hands before Thee without wrath or doubting. Thou hast seen the labours of Thy servants in this place for the benefit of those who may enter into the Church. And we this night dedicate it for the ordinance of baptism for the remission of sins and for the healing of the bodies of Thy Saints. We ask Thee, Holy Father, that whomsoever may step into this font, that the infirmities of their bodies may be healed. And we pray that those that shall attempt to pollute this place may be cursed before Thy face. We pray that Thou wouldst seal these prayers in heaven, Thy dwelling place, and we ask again, that whomsoever may step into this place may be healed. Yea, wilt Thou bless it for the health of Thy people, when they are sick. We ask Thee to seal these things in the name of Jesus Christ. Amen.

Example 2: Dedicatory prayer of "Deseret," LDS assembly rooms in South Tottenham, London, Sunday, July 26, 1908. The prayer was offered by Charles W. Penrose, president of the British and European Missions.

> Our Father, who art in heaven, with grateful hearts we come before Thee on this occasion. We thank Thee for Thy providences which have been over us, Thy children, and also that Thou hast blessed us with the privilege of acquiring this property wherein we can meet together and worship Thee in peace with none to molest or make us afraid, and where Thy servants who have been called to minister in Thy name in this part of Thy vineyard may have a comfortable resting place where they can confer together and hold council and have sweet communion, that they may be prepared to go forth in Thy name and minister in Thine ordinances to Thy name's honor and glory.
>
> We thank Thee, Our Father, with all our hearts, and we praise Thy holy name, for we realize that Thy hand has been over us for good and through Thy providence we have been successful in this undertaking. We have had many obstacles to contend with, but Thou hast removed them from our path. We recognize Thee as the giver of all good and we praise Thee and thank Thee with all our hearts. And now, Father, look down upon us on this occasion and accept of our offering. We realize that it is yet imperfect, that there are

many improvements to be made in this building, that many changes will have to take place in order to make it as it should be, a house of prayer and a habitation unto the Most High, and we desire to continue our labors here and have it so prepared that Thine angels may come into it whom thou hast appointed to minister unto the heirs of salvation. May no influence or power which is not of Thee have an abiding place here, but may ever part be holy unto the Lord.

And we now dedicate it unto Thee, O God. Wilt Thou bless the labors of Thy servants, and grant that this house shall be acceptable unto thee, that is may be a sacred edifice wherein Thy people may assemble and where Thy servants may abide and lodge when necessary. We dedicate to Thee, the Lord our God, the land on which this building rests and its surroundings which have been purchased by Thy servants. Wilt Thou grant that the ground may be holy unto Thee. We dedicate the foundations of the house and this hall with all its appurtenances and the rooms which are adjacent thereto. We dedicate the font which has been erected for the purpose of baptizing repentant believers, and the basement where it is erected, that when assemblies shall gather there to attend to the ordinance of baptism for the remission of sins it all may be holy before Thee. Grant that it may be purified by the power of Thy Spirit, that all may be sacred. We dedicate the hall by which we enter this place from the doors inward and outward and all the surrounding, and the statuary, and everything pertaining thereunto. And we pray that inasmuch as we may need to rent out portions of this building we may do so wisely, and if persons not of our faith shall occupy the same that they may do nothing to deface it or to cause Thy displeasure. We pray Thee that if anything is said or done in those rented places that is at all unseemly Thou wilt not impute it to Thy servants, who desire that all shall be so ordered as to be pleasing in Thy sight. We dedicate the stairways and the rooms that are above, whether used as bedrooms, or dining rooms, or sitting rooms, or prayer rooms or closets, and every part and particle thereof up to the roof, with the tower and all the appurtenances thereto, the windows, the furniture and everything adorning the walls, every part and particle of this house and all things that it contains we dedicate unto Thee.

We pray that Thy Spirit and power may be in every part and place in this building, for we desire that the whole building outside and inside, and all things that surround it pertaining to the building may be holy unto Thee, our God and Father. We pray that Thy blessings may be upon it all, and when people gather to worship it this hall, that Thy power may be upon them and upon all who minister in Thy name, that they may do so under the influence of Thy Spirit, that nothing may be done or said or attempted contrary to Thy holy will. We thank Thee for what Thou hast done for us in helping us to make this building as comfortable and beautiful as it is. And wilt Thou bless Thy servants who have been so diligent in laboring here, Thine elders sent out to preach the gospel, who have gone to with their might and have cleansed and purified and beautified the house. Bless Thy servant, President Soren Peterson, who has superintended this work and has shown zeal and perseverance characteristic of a servant of God. Grant that every encumbrance upon it may be speedily removed, that every part of it may be fully owned by Thy Church. Wilt Thou bless these Thy servants who have been so diligent in their labors and may they receive their reward in this life as well as in the life to come. Grant that when Thy saints come here to worship they may come in the spirit of holiness, humility and faith, that the power of God may be here and the fear of the Lord may be here, and may the Holy Ghost shed forth that sacred influence which was promised by our Redeemer and which we have felt so many times in the Temples of our God.

We thank Thee for the restoration of the gospel in these last days, for the visitation of angels, for the restoration of Thy holy priesthood, for the establishment of Thy kingdom, for the opening of the dispensation of the fullness of times, for the beginning of the restitution of all things, for the dawning beams of the millennial morn. We thank thee for the testimony of Jesus which Thou hast planted in our hearts, by which we know the truth, and wilt Thou help us to be firm and faithful to that testimony, that we may never waver from it in word or deed, that we as well as this house may be holy unto the Lord, that our bodies may be acceptable habitations for the Holy Spirit, even the tabernacles of the Lord, that we may be sanctified unto Thee in body and spirit and in every part of our being. We pray Thee, O Lord, to look upon Zion, Thy people who desire to be the pure in heart. Wilt Thou unite Thy people together that they may be able to stand up against their enemies, to maintain their rights and liberties and may their evil foes be confounded. Bless Thy servant President Joseph F. Smith. May Thy Spirit be upon him, his counselors, the Twelve, all the authorities in Thy Holy Priesthood, and all the societies that have been organized for the advancement of Thy work, that they may all be adequate to the duties that are required at their hands.

Bless Thy servants in all parts of the earth carrying the gospel of Jesus Christ unto the nations. Bless this, the European Mission. Bless Thy servant President Booth in the Turkish Mission, Thy servant President Steed in

South Africa, Thy servant President Ballif in the Swiss and German Mission, Thy servant President Cannon in Holland and Belgium, Thy servant President Rasmussen in Denmark and Norway, Thy servant President Sundwall in Sweden, and all Thy servants throughout these nations and throughout the United States and other lands, and upon the isles of the sea where Thy servants are laboring with great toil and diligence, and give them power to overcome every obstacle that may beset their paths, that they may gather in Israel from the four corners of the earth and be prepared for the coming of our Lord when He shall appear suddenly in His Holy Temple. Have mercy upon the nations of the world. Lovers of pleasure more than lovers of God, lead them unto Thee. And those who stand up against Thy Church and seek to do it harm, cause that they may be softened in their feelings. Guide the rulers and legislators of the nations that Thy servants may have liberty and freedom to preach the gospel among the peoples of the earth.

Accept of our prayers, our supplications, our songs. Let Thy Spirit inspire us and may Thy word be proclaimed in power. Let thy peace abide with us, be in our hearts, and go with us to our homes. Open the way for Thy servants laboring here to return in due time to their loved ones in the Valleys of the Mountains, and may the way be opened so that Thy saints may be able to gather with Thy people to the heights of Zion and build up cities and Temples and prepare the way for the coming of our Lord. We dedicate ourselves as well as this building, unto Thee, the Lord our God. Accept of us and direct us and finally crown us with eternal life in Thy glorious presence, through Jesus Christ, our Redeemer. Amen.

Example 3: Dedicatory prayer offered at the summit of Hartshead Pike, Sunday, May 4, 1980. The prayer was offered by Ellis Ivory, president of the England Manchester Mission.

O, dear God our Heavenly Father, we are most grateful that the sun shines on this day and on this land. And we are grateful to join as Saints in this Ashton Ward of Zion. And we are grateful for the Priesthood that is here.

But now, Heavenly Father, we do call upon the Heavenly Priesthood, Thy power and authority, to come down upon us this day and to touch our hearts and make us feel confident in power and humility, that we might go forth and perform the work that is before us.

And looking out upon this site today we see many homes and much beautiful land. But Father, we know that within these homes and in this land there dwells sin. We know that Satan certainly has much power and control over these people. Heavenly Father, bless us that we can do our part to stem this tide of wickedness and evil in the earth. We know our responsibilities, Father, and we feel them heavily and yet we are most grateful for them. We are grateful Father for missionaries who have affected our lives to enable us to be here, each and every one, sometime either directly or through our ancestors; that someone has cared enough, to have been bold enough, and have given up the pride of the world enough that we can now have the gospel and the peace that comes. And so, dear Heavenly Father, we would pray this day that we would be able to be strengthened and overcome fear, to overcome the pride of men and earthly accomplishments, even that we might truly be meek and humble servants of Thine, and that we will be able to go to our families, to distant relatives, and close, to our neighbors, to our friends and have the courage, Father, to show them how important this message is in their lives and how important it is for the world.

Heavenly Father, we pray that Thou wilt help us to build Thy Kingdom here, that indeed this ward will be a ward of Zion and that there will never be any fault-finding, that they will understand each other's imperfections and that we will not be ever critical of our leaders and especially not of Thy General Authorities, but that we will come quickly to obey every principle and every teaching, and every programme that comes forth from Thy servants.

And now, as we start on this day, this new meeting schedule, Father, we pray that we might truly catch the vision of it and that we will be able to see then the need for us to be even more dedicated, that we will give more time in building up the Kingdom, but that we might do it as missionaries and that we might do it to our families, that we might be able to in some way magnify our calling and magnify this ward, that indeed there will come a day when many wards will be here in this land and in this area, and that therefore there will be able to be more people to help stem the tide of this evil.

Heavenly Father, we pray for the inactive members of this ward, that they will be able to overcome sin that they will be able to overcome pride or materialism, or any other problems that stand in their way from living the commitments they have made at baptism. Heavenly Father, we have great need to join with Thee, and we would humbly pray that Thou wilt come down to us and lift us up that we might join in Thy hand and truly be partners then in building up Thy Kingdom. We pray for the missionaries who will serve here, that they will never be discouraged but that they will be bold and courageous and be able to go forth with the great tradition that has built the Kingdom thus far. We pray that Thy Spirit will truly be poured out upon all flesh and that through inspiration we will find those people who even this day are praying and who are striving and seeking for truth. Now these blessings we seek and pray for and this blessing of dedication to these people I pronounce humbly, by the power of Thy Holy Priesthood, and in the name of the Lord Jesus Christ, Amen.

Example 4: Dedicatory prayer of the LDS chapel in Oldham, Sunday, January 18, 1987. The prayer was offered by Martin A. Cook, president of the Ashton England Stake.

O, Holy Father, we dedicate this beautiful building in the name of the Author of mercy, the great I Am, the advocate with the Father, even Jesus Christ, Thine Only Begotten.

As we dedicate this building it seems to cry in silent force to the world, nay shouts across the filth and sewage of the world, that it can shroud the stranger in unlimited peace, offer knowledge, bring comfort and hospitality to the traveler. It calls to the weary and is a mark, a punctuation, in the lives of this people. [Now is] a time to pause and glean, a realization that here is a sanctuary for the spiritually halt, the blind, the hungry, the earnest seeker of truth, the depressed, the sick and the poor.

We dedicate these foundations to be sound and immovable and may those who walk here reflect its firmness and steadfastness as they labor to withstand Satan's shafts in the whirlwind. May we learn to build upon our own foundations, which foundation is the spirit and testament of the Savior. As we believe in Christ so will our actions vibrate in the lives of the on looker and infuse the Savior's influence, for we act relative to our belief on Him. How far we walk, how much we love, the example we set, the path we tread, how hard we labor, is motivated by the very depth of our witness and belief of the Son of God.

We dedicate these walls that they will stand firm against Satan's insatiable desire to tear down and destroy all things which might offer sanctuary to the homeless, spiritual tramp who wanders aimlessly to find comfort and warmth within this [place]. As these walls surround the spiritual vagrants of society, may we teach, admonish, motivate, uplift and love the lost and the weary, and envelop them into the safety and protection of these walls.

We dedicate the roof that it will repel the rains and ravages and turbulence of time. May it withstand the erosion of the elements, the hail and the snows of the disfavor of the world. May it deflect the ignorance of criticism into the drains of the depth. May its protecting cover establish a freedom from the cold of misunderstanding. May this canopy withstand the rains of oppression which fall upon the widows and the fatherless, and perpetrate the trueness of religion espoused by the Savior. May it bring comfort to all who seek its protection.

We dedicate these doors that they be hinged upon the principle of love and be ever open to those whose steps are eager to enter these portals. May the locks only lock against the vandals and not the visitor, be closed only against the inclemency and not the investigator, and open to the oppressed and not the ogre intent upon destruction, and may they be wide enough to offer welcome to sinner or saint.

We dedicate these windows that they may reflect the gospel purity, the uniqueness of those principles and ordinances long since lost to the world for hundreds of years. May those whose eyes penetrate its clearness perceive that the gospel famine did occur, that there was a falling away, that the Revelator John did predict an angel would restore another witness for Christ—for prophets do not lie. That Elijah has graced the earth again as promised by Malachi and brought hope to those in spiritual chains and given them an eternal future. We rejoice at the news of John the Baptist's visit to restore that precious passport to the kingdom. We have heard the voices of Peter, James and John ministering and pressing the keys of the dispensation of the fullness of times into Joseph [Smith's] hand, a Prophet of these latter days.

And so let the voices shout and proclaim the return of that which was lost and welcome the organization of Prophets and Apostles, whose presence and office was intended to remain until there was a unity of faith and whose very presence we announce, declare and testify to the world today.

We declare also truths and ordinances long since left out; more especially those ordinances forged in the Temples so built to give unto thy faithful children knowledge to return to thy presence. O, Holy Father, this ignorance has caused man and master to mourn—but no more, for we have the glad tidings.

We espouse the spiritual logic of our previous life and may it permeate the minds of many as they search for the answer to the question "from whence came we." For, if life is eternal, our beginning was not in our mortal birth—for eternity boasts [neither] beginning [nor] end. And so yet another truth, the truth of pre-earth life, we give to the world and trust it will discover the balm and joy such an understanding brings.

As we elevate our minds with restored truths we dedicate this spire which points to a better way, a more sure way, an understandable way—a way void of the clutter of tradition, heresy and rumor and in truth says "thus saith the Lord" for only Prophets can so say. We dedicate this heavenward pointing spire that it may ever so point and be the needle in the compass of our lives.

We dedicate these grounds that they may be ever pleasing to the eye and as the digger digs may the weeds be cast upon the waste. Cause that which is wholesome to come forth and our minds relinquish the desire to harbor complacency.

Invite change and knowledge, and cultivate a desire to enable our minds to spiritually spiral into higher realms. A testimony of the Savior is the spirit of prophecy and can come only from the gleaning of truths found in the scriptures so sadly neglected and unread.

May the Book of Mormon be snatched from the bowl of neglect and lifted onto a better view that our eyes may see more clearly and create our own escutcheon so Satan may be aware and see our personal defense is sure, as we allow the pure truths espoused seep into our souls and prompt our step.

As we dedicate a building we rededicate our lives and realize salvation comes only by service in finding lost souls who drift on an ocean of immoral sewage. We see the ocean swelling in filthiness as the tides constantly foul the shores of the mind of the wanderer. So we must not spin the coin of chance to choose our way, for Satan doth pretend [to] sleep. He will fool the slumberer, the unaware, the nonchalant and the empty mind.

May our believing cause the Lord's anger to be stilled and the necks of the unbelieving [be made] supple. As we measure our steps to our neighbor may they yield to the truths and efficacy of the greatest message man may hear as he turns towards the spiritual orchard of plenty wherein the fruits unsoured by Satan's touch turn the stomach from its hunger with the incomparable recipe of sweetness and taste the searcher might desire.

Our relief from sin is assured as we serve our fellow men with this food—unique in the spiritual kitchens of the world where many pseudo-spiritual chefs whisper "lo here lo there" is Christ. As we become the waiters to our Prophet the greatest of all chefs we bring the bread of life to the lonely and spread the sweet honey of salvation upon the seeker's loaf of life. Fill our minds and our souls with the sacredness of this saving act and the etching into their minds of the plan of salvation which gift is the greatest of all.

As we institute change into our lives may we pry from our eyes the blurring mote which stunts the sight and falsifies the vision and inculcates the desire to love our fellow men. Failure to do so indicates our inability to love the Savior, for how can we love someone we cannot see and fail to love he who sojourns by our side in the glare of the day.

And last of all we testify of our belief in the Savior Jesus Christ, our faith in His Atonement, our knowledge that he yet lives with a body to die no more, our understanding of his great sacrifice and pain as Elohim's spirit was withdrawn on that Golgotha hill, and as the blood dropped from his body in that awful garden we call Gethsemane. Our love for our Elder Brother we express with our deepest emotion, for in spite of his trembling at the very ordeal, He won the fight. In spite of the greatest pains ever borne He triumphed over death and is still our advocate with the Father.

We salute with reverence those past and present whose efforts to build the Church in this corner of England have proven valuable to the kingdom—may thy blessings be with them.

To all whose participation has given impetus to this memorable occasion we offer our grateful thanks and appreciation.

O, Holy Father we thank Thee for our very lives and recognize our unworthiness before thee. Forgive us for our errors and mistakes and give us strength to endure to the end.

This dedicatory prayer we offer in humility in the name of thy Son, Jesus Christ, amen.

Example 5: Dedicatory prayer of the Preston England Temple, Sunday, June 7, 1998. The prayer was offered by Gordon B. Hinckley, president of The Church of Jesus Christ of Latter-day Saints.

O God, our Eternal Father, we bow before Thee in solemn prayer as we dedicate this sacred house.

We worship Thee in spirit and in truth, Thou Great Elohim, the Almighty Judge of the nations, the Father of all mankind and the God of the universe.

We bow in reverence before Thy Beloved Son, the Lord Jesus Christ, who came to earth and gave His precious life in an act of Atonement that opened the gates of immortality and eternal life for each of us.

We bow in deepest gratitude for the gifts and blessings of the Holy Spirit which has borne witness of Thy divine reality and that of Thy Son.

We stand in respect and love for the Prophet Joseph Smith, the instrument in Thy hands in opening this great and final dispensation, the dispensation of the fullness of times, when Thou hast brought together in one the doctrines and practices of all previous dispensations.

Almighty God, forgive our sins on this day of dedication that we may come before Thee clean from all evil, and worthily as Thy children.

Through the centuries Thou hast smiled with favor upon England, "this sceptered isle." Great have been her ways, marvelous her destiny. She has bequeathed to the world the great principles of English law to enhance the dignity of man, and the priceless gift of the English Bible which since the year 1611 has stood as a testament of the Redeemer of the world.

This magnificent temple has been reared in this beautiful area where Thy chosen servants, in the days of their deep poverty and great sacrifice, first preached the restored gospel. Through 161 years of history this land of England, together with Scotland, Wales, and Ireland, has yielded a harvest of converts who have blessed and strengthened Thy Church. In early years thousands gave their lives when they left their homes, and with hope born of an abiding faith, sailed across the seas, and traversed a continent in search of Zion. Hallowed be their memory.

And now on this day which will long remain in our memories, acting in the authority of the eternal priesthood in us vested and in the name of Jesus Christ we dedicate unto Thee and unto Thy Son this the Preston England Temple of The Church of Jesus Christ of Latter-day Saints. We pray that Thou wilt accept it as the sacred offering of Thy thankful people. This is Thy house and we ask that Thou wilt sanctify it with Thy presence. From this day forth may Thy Holy Spirit dwell within these walls and touch the hearts of all who enter therein.

We dedicate the grounds on which it stands, with their trees and shrubs, flowers and lawns which add to the beauty of Thy house. We dedicate the structure from the footings of the temple to the figure of Moroni. We dedicate all of the components of the building that they may function harmoniously together to create a house that is "fitly framed."

We dedicate the Baptistry, the endowment rooms, the magnificent Celestial Room, the sealing rooms with their sacred altars, and every facility which is a part of Thy holy house.

Stay the hand of the vandal that he shall not deface or destroy. Temper the elements that they shall not damage or cause undue wear. May no unclean thing come within these hallowed walls. May Thy people come here with rejoicing in their hearts to enter into covenants with Thee, and be endowed with power from on high. May they kneel at these altars and be sealed together as families under the authority of the holy priesthood. May they return frequently to carry forward a great and selfless labor of vicarious work for the dead that the earth may not "be utterly wasted" at the coming of Thy Son. May the multitudes of the dead, through living proxies, receive the ordinances herein offered.

Now we pray for the temple president and his counselors and the matron and her assistants. We pray for all who will serve in these hallowed precincts. May each work with an eye single to Thy glory and the building of Thy kingdom.

We pray for those who serve in temples throughout the world that all may rejoice in the glorious opportunity that is theirs to assist Thee, dear Father, in Thy work of bringing "to pass the immortality and eternal life of man."

Bless Thy work in all the earth that it may roll forth "fair as the moon, clear as the sun and terrible as an army with banners." We invoke Thy blessings upon Thy servants, the missionaries, wherever they labor. Watch over them, protect them from every evil, lead them to those who will accept their message, and bind their testimonies upon the hearts of all who shall hear them.

We remember before Thee those called and ordained to lead Thy Church in these days of great opportunity. Sustain them, we pray Thee, give them strength, speak through them and reveal unto them Thy divine will concerning Thy work.

Bless the Saints of the United Kingdom, these wonderful people of England, Scotland, Wales, and Northern Ireland, as well as those of the Irish Republic. As they pay their tithes and offerings, wilt Thou open the windows of heaven and shower down blessings upon them. Bless their homes and families. Bless their children that they may grow up with a love for the truth. Bless them in body and mind and spirit.

Holy Father, we love Thee. We love Thy Divine Son. We love Thy holy work. Help us to be faithful. Help us to be true. Help us to walk always with integrity. May we always look to Thee with gratitude and love and faith. May we be found always walking in Thy paths.

And now as we conclude this prayer dedicating Thy holy house, by the same authority of the holy priesthood we dedicate the other structures that comprise this complex designed and built to serve Thy purposes—the Preston England Stake Center, the Missionary Training Center, the Family History facility, the Distribution Center, the Patron Housing and Temple Missionary Accommodation facilities, and the Grounds Building, that each may fulfill its appointed purposes and be preserved and protected from evil hands and unrighteous designs.

Our dear Father, on this sacred day of dedication, we rededicate ourselves and all that we have and are, to Thy holy work and that of Thy Beloved Son, and do it all in His name, even the name of the Lord Jesus Christ, Amen.

Appendix D
Oral History
The Book of Mormon, Proselytizing, and Conversion

In 1987, as part of the commemoration of the 150th anniversary of The Church of Jesus Christ of Latter-day Saints in the British Isles, the Religious Studies Center at Brigham Young University sponsored an oral history project designed to help document the experiences of British Latter-day Saints in the twentieth century. Funding from the Harold B. Lee Library and the Religious Studies Center, as well as additional university monies earmarked for the sesquicentennial, enabled the project. Eight interviewers contacted church members throughout England, Scotland, Wales, Northern Ireland, the Republic of Ireland, and the Isle of Man. Most of the interviewees had been Latter-day Saints for many years. Additional interviews were conducted with British church members visiting Salt Lake City, as well as with LDS British immigrants living in North America.

The interview project was conducted under the direction of the Joseph Fielding Smith Institute for Church History at BYU, with interviewers taken from among the university faculty. Transcription and editorial work was conducted by the James Moyle Oral History Program within the Church History Department of The Church of Jesus Christ of Latter-day Saints in Salt Lake City. Final typescripts and permanent copies of the interview tapes are on file in the LDS Church Archives, and copies of the transcripts are also available in the Harold B. Lee Library at BYU.

The James Moyle Oral History Program was partially funded by a grant to the Church History Department from the James Moyle Genealogical and Historical Association. Its primary objective was documenting, through recorded interviews, the history of the church in the twentieth century. Those interviewed include leaders who have influenced the development of church policies and programs, as well as rank-and-file members at the local level.

What follows are portions of two transcribed interviews conducted by Richard L. Jensen, then a senior research historian with the Joseph Fielding Smith Institute for Church History. Each interview sheds interesting light on the role of the Book of

Mormon within the proselytizing program in England in the mid-twentieth century, and suggests the impact of the text upon individual conversion.

Interview 1: Derek J. Plumbley, oral history interview by Richard L. Jensen, Salt Lake City, Utah, April 3, 1987

Derek Plumbley, son of Harry and Ellen Plumbley, was born on May 11, 1931 in Northwich, Cheshire. He graduated from the Winnington Park School in 1945 and then attended the Verdin Technical College, where in 1952 he earned a certificate in mechanical engineering. Plumbley served as an engine mechanic in the Royal Air Force from 1952 to 1954. While living in the Manchester area in 1956, Plumbley was contacted by missionaries and was baptized in May 1957. Plumbley has served as a member of the Manchester District presidency and as president of the Manchester Stake.

DP: It was in the latter end of '56 when a knock came on the door and two Mormon missionaries appeared. My wife was in. I was at work, of course, and they were just tracting. They were giving [copies of the] Book of Mormon out, and they'd gone out on a wet day—the area is known for its wet—with a knapsack full of [copies of the] Book of Mormon. They'd got rid of them all, except one, which was badly marked with rain, and the dye from the cover had run into the book. They stood on the end of our little road, which was a new little road with about twenty houses in it, debating whether to go back and throw the book away or try and get rid of it. Well, they decided to try and get rid of it, and it was mine. [chuckling] We were about the sixth house they called at and my wife took it—I don't know why—and gave them an appointment to come and visit me and convert me to Christianity. [laughing]

RJ: Not her, but you.

DP: [laughing] Oh no, only me. Having made the appointment, I felt obliged to let them in, although I didn't want to talk with them at all. And I don't know what kept them coming back or what kept me allowing them to come back in those first weeks.

They challenged me to read the Book of Mormon. I was an avid reader, as that was one of my great hobbies at the time. So I accepted that. I says, "I'll read anything once." Having started reading it, I suddenly realized what it was, of course, when I read the introduction and wished I'd never said anything. The idea of angels descending on people was just ridiculous, as far as I was concerned, and I just decided the book was rubbish anyway. I was basically at the point of terminating our interviews when they stopped coming, and they didn't appear again for six weeks, it must have been. So I thought it was all over and was quite glad.

But I kept on poking into the Book of Mormon while they were away. And when they did appear again, I was much more ready to listen, because by then I had realized that there was something in the book. So from then on I really gobbled it up, in a way. I didn't admit I was, even to myself, but I desperately wanted to know what they had. I was impressed by them as individuals. The thing that attracted me most was simply that they were throwing down, in a way, the doctrine of the orthodox churches, which I had already thrown down in my mind. So it was a perverse attraction, I suppose. [laughing]

RJ: They were allies almost.

DP: Yes. They were telling me three gods, instead of three in one, like the churches taught, because that was the approach in those days, to sort of take the orthodox doctrine and tear it to pieces before they began talking about the Restoration. And I suppose that was attractive. But when we got into the serious stuff, I was gradually reading the Book of Mormon and began to have spiritual experiences, which I didn't recognize as such at the time. I wouldn't have described them as that, but I knew something had happened.

RJ: What was happening?

DP: I was being deeply moved and carried away by the Book of Mormon, if you understand me. I was there. I could do that with any book, if you understand me. That's why I loved plays and books. I could get very involved. But I really did get involved. I suppose the first time was King Benjamin's speech from his tower. I had the deep conviction that if I'd been there, I would have signed on with the rest as a Christian, if you understand me, which rather threw me.

I went through a whole period of time when I would be with the missionaries, or reading the Book of Mormon, when I was filled with a very emotional feeling, something which I would describe as emotional at the time but which I now recognize as something else. I used to travel to work on the bus in those days and I would sit on the bus analyzing what had happened. By the time I got to work, I was quite convinced I was being duped and that the whole thing was a load of rubbish and I ought to get rid of them before I was conned. But as soon as I got home and began again to read the Book of Mormon, then it all came back.

I went through months of that. I thought I was going mad. I remember somebody saying, "Does it bring you peace?" And I said, "No, it never brought me a moment's peace. [laughing] It just brought me hassle and difficulty." I really didn't know where I was going for months, to be honest.

But Moroni frightened me. The Book of Mormon always did. I'm thinking of where he said, "I'll meet you one day and then you'll know I've told you the truth."

[laughing] When I got to that bit, I decided I'd have to join. So I was baptized in May of 1957.

The Book of Mormon is very special to me. It converted me. I mean, the missionaries helped me, of course. But my spiritual witness came from the Book of Mormon. When it says it's for the convincing of the Jew and the Gentile that Jesus is the Christ, I found Christ through the Book of Mormon totally, nothing else. I was reading Third Nephi, Christ's visit, the prayer scene where He gathers the children around Him, and I was so emotionally involved with Christ that I felt His love for the first time.

I may have accepted Him before and realized He was the Redeemer and that whoever they crucified at Jerusalem was the Christ, but this was the first time I felt I knew Him and what He was like as an individual. I saw Him as an individual and that came to me so powerfully that I literally couldn't bear it. I was so hot, literally hot, and it was winter, early in the year, February around this time, and very cold. I was in my shirt sleeves in front of a fire and I literally got up and put the book down and went outside into my little back garden and sat on the back gate in freezing temperatures for ten minutes or I wouldn't have been able to stand it.

And there were other things like that. I knew then, as I know now, that not only was He real, but He was a God of love and concern and that I could approach Him. And the questions that couldn't be answered just melted away. That's what I mean.

Interview 2: Albert Pickup, oral history interview by Richard L. Jensen, Worsthorne, Burnley, July 22, 1987

Albert Pickup, son of Hubert and Rose Hanna Pickup, was born on May 13, 1916, in Darwen, Lancashire. Early in his childhood, the Pickups moved to Burnley, where Albert obtained his education. Pickup left school at age fourteen. He was employed as a heavy goods vehicle driver during the 1930s, served in the Royal Engineers during World War II, and worked as a professional photographer until 1952. Pickup became acquainted with the Church of Jesus Christ of Latter-day Saints in the spring of 1948 and was baptized on September 26 of that year. Pickup served as a member of the Burnley town council from 1955 to 1983, during which time he served as town mayor and deputy mayor.

AP: We used this big studio downstairs as a social area. There were probably about fifteen people there. And when it came to drinks, Eunice, my girlfriend's girlfriend, said, "Oh, Arthur doesn't drink tea." I replied, "I'll give him coffee then." She said, "He doesn't drink coffee either." "Oh, why not?" "He's a Mormon." I said, "What's that?" [laughing] So that was the first mention to me of the word "Mormon," the first time I ever heard of it.

A few weeks later into the shop came two Mormon elders to have their films developed. I said, "Are you American?" "Yes." "What are you doing in Burnley?" "Oh, we're missionaries." I said something to the effect, "Well, we need missionaries. We're all heathens." I thought they'd tell me what the Mormon Church was. So I said, "Well, I'm interested in that. I'd like to hear something about it." They must have been amazed. [laughter] They were no doubt very pleased about that, and they came back after the shop had closed and began teaching me. So that was my first contact with the Church.

RJ: What do you remember about the way the missionaries taught you?

AP: I remember they didn't have discussions as such. I asked for most of what I got. I asked them for the information. But I had to ask for a Book of Mormon, I asked for a Doctrine and Covenants, I asked them if I could pay tithing, and I had to ask, eventually, if I could be baptized. [laughing]

RJ: Well, certainly not the way it would be done now.

AP: That's right, yes.

RJ: So you asked if you could pay tithing.

AP: Yes.

RJ: How would you have learned about that?

AP: In talking. They used to come socially, ostensibly for social occasions rather than teaching occasions.

RJ: So it was almost as if you were prying things out of them.

AP: Yes.

RJ: Did you think that that was more effective in your case than it would have been had they presented it more forthrightly?

AP: I think it might have been. I'll tell you one thing that I remember. I had a young lady working as an assistant at that time, and I remember distinctly in the darkroom one day talking about a pamphlet which included the Joseph Smith story. I said, "I think it makes sense, in all ways, but I can't accept the gold plates. That doesn't make sense, the gold plates. Apart from that, it seems all right." It didn't worry me for very long.

RJ: How did that fit in with the missionaries' time with you? This pamphlet, was that . . .

AP: Well, they just left it.

RJ: They left it and you had a hard time accepting that.

AP: The gold plates, yes. I asked them about it and they explained it away. As I say, there were no formal discussions as such. It was all conversation, just chatting and asking questions and things like that.

RJ: Could you describe the way in which you came to the point that you wanted things to happen, that you wanted to read the Book of Mormon, that you wanted to pay tithing, that you wanted to be baptized?

AP: The Book of Mormon was a start. When I started to read the Book of Mormon, that started me off, and the Doctrine and Covenants brought an awful lot of questions up, and those included tithing.

RJ: What did you think at that time? When did you start concluding that there really was something here?

AP: I think from the very first discussion I was attracted. I didn't have to fight at that time against it, except it took me a long while to accept Joseph Smith. I think probably it was three years before I really accepted that. And that came really through logic, mainly.

RJ: No overwhelming feeling, no . . .

AP: No burning in the bosom, no. No, it was just common sense, I think, in the first place, regarding the things which were said and done. I remember saying at that time that they seemed to have an answer for everything. Whatever it was, there was an answer to it. But I just had difficulty accepting Joseph Smith as a prophet until I accepted the Book of Mormon as true. And as it was true, then the prophet who wrote it [really] was a prophet. But that was later. At first it just seemed right to me.

RJ: So you were a member of the Church, then, for a couple of years before you could really accept Joseph Smith as a prophet.

AP: Yes, that was right.

Notes

Abbreviations

BYU	Brigham Young University, Provo, Utah
CN	*LDS Church News*
CRO	Cheshire Record Office
DC	*Doctrine and Covenants*
FHL	Family History Library, The Church of Jesus Christ of Latter-day Saints
HBLL	Harold B. Lee Library, Brigham Young University, Provo, Utah
HC	*History of The Church of Jesus Christ of Latter-day Saints*
JD	*Journal of Discourses*
JWML	J. Willard Marriott Library, University of Utah, Salt Lake City, Utah
LDS	The Church of Jesus Christ of Latter-day Saints
LRO	Lancashire Record Office
LDSMS	*The Latter-day Saints' Millennial Star*
PRO	Public Record Office

Chapter 1. "Among These Dark Satanic Mills"

1. Matthew L. Rasmussen, "The Advent of Mormonism in Lancashire's Upper Ribble Valley," unpublished MA dissertation, University of Lancaster, 2004, 29–34.
2. Grant Underwood, *The Millenarian World of Early Mormonism* (Urbana, Illinois: University of Illinois Press, 1993), 137.
3. Alan Rogers, *Approaches to Local History*, 2nd edition (New York: Longman, 1977), 2.
4. Hugh McLeod, *Religion and Society in England, 1850–1914* (New York: St. Martin's Press, 1996), 34.
5. Orson F. Whitney, *Life of Heber C. Kimball*, 2nd collector's edition reprint (Salt Lake City, Utah: Bookcraft, 1996), 187–88.
6. Heber C. Kimball, "Temple and Endowment—Raising Grain and Building Storehouses—Dedication," *Journal of Discourses* (hereafter JD), vol. 5: 22, Liverpool, 1857.
7. James R. Moss, "The Kingdom Builders," *Ensign*, December 1979, 27.
8. Ibid.
9. For further insight into the Mormon maritime experience in Liverpool, see Fred E. Woods, "The Tide of Mormon Migration Flowing Through the Port of Liverpool, England," *British Journal of Mormon Studies*, no. 1 (2008): 60–85.

10. Sheri L. Dew, *Go Forward with Faith: The Biography of Gordon B. Hinckley* (Salt Lake City, Utah: Deseret Book Company, 1996), 61–69.
11. LDS Church Archives, Elders Labor Record, Liverpool Conference, 1908–1939, LR 4949 21. Other records indicate that while in Lancashire Hinckley distributed 8,785 tracts and pamphlets, attended 191 meetings, held 200 gospel conversations, and spent over 400 hours with local church members (Dew, *Biography*, 69).
12. Sarah Jane Weaver, "Into All the World: Most Traveled President in History," *LDS Church News* (hereafter CN), week ending 2 February 2008.
13. Gerry Avant, "Reflecting on Mission, Turning Point in Life," CN, week ending 2 February 2008.
14. Chris Morales, "One Last Goodbye: Well-Wishers Pay Tribute with Tears of Joy, Gratitude," CN, week ending 9 February 2008.
15. John K. Walton, *Lancashire: A Social History, 1558–1939* (Manchester: Manchester University Press, 1987), 2.
16. It should be noted, however, that the Great Basin became the destination of the saints under the leadership of Joseph Smith's successor, Brigham Young. Before his death in 1844, Smith directed the saints to establish Zion at various locations in the states of Ohio, Missouri, and Illinois.
17. See Robert Curie, Alan Gilbert, and Lee Horsley, *Churches and Churchgoers: Patterns of Church Growth in the British Isles since 1700* (Oxford: Clarendon Press, 1977), 97 for a discussion of the effect of LDS emigration policy on its membership statistics in Britain.
18. Robert Lively asserts that the success of the British Mission in the mid-nineteenth century occurred "in direct relation to the stability of the church in America and its consequent ability to provide leadership and missionaries for the mission in Great Britain." See Robert L. Lively, "Some Sociological Reflections on the Nineteenth-Century British Mission," in *Mormons in Early Victorian Britain*, ed. Richard L. Jensen and Malcolm Thorp (Salt Lake City, Utah: University of Utah Press, 1989), 17.
19. Susan Easton Black, "Profile of a British Saint, 1837–1848," in *Regional Studies in Latter-day Saint Church History: The British Isles*, ed. Donald Q. Cannon (Provo, Utah: Department of Church History and Doctrine, Brigham Young University, 1990), 103.
20. Ibid., 104.
21. David J. Whittaker, "Mormonism in Victorian Britain: A Bibliographic Essay," in *Mormons in Early Victorian Britain*, ed. Richard L. Jensen and Malcolm R. Thorp, (Salt Lake City, Utah: University of Utah Press, 1989), 262.
22. Ibid., 262.
23. Dean L. May, "Mormons," in *Harvard Encyclopedia of American Ethnic Groups*, ed. Stephan Thernstrom (Cambridge, Massachusetts: Harvard University Press, 1980), 720–31. See also Thomas O'Dea, foreward to Nels Anderson, *Desert Saints: The Mormon Frontier in Utah* (Chicago: University of Chicago Press, 1966), xiv.
24. Elen Pifer, ed., *Vladimir Nabokov's Lolita: A Casebook* (New York: Oxford University Press, 2003), 201.
25. Curie, Gilbert, and Horsley, *Churches and Churchgoers*, 97.

26. Dean L. May, "Writing from within a Religious Tradition: A Mormon Perspective," *Journal of Mormon History* 28 (2002): 117.
27. Ibid.
28. Curie, Gilbert, and Horsley, *Churches and Churchgoers*, 98.
29. James B. Allen, Ronald K. Esplin, and David J. Whittaker, *Men With a Mission*, 53.
30. "Statistical Report of the Church in the British Islands, for the Half-Year Ending June 1st, 1851," *The Latter-Day Saints Millennial Star* (hereafter LDSMS) 13 (1851): 207.
31. James R. Moss, "The Kingdom Builders," *Ensign*, December 1979, 27.
32. Davies, *Mormon Spirituality*, 17–18.
33. Taylor, *Expectations Westward*, 154.
34. Leonard J. Arrington and Davis Bitton, *The Mormon Experience: A History of the Latter-day Saints* (New York: Alfred A. Knoph, 1979), 129.
35. Letter from Franklin D. Richards to John Taylor, March 2, 1855, quoted in *Truth Will Prevail: The Rise of The Church of Jesus Christ of Latter-day Saints in the British Isles 1837–1987*, ed. Bloxham, Moss, and Porter (Salt Lake City, Utah: Deseret Book, 1987), 177–78.
36. Letter from Brigham Young to Franklin D. Richards, September 30, 1855, LDSMS 17 (1855): 814–15, cited in Fred E. Woods, "Conveyance and Contribution: Mormon Scots Gather to an American Zion," *History Scotland*, no. 5 (August 2005): 3.
37. Edward P. Thompson, *The Making of the English Working Class* (New York: Vintage Books, 1963), 390, 801–2. See also W.H.G. Armytage, *Heavens Below; Utopian Experiments in England 1560–1960* (London: Routledge and K. Paul, 1961), 264.
38. Malcolm Thorp, "The Religious Backgrounds of Mormon Converts in Britain 1837–52," *Journal of Mormon History* 4 (1977): 64.
39. Thorp, "Religious Backgrounds," 65.
40. W.H.G. Armytage, "Liverpool, Gateway to Zion," *Pacific Northwest Quarterly* 48 (1957): 39.
41. Thorp, "Religious Backgrounds," 64.
42. Frederick S. Buchanan, "The Ebb and Flow of Mormonism in Scotland 1840–1900," *BYU Studies* 27 (1987): 30.
43. Bertrand Russell, *A History of Western Philosophy; and Its Connection with Political and Social Circumstances from the Earliest Times to the Present Day* (London: G. Allen and Unwin, 1946), xiv.
44. Mormon theology does not call for a separation between the spiritual and the temporal. As stated in a revelation received by Joseph Smith in 1830, "all things . . . are spiritual and not at any time [has the Lord] given . . . a law which was temporal." See Doctrine and Covenants (hereafter DC) 29:34.
45. Walton, *A Social History*, 1.
46. See appendix B, "A Timely Warning to the People of England," for evidence of this apocalyptic ethos. This broadside tract, written by Apostle Orson Hyde in Preston on August 19, 1837, and reproduced in Manchester in 1940, was widely distributed throughout Britain and represents an early eschatological perspective of Lancashire.
47. Hyde, "A Timely Warning," appendix B.

48. Heber C. Kimball, "Emigration—The Saints Warned to Repent or Judgments Will Come Upon Them," JD 4: 107.

Chapter 2. The Gathering

1. Fawn Brodie, *No Man Knows My History: The Life and Times of Joseph Smith the Mormon Prophet* (New York: Alfred A. Knopf, 1960), viii.
2. Joseph Smith and B. H. Roberts, *History of The Church of Jesus Christ of Latter-day Saints*, 2nd edition (hereafter HC) (Salt Lake City, Utah: Deseret Book Company, 1958), 2: 52.
3. *Teachings of Presidents of the Church: Joseph Smith* (Salt Lake City, Utah: The Church of Jesus Christ of Latter-day Saints, 2007), 520.
4. Joseph Fielding Smith, ed., *Teachings of the Prophet Joseph Smith* (Salt Lake City, Utah: Deseret News Press, 1938), 331.
5. Milton V. Backman, *The Heavens Resound: A History of the Latter-day Saints in Ohio, 1830–1838* (Salt Lake City, Utah: Deseret Book, 1983), 213.
6. LDSMS 1 (1840): 1
7. Beth Oyler, *Index to the Millennial Star*, vols. 1–80, 1840–1918, Special Collections, J. Willard Marriott Library (hereafter JWML), University of Utah.
8. Grant Underwood, *The Millenarian World of Early Mormonism* (Urbana, Illinois: University of Illinois Press, 1993), 127–38.
9. LDSMS 1 (1840): 5.
10. Ibid., 5–6.
11. Ibid., 263.
12. "A Proclamation, to the Saints Scattered Abroad," LDSMS 1 (1840): 271.
13. Joseph Smith, "The Purpose of the Gathering of Israel," in *Teachings of the Prophet Joseph Smith*, ed. Joseph Fielding Smith (Salt Lake City, Utah: Deseret Book Company, 1977), 307–308.
14. "Proclamation," LDSMS 1 (1840): 271.
15. Ibid., 273.
16. Ibid., 274.
17. HC 4: 346.
18. Editorial, LDSMS 5 (1844): 46–47.
19. "Mark of Respect Shown By the Latter-day Saints in Liverpool," Supplement to the LDSMS 5 (1844): 15.
20. LDS Church Archives, letter from Richard Halewood to siblings in Nauvoo, September 16, 1844, MS 15543.
21. DC 42:9, 36, 62, 67.
22. DC 124:51.
23. "Why Do the Saints Leave Nauvoo?" LDSMS 7 (1846): 73.
24. Ibid.
25. LDS Church Archives, manuscript history of the Liverpool Branch, 1846, LR 4948 2.
26. *Church History in the Fulness of Times* (Salt Lake City, Utah: The Church of Jesus Christ of Latter-day Saints, 2000), 294–95.
27. LDS Church Archives, manuscript history of the Liverpool Branch, 1862, LR 4948 2.

28. Brodie, *No Man Knows My History*, 283.
29. Richard L. Bushman, "Making Space for the Mormons," in *Believing History: Latter-day Saint Essays* (New York: Columbia University Press, 2004), 180.
30. HC 5: 85.
31. HC 6: 222.
32. "Elder Hedlock's Statement," LDSMS 7 (1846): 46.
33. "Address by Elder Hedlock," LDSMS 7 (1846): 123.
34. "Notices," LDSMS 8 (1846): 96.
35. Correspondence from Wilford Woodruff, LDSMS 7 (1846): 42.
36. "Tenth Letter of Orson Spencer to the Rev. W. Crowel, A.M." LDSMS 9 (1847): 308–11.
37. "Pioneers' Day," *Deseret Evening News*, July 26, 1880, 2, cited in *Church History in the Fulness of Times* (Salt Lake City, Utah: The Church of Jesus Christ of Latter-day Saints, 2000), 333. See also LDSMS 50 (1888): 561.
38. LDSMS 10 (1848): 40–41.
39. LDS Family History Library, record of members, Upholland Branch, 1848–1900, 87037 items 3–4.
40. Year-end statistical reports, LDSMS, 1849–1868.
41. LDS Church Archives, letter from George Reynolds to George Q. Cannon, August 20, 1864, manuscript history of the Liverpool Branch, LR 4948 2.
42. Moses 7:18.
43. LDSMS 14 (1852): 617.
44. Author's private collection, letter from Matthew and Jane Ellison to Betty Ellison, April 26, 1864, photocopy of original.
45. The details of the Spencer family are taken from an oral history interview with Dorothy Spencer Taylor, a direct descendent, conducted by the author at Clitheroe, Lancashire, April 7, 2004. Where possible, details concerning the family's migration have been verified by LDS genealogical resources, including its official website (www.familysearch.org) and the Mormon Immigration Index.
46. Family Group Record for Richard and Mary Spencer, http://www.familysearch.org/Eng/Search/frameset_search.asp, accessed on August 26, 2006.
47. *Mormon Immigration Index* (Intellectual Reserve, Inc., The Church of Jesus Christ of Latter-day Saints), CD-ROM.
48. Taylor, oral history.
49. LDS Church Archives, manuscript history of the Liverpool Branch, 1842, LR 4948 2.
50. LDS Church Archives, manuscript history of the Liverpool Branch, 1857, LR 4849 2.
51. LDS Family History Library (hereafter FHL), Upholland Branch council meeting minutes, August 14, 1855, 87037.
52. Ibid.
53. FHL, Upholland Branch council meeting minutes, 14 January 1856, 87037.
54. Heber C. Kimball, "Emigration—Saints Warned to Repent or Judgments Will Come Upon Them," JD 4: 107.
55. C. Mark Hamilton, *Nineteenth-Century Mormon Architecture and City Planning* (New York: Oxford University Press, 1995), 14.
56. "Purpose of Gathering," LDSMS 66 (1904): 40.

57. Letter from the First Presidency, LDSMS 55 (1893): 148–49.
58. Ibid.
59. Ibid.
60. "Trials Not Ended by Emigration," LDSMS 58 (1896): 120–21.
61. "The Gathering—Its Advantages," LDSMS 60 (1898): 351. For further discussion of the pivotal role played by George Q. Cannon in the reversal of the gathering doctrine, see Leonard J. Arrington and Davis Bitton, *The Mormon Experience: A History of the Latter-day Saints* (Urbana and Chicago, Illinois: University of Illinois Press, 1992), 140.
62. LDSMS 60 (1898): 351.
63. Ibid., 264.
64. LDSMS 62 (1900): 312.
65. "Purpose of Gathering," LDSMS 66 (1904): 40.
66. Ibid., 41.
67. LDSMS 71 (1909): 45–46.
68. LDSMS 66 (1904): 40.
69. Ibid.
70. DC 97:21.
71. Theologically, the saints justified the practice of proxy ordinances with the biblical precedent in 1 Corinthians 15:29, wherein the Apostle Paul refers to baptisms for the dead.
72. "The Purpose of Gathering," LDSMS 66 (1904): 41.
73. Ibid., 42.
74. Ibid., 40–41.
75. Statistics taken from 1877–1932 year-end statistical reports in the *Millennial Star* as compiled in Gordon Irving, *Information about British Mission Conferences*, LDS Church Archives, MS 17882.
76. "An Old Canard Revived," LDSMS 69 (1907): 536–37; "Following Up The Falsehood," LDSMS 69 (1907): 552–54; "Collapse of the 'Fifty-Four Girls' Canard," LDSMS 70 (1908): 616–18; "Statement by President Joseph F. Smith," LDSMS 73 (1911): 401–3.
77. The *Encyclopedia of Mormonism* indicates that, for Latter-day Saints, "the lost tribes are Israelites other than either the Jewish people or the Lamanites of the Book of Mormon." Their identification and emergence is significant to Mormonism because they are predicted to have a vital part to play "in the events of the last days." Mormon doctrine holds that Moses appeared to Joseph Smith in 1836 and transferred the "keys of the gathering of Israel."
78. "Gathering Pre-Ordained," LDSMS 80 (1918): 183.
79. Richard L. Jensen, "The Gathering to Zion," in *Truth Will Prevail*, ed. V. Ben Bloxham, James R. Moss, and Larry C. Porter, 197.
80. "Editorial: Stay Where You Are!" LDSMS 83 (1921): 584, 586.
81. "London Temple Progress," LDSMS, 118 (1956): 248.
82. Richard L. Evans, *A Century of "Mormonism" in Great Britain* (Salt Lake City, Utah: Deseret News Press, 1937), 240–41.
83. Evans, *A Century*, 241.
84. Letter from the First Presidency to the British Mission, August 28, 1945, as cited in "On Emigration to Zion," LDSMS 112 (1950): 199.

85. LDSMS 109 (1947): 383.
86. LDS Church Archives, "Manchester Stake 1960–1961," bound mimeograph, privately published by Robert Gordon Larsen, 1961, MS 17882.
87. LDSMS 121 (1959): 4.
88. Ibid., 243.
89. Isaiah 54:2; 3 Nephi 22:2.
90. Bruce R. McConkie, "Building Zion," *Liahona*, September 1977, 12.
91. *Official Report of the First British Area General Conference of The Church of Jesus Christ of Latter-day Saints* (The Church of Jesus Christ of Latter-day Saints, 1972), 6.
92. Ibid., 5.
93. LDSMS 122 (1960): 195.
94. *Deseret News 1999–2000 Church Almanac* (Salt Lake City, Utah: Deseret News, 2000), 400.
95. McConkie, *Liahona*, 12.
96. LDS Church Archives, Bessie Corless Morill and Gerturde Corless, oral history interview by Richard L. Jensen, 1987, typescript, 28, 32, James Moyle Oral History Program, History Department of The Church of Jesus Christ of Latter-day Saints, Salt Lake City, Utah, OH 868.

Chapter 3. Establishment and Expansion

1. Richard L. Evans, *A Century of "Mormonism" in Great Britain* (Salt Lake City, Utah: Deseret News Press, 1937), 244.
2. LDS Church Archives, Joseph Fielding to Hannah Fielding, March 27, 1839, MS 749 2. Note Fielding's citing of Luke 10:2.
3. DC 124:128.
4. HC 2: 488.
5. Ibid., 529.
6. Ibid., 489.
7. Some scholars are of the opinion that Joseph Smith dispatched Kimball to England as means of preventing him from siding with the growing numbers of opponents among the Twelve. This notion seems unlikely, however, when one considers that Orson Hyde, another member of the Twelve who was rather conspicuously at odds with the prophet during this time, was likewise sent to England as one of Kimball's missionary associates.
8. Orson Whitney's *The Life of Heber C. Kimball* (Salt Lake City, Utah: The Kimball Family, 1888) is perhaps the most noteworthy example. Whitney does not seek to mask his esteem for Kimball as both his grandfather and a member of the First Presidency of the church. By contrast, Stanley B. Kimball's *Heber C. Kimball: Mormon Patriarch and Pioneer* (Urbana, Illinois: University of Illinois Press, 1981) is noticeably more objective in its evaluation, although the author is also a direct descendent of Heber C. Kimball.
9. Whitney, *Kimball*, 191.
10. Ibid., 104. Note Kimball's reference to Isaiah 33:19.
11. Whitney, *Kimball*, 104.
12. Ibid., 105.

13. Ibid.
14. Kimball's own account suggests he was informed of his call to missionary service by Joseph Smith in the temple at Kirtland, Ohio, on Sunday, June 4, 1837. However, his ministerial certificate is dated June 2 and indicates Kimball's call to serve was determined "at a conference of the elders and heads of the Church." As a member of the Quorum of the Twelve Apostles, it seems likely that Kimball would have participated in the council that determined his presidency of the mission to England. Accordingly, Kimball's appointment to the British Mission may not have been as spontaneous as his personal reflections suggest.
15. LDS Church Archives, letter of recommendation for missionary service, issued to Heber C. Kimball, June 2, 1837, by Joseph Smith, Sidney Rigdon, and Hyrum Smith, MS 3458.
16. Whitney, *Kimball*, 104.
17. Ibid.
18. Brigham Young, "Why Success Attends the Ministerial Labours of Some Elders, and Not Those of Others," JD 4: 305.
19. See appendix A for a transcription of a letter written by Kimball to the converts of Chatburn and Downham that partially elucidates this matter.
20. HC 2: 493.
21. HC 4: 541.
22. Whitney, *Kimball*, 148.
23. HC 2: 505.
24. Stanley Kimball, *Heber C. Kimball: Mormon Patriarch and Pioneer* (Urbana, Illinois: University of Illinois Press, 1981), 54, note 18.
25. Kimball, *Heber C. Kimball*, 47.
26. Heber C. Kimball and Orson Hyde to Isaac Russell, September 7, 1837, as cited in Malcolm Thorp, "The Setting for the Restoration in Britain: Political, Social, and Economic Conditions," ed. Ben Bloxham, James Moss, and Larry Porter, *Truth Will Prevail: The Rise of The Church of Jesus Christ of Latter-day Saints in the British Isles, 1837–1987* (Salt Lake City, Utah: Intellectual Reserve, 1987), 67.
27. Michael Sanderson, "Literacy and Social Mobility in the Industrial Revolution in England," in *Past and Present*, 56 (1972): 85. This estimate is based on the literacy scores for the 1830s in the parishes of Whalley, Ribchester, Blackburn, Penwortham, and Leyland.
28. It is important to note that Alston was largely transformed in the early nineteenth century by a Primitive Methodist mission. See John Petty, *The History of the Primitive Methodist Connexion: From Its Origin to the Conference of 1860, the First Jubilee Year of the Connexion* (London: John Dickenson, 1880), 203–5. The extent to which Primitive Methodism influenced popular religious attitudes prior to the coming of the Mormons deserves further research.
29. See Gordon K. Thomas, "The Book of Mormon in the English Literary Context of 1837," *BYU Studies* 27 (1987): 37–46, for a brief but novel analysis of the reasons why the Book of Mormon may have been deemed controversial at the outset of the British Mission.
30. For further discussion of the Book of Mormon as a "sacred sign," see Terryl Givens, *By the Hand of Mormon: The American Scripture that Launched a New World Religion* (Oxford; New York: Oxford University Press, 2002), 62–88.

31. Oral history suggests that by the mid-twentieth century the Book of Mormon was central to the LDS proselytizing program. See appendix D for two examples of the pronounced role of the Book of Mormon in individual conversionary experiences.
32. LDS Church Archives, letter from Willard Richards to John Child, February 27, 1841, MS 7120.
33. Special Collections, JWML, University of Utah, Samuel Hawthornthwaite, "Mr. Hawthornthwaite's Adventures among the Mormons As an Elder During Eight Years" (self published in Manchester, 1857), 78.
34. LDS Church Archives, manuscript history of the Liverpool Branch, July 23, 1840, LR 4949 2.
35. LDS Church Archives, Richards to Child, 1841.
36. FHL, record of members of the Chatburn Branch, 1838–1854, 86990; record of members of the Clitheroe Branch, 1838–1885, 86992.
37. Matthew L. Rasmussen, "The Advent of Mormonism in Lancashire's Upper Ribble Valley," unpublished master's thesis, University of Lancaster, 63–64.
38. Milton V. Backman, *The Heavens Resound: A History of the Latter-day Saints in Ohio, 1830–1838* (Salt Lake City, Utah: Deseret Book Press, 2002), 82–100, 211–36.
39. W.H.G. Armytage, "Liverpool, Gateway to Zion," *Pacific Northwest Quarterly* 48 (1957): 39.
40. Armytage's reference to angels stems from a revelation received by Joseph Smith on July 12, 1843. See HC 5: 502 and DC 132:15–16. The deification of man, also referred to by Armytage, was not taught by Joseph Smith until April 7, 1844 at a sermon in Nauvoo, Illinois. See "The King Follett Sermon," *Ensign*, May 1971, 13.
41. James B. Allen, Ronald K. Esplin, and David J. Whittaker, *Men with a Mission 1837–1841: The Quorum of the Twelve Apostles in the British Isles* (Salt Lake City, Utah: Deseret Book Company, 1992), 135–37.
42. Lewis R. Rambo, *Understanding Religious Conversion* (New Haven, Connecticut: Yale University Press, 1994), 168–69.
43. LDS Church Archives, autobiographical sketch of Mary Haskin Parker Richards, MS 13843.
44. Whitney, *Kimball*, 171.
45. Richard Carwardine, *Transatlantic Revivalism: Popular Evangelicalism in Britain and America, 1790–1865* (London: Greenwood Press, 1978), 67.
46. Malcolm Thorp, "Setting for the Restoration," in *Truth Will Prevail*, 44.
47. *Preston Chronicle*, March 17, 1838, as cited in *Truth Will Prevail*, 95.
48. Rambo, *Conversion*, 167.
49. Ibid.
50. See appendix A for the full text of this letter, which reveals Kimball's paternal outlook on his converts from Chatburn and Downham.
51. LDS Church Archives, letter from Heber C. Kimball to Edward Martin, September 11, 1840, MS 6135 folder 3. Note Kimball's reference to Revelation 3:40.
52. LDS Church Archives, letter from Vilate Kimball to Heber C. Kimball, September 1840, MS 3276 2.
53. LDS Church Archives, Richards, autobiography, MS 13843.

54. Heber C. Kimball, "Emigration—The Saints Warned to Repent or Judgments Will Come Upon Them," JD 4: 105, 107.
55. Journal of Joseph Fielding, 57, as cited in *Truth Will Prevail*, 92.
56. Heber C. Kimball to Parley P. Pratt, LDSMS 1 (1840): 37.
57. Cheshire Records Office (hereafter CRO), 1804 visitation returns, Downham, Mf 44/11, as cited in *The Church of England in Industrializing Society: The Lancashire Parish of Whalley in the 18th Century*, ed. M. F. Snape (Woodbridge, Suffolk: The Boydell Press, 2003), 193.
58. CRO, 1804 visitation returns, Altham and Accrington, Mf 44/10, as cited in *Church in Industrializing Society*, 193.
59. Whitney, *Kimball*, 169–70.
60. LDSMS 1 (1840): 38.
61. Snape, *Church in Industrializing Society*, 193–99.
62. CRO, EDC 5 1731/21, as cited in *Church in Industrializing Society*, 12.
63. Thomas Whitaker, *An History of the Original Parish of Whalley and Honour of Clitheroe*, vol. 2 (London, 1872–76), 244.
64. Hugh McLeod, *Religion and Society in England, 1850–1914* (New York: St. Martin's Press, 1996), 32.
65. Oral history interview with Right Honourable Ralph Assheton, Lord of Clitheroe, Downham Hall, April 1, 2004. It should be noted that although the influence of the Asshetons within the Pendle region extends back to the sixteenth century, it was only after 1800 that the family took up permanent residence in the upper Ribble Valley.
66. Assheton, oral history, April 1, 2004.
67. Assheton family library, Downham Hall, Downham, Lancashire, rent book, 1838.
68. Geoffrey Timmins, *The Last Shift: The Decline of Handloom Weaving in Nineteenth-Century Lancashire* (Manchester: Manchester University Press, 1993), 91–103.
69. Diary of Robert Campbell, as cited in *Men With A Mission*, ed. Allen, Esplin, and Whittaker (Salt Lake City, Utah: Deseret Book Company, 1992), 339.
70. LDS Church Archives, Parley Parker Pratt to Mary Ann Pratt, April 6, 1840, MS 81.
71. LDS Church Archives, manuscript history of the Liverpool Branch, 1840, LR 4948 2.
72. LDS Church Archives, manuscript history of the Douglas Branch, 1840, LR 2301 2.
73. LDS Church Archives, Heber C. Kimball to John Taylor, November 9, 1840, MS 20533.
74. H. George Bickerstaff, "Gifts of the Spirit," in *Encyclopedia of Mormonism*, ed. Daniel H. Ludlow (New York: Macmillan Publishing Company, 1992), 2: 546.
75. Mark 16:7
76. *Encyclopedia of Mormonism*, 2: 545.
77. Allen, Esplin, and Whittaker, *Men With A Mission*, 197.
78. Scott G. Kenney, ed., *Wilford Woodruff's Journal, 1833–1898* (Midvale, Utah: Signature Books), 1: 506.
79. DC 88:81.
80. Allen, Esplin, and Whittaker, *Men With A Mission*, 61.
81. http://www.familysearch.org, ancestral file for Henry Stocks.
82. LDS Church Archives, journal of Henry Stocks, 1844–70, MS 9274.
83. Ibid., July 1846.
84. Ibid., March 1849.

85. Ibid., August 1849.
86. Ibid.
87. Ibid., November 1849.
88. Ibid., April 1850.
89. Ibid., June 1850.
90. Ibid., July 1850.
91. Ibid., September 1850.
92. Ibid.
93. Ibid.
94. Ibid., November 1850.
95. Ibid., February 1851.
96. Ibid., July 1853.
97. Ibid., February 1854.
98. Rambo, *Conversion*, 168–69.
99. Douglas Davies, *An Introduction to Mormonism* (Cambridge: Cambridge University Press, 2003), 16.

Chapter 4. Consolidation and Decline

1. LDSMS 11 (1849): 346.
2. LDS Church Archives, manuscript history of the Liverpool Conference, LR 4949 2.
3. LDS Church Archives, manuscript history of the Preston Conference, December 1, 1851, LR 7179 2.
4. LDS Church Archives, manuscript history of the Clitheroe Branch, January 7, 1857, LR 2421 2.
5. LDS Church Archives, manuscript history of the Preston Conference, June 30, 1855, LR 7179 2.
6. *Church History in the Fulness of Times*, (Church Educational System, The Church of Jesus Christ of Latter-day Saints, 2000), 358.
7. LDS Church Archives, manuscript history of the Liverpool Conference, July 8, 1856.
8. LDS Church Archives, statistical report, manuscript history of the Preston Conference, December 31, 1857, LR 7180 2.
9. "The Mormons in England," *New York Times*, August 1, 1867, 2.
10. LDSMS 30 (1868): 393.
11. Letter from Henry Leigh to Joseph F. Smith, June 3, 1874, LDSMS 36 (1874): 363.
12. Letter from Bedson Eardley and William Barton to Joseph F. Smith, October 15, 1874, LDSMS 36 (1874): 668–69.
13. Michael F. Snape, *The Church of England in Industrializing Society: The Lancashire Parish of Whalley in the 18th Century* (Woodbridge, Suffolk: The Boydell Press 2003), 193–99.
14. FHL, membership register of the Preston Conference, 1837–1862, 87028.
15. L. Tom Perry Special Collections, Harold B. Lee Library (hereafter HBLL), Brigham Young University, journal of William Athole McMaster, MSS 160.
16. LDS Church Archives, journal of Jesse Bigler Martin, 1853–1854, MS 8209.
17. Jesse Martin, journal, December 1853.

18. FHL, membership register of the Preston Branch, 87028.
19. FHL, Liverpool Conference Elders Record 1898–1902, membership register of the Preston Branch, 87028.
20. 1853–1854 membership data taken from year-end statistical reports, LDSMS 16 (1854): 78; 17 (1855): 75. 1855–1859 membership data taken from LDS Church Archives, European Mission statistical reports 1855–1876, CR 271 4.
21. LDS Church Archives, European Mission statistical reports 1855–1876, CR 271 4.
22. Letter from Septimus Sears to George Q. Cannon, February 18, 1865, LDSMS 27 (1865): 157.
23. This conclusion was arrived at through comparative analysis of twelve separate missionary journals kept between 1870 and 1895. Of these twelve missionaries, nine were born in the English North West or lived there for some time prior to emigration. Two were born in Utah to parents who hailed from either Lancashire or Cheshire. Only one missionary of those surveyed was neither from Lancashire nor of immediate Lancastrian descent.
24. LDS Church Archives, letter from George Reynolds to Eliza Hickock, June 13, 1871, MS 13759.
25. LDS Church Archives, letter from George Reynolds to Daniel H. Wells, July 13, 1871, MS 13759.
26. LDS Church Archives, letter from George Reynolds to Septimus W. Sears, June 14, 1871, MS 13759.
27. LDS Church Archives, letter from George Reynolds to G.E.G. Taylor, June 14, 1871, MS 13759.
28. LDS Church Archives, letter from George Reynolds to Septimus W. Sears, June 14, 1871, MS 13759.
29. LDS Church Archives, journal of Frederick William Chappell, June 21, 1890, MS 13921.
30. LDS Church Archives, journal of Daniel Kent Greene, June 11, 1887, MS 16828.
31. Daniel Kent Greene, journal, 1887, MS 16828.
32. LDS Church Archives, letter from George Reynolds to G.E.G. Taylor, June 14, 1871, MS 13759.
33. LDS Church Archives, journal of William Bell Barton, June 1874, MS 17150.
34. LDS Church Archives, letter from George Reynolds to Thomas McIntyre, June 3, 1871, MS 13759.
35. Letter from John T. Caine to Joseph F. Smith, June 23, 1875, LDSMS 37 (1875): 413.
36. Ibid., 413.
37. Ibid.
38. Letter from George Crane to William Budge, August 21, 1880, LDSMS 42 (1880): 555.
39. Ibid.
40. LDS Church Archives, journal of George Parkinson, April 22–24, 1883, MS 15190.
41. Ibid., May 2, 1883.
42. LDS Church Archives, journal of Thomas Jackson, December 1880, MS 8363.
43. Frederick William Chappell, journal, July 5, 1890.
44. LDS Church Archives, journal of George Clark Rigby, October 17, 1893, MS 19195.
45. LDS Church Archives, Horace E. Hayes, oral history interview by Chad M. Orton, 1988, typescript, 1–2, James Moyle Oral History Program, Church History Department, The Church of Jesus Christ of Latter-day Saints, OH 1243.

46. Matthew 10:35–36.
47. Thomas Jackson, journal, December 1880–September 1881.
48. LDS Church Archives, journal of William Jones, 1893–1895, MS 15511.
49. George Parkinson, journal, May 13, 1883.
50. Ibid., May 20, 1883.
51. Thomas Sleight, journal, 1886.
52. Daniel Kent Greene, journal, June 1887.
53. George Parkinson notes the visit of LDS leader Orson F. Whitney to Preston, where he delivered a lecture titled "The Faith and Practice of the Latter-day Saints in Utah." See George Parkinson, journal, February 18, 1883.
54. The clearest examples are found in the LDS Church Archives, journal of Stephen Longstroth Richards, 1877–1878, MS 16661; and the journal of Brigham Davies, 1893–1894, MS 15924.
55. Frederick Chappell, journal, June 22, 1890.
56. Ibid., August 31, 1890.
57. Brigham Davies, journal, May 29, 1893.
58. Frederick Chappell, journal, August 31, 1890.
59. Ibid., August 20, 1890.
60. Ibid., August 10, 1890.
61. LDS Church Archives, journal of Henry Whittaker Lunt, April 19, 1893, MS 9639.
62. George Parkinson, journal, February 11, 1883.
63. Ibid., February 6–7 1883.
64. Ibid., February 10, 1883.
65. Letter from Bedson Eardley and William Barton to Joseph F. Smith, October 15, 1874, LDSMS 36 (1874): 668–69.
66. George Parkinson, journal, February 2, 1883.
67. Ibid.
68. Ibid., May 1, 1883.
69. Daniel Greene, journal, March 17, 1888.
70. Henry Whittaker Lunt, journal, December 15, 1893.
71. Ibid.

Chapter 5. Opponents, Apostates, and Dissenters

1. Special Collections, JWML, University of Utah, John Bowes, "Mormonism Exposed, in Its Licentious Abominations, Refuted in Its Principles, and in the Claims of Its Head, the Modern Mohammed, Joseph Smith, Who Is Proved To Be a Deceiver and No Prophet of God" (London: E. Ward, n.d.), 1–71.
2. DC 1:30.
3. James E. Talmage, *The Great Apostasy: Considered in the Light of Scriptural and Secular History* (Salt Lake City, Utah, Deseret News, 1909), iii.
4. Anthony Hewitson, *Our Churches and Chapels, Their Parsons, Priests, & Congregations; Being a Critical and Historical Account of Every Place of Worship in Preston* (Preston, Lancashire: Preston Chronicle Office, Fishergate, 1869), 110.

5. Malcolm R. Thorp, "Sectarian Violence in Early Victorian Britain: The Mormon Experience 1837–1860," *Bulletin of the John Rylands Library*, 70 (1988): 144.
6. Craig L. Foster, *Penny Tracts and Polemics: A Critical Analysis of Anti-Mormon Pamphleteering in Great Britain 1837–1860* (Salt Lake City, Utah: Greg Kofford Books, 2002), 205–6. See also Malcolm R. Thorp, "Winifred Graham and the Mormon Image," *Journal of Mormon History* 6 (1979): 107–21.
7. Leonard J. Arrington, "Mormonism: Views from Without and Within," *BYU Studies* 14 no. 2 (1974): 140.
8. LDSMS 19 (1857): 723–25.
9. LDSMS 18 (1856): 648–51.
10. HC 4: 540.
11. Hewitson, *Our Churches and Chapels*, 112.
12. Stephen J. Fleming, "The Religious Heritage of the British Northwest and the Rise of Mormonism," *Church History* 77 no. 1 (2008): 73–74.
13. LDS Church Archives, letter from the Reverend James Fielding to Joseph Fielding, August 27, 1838, MS 749 1.
14. Foster, *Penny Tracts*, 51–52.
15. Allen, Esplin, and Whittaker, *Men With a Mission*, 240.
16. For further discussion of the significance of pamphlet production during Mormonism's formative years, see David J. Whittaker, "Early Mormon Pamphleteering," unpublished Ph.D. thesis, Brigham Young University, 1982, 1–92.
17. LDS Church Archives, journal of Frederick William Chapell, October 1890, MS 13921; journal of George Clark Rigby, January 1895, MS 19195. Specific mention of Hyde's pamphlet is made in both journals.
18. LDS Church Archives, Sylvia Mills Whalley, oral history interview by Richard L. Jensen, Ashton-under-Lyne, Greater Manchester, July 24, 1987, typescript, 6, James Moyle Oral History Program, Church History Department, The Church of Jesus Christ of Latter-day Saints, OH 879.
19. See appendix B for a transcription of the full text of Hyde's pamphlet.
20. Warren A. Jennings, "The Lynching of an American Prophet," *BYU Studies* 40 no. 1 (2001): 205–6.
21. HC 4: 416–17, 444–45; HC 5: 61.
22. Letter from David Wells Kilbourne to the Reverend Thomas Dent, June 29, 1844, in Jennings, "Lynching," 207.
23. Kilbourne to Dent, 210.
24. Kilbourne to Dent, 211.
25. LDS Church Archives, letter from William and Ann Parry to unnamed children, September 15, 1844, MS 15543.
26. Ibid.
27. LDS Church Archives, letter from Richard Halewood to Richard Moon, September 16, 1844, MS 15543.
28. HC 4: 540.
29. Malcolm R. Thorp, "Sectarian Violence in Early Victorian Britain: The Mormon Experience, 1837–1860," in *Bulletin of the John Rylands University Library of Manchester*, 70

(1988): 135–47. Additional work of note includes Thorp, "Early Mormon Confrontations with Sectarianism, 1837–40," in *Mormonism in Early Victorian Britain*, ed. Richard L. Jensen and Malcolm R. Thorp, 49–69; and Thorp, "The Mormon Peril: The Crusade against the Saints in Britain, 1910–1914," *Journal of Mormon History* 2 (1975): 69–88.

30. Thorp, "Sectarian Violence," 138.
31. Ibid., 144.
32. For a regional study of anti-Mormonism in the West Midlands, see John Cotterill, "Midland Saints: the Mormon Mission in the West Midlands, 1837–77," unpublished Ph.D. thesis, University of Keele, 1985, 306–71.
33. LDS Church Archives, manuscript history of the Chester Branch, January 2, 1844, LR 1640 2.
34. LDS Church Archives, manuscript history of the Chester Branch, 1850.
35. LDS Church Archives, journal of Henry Stocks, September 17, 1850, MS 9274.
36. Ibid., November 4, 1850.
37. Ibid., March 7, 12, 1851.
38. Andrew Hepburn's own arguments concerning Mormonism were later delineated in his pamphlet "Mormonism Exploded, or, the Religion of the Latter-day Saints: Proved to be a System of Imposture, Blasphemy, and Immorality," (London: Simpkin, Marshall, & Co., 1855).
39. Henry Stocks, journal, March 16, 1851.
40. Ibid., April 8, 1851.
41. Ibid., June 25, 1851.
42. Ibid., June 29, 1851.
43. LDS Church Archives, manuscript history of the Chester Branch, June 29, 1851, LR 1640 2.
44. Luke 9:5.
45. Henry Stocks, journal, July 22, 1851.
46. B.H. Roberts, *The Life of John Taylor, Third President of The Church of Jesus Christ of Latter-day Saints* (Salt Lake City, Utah: G.Q. Cannon, 1892), 89–91.
47. LDS Church Archives, manuscript history of the Douglas Branch, September 1840, LR 2301 2.
48. Ibid., October 1840.
49. LDSMS 1 (1840): 214.
50. LDSMS 2 (1841): 6.
51. LDS Church Archives, manuscript history of the Douglas Branch, December 1840.
52. LDSMS 19 (1857): 600. See also LDS Church Archives, manuscript history of the Douglas Branch, 1857, LR 2301 2.
53. LDS Church Archives, manuscript history of the Douglas Branch, 1863.
54. Letter from Henry Leigh to Joseph F. Smith, LDSMS 36 (1874): 365.
55. Ibid.
56. Ibid.
57. LDSMS 16 (1854): 283–85, 359, 389–92.
58. Key among these critics was Samuel Hawthornthwaite, whose anti-Mormon pamphlet—which features the Alston Marsden case—is analyzed later in the chapter.
59. LDS Church Archives, journal of William George Phillips, July 1887, MS 14471.

60. Ibid., July 1887.
61. LDSMS 50 (1888): 732–35.
62. Ibid., 667–68.
63. LDSMS 50 (1888): 763–64.
64. LDSMS 45 (1883): 840.
65. LDSMS 50 (1888): 486.
66. William Phillips, journal, July 1887.
67. LDSMS 50 (1888): 732.
68. Ibid., 733.
69. "Private Lecture on 'Mormonism.'—A Protest," *Bolton Weekly Guardian*, February 15, 1889, reprinted in LDSMS 51 (1889): 150.
70. *Eccles Advertiser*, July 27, 1889, reprinted in LDSMS 51 (1889): 517–18.
71. LDSMS 51 (1889): 660–62.
72. Anti-Mormon persecution by former members was not restricted to the nineteenth century. See LDS Church Archives, Bessie Corless Morrill, oral history interview by Richard L. Jensen, 1987, typescript, 15, James Moyle Oral History Program, Church History Department, The Church of Jesus Christ of Latter-day Saints, OH 868. Morrill's interview references mid-twentieth-century disturbances caused by disgruntled former members, including a particularly compelling example of a former member preaching against the Latter-day Saints in Preston in 1967. Identical to his nineteenth-century predecessors, this individual's protests also involved the sale of anti-Mormon literature.
73. The Latter-day Saints' sensitivity to individual apostasy was no doubt heightened by their belief in the "Great Apostasy"—the corruption that devastated the original church established by Christ and the apostles of the New Testament.
74. Special Collections, JWML, University of Utah, J. Benjamin Franklin, "A Cheap Trip to the Great Salt Lake City, an Annotated Lecture Delivered before the President of America and Representatives; the Mayors of Liverpool and Manchester" (Ipswich, Suffolk: J. Scoggins, 1864).
75. Ibid., 4.
76. Special Collections, JWML, University of Utah, Samuel Hawthornthwaite, "Mr. Hawthornthwaite's Adventures among the Mormons As an Elder during Eight Years" (self-published in Manchester, 1857), 4.
77. Ibid., 50.
78. Franklin, "A Cheap Trip," 8.
79. Ibid., 2.
80. DC 89:9–11.
81. Franklin, "A Cheap Trip," 4.
82. Hawthornthwaite, "Adventures," 29.
83. Ibid., 80.
84. Ibid., 111–12.
85. This is likely a mistaken reference to the "six points" of Chartism outlined in 1837 by the London Working Men's Association: 1) manhood suffrage, 2) secret ballot, 3) no property qualification, 4) payment of members, 5) equal electoral districts, and 6) annual parliaments.

86. Hawthornthwaite, "Adventures," 77–78.
87. Franklin, "A Cheap Trip," 4.
88. Lewis R. Rambo, *Understanding Religious Conversion* (New Haven, Connecticut: Yale University Press, 1994), 170.
89. Hawthornthwaite, "Adventures," 4.
90. Franklin, "A Cheap Trip," 5.
91. Hawthornthwaite, "Adventures," 4.
92. LDS Church Archives, Robert Aveson, "Apostasy, Its Cause and Effect," unpublished pamphlet, MS 261.
93. Ibid.
94. Ibid.
95. FHL, membership register of the Ashton-under-Lyne Branch 1837–1889, 86976, item 9.
96. FHL, membership register of the Middlewich Branch 1840–1865, 87044, item 1.
97. FHL, record of members of the Chatburn Branch 1837–1854, 86990, item 29.
98. LDSMS 31 (1869): 779.
99. LDSMS 12 (1850): 280–83.
100. Letter from Andrew Ferguson to Franklin D. Richards, August 28, 1854, LDSMS 16 (1854): 606.

Chapter 6. Revivals and Reversals

1. These British Mission statistics (1877–1892) are taken from the year-end statistical reports of the *Millennial Star*. For a more accessible compilation of these reports, see LDS Church Archives, Gordon Irving, "Information about British Mission Conferences, 1877–1932."
2. Irving, "Information about British Mission Conferences," 45, 47.
3. The resurgence may be explained in part by what Hugh McLeod identified as the "ethos of experimentation and of moral and intellectual individualism that was particularly characteristic of the 1890s." See McLeod, *Religion and Society in England 1850–1914* (New York: St. Martin's Press, 1996), 54.
4. Richard L. Jensen, "The British Gathering to Zion," in *Truth Will Prevail*, ed. Bloxham, Moss, and Porter, 189. For a more recent perspective, see David M. Morris, "The Rhetoric of the Gathering and Zion: Constancy through Change 1830–1920," *International Journal of Mormon Studies* 1 (2008): 165–66.
5. Notwithstanding the change in policy, the membership in Lancashire continued to pursue emigration in the first decade of the 1900s, albeit at a slower rate. Between 1900 and 1910 approximately six hundred Latter-day Saints emigrated from the North West, a twenty-five percent decline from the 1880s.
6. "Apostle Francis M. Lyman's Address," LDSMS 63 (1901): 369–70.
7. "Among the Conferences," LDSMS 63 (1901): 374–75.
8. LDS Church Archives, British Mission Statistics 1877–1932, as compiled in Irving, "Information about British Mission Conferences," 39, 45, 47. Between 1892 and 1911, membership in the Liverpool Conference grew from 115 to 1,009. During the same period, membership in the Manchester Conference increased from 157 to 649.

9. For a useful list of membership statistics in Britain from 1837 to 1970, see Robert Currie, Alan Gilbert, and Lee Horsley, *Churches and Churchgoers: Patterns of Church Growth in the British Isles since 1700* (Oxford: Clarendon Press, 1977), 156–58.
10. "Apostle Francis M. Lyman's Address," LDSMS 63 (1901): 369.
11. Ibid., 370.
12. LDS Church Archives, journal of George C. Parkinson, February 10, 1883.
13. LDS Church Archives, journal of Brigham Davies, July 5, 1893.
14. The 1908 placement of the Liverpool Conference headquarters in Preston helped maintain the town's status as the center of British Mormonism. See LDSMS 70 (1908): 638.
15. FHL, membership register of the Manchester Branch 1901–1909, 87044, item 3.
16. Ibid.
17. FHL, membership register of the Barrow Branch 1904–1909, 86977, item 10.
18. Ibid.
19. This is not to suggest that the death of Mary Shepherd Gregson was the primary justification for the amalgamation of the Barrow and Lancaster Branches. The Lancaster Branch, regarded as "one of the most prosperous fields of the [Liverpool] conference" by mission leadership in 1902, was greatly weakened by emigration in 1904. The merger of the two congregations was likely motivated by the need to secure the viability of both branches. See LDS Church Archives, manuscript history of the Lancaster Branch 1904, LR 4948 2.
20. Lyman defined the boundaries of the Manchester and Liverpool Conferences as follows: "Manchester includes [Cheshire] and that part of [Lancashire] that lies within straight lines drawn from the east side of Warrington to the south side of Darwen, and from that point to the south side of Bacup and on to the boundary of the county. The Liverpool Conference has the remainder of [Lancashire], including Warrington, Darwen, Bacup, together with Westmoreland [sic] and the Isle of Man." These instructions were inserted into the membership registers kept throughout Britain beginning in 1901, the first year of Lyman's presidency. For an example, see FHL, membership register of the Lancaster Branch, 87008, item 10.
21. "British Mission Statistics," LDSMS 65 (1903): 87.
22. "British Mission Statistics," LDSMS 67 (1905): 205; 68 (1906): 119.
23. *Church History in the Fulness of Times* (Salt Lake City, Utah: Church Educational System, The Church of Jesus Christ of Latter-day Saints, 2000), 456.
24. LDSMS 69 (1907): 693.
25. Charles W. Penrose, "To the Missionaries in the British Isles," LDSMS 69 (1907): 24–25.
26. The titles of the tracts are as follows: 1) Introduction—Necessity of Obedience; 2) Character of the Godhead; 3) The Atonement—First Principles of the Gospel; 4) The Gift of the Holy Ghost; 5) Divine Authority; 6) A Departure from the Faith; 7) The Restoration of the Gospel; 8) The Book of Mormon; 9) Modern Revelation; 10) Salvation for the Dead; 11) Baptism for the Dead; and 12) Fruits of the Gospel.
27. The content of these twelve tracts were made available to the British church between March and September 1898. The complete text can be found in LDSMS 60 (1898): 201–4; 217–21; 235–39; 265–69; 296–300; 312–16; 328–32; 361–66; 401–5; 523–27; 588–92; 595–99. Penrose's year-end report for 1908 notes that the Liverpool office printed

1,225,000 copies of "Rays of Living Light." The tracts, Penrose noted, were consistently "in great demand." See LDSMS 70 (1908): 860. Evidence of the earliest distribution of these tracts in Lancashire can be found in FHL, "Elders' Tracting Record 1899," membership register of the Preston Branch, 87028.

28. LDSMS 60 (1898): 204.
29. Robert Price, "Results of an Open-Air Meeting" LDSMS 69 (1907): 93–94.
30. Walter M. Douglas, "How I Found the Truth," LDSMS 69 (1907): 172.
31. LDSMS 69 (1907): 24.
32. Ibid., 25.
33. Ibid., 510.
34. Ibid., 204.
35. LDSMS 70 (1908): 462.
36. British Mission statistics report the baptism of just over 1,200 converts in 1908. The contribution of the Liverpool Conference was thus unparalleled anywhere in the British Mission, with 218 converts reported. The contribution of the Manchester Conference was noticeably more modest. With 72 converts reported in 1908, the Manchester Conference was below even the national conference average of 94. See Irving, "Information about British Mission Conferences," 39, 45.
37. "The Lord's Work in the Past Year," LDSMS 70 (1908): 859.
38. "Special to our Missionaries," LDSMS 71 (1909): 9.
39. *Cheshire Post*, April 28, 1907, reprinted in LDSMS 69 (1907): 236.
40. *Gloucestershire Echo*, September 30, 1907, reprinted in LDSMS 69 (1907): 635.
41. LDSMS 69 (1907): 636–39.
42. LDSMS 70 (1908): 520–23; 533–34.
43. Ibid., 584.
44. Malcolm R. Thorp, "'The Mormon Peril': The Crusade against the Saints in Britain 1910–1914," *Journal of Mormon History* 2: 70.
45. Malcolm R. Thorp, "Winifred Graham and the Mormon Image in England," *Journal of Mormon History* 6: 115–19.
46. *Christian Statesman*, February 1917, 51: 84.
47. Thorp, "The Mormon Peril," 87. Columnist Abby Clay received specific mention in an oral history interview with Elsie Rickard, a convert from Wigan. See LDS Church Archives, Elsie Rickard, oral history interview by Chad M. Orton, 1986, typescript, 4, James Moyle Oral History Program, Church History Department, The Church of Jesus Christ of Latter-day Saints, CR 884 85.
48. Irving, "Information about British Mission Conferences," 39.
49. Brian Q. Cannon and Jacob W. Olmstead, "'Scandalous Film': The Campaign to Suppress Anti-Mormon Motion Pictures 1911–12," *Journal of Mormon History* 29: 47.
50. Raymond Wells, missionary journal, July 14, 1913, author's private collection, photocopy of original.
51. Ibid., July 17, 1913.
52. "Mormons Ejected: Scene at Garston Cinematograph Entertainment," *Liverpool Post and Mercury*, December 12, 1911; "The Anti-'Mormon' Moving Pictures and Play," LDSMS 73 (1911): 808–11.

53. Special Collections, JWML, University of Utah, Rudger Clawson Papers, Letters to the First Presidency, November 7, 1911.
54. Ibid., February 21, 1912.
55. Liverpool Conference Statistics 1912, in Irving, "Information about British Mission Conferences," 45.
56. R.C.K. Ensor, *England 1870–1914* (Oxford: Clarendon Press, 1936), 532.
57. Thorp, "The Mormon Peril," 88.
58. LDS Church Archives, V. Adelaide Tope, oral history interview by Richard L. Jensen, 1987, typescript, 2, James Moyle Oral History Program, Church History Department, The Church of Jesus Christ of Latter-day Saints, OH 885.
59. Ibid.
60. LDS Church Archives, Sylvia Mills Whalley, oral history interview by Chad M. Orton, 1987, typescript, 4, James Moyle Oral History Program, Church History Department, The Church of Jesus Christ of Latter-day Saints, OH 879.
61. LDS Church Archives, Horace Hayes, oral history interview by Chad M. Orton, 1988, typescript, 72, James Moyle Oral History Program, Church History Department, The Church of Jesus Christ of Latter-day Saints, OH 1243.
62. Ibid., 17.
63. Ibid.
64. Ibid., 17–18.
65. Ibid., 19.
66. LDS Church Archives, Gertrude Corless, oral history interview by Richard L. Jensen, 1987, typescript, 5, James Moyle Oral History Program, Church History Department, The Church of Jesus Christ of Latter-day Saints, OH 868.
67. Rickard, oral history, 4.
68. Hayes, oral history, 19.
69. LDS Church Archives, Derek J. Plumbley, oral history interview by Richard L. Jensen, 1987, typescript, 6, James Moyle Oral History Program, Church History Department, The Church of Jesus Christ of Latter-day Saints, OH 820.
70. Rickard, oral history, 4.
71. Ibid.
72. Gertrude Corless, oral history, 13.
73. Tope, oral history, 14.
74. Hayes, oral history, 146.
75. Ibid., 77.
76. LDS Church Archives, Rodney A. Fullwood, oral history interview by Richard L. Jensen, 1988, typescript, 26, James Moyle Oral History Program, Church History Department, The Church of Jesus Christ of Latter-day Saints, OH 830; LDS Church Archives, Sarah Jane Cookman, oral history interview by Patricia Edwina Robinson, 1986, typescript, 2, 6, British Isles Oral History Project, Church Educational System, The Church of Jesus Christ of Latter-day Saints, CR 884 11. An additional example is found in Hayes, oral history, 103.
77. Hayes, oral history, 144.
78. Plumbley, oral history, 6.

79. Douglas D. Alder, "The Mormon Ward: Congregation or Community?" *Journal of Mormon History* 5: 77.
80. In the early 1900s, "mutual improvement" societies were flourishing throughout Britain—sponsored by many Christian denominations. Comparable programs established by the LDS Church during this period should not be considered a strictly "Mormon" phenomenon. For further discussion, see McLeod, *Religion and Society*, 24.
81. Plumbley, oral history, 6.
82. Cookman, oral history, 3.
83. LDS Church Archives, Albert Pickup, oral history interview by Richard L. Jensen, 1987, typescript, 19, James Moyle Oral History Program, Church History Department, The Church of Jesus Christ of Latter-day Saints, OH 932.
84. LDS Church Archives, Bessie C. Morrill, oral history interview by Richard L. Jensen, 1987, typescript, 13, James Moyle Oral History Program, Church History Department, The Church of Jesus Christ of Latter-day Saints, OH 868.
85. Pickup, oral history, 75.
86. LDS Church Archives, England Manchester Mission Historical Summary, 1994, LR 15512 3.
87. Eventually, the number of missions in Britain would be as high as eight. By the late 1970s there were two missions headquartered in London and one in Bristol, Birmingham, Leeds, Manchester, and Edinburgh.
88. LDSMS 110 (1948): 229
89. Pickup, oral history, 58.
90. Richard Mavin, "The Woodbury Years: An Insider's Look at Baseball Baptisms in Britain," *Sunstone*, March 1996, 58.
91. Ibid.
92. Pickup, oral history, 59.
93. D. Michael Quinn, interview, "The Mormons," Public Broadcasting System, http://www.pbs.org/mormons/interviews/quinn.html#2.
94. Mavin, "An Insider's Look," 58.
95. *Deseret News Almanac*, summary of church membership, 1960–80.
96. England Manchester Mission annual reports, 1985.
97. Ibid., 1986–89.
98. Ibid., 1997.
99. The main sources of statistical information pertaining to LDS growth in Lancashire—*The Latter-day Saints' Millennial Star* and Gordon Irving's "Information about British Mission Conferences"—ceased regular reporting of convert baptisms in 1932.
100. Between 1986 and 1988 a massive oral history project was co-sponsored by Brigham Young University and the James Moyle Oral History Program of the Church History Department of The Church of Jesus Christ of Latter-day Saints. In commemoration of British Mormonism's sesquicentennial, oral historians recorded and transcribed interviews with hundreds of British Latter-day Saints. This chapter draws only from those interviews with members from Lancashire and the English North West. For a more comprehensive analysis of British Latter-day Saint oral histories, see Jerome M. Perkins, "The Story of the British Saints in Their Own Words, 1900–50" in *Regional Studies in*

Latter-day Saint Church History: the British Isles, ed. Cynthia Doxey, Robert C. Freeman, Richard Neitzel Holzapfel, and Dennis A. Wright (Provo, Utah: Religious Studies Center, Brigham Young University, 2007), 149–69.

Chapter 7. A Home for the Saints

1. Gerry Avant, "Site Acquired for Second Temple in England," CN, October 24, 1992, 3.
2. The site selection was confirmed by President Thomas S. Monson, then a counselor in the First Presidency. See Heidi Swinton, *To the Rescue: The Biography of Thomas S. Monson* (Salt Lake City: Deseret Book Company, 2010), 435.
3. David M. Pickup, *The Pick and Flower of England: The Illustrated Story of the Mormons in Victorian England and the Story of the Preston Temple* (Burnley, Lancashire: Living Legend Press, 1997), 132–33.
4. One of the most dramatic consequences of the temple was a sharp increase in local membership numbers, which precipitated the division of the Preston Stake in 2005 and the creation of a new stake based in Chorley. The Chorley Stake was the thirty-seventh stake organized by the church in Britain and the first since the formation of the York and Watford Stakes in 1996. For a complete listing of stakes in the United Kingdom and their dates of organization, see *2007 Church Almanac* (Salt Lake City, Utah: Deseret Morning News, 2006), 476–77.
5. Harold W. Turner, *From Temple to Meeting House: The Phenomenology and Theology of Places of Worship* (The Hague: Mouton Publishers, 1979), 323–45.
6. Douglas J. Davies, *The Mormon Culture of Salvation: Grace, Force, and Glory* (Aldershot, Hampshire: Ashgate Publishing Limited, 2000), 72–73.
7. President Joseph F. Smith, opening address, General Conference of The Church of Jesus Christ of Latter-day Saints, October 1903, *Conference Report* (Salt Lake City, Utah: Deseret News Press, 1903), 4.
8. Ibid.
9. Admittedly, this is an oversimplification of one of Mormonism's enduring paradoxes, what Terryl Givens describes as an inherent tension between Mormonism's "sequestered exclusivity and optimistic universalism." See Givens, *People of Paradox: A History of Mormon Culture* (New York: Oxford University Press, 2007), 105.
10. Smith's original "Plat for the City of Zion" anticipated the erection of twelve temples on two centrally located city blocks. Each temple was intended to serve many purposes beyond the performance of sacred rites. Instructions in the margins of this plan indicate these structures were to operate jointly as temples, schools, and houses of worship. The plans never materialized—they were reserved for the settlement in Jackson County, Missouri, the divinely appointed place for the "center stake of Zion." The saints' subsequent settlements in Nauvoo, Illinois, and the Great Basin were pared-down versions of Smith's original intention. Aspects of this general pattern are still evident in hundreds of Mormon settlements in the western United States, Canada, and Mexico. For further insight into Smith as a city planner, see Richard L. Bushman, *Believing History: Latter-day Saint Essays* (New York: Columbia University Press, 2004), 173–98.
11. Bushman, *Believing History*, 185–86.

12. As Terryl Givens notes, Webster's 1828 *Dictionary* reveals the cultural ambiguity of the term "temple" in Joseph Smith's day, then defined simply as "a church; an edifice erected among Christians as a place of public worship." Indeed, the full development of the temple as a sacred space with a clearly specified purpose would take a generation to develop.
13. LDS Church Archives, letter from John Druce to John Snider, September 15, 1844, MS 15543.
14. LDSMS 6 (1845): 43.
15. Pickup, *Pick and Flower*, 33–35, 52–55.
16. For a description of the Vauxhall Chapel and a history of its occupancy, see Anthony Hewitson, *Our Churches and Chapels, Their Parsons, Priests, & Congregations; Being a Critical and Historical Account of Every Place of Worship in Preston* (Preston, Lancashire: Preston Chronicle Office, Fishergate, 1869), 82–88. On pages 112–13 Hewitson lists the many locations in Preston where the Latter-day Saints worshipped between 1837 and 1869.
17. James B. Allen, Ronald K. Esplin, and David J. Whittaker, *Men With a Mission 1837–1841: The Quorum of the Twelve Apostles in the British Isles* (Salt Lake City, Utah: Deseret Book Company, 1992), 39–41.
18. Orson F. Whitney, *Life of Heber C. Kimball*, 2nd collector's edition reprint (Salt Lake City, Utah: Bookcraft, 1996), 142.
19. Ibid., 156.
20. FHL, membership register of the Clitheroe Branch 1838–1885, 86992, items 14–16.
21. Family group record of John Ormerod, http://www.familysearch.org.
22. In 1850 John Ormerod was serving as either branch clerk or branch president, strong evidence of his devotion to Mormonism at the time of his marriage to Ellen.
23. "Celestial" or "eternal" marriage is the climactic temple ceremony in Mormonism and is deemed essential for exaltation. See DC 131:1–4.
24. Although failure to emigrate was regarded a sign of faithlessness throughout much of the nineteenth century, John Ormerod appears to have been an important exception. Branch records indicate he was active throughout his life and presided over the saints in Clitheroe for decades. Eventually, Ormerod became the sole church representative in the upper Ribble Valley. As a branch leader, Ormerod held open the door to Zion for his fellow Latter-day Saints for over forty years. Ormerod failed to emigrate before church policy concerning the gathering shifted, effectively denying him the opportunity. With characteristic obedience, Ormerod stayed in Low Moor, Clitheroe, until his death in 1901. Notifying readers of the *Millennial Star* of his father's passing, John Franklin Ormerod wrote, "I beg to assure you that he has always been, and died, a faithful believer in the true religion of Jesus Christ." This statement verifies the enduring commitment of one of the few Latter-day Saints whose life spanned the entire breadth of the gathering. See LDSMS 63 (1901): 588.
25. Moroni 8:9–12.
26. Whitney, *Kimball*, 156.
27. Family group record for Heber C. Kimball and Mary Smithies, http://www.familysearch.org.

28. FHL, membership register of the Clitheroe Branch, 86992, items 14–16.
29. Ibid.
30. Ibid.
31. Pickup, *Pick and Flower*, 59.
32. PRO, HO 129/479, 1851 census returns for Clitheroe, microfilm reproduction, LDS Family History Library, 2206701.
33. LDS Church Archives, Oldham ward dedication material, 1987, MS 9595.
34. LDS Church Archives, manuscript history of the Liverpool Branch, September 6, 1844, LR 4948 2. The "temple boxes" mentioned were for the collection of funds dedicated to the construction of the Nauvoo Temple.
35. LDS Church Archives, manuscript history of the Liverpool Branch, April 25, 1852. Shortly after vacating the hall, it was destroyed by fire and rebuilt in 1853. See www.liverpoolwalks.co.uk/003/hallv.htm-site, accessed September 25, 2009. The saints' avoidance of the disaster was no doubt regarded as providential.
36. "The Mormons in England," *New York Times*, August 1, 1867, 2.
37. LDS Church Archives, Elsie Rickard, oral history interview by Chad M. Orton, 1986, typescript, 2, James Moyle Oral History Program, Church History Department, The Church of Jesus Christ of Latter-day Saints, CR 884 85.
38. LDS Church Archives, Horace Hayes, oral history interview by Chad M. Orton, 1988, typescript, 2, James Moyle Oral History Program, Church History Department, The Church of Jesus Christ of Latter-day Saints, OH 1243.
39. LDS Church Archives, Gertrude Corless, oral history interview by Richard L. Jensen, 1987, typescript, 10, James Moyle Oral History Program, Church History Department, The Church of Jesus Christ of Latter-day Saints, OH 868.
40. Hayes, oral history, 34.
41. Ibid., 19.
42. LDS Church Archives, "Manchester Stake 1960–1961," bound mimeograph, published privately by Robert Gordon Larsen, 1961, MS 17882, 16.
43. Hayes, oral history, 53.
44. Ibid., 38.
45. Ibid., 36.
46. LDS Church Archives, Sylvia Mills Whalley, oral history interview by Chad M. Orton, 1987, typescript, 4, James Moyle Oral History Program, Church History Department, The Church of Jesus Christ of Latter-day Saints, OH 879.
47. Ronald G. Watt and Kenneth W. Godfrey, "'Old 42': The British and European Mission Headquarters in Liverpool, England, 1844–1904," *Mormon Historical Studies* 10 (Spring 2009): 88.
48. Ronald W. Walker, "Heber J. Grant's European Mission, 1903–1906," *Journal of Mormon History* 14 (1988): 19–20.
49. Andrew Jenson, *Encyclopedic History of The Church of Jesus Christ of Latter-day Saints* (Salt Lake City, Utah: Deseret News Press, 1941), 94.
50. LDSMS 94 (1932): 122.
51. LDSMS 95 (1933): 340. Gordon Square was in an area of London where other religious denominations maintained their headquarters, including the Society of Friends

on nearby Euston Road. Gordon Square also currently houses the most important Nonconformist archive, Dr. William's Library. The removal of the Latter-day Saints' administrative offices to this location gave Mormonism increased visibility and a more established place among the major Nonconformist faiths—something they would not have been able to accomplish had they remained in Liverpool.

52. LDSMS 95 (1933): 340, 345.
53. LDSMS 66 (1904): 282.
54. LDS Church Archives, V. Adelaide Tope, oral history interview by Richard L. Jensen, 1987, typescript, 5, James Moyle Oral History Program, Church History Department, The Church of Jesus Christ of Latter-day Saints, OH 885.
55. LDSMS 95 (1933): 346.
56. LDSMS 98 (1936): 63.
57. Tope, oral history, 2.
58. LDSMS 73 (1911): 155–57.
59. LDS Church Archives, Oldham ward dedication material, 1987, MS 9595.
60. Larsen, "Manchester Stake," 17.
61. LDS Church Archives, Albert and Jeanie Pickup, oral history interview by Richard L. Jensen, 1987, typescript, 21, 70, James Moyle Oral History Program, Church History Department, The Church of Jesus Christ of Latter-day Saints, OH 932.
62. Ibid., 21.
63. Ibid., 16.
64. LDS Church Archives, Derek J. Plumbley, oral history interview by Richard L. Jensen, 1987, typescript, 17, James Moyle Oral History Program, Church History Department, OH 820.
65. Although identical in meaning and usage, the term "district" replaced "conference" in LDS vocabulary beginning in 1927. As James E. Talmage, then president of the British and European Missions, explained: "There has been something akin to incongruity in the double usage of the term *Conference* as designating (1) a church assemblage of people, and (2) a geographical area of specified boundaries constituting a territorial unit in a Mission. The custom of using this word *Conference* with plainly different meanings is objectionable on the grounds of inconsistency and of the inevitable uncertainty or confusion arising therefrom. By recent action of the First Presidency and the Council of the Twelve the term *District* shall be substituted for the word *Conference* when reference is made to a territorial division of a Mission." See LDSMS 89 (1927): 216. As explained in chapter two, the district was the organizational forerunner to the stake, the first being organized in Manchester in 1960.
66. Plumbley, oral history, 17.
67. DC 93:36.
68. Whalley, oral history, 13.
69. This preference may have originated with Joseph Smith's 1841 proclamation that vicarious baptisms be performed solely within the temple. See HC 4:426. This material was taken from the minutes of a church conference held in Nauvoo, Illinois, on October 3, 1841, and published in *Times and Seasons*, October 15, 1841, 578. Prior to this declaration, baptisms for the dead were practiced in the Mississippi River. In a similar strain, early convert

baptisms in Britain were performed in natural, open-air settings until mission leadership began to encourage the use of indoor baptismal facilities. Carol Wilkinson identifies the most probable baptismal site of the early converts of the upper Ribble Valley in "Mormon Baptismal Site in Chatburn, England," *Mormon Historical Studies* 7 (2006): 83–88.

70. LDS Church Archives, manuscript history of the Liverpool Branch, July 13, 1849, LR 4948 2. See appendix C for a complete transcription of the prayer offered by Milo Andrus.
71. Ibid.
72. Pickup, oral history, 21.
73. LDS Church Archives, Phillip Ambrose, oral history interview by Branda Roak, 1986, typescript, 3, British Isles Oral History Project, Church Educational System, The Church of Jesus Christ of Latter-day Saints, CR 884 94.
74. LDS Church Archives, May T. Gartland, oral history interview by Richard L. Jensen, 1987, typescript, 9, James Moyle Oral History Program, Church History Department, The Church of Jesus Christ of Latter-day Saints, OH 885.
75. Whalley, oral history, 6.
76. LDS Church Archives, manuscript history of the Liverpool Branch, February 10, 1862, LR 4948 2.
77. Ronan James Head, "Creating a Mormon Mecca in England: The Gadfield Elm Chapel," *Mormon Historical Studies*, 7 (2006): 89–102. See also Richard Woolley Jackson, *Places of Worship: 150 Years of Latter-day Saint Architecture* (Provo, Utah: Religious Studies Center, Brigham Young University, 2003), 52.
78. James R. and LaVelle R. Moss, "Names and Places: Locales of British LDS Interest," *Ensign*, July 1987, 16.
79. "Gadfield Elm: The Oldest LDS Chapel in Europe," *Ensign*, October 1986.
80. A structure similar to the one in Oldham was planned, but never built, in Liverpool. The LDS Church Archives retains the architectural plans for the proposed "mission room," drafted in 1907 by Bullen Brothers & Sons, a Liverpool building firm. The front elevation of the Liverpool chapel bears a strong resemblance to photographs of the exterior of the Oldham chapel. It is probable that the professionally rendered plans, although unused in Liverpool, were acquired by the saints in Oldham, who followed the design when determining the dimensions and features of their own chapel. See LDS Church Archives, architectural drawing of proposed mission room at 295 Edge Lane, Liverpool, January 16, 1907, MS 11588.
81. LDSMS 71 (1909): 197.
82. As Terryl Givens notes, "A people's religious structures are visible manifestation of religious values, or, more specifically, a way of ordering those values." While this is certainly true regarding LDS temples, it is also an important element in LDS chapel building, both in the United States and in Britain. See Givens, *People of Paradox*, 107–15.
83. LDSMS 71 (1909): 197.
84. Larsen, "Manchester Stake," 9.
85. Pickup, oral history, 71–72.
86. Larsen, "Manchester Stake," 23.
87. Whalley, oral history, 48.

88. Jackson, *Places of Worship*, 313.
89. LDS Church Archives, dedicatory prayer of Oldham chapel offered by Martin A. Cook, January 18, 1987, LR 6490 21.
90. Givens, *People of Paradox*, 244–45.
91. Paul Lawrence Anderson, "Mormon Moderne: New Directions in Latter-day Saint Architecture, 1890–1955," unpublished manuscript cited in Givens, *People of Paradox*, 244.
92. Plumbley, oral history, 25.
93. Corless, oral history, 14.
94. Larsen, "Manchester Stake," 23.
95. Author's field notes, Ellesmere Port, April 1997.
96. Corless, oral history, 14.
97. Larsen, "Manchester Stake," 9.
98. Pickup, oral history, 69.
99. Pickup, oral history, 73.
100. Plumbley, oral history, 26.
101. The chapel as a religious symbol finds abundant substantiation in the dedicatory prayers offered by church leaders (see appendix C). For a useful discussion of the evolution of dedicatory prayers for LDS temples, see Samuel Brown, "A Sacred Code: Mormon Temple Dedication Prayers 1836–2000," *Journal of Mormon History* 32 (2006): 173–96.
102. See appendix C, dedicatory prayer of the Oldham Chapel.
103. LDS Church Archives, Rodney A. Fullwood, oral history interview by Richard L. Jensen, 1987–88, typescript, 25, James Moyle Oral History Program, Church History Department, OH 830.
104. Plumbley, oral history, 28.
105. Michael H. Madsen, "The Sanctification of Mormonism's Historical Geography," *Geographies of Religions and Belief Systems* 1 (2006): 52.

Chapter 8. "In England's Green and Pleasant Land"

1. P.A.M. Taylor, *Expectations Westward: The Mormons and the Emigration of their British Converts in the Nineteenth Century* (Edinburgh and London: Oliver and Boyd, 1965). See also Hugh McLeod, *Religion and Society in England, 1850–1914* (New York: St. Martin's Press, 1996), 52.
2. LDS Church Archives, Rodney Atkinson Fullwood, oral history interview by Richard L. Jensen, typescript, 27, James Moyle Oral History Program, Church History Department, The Church of Jesus Christ of Latter-day Saints, OH 830.
3. Douglas J. Davies, "Aspects of Latter-day Saint Eschatology," in *A Sociological Yearbook of Religion in Britain*, ed. Michael Hill (London: SCM Press, 1973) 6: 133.
4. Eric Eliason, "The Cultural Dynamics of Historical Self-Fashioning: LDS Pioneer Nostalgia, American Culture, and the International Church," *Journal of Mormon History* 28: 160–62.
5. LDS Church Archives, Jeannie Pickup, oral history interview by Richard L. Jensen, 1987, typescript, 69, James Moyle Oral History Program, Church History Department, The Church of Jesus Christ of Latter-day Saints, OH 932.

6. A notable exception is the Salt and Woodruff families of Chisworth, Cheshire. Merged through marriage, one strand of this family remained active in their Mormon faith from the early 1840s through the 1960s. That the Chisworth's remained in England when so many of the faithful were gathering to Zion stems from their property ownership. Unwilling to part with the family farm, the Salt/Woodruff family helped sustain the local congregation until the organization of the Manchester Stake in 1960. See LDS Family History Library, membership register of the Chisworth Branch, Manchester District, 1876–1931, 205633 item 2; membership register of the Hyde Branch, 1840–1947, 87005 items 1–4; and LDS Church Archives, Robert Gordon Larsen, "Manchester Stake 1960–1961," MS 17882.
7. Author's field notes, Preston Stake Conference, Chorley, Lancashire, June 17, 2001. See also Don L. Searle, "The Church in the United Kingdom and Ireland," *Ensign*, June 1998, 40.
8. See Craig L. Marshall, "Mormon Religiosity and Higher Education," unpublished Ph.D. thesis, University of Nottingham, 1996, for a discussion of the role of the LDS Church Educational System upon this pursuit.
9. Bernard Walsh, oral history interview by the author, Chorley, Lancashire, June 10, 2006.
10. http://globalmormonism.byu.edu.
11. Ibid.
12. Ibid.
13. Reid L. Neilson, *Early Mormon Missionary Activities in Japan, 1901–1904* (Salt Lake City, Utah: University of Utah Press, 2010), 146–49.
14. http://globalmormonism.byu.edu.
15. Arnold K. Garr, "Latter-day Saints in Tubuai, French Polynesia, Yesterday and Today," in *Regional Studies in Latter-day Saint Church History*, ed. Reid Neilson, Steven C. Harper, Craig K. Manscill, and Mary Jane Woodger (Provo: Utah, Religious Studies Center, Brigham Young University, 2008), 6–9.
16. Ibid., 13.
17. LDSMS 52: (1890) 269.
18. LDS Church Archives, manuscript history of the Preston Branch, LR 7179 2.
19. Ibid.
20. LDS Church Archives, Bessie Morrill and Gertrude Corless, oral history interview by Richard L. Jensen, 1987, typescript, 21, James Moyle Oral History Program, Church History Department, The Church of Jesus Christ of Latter-day Saints, OH 868.
21. Orson F. Whitney, *Life of Heber C. Kimball, An Apostle; the Father and Founder of the British Mission* (Salt Lake City, Utah: Juvenile Instructor Office, 1888), 447.
22. John Navone, *Towards a Theology of Story* (Slough, England: St. Paul Publications, 1977), 33–34, 41.
23. Douglas J. Davies, "Pilgrimage in Mormon Culture," in *Social Anthropology of Pilgrimage*, ed. Jha Makhan (New Delhi: Inter-India Publications, 1991), 315–16, 323–25.
24. Armand Mauss, "Can There Be a 'Second Harvest?': Controlling the Costs of Latter-day Saint Membership in Europe," *International Journal of Mormon Studies* 1: 1–59.

25. "Official Report of the First Manchester England Area Conference of The Church of Jesus Christ of Latter-day Saints" (Salt Lake City, Utah: The Church of Jesus Christ of Latter-day Saints), 3.
26. Ibid., 5.
27. LDSMS 95 (1933): 91.
28. Ibid., 424.
29. Ibid.
30. Isaiah 11:12.

Bibliography

Abbreviations

Church History Library, The Church of Jesus Christ of Latter-day Saints, Salt Lake City (hereafter cited as Church History Library).

Family History Library, The Church of Jesus Christ of Latter-day Saints, Salt Lake City (hereafter cited as Family History Library).

L. Tom Perry Special Collections, Harold B. Lee Library, Brigham Young University, Provo, Utah (hereafter cited as Perry Special Collections).

Special Collections, J. Willard Marriott Library, University of Utah, Salt Lake City (hereafter cited as U of U Special Collections).

Accrington (Lancashire) Branch. Manuscript history. LR 10476 2. Church History Library.

———. Membership register, 1841–1853. 86975, items 1–2. Family History Library.

Adlington (Lancashire) Branch. Manuscript history. LR 10490 2. Church History Library.

Albrect, Stan L. "The Making of British Saints in Historical Perspective." *BYU Studies* 27 (1987): 119–35.

Alder, Douglas D. "The Mormon Ward: Congregation or Community?" *Journal of Mormon History* 5 (1978): 61–78.

Allen, James B., Ronald K. Esplin, and David J. Whittaker. *Men With a Mission 1837–1841: The Quorum of the Twelve Apostles in the British Isles*. Salt Lake City, Utah: Deseret Book Company, 1992.

Alston (Cumberland) Branch. Manuscript history. LR 10597 2. Church History Library.

Altholz, Josef L. *The Religious Press in Britain, 1760–1900*. New York: Greenwood Press, 1989.

Ames, Edward Scribner. "Stages in Religious Conversion." In *Readings in the Psychology of Religion*, edited by Orlo Strunk. New York: Abingdon Press, 1959, 140–43.

Anastasiou, Andre K. Autobiography, 1976. MS 4646. Church History Library.

Anderson, Nels. *Desert Saints: The Mormon Frontier in Utah*. Chicago, Illinois: University of Chicago Press, 1966.

Anderson, Olive. "Emigration and Marriage Break-up in Mid-Victorian England." *Economic History Review* 50 (1997): 104–9.

Armytage, W. H. G. *Heavens Below: Utopian Experiments in England 1560–1960*. London: Routledge and K. Paul, 1961.

———. "Liverpool, Gateway to Zion." *Pacific Northwest Quarterly* 48 (1957): 39–44.

Arrington, Leonard J. "Mormonism: Views from Without and Within." *BYU Studies* 14 (1974): 140–53.

———, and Davis Bitton. *The Mormon Experience: A History of the Latter-day Saints*. Urbana and Chicago, Illinois: University of Illinois Press, 1992.

Ashton-under-Lyne (Lancashire) Branch. Membership register, 1837–1889. 86979, item 9. Family History Library.

Assheton, Ralph, Right Honorable Lord Clitheroe. Register of village rentals, 1838. Downham Hall, Downham, Lancashire. Assheton Family Estate Records.

Avant, Gerry. "Reflecting on Mission, Turning Point in Life." *LDS Church News*. February 2, 2008.

Aveson, Robert. "Apostasy, its Cause and Effect." Unpublished pamphlet. MS 261. Church History Library.

Backman, Milton V. *The Heavens Resound: A History of the Latter-day Saints in Ohio 1830–1838*. Salt Lake City, Utah: Deseret Book Company, 1983.

Balmer, Randall. "'Faith in the Religion of Their Fathers': Passing Mormonism from One Generation to the Next." *Journal of Mormon History* 30 (2004): 37–57.

Barrow-in-Furness (Lancashire) Branch. Manuscript history. LR 530 2. Church History Library.

———. Membership register, 1904–1909. 86977, item 10. Family History Library.

Barton, William Bell. Journal, 1874–1876. MS 17150. Church History Library.

Birkenhead (Cheshire) Branch. Manuscript history. LR 729 2. Church History Library.

———. Membership register, 1852–1873, 1907–1914, 1905–1947. 86980, items 18–20. Family History Library.

Blackburn (Lancashire) Branch. Manuscript history. LR 751 2. Church History Library.

———. Membership register, 1837–1948. 86982 items 11–17. Family History Library.

Black, Susan Easton. "A Profile of a British Saint, 1837–1848." In *Regional Studies in Latter-day Saint Church History: The British Isles*, edited by Donald Q. Cannon. Provo, Utah: Department of Church History and Doctrine, Brigham Young University, 1990, 103–13.

Blackpool (Lancashire) Branch. Manuscript history. LR 770 2. Church History Library.

———. Membership register, 1899–1908. 86982, item 18. Family History Library.

Bloxham, Ben V., James R. Moss, James Porter, eds. *Truth Will Prevail: The Rise of The Church of Jesus Christ of Latter-day Saints in the British Isles, 1837–1987*. Solihull, Warwickshire: The Church of Jesus Christ of Latter-day Saints, 1987.

Boden, Heber C. Journal, 1893–1895. MS 8797 1 1. Church History Library.

Bolton (Lancashire) Branch. Manuscript history. LR 841 2. Church History Library.

———. Membership register, 1838–1887. 86983 items 5–6. Family History Library.

Boone, David F. "'The King of Kings Needs a Few Men': British Saints during World War II." In *Regional Studies in Latter-day Saint Church History: The British Isles*, edited by Cynthia Doxey. Provo, Utah: Religious Studies Center, Brigham Young University, 2007, 193–217.

Bootle (Lancashire) Branch. Manuscript history. LR 945 2. Church History Library.

———. Membership register, 1901–1912. 86983, item 7. Family History Library.

Bowes, John. "Mormonism Exposed, in Its Licentious Abominations, Refuted in Its Principles, and in the Claims of Its Head, the Modern Mohammed, Joseph Smith, Who Is Proved To Be a Deceiver and No Prophet of God." Pamphlet. London: E. Ward, n.d. U of U Special Collections.

Bradley, Martha Sontag. "Creating the Sacred Space of Zion." *Journal of Mormon History* 31 (2005): 1–30.

Breightmet Fold (Lancashire) Branch. Membership register, 1840–1861. 86984, item 19. Family History Library.

Brenchley, Julius, and Jules Remy. "A Journey to the Great-Salt-Lake City; With a Sketch of the History, Religion, and Customs of the Mormons." Pamphlet. London: W. Jeffs, 1861. Perry Special Collections.

Brodie, Fawn. *No Man Knows My History: The Life and Times of Joseph Smith the Mormon Prophet*. New York: Alfred A. Knopf, 1960.

Brown, Kenneth D. *A Social History of the Nonconformist Ministry in England and Wales 1800–1930*. Oxford: Clarendon Press, 1988.

Brown, Samuel. "A Sacred Code: Mormon Temple Dedication Prayers 1836–2000." *Journal of Mormon History* 32 (2006): 173–96.

Buchanan, Frederick S. "The Ebb and Flow of Mormonism in Scotland 1840–1900." *BYU Studies* 27 (1987): 27–51.

Bullen Brothers and Sons Ltd. Architectural drawing, Liverpool mission room, 1907. MS 11588. Church History Library.

Burnley (Lancashire) Branch. Manuscript history. LR 1234 2. Church History Library.

———. Membership register, 1840–1948. 86989, items 13–18. Family History Library.

Bury (Lancashire) Branch. Manuscript history. LR 1243 2. Church History Library.

———. Membership register, 1839–1888, 1900–1946. 86989, items 24–26. Family History Library.

Bushman, Claudia, and Richard Bushman. *Building the Kingdom: A History of the Mormons in America*. Oxford: Oxford University Press, 2000.

Bushman, Richard. *Believing History*, edited by Reid L. Nielson and Jed Woodworth. New York: Columbia University Press, 2004.

Cannon, Brian Q., and Jacob W. Olmstead. "'Scandalous Film': The Campaign to Suppress Anti-Mormon Motion Pictures 1911–12." *Journal of Mormon History* 29 (2003): 42–76.

Cannon, Donald Q. "Joseph Smith and the Globalization of Mormonism." *Journal of Mormon History* 32 (2006): 1–24.

———, ed. *Regional Studies in Latter-day Saint Church History: British Isles*. Provo, Utah: Department of Church History and Doctrine, Brigham Young University, 1990.

Cannon, M. Hamlin. "The English Mormons in America." *American Historical Review* 57 (1952): 893–908.

Carlisle (Cumberland) Branch. Membership register, 1843–1948. 86990, items 14–15; 86995, item 23. Family History Library.

Carwardine, Richard. *Transatlantic Revivalism: Popular Evangelicalism in Britain and America 1790–1865*. Westport, Connecticut: Greenwood Press, 1978.

Chappell, Frederick William. Journal, 1890–1891. MS 13921. Church History Library.
Chatburn (Lancashire) Branch. Manuscript history. LR 2419 2. Church History Library.
———. Membership register, 1838–1854. 86990, item 29. Family History Library.
Chester (Cheshire) Branch. Manuscript history. LR 1640 2. Church History Library.
———. Membership register, 1841–1909. 86991, items 19–21. Family History Library.
Chorley (Lancashire) Branch. Manuscript history. LR 1703 2. Church History Library.
———. Membership register, 1898–1910. 86992, item 5. Family History Library.
Church History in the Fulness of Times. Salt Lake City, Utah: The Church of Jesus Christ of Latter-day Saints, 2000.
"The Church Today in the British Isles." *Ensign*. July 1987.
Clitheroe (Lancashire) Branch. Manuscript history. LR 2421 2. Church History Library.
———. Membership register, 1838–1885. 86992, items 14–16. Family History Library.
Cook, Martin A. Dedicatory prayer, January 18, 1987. LR 6490 21. Church History Library.
Cotterill, John. "Midland Saints: the Mormon Mission in the West Midlands 1837–77." Ph.D. diss., University of Keele, 1985.
Cowan, Richard O. *The Church in the Twentieth Century*. Salt Lake City, Utah: Bookcraft, 1985.
———. "The Church Comes of Age in Britain." In *Regional Studies in Latter-day Saint Church History: The British Isles*, edited by Donald Q. Cannon. Provo, Utah: Department of Church History and Doctrine, Brigham Young University, 1990, 193–214.
———. *Temples to Dot the Earth*. Salt Lake City, Utah: Bookcraft, 1989.
Cowley, Mathias F., ed. *Wilford Woodruff: Fourth President of The Church of Jesus Christ of Latter-day Saints*. Salt Lake City, Utah: Bookcraft, 1964.
Crosby (Lancashire) Branch. Manuscript history. LR 2054 2. Church History Library.
Cross Moor (Lancashire) Branch. Membership register, 1842–1857. 86993, item 5. Family History Library.
Curie, Robert, Alan D. Gilbert, and Lee Horsley. *Churches and Churchgoers: Patterns of Church Growth in the British Isles Since 1700*. Oxford: Clarendon Press, 1977.
Cuthbert, Derek A. "Breakthrough in Britain." *Ensign*. July 1987.
Davies, Brigham. Journal, 1893–1894. MS 15924. Church History Library.
Davies, Douglas J. "Aspects of Latter-day Saint Eschatology." In *A Sociological Yearbook of Religion in Britain*, vol. 6, edited by Michael Hill. London: SCM Press, 1973, 122–35.
———. *An Introduction to Mormonism*. Cambridge: Cambridge University Press, 2003.
———. *The Mormon Culture of Salvation: Force, Grace and Glory*. Aldershot, Hampshire: Ashgate Publishing Limited, 2000.
———. "Mormon History, Text, Color, and Rites." *Journal of Religious History* 31 (2007): 305–15.
———. *Mormon Spirituality: Latter-day Saints in Wales and Zion*. Nottingham: University of Nottingham Press, 1987.
———. "Pilgrimage in Mormon Culture." In *Social Anthropology of Pilgrimage*, edited by Makhan Jha. New Delhi: Inter-India Publications, 1991, 310–25.
Deseret News Church Almanac. Salt Lake City, Utah: Deseret News Press, 1974–1980.
Dew, Sheri L. *Go Forward with Faith: The Biography of Gordon B. Hinckley*. Salt Lake City, Utah: Deseret Book Company, 1996.

Disley (Cheshire) Branch. Membership register, 1850–1894. 86995, item 1. Family History Library.

Douglas (Isle of Man) Branch. Manuscript history. LR 2301 2. Church History Library.

Doxey, Cynthia. "The Church in Britain and the 1851 Religious Census." *Mormon Historical Studies* 4 (2003): 107–38.

———, Robert C. Freeman, Richard Neitzel Holzapfel, and Dennis A. Wright, eds. *Regional Studies in Latter-day Saint Church History: The British Isles*. Provo, Utah: Religious Studies Center, Brigham Young University, 2007.

Druce, John. Correspondence, September 15, 1844. MS 15543. Church History Library.

Eccles (Lancashire) Branch. Manuscript history. LR 2484 2. Church History Library.

Eliason, Eric A. "The Cultural Dynamics of Historical Self-Fashioning: LDS Pioneer Nostalgia, American Culture, and the International Church." *Journal of Mormon History* 28 (2002): 140–73.

Ellesmere Port (Cheshire) Branch. Manuscript history. LR 14106 2. Church History Library.

Ellison, Matthew, and Jane Ellison. Correspondence, April 26, 1864. Photocopy of original in author's possession.

Elton (Cheshire) Branch. Membership register, 1840–1849. 86997, item 4. Family History Library.

Ensor, R. C. K. *England 1870–1914*. Oxford: Clarendon Press, 1936.

Esplin, Ronald K. "A Great Work Done in That Land." *Ensign*. July 1987.

———. "The Significance of Nauvoo for Latter-day Saints." *Journal of Mormon History* 16 (1990): 71–88.

European Mission. Statistical reports, 1855–1876. CR 271 4. Church History Library.

Evans, Richard L. *A Century of "Mormonism" in Great Britain*. Salt Lake City, Utah: Deseret News Press, 1937.

Farnworth (Lancashire) Branch. Membership register, 1851–1894. 86998, item 3. Family History Library.

Fielding, James. Correspondence, August 27, 1838. MS 749 1. Church History Library.

———. Correspondence, March 27, 1839, MS 749 2. Church History Library.

Flake, Kathleen. "Re-Placing Memory: Latter-day Saint Use of Historical Monuments and Narrative in the Early Twentieth Century." *Religion and American Culture* 13 (2003): 69–109.

Fleming, Stephen J. "The Religious Heritage of the British Northwest and the Rise of Mormonism." *Church History* 77 (2008): 73–104.

Foster, Craig L. *Penny Tracts and Polemics: A Critical Analysis of Anti-Mormon Pamphleteering in Great Britain 1837–1860*. Salt Lake City, Utah: Greg Kofford Books, 2002.

Franklin, Benjamin J. "A Cheap Trip to the Great Salt Lake City, An Annotated Lecture Delivered before the President of America and Representatives; the Mayors of Liverpool and Manchester." Pamphlet. Ipswich, Suffolk: J. Scoggins, 1864. U of U Special Collections.

Gilbert, A. D. *Religion and Society in Industrial England: Church, Chapel and Social Change, 1740–1914*. New York: Longman Press, 1976.

Givens, Terryl L. *By the Hand of Mormon: The American Scripture that Launched a New World Religion*. Oxford: Oxford University Press, 2002.

———. *People of Paradox: A History of Mormon Culture*. Oxford: Oxford University Press, 2007.

Great Harwood (Lancashire) Branch. Membership register, 1899–1914. 87000, item 14. Family History Library.

Green, Arnold H. "Gathering and Election: Israelite Descent and Universalism in Mormon Discourse." *Journal of Mormon History* 25 (1999): 195–228.

Green, Daniel Kent. Journal, 1887. MS 16828. Church History Library.

Greene, Simon J. D. *Religion in the Age of Decline: Organization and Experience in Industrial Yorkshire 1870–1920*. Cambridge: Cambridge University Press, 1996.

Halewood, Richard. Correspondence, December 16, 1844. MS 15543. Church History Library.

Halshaw Moor (Lancashire) Branch. Membership register, 1842–1887. 87001, item 12. Family History Library.

Hamilton, C. Mark. *Nineteenth Century Mormon Architecture and City Planning*. New York: Oxford University Press, 1995.

Handforth-with-Bosden (Cheshire) Branch. Membership register, 1847–1863. 87001, item 22. Family History Library.

Harris, Jan G. "Mormons in Victorian England." Master's thesis, Brigham Young University, 1987.

———. "Mormons in Victorian Manchester." *BYU Studies* 27 (1987): 47–56.

Harrison, J. F. C. *The Second Coming: Popular Millenarianism 1780–1850*. London: Routledge and Kegan Paul, 1979.

———. "The Popular History of Early Victorian Britain: A Mormon Contribution." In *Mormons in Early Victorian Britain*, edited by Malcolm R. Thorp and Richard L. Jensen. Salt Lake City, Utah: University of Utah Press, 1989, 1–15.

Hawthornthwaite, Samuel. "Mr. Hawthornthwaite's Adventures among the Mormons As an Elder During Eight Years" (Manchester: Self-published, 1857). U of U Special Collections.

Head, Ronan James. "Creating a Mormon Mecca in England: The Gadfield Elm Chapel." *Mormon Historical Studies* 7 (2006): 89–102.

Heelas, Paul, and Linda Woodhead. *The Spiritual Revolution: Why Religion is Giving Way to Spirituality*. Oxford: Blackwell Press, 2005.

Hepburn, Andrew Balfour. "Mormonism Exploded, or, The Religion of the Latter-day Saints: Proved to by a System of Imposture, Blasphemy, and Immorality: With the Autobiography and Portrait of the Author, Two Parts." London: Simpkin, Marshall and Company, 1855. Perry Special Collections.

Hewitson, Anthony. *Our Churches and Chapels, Their Parsons, Priests, & Congregations; Being a Critical and Historical Account of Every Place of Worship in Preston*. Published commentary. Preston, Lancashire: Preston Chronicle Office, 1869. Family History Library.

Heywood (Lancashire) Branch. Membership register, 1840–1912. 87002, items 19–22. Family History Library.

Hill, Marvin S. *Quest for Refuge: The Mormon Flight from American Pluralism*. Salt Lake City, Utah: Signature Books, 1989.

Hinckley, Gordon B. Dedicatory prayer of the Preston England Temple, June 7, 1998. *LDS Church News*, June 13, 1998.

Hinckley, Gordon B. "Taking the Gospel to Britain: A Declaration of Vision, Faith, Courage, and Truth." *Ensign*. July 1987.

Housley, Paul Simpson, Jamie Scott, eds. *Sacred Places and Profane Spaces: Essays in the Geographies of Judaism, Christianity, and Islam*. New York: Greenwood Press, 1991.

Hyde (Cheshire) Branch. Manuscript history. LR 3993 2. Church History Library.

———. Membership register, 1840–1947. 87005, items 1–4. Family History Library.

Hyde, Orson. "A Timely Warning to the People of England: Of Every Sect and Denomination, and to Every Individual into Whose Hands It May Fall." Pamphlet. Manchester: Reprinted by W. R. Thomas, Spring Gardens, n.d. Perry Special Collections.

Irving, Gordon. "Information about British Mission Conferences 1877–1932." Church History Library.

Ivory, Ellis. Dedicatory prayer, May 4, 1980. LR 15512 21. Church History Library.

Jackson, Richard H., and Roger Henrie. "Perception of Sacred Space." *Journal of Cultural Geography* 3 (1983): 94–107.

Jackson, Richard W. *Places of Worship: 150 Years of LDS Architecture*. Provo, Utah: Religious Studies Center, Brigham Young University, 2003.

Jackson, Thomas. Journal, 1880–1881. MS 8363. Church History Library.

Jenkins, Russell. "Gates of Heaven Open (For a Limited Time Only)." *The Times*. May 15, 1998.

Jennings, Warren A. "The Lynching of an American Prophet." *BYU Studies* 40 (2001): 205–16.

Jensen, Richard J. "Without Purse or Scrip: Financing LDS Missionary Work in Europe in the Nineteenth Century." *Journal of Mormon History* 12 (1985): 3–14.

Jensen, Richard L. "The British Gathering to Zion." In *Truth Will Prevail: The Rise of The Church of Jesus Christ of Latter-day Saints in the British Isles 1837–1987*, edited by V. Ben Bloxham, James R. Moss, and Larry C. Porter. Solihull, Warwickshire: The Church of Jesus Christ of Latter-day Saints, 1987, 165–98.

———, and Malcolm R. Thorp, eds. *Mormons in Early Victorian Britain*. Salt Lake City, Utah: University of Utah Press, 1989.

Jenson, Andrew. *Encyclopedic History of The Church of Jesus Christ of Latter-day Saints*. Salt Lake City, Utah: Deseret News Press, 1941.

Johnson, Dale A. *The Changing Shape of English Nonconformity 1825–1925*. New York: Oxford University Press, 1999.

Johnson, G. Wesley, and Marian Ashby Johnson. "On the Trail of Twentieth-Century Mormon Outmigration." *BYU Studies* 46 (2007): 41–83.

Jones, William. Journal, 1893–1895. MS 15511. Church History Library.

Kedar, Benjamin Z., and R. J. Werblowsky, eds. *Sacred Space: Shrine, City, Land*. New York: New York University Press, 1998.

Kendal (Westmorland) Branch. Manuscript history. LR 4399 2. Church History Library.

———. Membership register, 1840–1852. 87007, item 5. Family History Library.

Kersley (Lancashire) Branch. Membership register, 1842–1876. 87007, item 17. Family History Library.

Kimball, Heber C. Correspondence, September 11, 1840. MS 6135, folder 3. Church History Library.

Kimball, Stanley B. *Heber C. Kimball: Mormon Patriarch and Pioneer*. Urbana, Illinois: University of Illinois Press, 1981.

———. Correspondence, November 9, 1840. MS 20533. Church History Library.

Kimball, Vilate. Correspondence, September 1840. MS 3276 2. Church History Library.

Lancaster (Lancashire) Branch. Manuscript history. LR 4948 2. Church History Library.

———. Membership register, 1884–1929. 87008, items 9–10. Family History Library.

Lane, Belden C. "Giving Voice to Place: Three Models for Understanding American Sacred Space." *Religion and American Culture* 11 (2001): 53–81.

———. *Landscapes of the Sacred: Geography and Narrative in American Spirituality*. New York: Paulist Press, 1988.

Larsen, Robert Gordon. "Manchester Stake 1960–1961." MS 17882. Church History Library.

Launius, Roger D. "Mormon Memory, Mormon Myth, and Mormon History." *Journal of Mormon History* 21 (1995): 1–24.

Leigh (Lancashire) Branch. Manuscript history. LR 4822 2. Church History Library.

———. Membership register, 1840–1901. 87036, items 31–33. Family History Library.

Leyland Moss (Lancashire) Branch. Membership register, 1838–1854. 87010, item 14. Family History Library.

Lively, Robert L. "Some Sociological Reflections on the Nineteenth-Century British Mission." In *Mormons in Early Victorian Britain*, edited by Malcolm R. Thorp and Richard L.

Liverpool Branch. Manuscript history. LR 4948 2. Church History Library.

———. Membership register, 1840–1960. 87012, items 1–6. Family History Library.

Liverpool Conference. Manuscript history. LR 4949 2. Church History Library.

———. Membership register, 1872–1921. 87012, items 7–11. Family History Library.

———. Record of missionaries, 1909–1939. LR 4949 21. Church History Library.

Longton (Lancashire) Branch. Membership register, 1837–1854. 87016, item 1. Family History Library.

Lunt, Henry Whittaker. Journal, 1893–1894. MS 9639. Church History Library.

Lymm (Cheshire) Branch. Membership register, 1841–1881. 87016, item 24. Family History Library.

Macclesfield (Cheshire) Branch. Membership register, 1840–1869. 87017, items 1–3. Family History Library.

Madsen, Michael H. "The Sanctification of Mormonism's Historical Geography." *Geographies of Religions and Belief Systems* 1 (2006): 51–73.

Manchester Branch. Manuscript history. LR 5221 2. Church History Library.

———. Membership register, 1838–1946. 87017, items 7–13; 87044, item 3. Family History Library.

Manchester Conference. Manuscript history. LR 5219 2. Church History Library.

Manchester District. Membership register, 1876–1931. 205633, item 2. Family History Library.

Marshall, Craig L. "Mormon Student Religiosity and Higher Education." Ph.D. diss., University of Nottingham, 1996.

Martin, Jesse Bigler. Journal, 1853–1854. MS 8209. Church History Library.

Maudsley, Sutcliffe. Portraits, 1844. MSS 787. Perry Special Collections.

Mauss, Armand L. *The Angel and the Beehive: The Mormon Struggle with Assimilation*. Urbana, Illinois: University of Illinois Press, 1994.

———. *All Abraham's Children: Changing Mormon Conceptions of Race and Lineage*. Urbana, Illinois: University of Illinois Press, 2003.

———. "Can There Be a 'Second Harvest'?: Controlling the Costs of Latter-day Saint Membership in Europe." *International Journal of Mormon Studies* 1 (2008): 1–59.

———. "In Search of Ephraim: Traditional Mormon Conceptions of Lineage and Race." *Journal of Mormon History* 25 (1999): 131–73.

Mavin, Richard. "The Woodbury Years: An Insider's Look at Baseball Baptisms in Britain." *Sunstone*, March 1996, 56–60.

May, Dean L. "Rites of Passage: The Gathering as Cultural Credo." *Journal of Mormon History* 29 (2003): 1–41.

———. "Writing from within a Religious Tradition: A Mormon Perspective." *Journal of Mormon History* 28 (2002): 111–29.

McCord, James. Architectural elevation, Nauvoo Temple, 1842. MS 13936. Church History Library.

McLeod, Hugh. *Religion and Society in England 1850–1914*. New York: St. Martin's Press, 1996.

———. *Class and Religion in the Late Victorian City*. London: Croom Helm, 1974.

———. *The Religious Crisis of the 1960s*. Oxford: Oxford University Press, 2007.

McMaster, William Athole. Journal, 1849–1886. MSS 160. Perry Special Collections.

Middleton (Lancashire) Branch. Manuscript history. LR 5527 2. Church History Library.

———. Membership register, 1842–1865. 87019, items 7–8. Family History Library.

Middlewich (Cheshire) Branch. Membership register, 1840–1865. 87044, item 1. Family History Library.

"Missionary Journal: Five Church Leaders Look Back at Their British Isles Mission Experiences." *Ensign*. July 1987.

Mitchell, Hildi. "'Being There': British Mormons and the History Trail." *Anthropology Today* 17 (2001): 9–14.

———. "Postcards from the Edge of History: Narrative and the Sacralization of Mormon Historical Sites." In *Pilgrim Voices: Narrative and Authorship in Christian Pilgrimage*, edited by Simon Coleman and John Elsner. Oxford: Berghahn Books, 2003, 133–57.

Mormon Immigration Index. CD/ROM. Intellectual Reserve Inc. The Church of Jesus Christ of Latter-day Saints.

Morales, Chris. "One Last Goodbye: Well-Wishers Pay Tribute with Tears of Joy, Gratitude." *LDS Church News*. February 9, 2008.

Morris, David M. "The Rhetoric of the Gathering and Zion: Consistency through Change 1831–1920." *British Journal of Mormon Studies* 1 (2008): 153–169.

Moss, James R. "The Kingdom Builders." *Ensign*. December 1979.

———, and LaVelle R. Moss. "Names and Places: Locales of British LDS Interest." *Ensign*. July 1987.
Mossley (Lancashire) Branch. Membership register, 1848–1874. 87041, item 1. Family History Library.
Mottram (Cheshire) Branch. Membership register, 1841–1857. 87020, item 3. Family History Library.
Mulder, William. "Mormonism's 'Gathering': An American Doctrine with a Difference." *Church History* 23 (1954): 248–64.
Navone, John. *Towards a Theology of Story*. Slough, England: St. Paul Publication, 1977.
Neilson, Reid L. *Early Mormon Missionary Activities in Japan, 1901–1924*. Salt Lake City, Utah: University of Utah Press, 2010.
———, Steven C. Harper, Craig K. Manscill, and Mary Jane Woodger, eds. *Regional Studies in Latter-day Saint Church History: The Pacific Isles*. Provo, Utah: Religious Studies Center, Brigham Young University, 2008.
Nelson (Lancashire) Branch. Manuscript history. LR 5993 2. Church History Library.
———. Membership register, 1902–1944. 87020, items 9–11. Family History Library.
Newton-le-Willows (Lancashire) Branch. Membership register, 1842–1880. 87022, items 5–6. Family History Library.
Nora, Pierre. "Between Memory and History: Les Lieux de Mémoire." *Representations* 26 (1989): 7–24.
Official Report of the First British Area General Conference of The Church of Jesus Christ of Latter-day Saints: Held in the Belle Vue Exhibition Centre and the Free Trade Hall in Manchester, England, August 27–29, 1971. Church History Library.
Official Report of the First Manchester England Area Conference of The Church of Jesus Christ of Latter-day Saints: Held in the Belle Vue Exhibition Center in Manchester, England, June 19–20, 1976. Church History Library.
Oldham (Lancashire) Branch. Manuscript history. LR 6490 2. Church History Library.
———. Membership register, 1840–1947. 87027, items 2–6. Family History Library.
Oldham Ward. Chapel dedication material, 1987. MS 9595. Church History Library.
Olsen, Steven L. "Historical Sites as Institutional Memory." In *Telling the Story of Mormon History*, edited by William G. Hartley. Provo, Utah: Proceedings of the 2002 Symposium of the Joseph Fielding Smith Institute for Latter-day Saint History at Brigham Young University, 121–24.
Oyler, Beth. *Index to the Millennial Star 1840–1918*. U of U Special Collections.
Pace, Garland. Journal, 1908–1910. MS 14452. Church History Library.
Parkinson, George C. Journal, 1883–1884. MS 15190. Church History Library.
Parry, William and Ann Parry. Correspondence, 1844. MS 15543. Church History Library.
Phillips, William George. Journal, 1887. MS 14471. Church History Library.
Pickup, David M. W. *The Pick and Flower of England: The Illustrated History of the Mormons in Victorian England and the Story of the Preston Temple*. Burnley, Lancashire: Living Legend, 1997.
Plumbley (Cheshire) Branch. Membership register, 1840–1849. 87027, item 24. Family History Library.

Plumbley, Derek J. Oral history, 1987. OH 820. Church History Library.
Poynton (Cheshire) Branch. Membership register, 1843–1854. 87028, item 11. Family History Library.
Pratt, Parley Parker. Correspondence, April 6, 1840. MS 81. Church History Library.
Pred, Allan Richard. *Making Histories and Constructing Human Geographies: The Local Transformation of Practice, Power Relations, and Consciousness*. Boulder, Colorado: Westview Press, 1990.
Preston (Lancashire) Branch. Manuscript history. LR 7179 2. Church History Library.
———. Membership register, 1837–1948. 87028, items 12–16. Family History Library.
Preston (Lancashire) Conference. Manuscript history. LR 7180 2. Church History Library.
———. Membership register, 1837–1968. 87028, item 17. Family History Library.
Priestly, John B. *The Edwardians*. London: Heineman Press, 1970.
Rambo, Lewis R. *Understanding Religious Conversion*. New Haven, Connecticut: Yale University Press, 1993.
Radcliffe (Lancashire) Branch. Manuscript history. LR 10142 2. Church History Library.
———. Membership register, 1847–1909. 87029, items 1–3. Family History Library.
Rasmussen, Matthew L. "The Advent of Mormonism in Lancashire's Upper Ribble Valley." Master's thesis, University of Lancaster, 2004.
———. "A Home for the Saints: Developments in Worship Accommodation in Lancashire, England." *International Journal of Mormon Studies* 4 (2011): 66–107.
Rawtenstall (Lancashire) Branch. Manuscript history. LR 7344 2. Church History Library.
———. Membership register, 1855–1907. 87029, items 10–13. Family History Library.
Reynolds, George. Correspondence. Letterpress copybook, 1871–1872, MS 13759. Church History Library.
Richards, Mary Haskin Parker. Autobiography, MS 13848. Church History Library.
Richards, Stephen Longstroth. Journal, 1877–1878. MS 16661. Church History Library.
Richards, Willard. Correspondence, February 27, 1841. MS 7120. Church History Library.
Rigby, George Clark. Journal, 1893–1895. MS 19195. Church History Library.
Roberts, Brigham H. *The Life of John Taylor, Third President of The Church of Jesus Christ of Latter-day Saints*. Salt Lake City, Utah: G. Q. Cannon, 1892.
Rochdale (Lancashire) Branch. Membership register, 1863–1948. 87029, items 20–24. Family History Library.
Rogers, Alan. *Approaches to Local History*, 2nd edition. New York: Longman Press, 1977.
Runcorn (Cheshire) Branch. Manuscript history. LR 7698 2. Church History Library.
Russell, Bertrand. *A History of Western Philosophy; and its Connection With Political and Social Circumstances from the Earliest Times to the Present Day*. London: G. Allen and Unwin, 1946.
———. Membership register, 1867–1883. 87029, item 35. Family History Library.
Sanderson, Michael. "Literacy and Social Mobility in the Industrial Revolution in England." *Past and Present* 56 (1972): 75–104.
Searle, Don L. "The Church in the United Kingdom and Ireland." *Ensign*. June 1998.
Shepherd, Gary, Gordon Shepherd. *A Kingdom Transformed: Themes in the Development of Mormonism*. Salt Lake City, Utah: University of Utah Press, 1984.

Sherrill, Rowland. "American Sacred Space and the Contest of History." In *American Sacred Space*, edited by David Chidester and Edward T. Linenthal. Bloomington, Indiana: Indiana University Press, 1995, 313–40.

Smart, Paul F. "The History of the Early Members of The Church of Jesus Christ of Latter-day Saints in Preston, Lancashire, England." Master's thesis, Brigham Young University, 1989.

Smith, George D., ed. *An Intimate Chronicle: The Journals of William Clayton*. Salt Lake City, Utah: Signature Books, 1995.

Smith, Joseph, and B. H. Roberts. *History of The Church of Jesus Christ of Latter-day Saints*, 2nd edition. Salt Lake City, Utah: Deseret Book Company, 1958.

Smith, Joseph, Hyrum Smith, Sidney Rigdon. Recommendation for missionary service issued to Heber C. Kimball, June 2, 1837. MS 3458. Church History Library.

Smith, Joseph Fielding. *Essentials in Church History*, 22nd enlarged edition. Salt Lake City, Utah: Deseret Book Company, 1967.

———, ed. *Teachings of the Prophet Joseph Smith*. Salt Lake City, Utah: Deseret News Press, 1938.

Snape, Michael F. *The Church of England in Industrializing Society: The Lancashire Parish of Whalley in the 18th Century*. Woodbridge, Suffolk: The Boydell Press, 2003.

Southport (Lancashire) Branch. Membership register, 1911. 87032, item 43. Family History Library.

St. Helens (Lancashire) Branch. Manuscript history. LR 7765 2. Church History Library.

———. Membership register, 1841–1879. 87030, item 7. Family History Library.

Skelmersdale (Lancashire) Branch. Manuscript history. LR 13537 2. Church History Library.

Sleight, Thomas. Journal, 1884–1886. MS 9406. Church History Library.

Southport (Lancashire) Branch. Manuscript history. LR 8568 2. Church History Library.

Stalybridge (Cheshire) Branch. Membership register, 1849–1862. 87033, item 18. Family History Library.

Stark, Rodney. *The Rise of Mormonism*. New York: Columbia University Press, 2005.

Strunk, Orlo, ed. *Readings in the Psychology of Religion*. New York: Abingdon Press, 1959.

Stockport (Cheshire) Branch. Manuscript history. LR 8721 2. Church History Library.

———. Membership register, 1839–1913. 87034, items 10–11. Family History Library.

Stocks, Henry. Journal, 1844–1870. MS 9274. Church History Library.

Swinton (Lancashire) Branch. Membership register, 1876–1914. 87035, item 40. Family History Library.

Talmage, James E. *The Great Apostasy: Considered in the Light of Scriptural and Secular History*. Salt Lake City, Utah: Deseret News 1909.

Taylor, Phillip A. M. *Expectations Westward: The Mormons and the Emigration of their British Converts in the Nineteenth Century*. Edinburgh and London: Oliver and Boyd, 1965.

Teachings of the Presidents of the Church: Joseph Smith. Salt Lake City, Utah: The Church of Jesus Christ of Latter-day Saints, 2008.

Thernstrom, Stephan, ed. *Harvard Encyclopedia of American Ethnic Groups*. Cambridge, Massachusetts: Harvard University Press, 1980.

Tintwistle (Cheshire) Branch. Membership register, 1842–1857. 87043, item 1. Family History Library.

Thomas, Gordon K. "The Book of Mormon in the English Literary Context of 1837." *BYU Studies* 27 (1987): 37–45.

Thompson, Edward P. *The Making of the English Working Class*. New York: Vintage Books, 1963.

Thorp, Malcolm R. "The British Government and the Mormon Question 1910–1922." *Journal of Church and State* 21 (1979): 305–23.

———. "The Field is White Already to Harvest," Appendix A. In *Men With a Mission 1837–1841: The Quorum of the Twelve Apostles in the British Isles*, edited by James B. Allen, Ronald K. Esplin, and David J. Whittaker. Salt Lake City, Utah: Deseret Book Company, 1992, 323–44.

———. "The Mormon Peril: The Crusade against the Saints in Britain 1910–1914." *Journal of Mormon History* 2 (1975): 69–88.

———. "Popular Mormon Millennialism in Nineteenth Century Britain." *Journal of Mormon History* 32 (2005): 89–111.

———. "The Religious Backgrounds of Mormon Converts in Britain 1837–52." *Journal of Mormon History* 4 (1977): 51–66.

———. "Sectarian Violence in Early Victorian Britain: The Mormon Experience 1837–1860." *Bulletin of the John Rylands University Library* 70 (1988): 136–47.

———. "The Setting for the Restoration in Britain: Political, Social, and Economic Conditions." In *Truth Will Prevail: The Rise of The Church of Jesus Christ of Latter-day Saints in the British Isles 1837–1987*, edited by V. Ben Bloxham, James R. Moss, and Larry C. Porter. Solihull, Warwickshire: The Church of Jesus Christ of Latter-day Saints, 1987, 44–70.

———. "Winifred Graham and the Mormon Image." *Journal of Mormon History*, 6 (1979): 107–21.

Timmins, Geoffrey. *The Last Shift: The Decline of Handloom Weaving in Nineteenth-Century Lancashire*. Manchester: Manchester University Press, 1993.

———. *Made in Lancashire: A History of Regional Industrialization*. Manchester: Manchester University Press, 1998.

Tobler, Douglas F. "Truth Prevailing: The Significance of the Nineteenth-Century LDS Experience in Britain." *Ensign*. July 1987.

Todmorden (Lancashire) Branch. Manuscript history, LR 9169 2. Church History Library.

———. Membership register, 1841–1854. 87036, item 18. Family History Library.

Tottington (Lancashire) Branch. Membership register, 1841–1875. 87036, items 19–22. Family History Library.

Turner, Harold W. *From Temple to Meeting House: The Phenomenology and Theology of Places of Worship*. New York: Mouton Publishers, 1978.

Tyldesley (Lancashire) Branch. Membership register, 1852–1887. 87036, items 31–33. Family History Library.

Ulverston (Lancashire) Branch. Manuscript history, LR 9502 2. Church History Library.

Underwood, Grant. "Millenarianism and the Early Mormon Mind." *Journal of Mormon History* 9 (1982): 41–52.

———. *The Millenarian World of Early Mormonism*. Urbana, Illinois: University of Illinois Press, 1993.

Upholland (Lancashire) Branch. Membership register, 1848–1890. 87037, items 3–4. Family History Library.

Van Orden, Bruce A. "The Decline in Convert Baptisms and Member Emigration from the British Mission after 1870." *BYU Studies* 27 (1987): 97–105.

———. "George Reynolds: Secretary, Sacrificial Lamb, and Seventy." Ph.D. diss., Brigham Young University, 1986.

Walker, Ronald W. "Heber J. Grant's European Mission 1903–06." *Journal of Mormon History* 14 (1988): 17–34.

Wallasey (Cheshire) Branch. Manuscript history, LR 9895 2. Church History Library.

Walton, John K. *A Social History of Lancashire*. Manchester: Manchester University Press, 1987.

Warrington (Cheshire) Branch. Manuscript history, LR 9920 2. Church History Library.

———. Membership register, 1881–1883. 87037, item 22. Family History Library.

Watt, George D., ed. *Journal of Discourses, by Brigham Young, President of The Church of Jesus Christ of Latter-day Saints, His Two Counsellors, and the Twelve Apostles, Reported by G. D. Watt, and Humbly Dedicated to the Latter-day Saints in All the World*. Liverpool: S. W. Richards, 1857.

Watt, Ronald G., and Kenneth W. Godfrey, "'Old 42': The British and European Mission Headquarters in Liverpool, England, 1855–1904." *Mormon Historical Studies* 10 (2009): 87–99.

Watts, Michael R. *The Dissenters*, 2 vols. Oxford: Clarendon Press, 1978–1995.

Weaver, Sarah Jane. "Into All the World: Most Travelled President in History." *LDS Church News*. February 2, 2008.

Wells, Raymond. Journal, 1913. Typescript of original in author's possession.

Westleigh (Lancashire) Branch. Membership register, 1840–1887. 87038, item 14. Family History Library.

Whitaker, Thomas D. *An History of the Original Parish of Whalley and Honour of Clitheroe*, volume 2, 4th edition. London: Routledge, 1872.

Whitney, Orson F. *The Life of Heber C. Kimball*, 2nd collector's edition. Salt Lake City, Utah: Bookcraft, 1996.

Whittaker, David J. "Early Mormon Pamphleteering." Ph.D. diss., Brigham Young University, 1982.

———. "Mormonism in Victorian Britain: A Bibliographic Essay." In *Mormons in Early Victorian Britain*, edited by Malcolm R. Thorp and Richard L. Jensen. Salt Lake City, Utah: University of Utah Press, 1989, 258–71.

Wigan (Lancashire) Branch. Manuscript history, LR 10175 2. Church History Library.

———. Membership register, 1854–1948. 87038, items 33–35. Family History Library.

Wilkinson, Carol. "Mormon Baptismal Site in Chatburn, England." *Mormon Historical Studies* 7 (2006): 83–88.

Woodruff, Wilford. *Wilford Woodruff's Journal, 1833–1898*. 9 Volumes. Edited by Scott G. Kenney. Midvale, Utah: Signature Books, 1983.

Woods, Fred E. "Conveyance and Contribution: Mormon Scots Gather to an American Zion." *History Scotland* 5, no. 4 (August 2005): 37–42.

———. "The Tide of Mormon Migration Flowing Through the Port of Liverpool, England." *British Journal of Mormon Studies*, 1 (2008): 60–85.

Woolley, Kenneth R. Correspondence, 1906–1908. Photocopies of original in author's possession.

Young, Brigham. *Discourses of Brigham Young*. Edited by John A. Widtsoe. Salt Lake City, Utah: Deseret Book Company, 1943.

Newspapers, Almanacs, and Popular Periodicals

Bolton Weekly Guardian. Bolton, Lancashire

Church Almanac. Salt Lake City, Utah

Conference Reports. Salt Lake City, Utah

Deseret Evening News. Salt Lake City, Utah

Eccles Advertiser. Eccles, Lancashire

Ensign. Salt Lake City, Utah

The Guardian. Manchester, England

The Latter-day Saints' Millennial Star, Liverpool, England

The Latter-day Saints' Millennial Star, London, England

The Latter-day Saints' Millennial Star, Manchester, England

LDS Church News. Salt Lake City, Utah

Liahona. Salt Lake City, Utah

The New York Times. New York, New York

Preston Chronicle. Preston, Lancashire

The Times. London, England

Times and Seasons. Nauvoo, Illinois

Index